VIZ GRAPHIC NOVEL
NO NEED FOR TENCHI!™
UNREAL GENIUS

This volume contains NO NEED FOR TENCHI! PART FIVE
in its entirety.

STORY AND ART BY
HITOSHI OKUDA

ENGLISH ADAPTATION BY
FRED BURKE

Translation/Lillian Olsen
Touch-Up Art & Lettering/Dan Nakrosis
Cover Design/Hidemi Sahara
Edited by/Annette Roman & Carl Gustav Horn

Senior Editor/Trish Ledoux
Director of Sales & Marketing/Oliver Chin
Managing Editor/Hyoe Narita
Editor-in-Chief/Satoru Fujii
Publisher/Seiji Horibuchi

Printed in Canada

Published by Viz Communications, Inc.
P.O. Box 77010 • San Francisco, CA 94107

10 9 8 7 6 5 4 3 2 1
First printing, April 1999

Vizit us at our World Wide Web site at www.viz.com and
our Internet magazine, j-pop.com, at www.j-pop.com!

NO NEED FOR TENCHI! GRAPHIC NOVELS TO DATE
NO NEED FOR TENCHI!
SWORD PLAY
MAGICAL GIRL PRETTY SAMMY
SAMURAI SPACE OPERA
UNREAL GENIUS

VIZ GRAPHIC NOVEL

◆◆◆◆◆◆◆◆◆◆◆◆◆

NO NEED FOR TENCHI!™

UNREAL GENIUS

STORY AND ART BY
HITOSHI OKUDA

CONTENTS

Tales of Tenchi #1
CAPTIVE OF LOVE

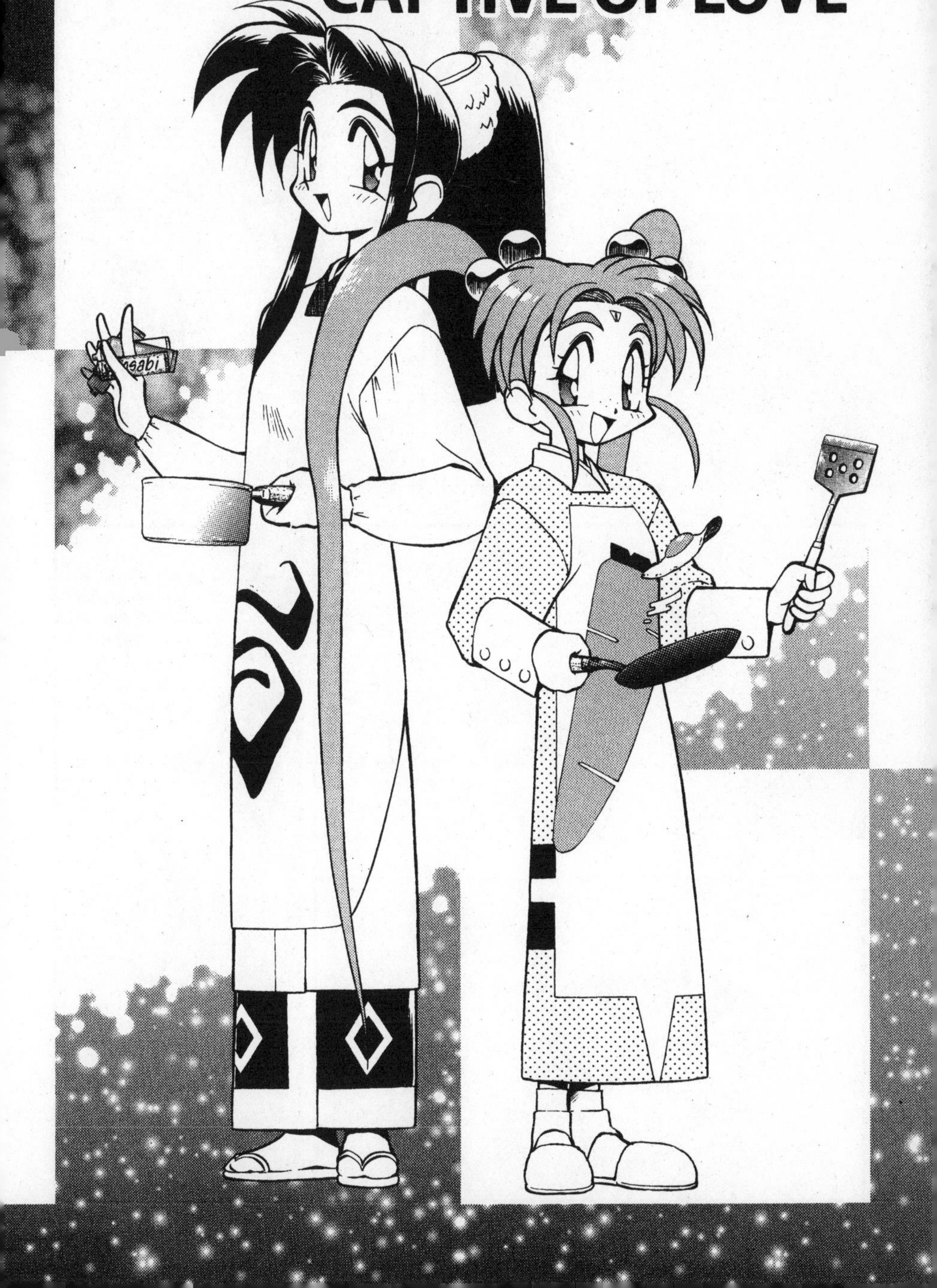

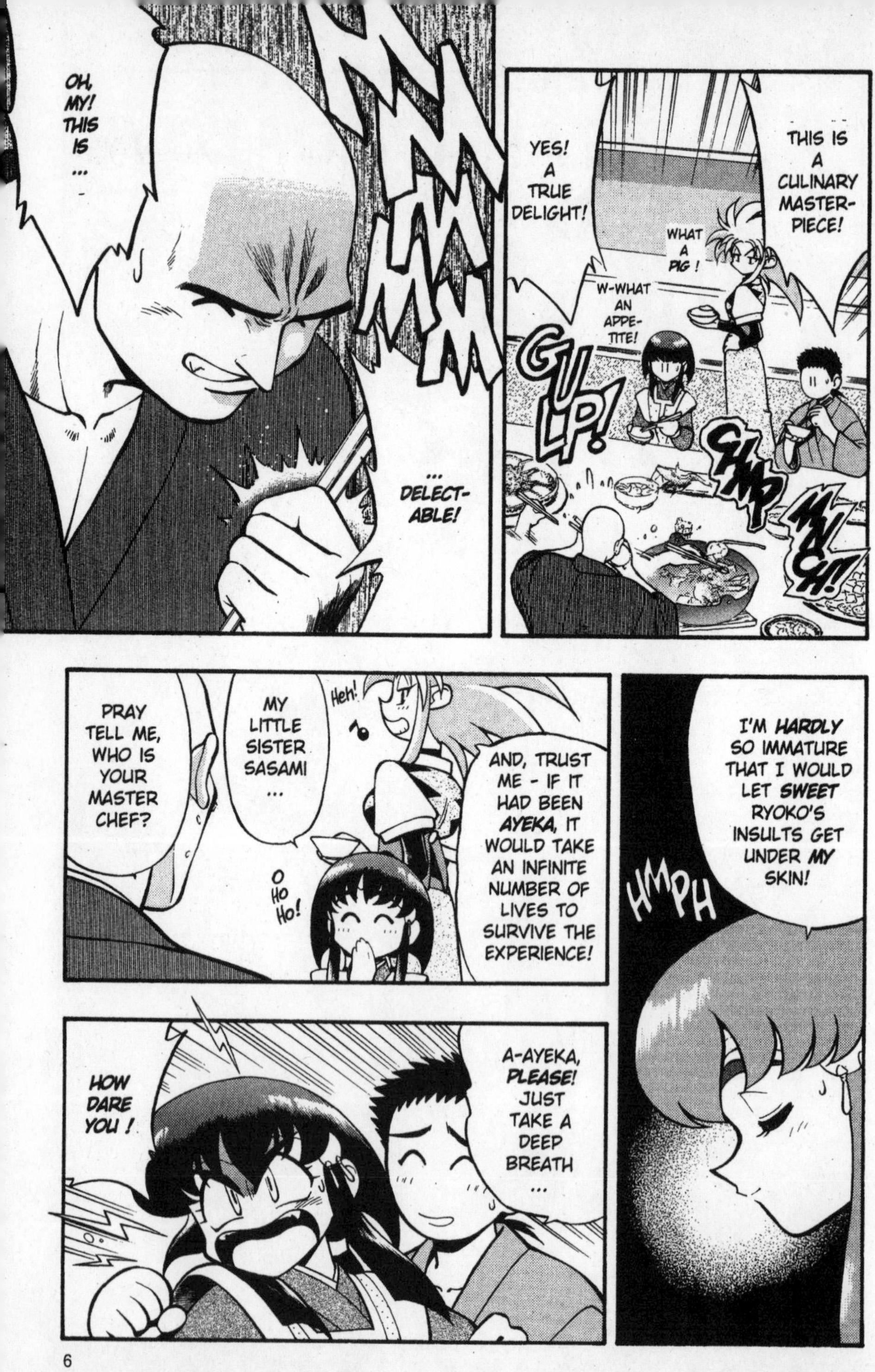

OH, MY! THIS IS ...
... DELECTABLE!
YES! A TRUE DELIGHT!
THIS IS A CULINARY MASTER-PIECE!
WHAT A PIG!
W-WHAT AN APPE-TITE!
GULP!
CHOMP
MUNCH!!
PRAY TELL ME, WHO IS YOUR MASTER CHEF?
MY LITTLE SISTER SASAMI ...
Heh!
AND, TRUST ME - IF IT HAD BEEN AYEKA, IT WOULD TAKE AN INFINITE NUMBER OF LIVES TO SURVIVE THE EXPERIENCE!
O HO HO!
HOW DARE YOU!
A-AYEKA, PLEASE! JUST TAKE A DEEP BREATH ...
I'M HARDLY SO IMMATURE THAT I WOULD LET SWEET RYOKO'S INSULTS GET UNDER MY SKIN!
HMPH

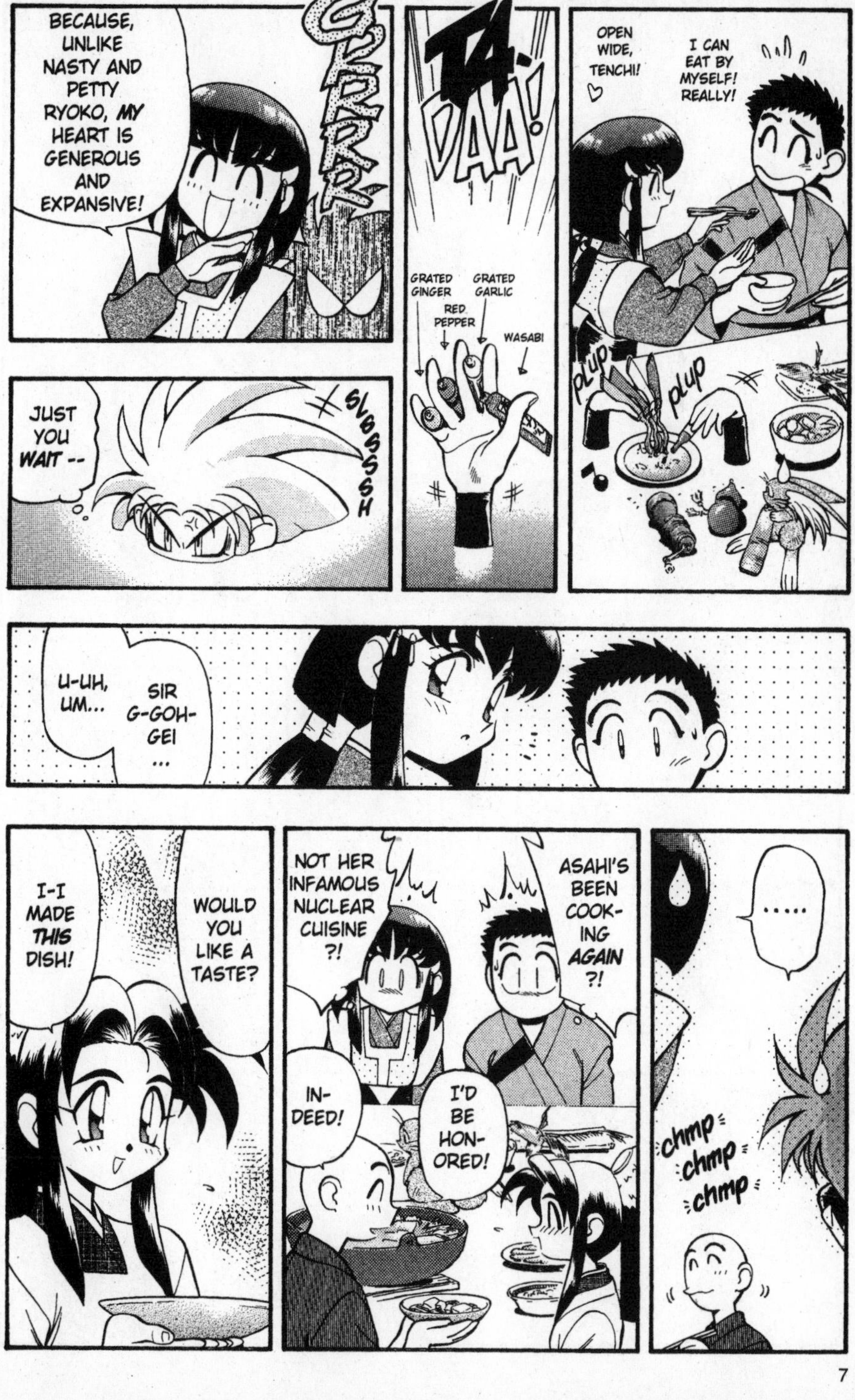
BECAUSE, UNLIKE NASTY AND PETTY RYOKO, MY HEART IS GENEROUS AND EXPANSIVE!
GRRRR
JUST YOU WAIT --
SLSSSSSH
TA-DAA!
GRATED GINGER
RED PEPPER
GRATED GARLIC
WASABI
OPEN WIDE, TENCHI!
I CAN EAT BY MYSELF! REALLY!
plup
plup
U-UH, UM...
SIR G-GOH-GEI ...
I-I MADE THIS DISH!
WOULD YOU LIKE A TASTE?
NOT HER INFAMOUS NUCLEAR CUISINE ?!
ASAHI'S BEEN COOK-ING AGAIN ?!
IN-DEED!
I'D BE HON-ORED!
.....
chmp
chmp
chmp

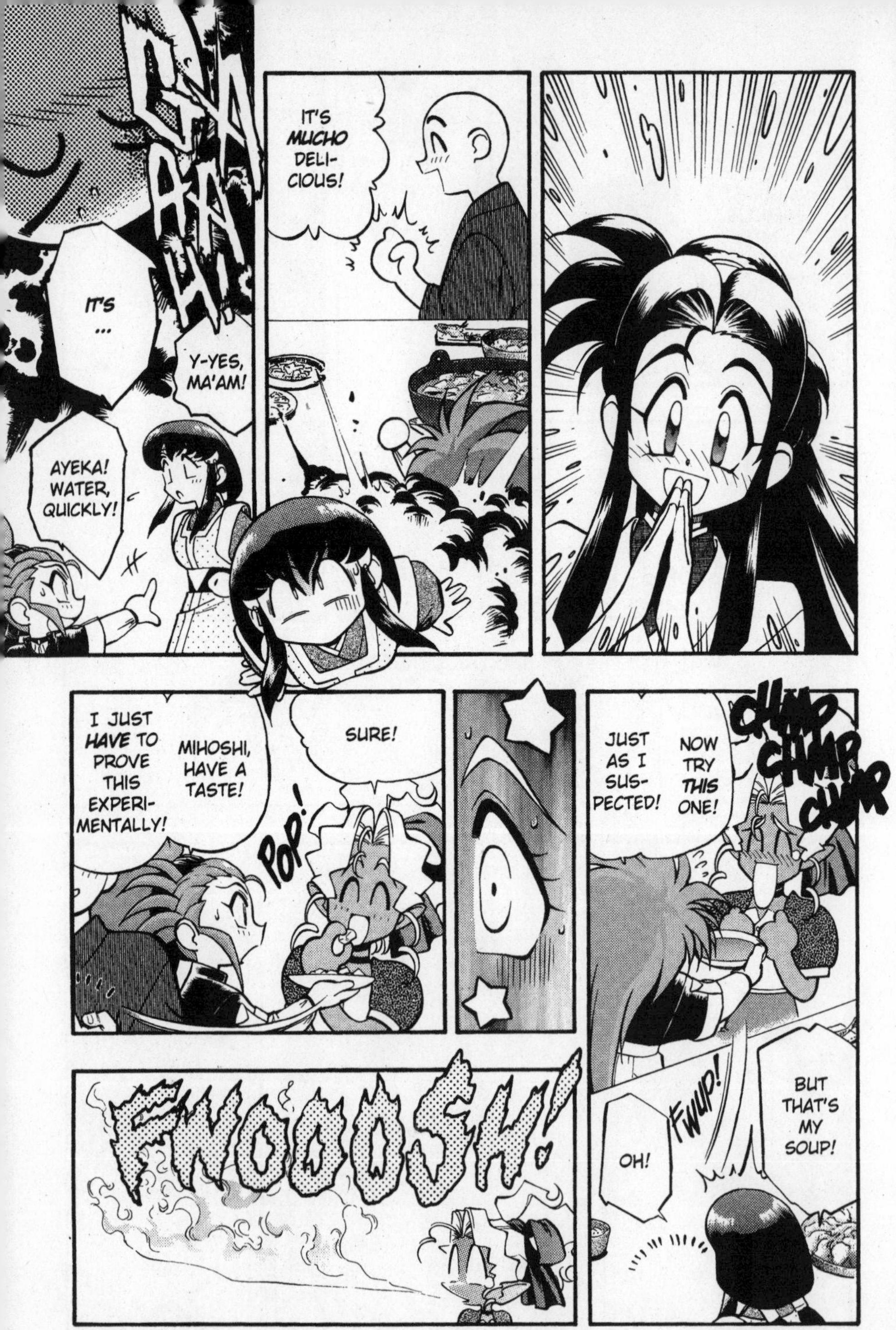
IT'S ...
Y-YES, MA'AM!
AYEKA! WATER, QUICKLY!
IT'S MUCHO DELICIOUS!
I JUST HAVE TO PROVE THIS EXPERIMENTALLY!
MIHOSHI, HAVE A TASTE!
SURE!
POP!
JUST AS I SUSPECTED!
NOW TRY THIS ONE!
CHOMP CHOMP CHOMP
FWOOOSH!
OH!
FWUP!
BUT THAT'S MY SOUP!

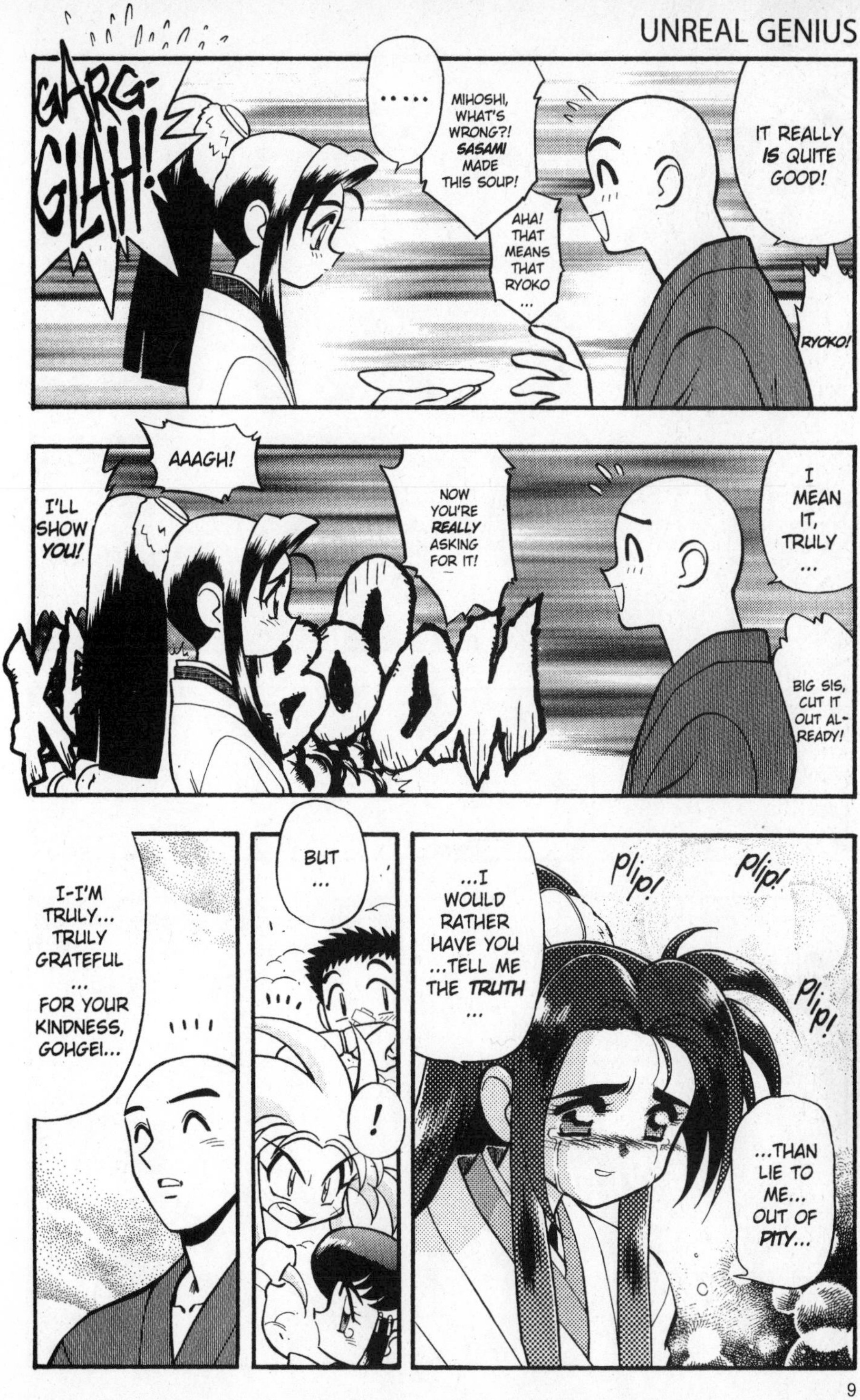
GARG-GLAH!
.....
MIHOSHI, WHAT'S WRONG?! SASAMI MADE THIS SOUP!
AHA! THAT MEANS THAT RYOKO ...
IT REALLY IS QUITE GOOD!
RYOKO!
I'LL SHOW YOU!
AAAGH!
NOW YOU'RE REALLY ASKING FOR IT!
KA-BOOM
I MEAN IT, TRULY ...
BIG SIS, CUT IT OUT AL-READY!
I-I'M TRULY... TRULY GRATEFUL ... FOR YOUR KINDNESS, GOHGEI...
BUT ...
!
...I WOULD RATHER HAVE YOU ...TELL ME THE TRUTH ...
plip! plip! plip!
...THAN LIE TO ME... OUT OF PITY...

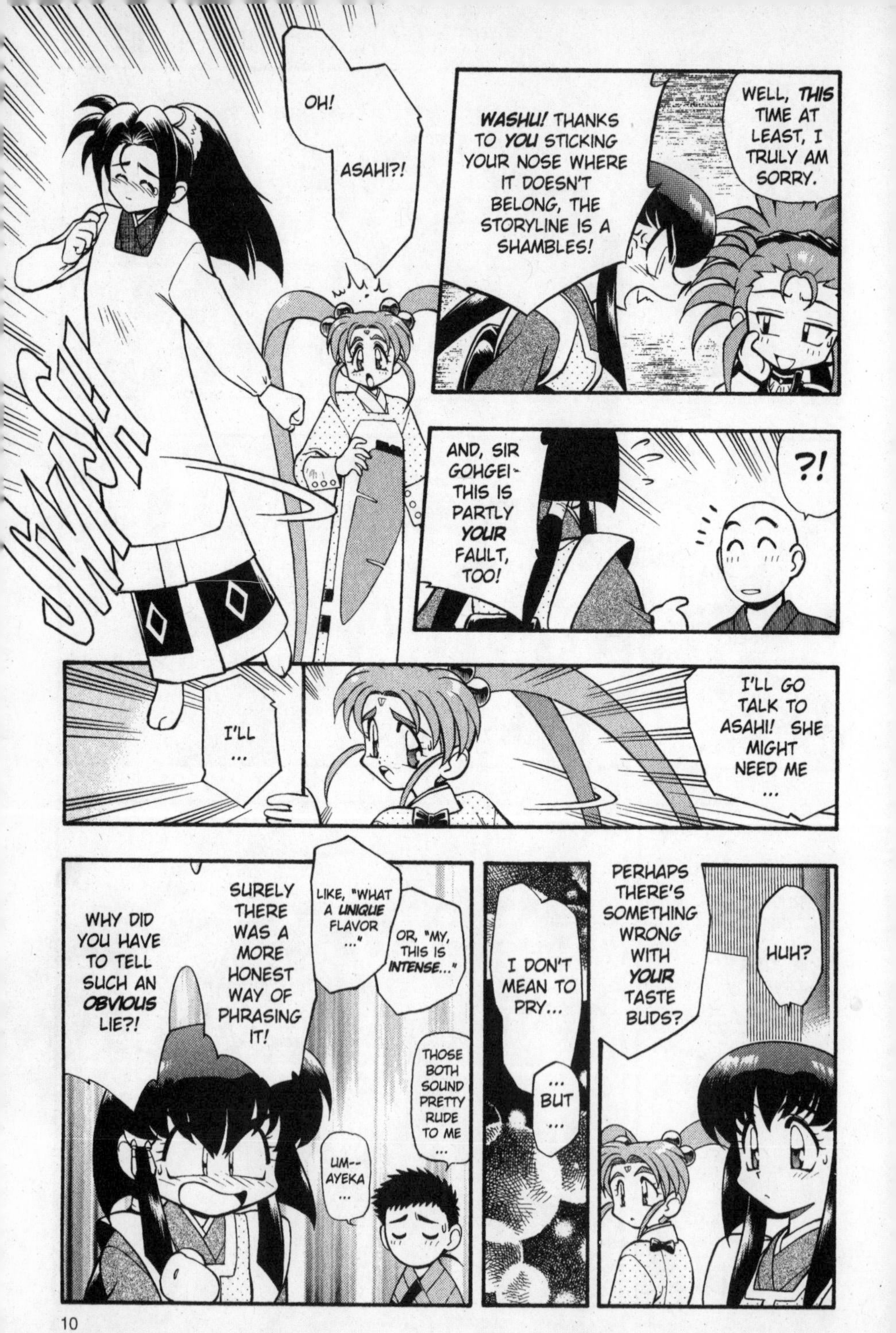

OH!
ASAHI?!
SWISH!
WASHU! THANKS TO YOU STICKING YOUR NOSE WHERE IT DOESN'T BELONG, THE STORYLINE IS A SHAMBLES!
WELL, THIS TIME AT LEAST, I TRULY AM SORRY.
AND, SIR GOHGEI- THIS IS PARTLY YOUR FAULT, TOO!
?!
I'LL ...
I'LL GO TALK TO ASAHI! SHE MIGHT NEED ME ...
WHY DID YOU HAVE TO TELL SUCH AN OBVIOUS LIE?!
SURELY THERE WAS A MORE HONEST WAY OF PHRASING IT!
LIKE, "WHAT A UNIQUE FLAVOR ..."
OR, "MY, THIS IS INTENSE..."
UM-- AYEKA ...
THOSE BOTH SOUND PRETTY RUDE TO ME ...
I DON'T MEAN TO PRY...
... BUT ...
PERHAPS THERE'S SOMETHING WRONG WITH YOUR TASTE BUDS?
HUH?

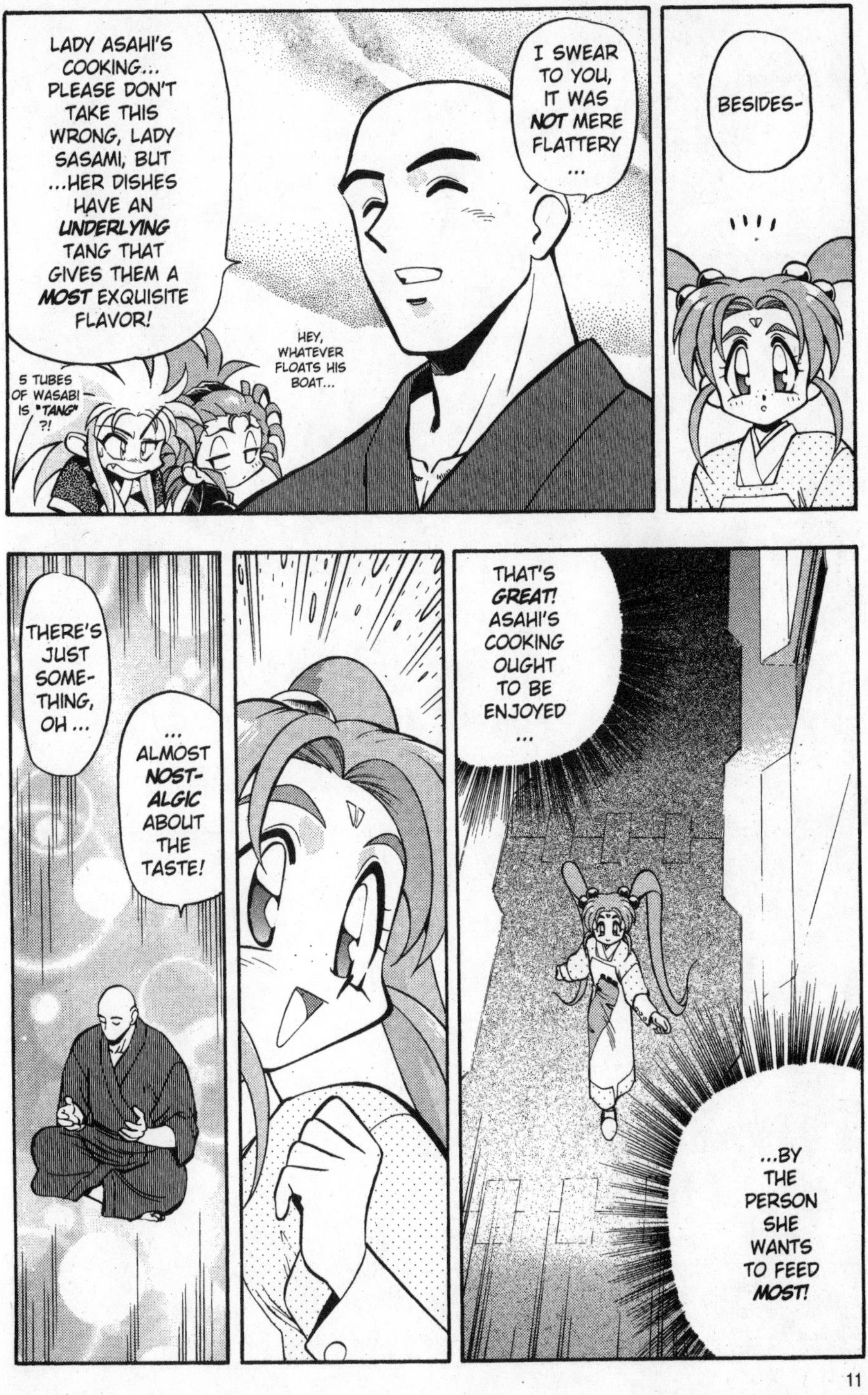
LADY ASAHI'S COOKING... PLEASE DON'T TAKE THIS WRONG, LADY SASAMI, BUT ...HER DISHES HAVE AN UNDERLYING TANG THAT GIVES THEM A MOST EXQUISITE FLAVOR!
5 TUBES OF WASABI IS "TANG"?!
HEY, WHATEVER FLOATS HIS BOAT...
I SWEAR TO YOU, IT WAS NOT MERE FLATTERY ...
BESIDES-
THERE'S JUST SOME-THING, OH ...
... ALMOST NOST-ALGIC ABOUT THE TASTE!
THAT'S GREAT! ASAHI'S COOKING OUGHT TO BE ENJOYED ...
...BY THE PERSON SHE WANTS TO FEED MOST!

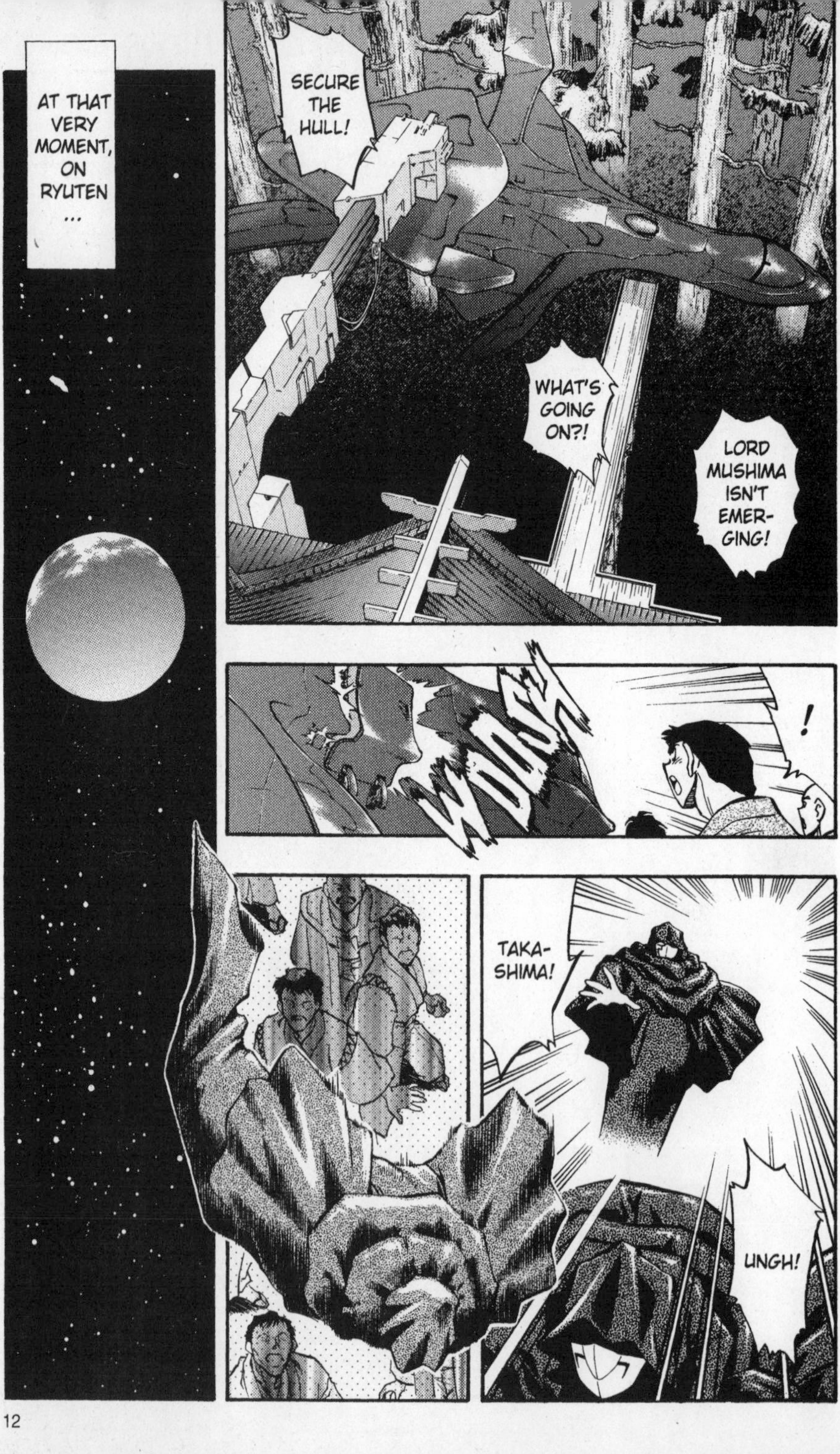
AT THAT VERY MOMENT, ON RYUTEN ...
SECURE THE HULL!
WHAT'S GOING ON?!
LORD MUSHIMA ISN'T EMERGING!
WOOSH
!
TAKA-SHIMA!
UNGH!

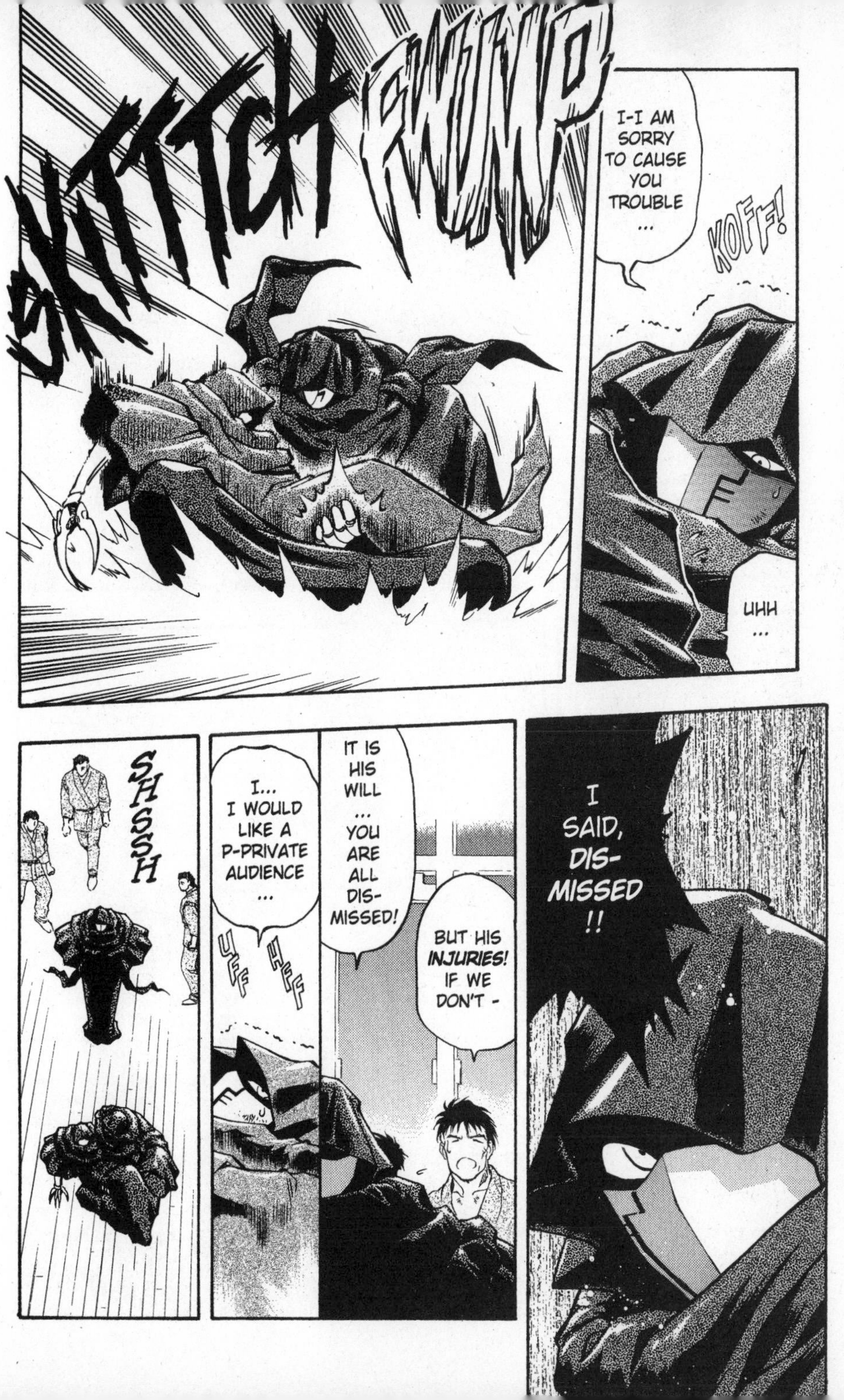
SKITTTCH
FWUMP
I-I AM SORRY TO CAUSE YOU TROUBLE ...
KOFF!
UHH ...
SHSSH
I... I WOULD LIKE A P-PRIVATE AUDIENCE ...
IT IS HIS WILL ... YOU ARE ALL DIS-MISSED!
UFF
HEFF
BUT HIS **INJURIES!** IF WE DON'T -
I SAID, DIS-MISSED !!

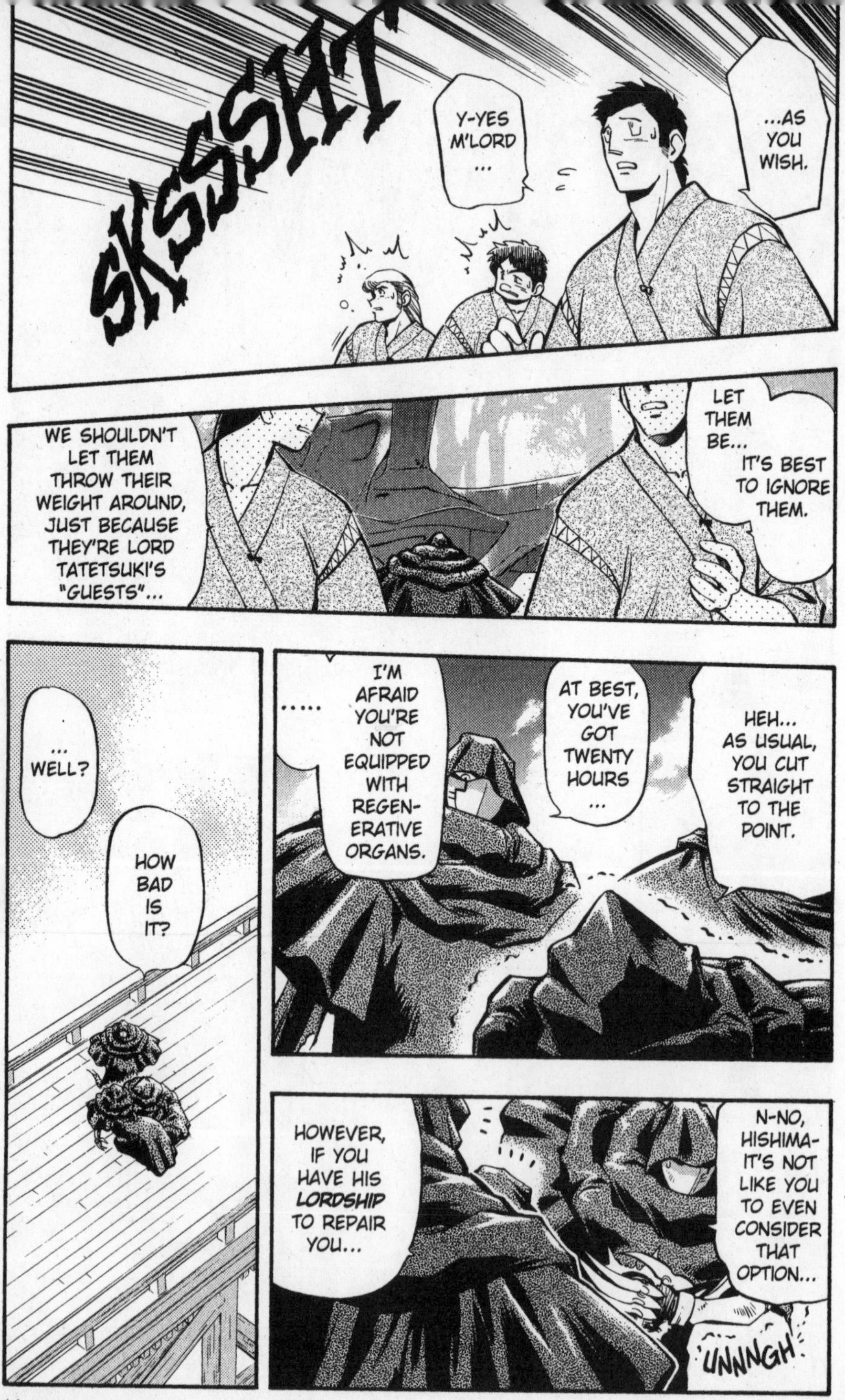
SKSSSHT
Y-YES M'LORD ...
...AS YOU WISH.
WE SHOULDN'T LET THEM THROW THEIR WEIGHT AROUND, JUST BECAUSE THEY'RE LORD TATETSUKI'S "GUESTS"...
LET THEM BE... IT'S BEST TO IGNORE THEM.
... WELL?
HOW BAD IS IT?
.....
I'M AFRAID YOU'RE NOT EQUIPPED WITH REGEN-ERATIVE ORGANS.
AT BEST, YOU'VE GOT TWENTY HOURS ...
HEH... AS USUAL, YOU CUT STRAIGHT TO THE POINT.
HOWEVER, IF YOU HAVE HIS *LORDSHIP* TO REPAIR YOU...
N-NO, HISHIMA-IT'S NOT LIKE YOU TO EVEN CONSIDER THAT OPTION...
UNNNGH

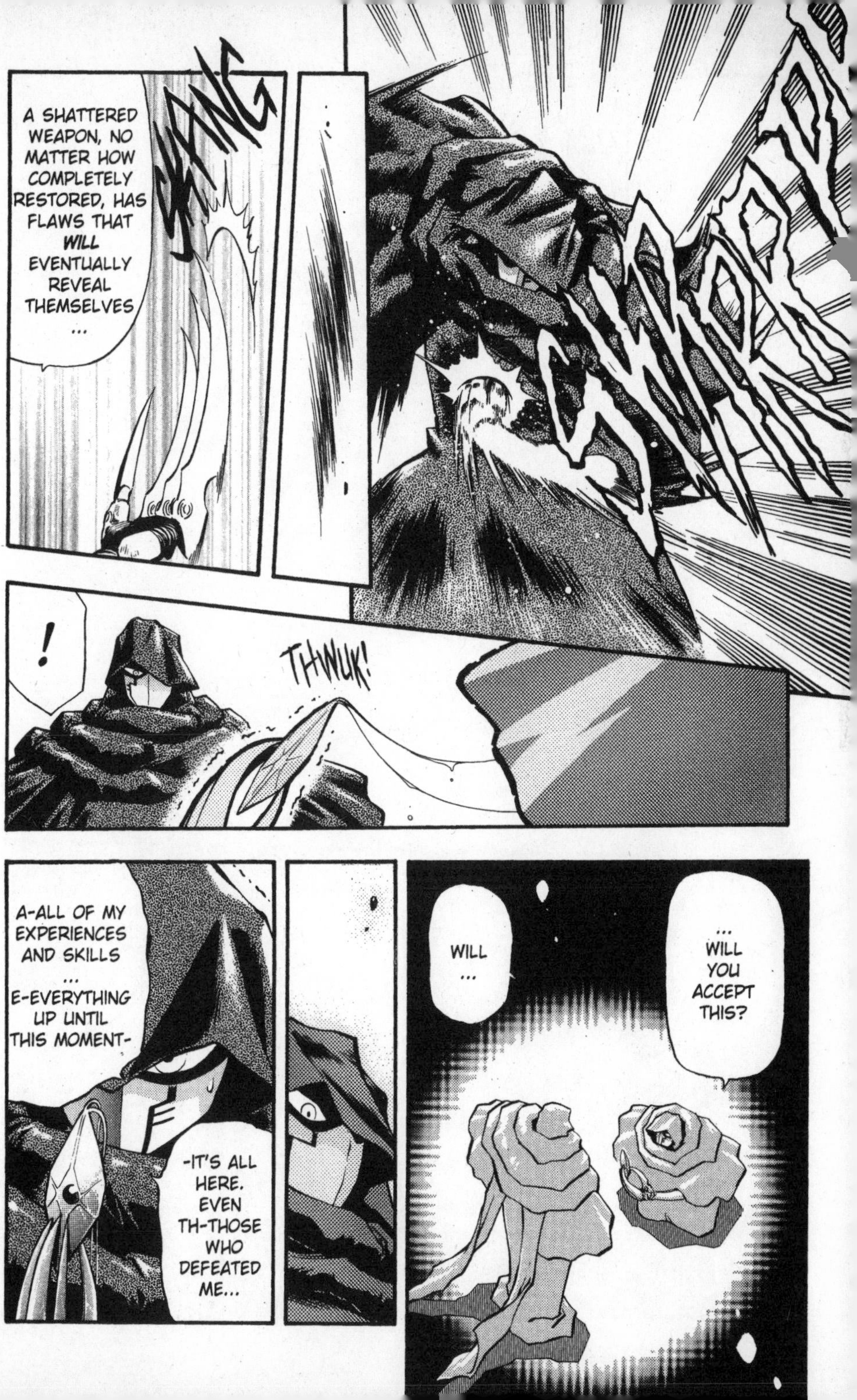
A SHATTERED WEAPON, NO MATTER HOW COMPLETELY RESTORED, HAS FLAWS THAT **WILL** EVENTUALLY REVEAL THEMSELVES ...
SHING
SHHRAK
!
THWUK!
A-ALL OF MY EXPERIENCES AND SKILLS ... E-EVERYTHING UP UNTIL THIS MOMENT-
-IT'S ALL HERE. EVEN TH-THOSE WHO DEFEATED ME...
WILL ...
... WILL YOU ACCEPT THIS?

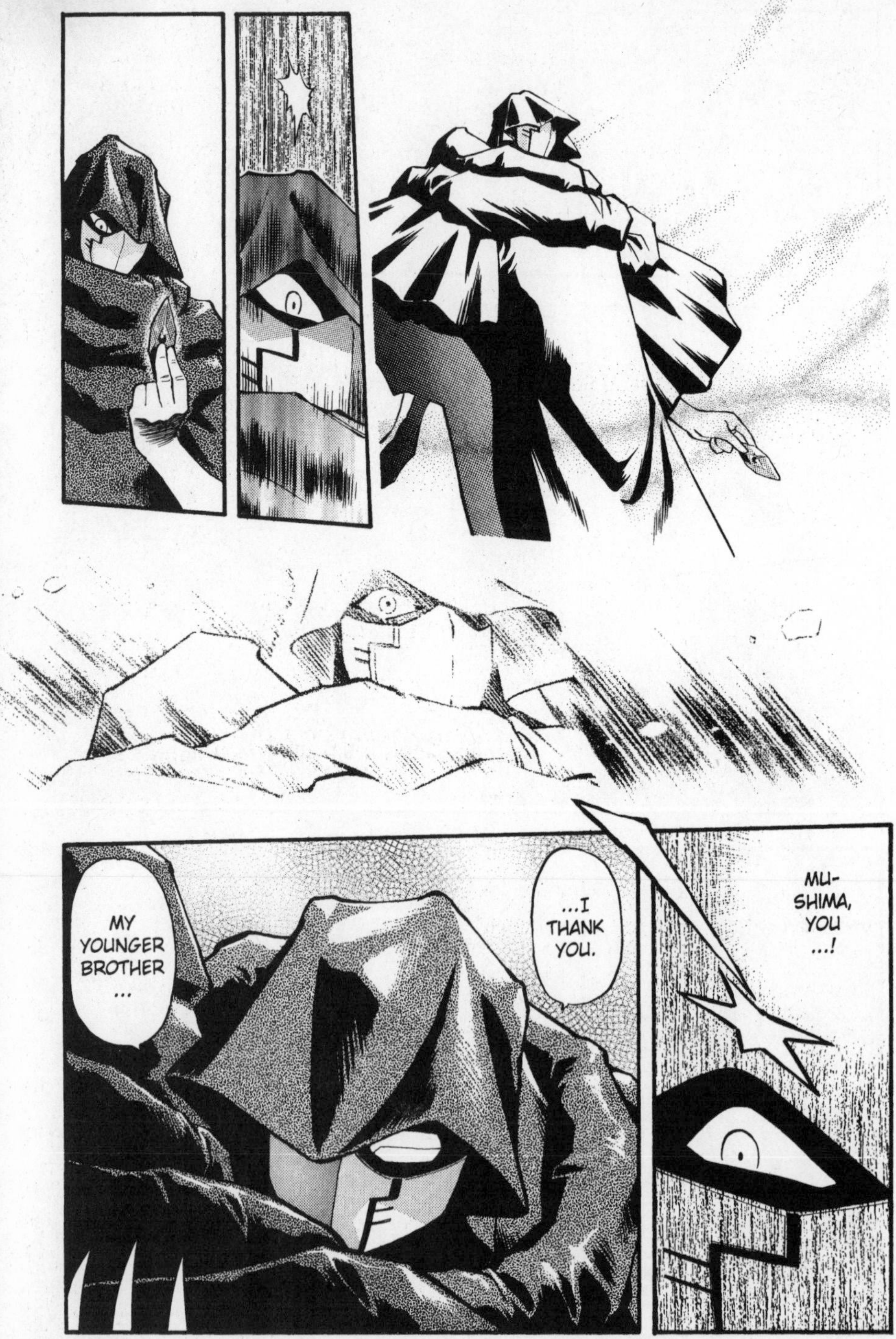
MY YOUNGER BROTHER ...
...I THANK YOU.
MU-SHIMA, YOU ...!

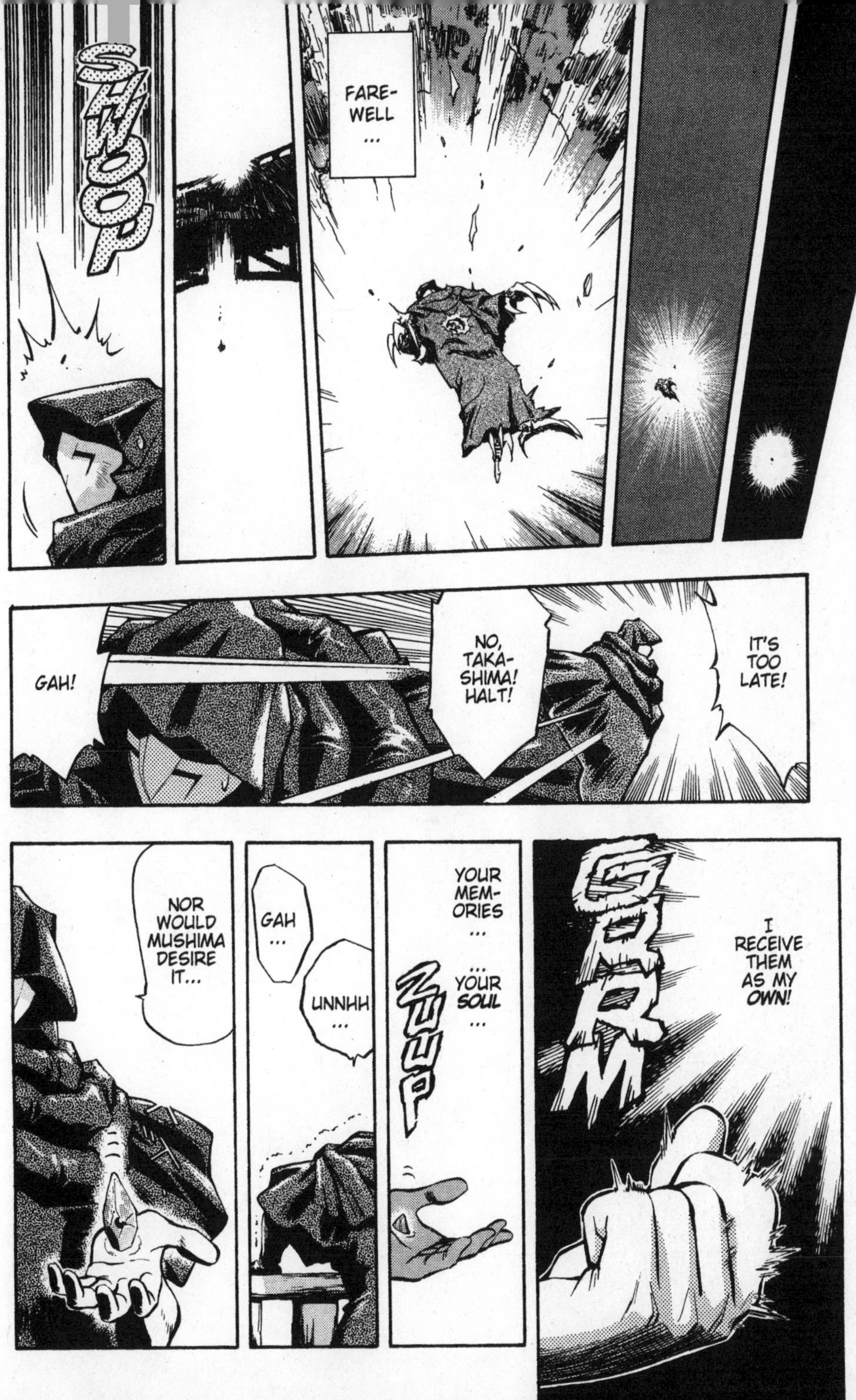
SHWOOP
FARE-WELL ...
GAH!
NO, TAKA-SHIMA! HALT!
IT'S TOO LATE!
NOR WOULD MUSHIMA DESIRE IT...
GAH ...
UNNHH ...
YOUR MEM-ORIES ...
... YOUR SOUL ...
ZUUUP
GRRM
I RECEIVE THEM AS MY OWN!

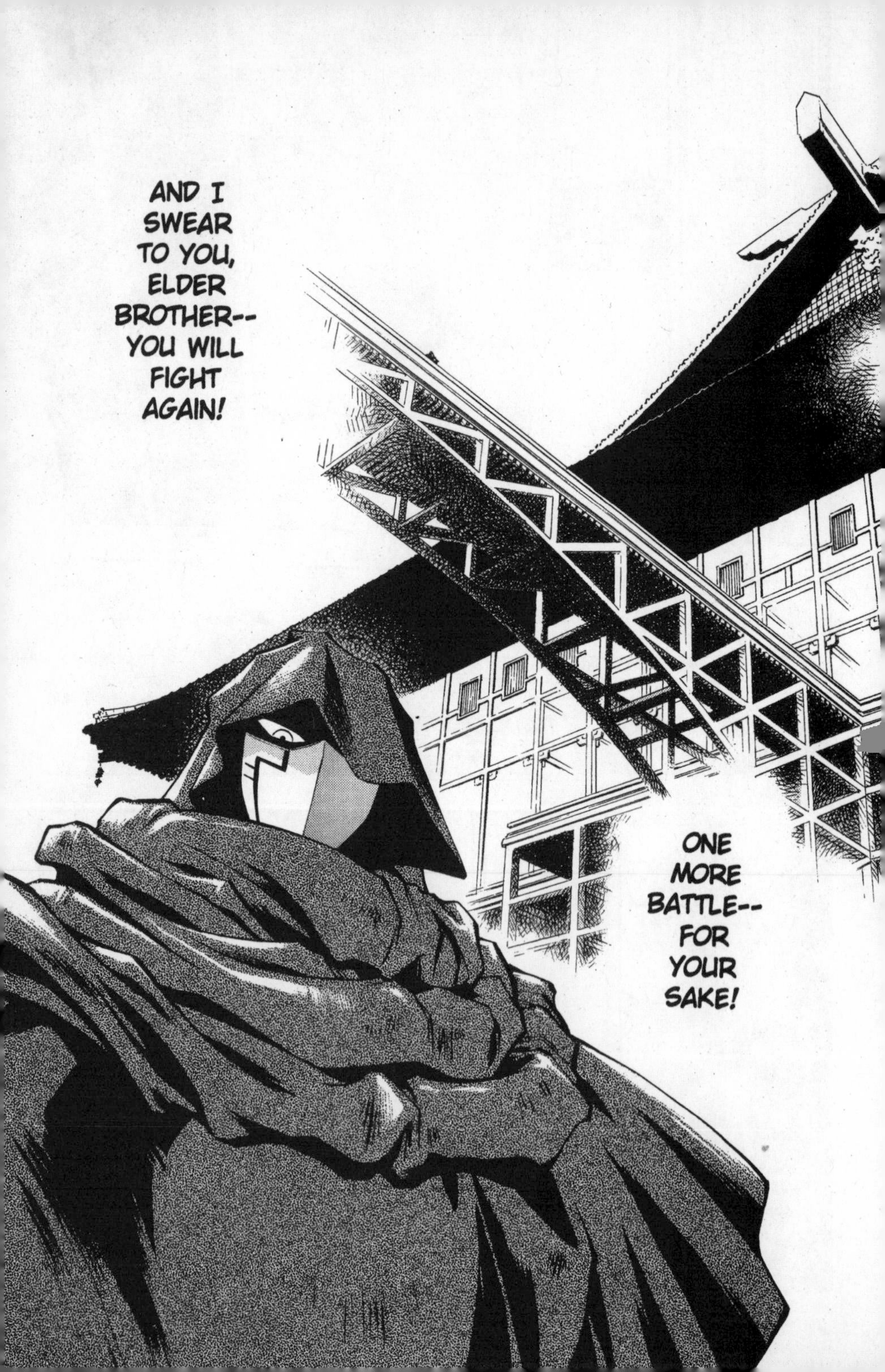
AND I SWEAR TO YOU, ELDER BROTHER-- YOU WILL FIGHT AGAIN!
ONE MORE BATTLE-- FOR YOUR SAKE!

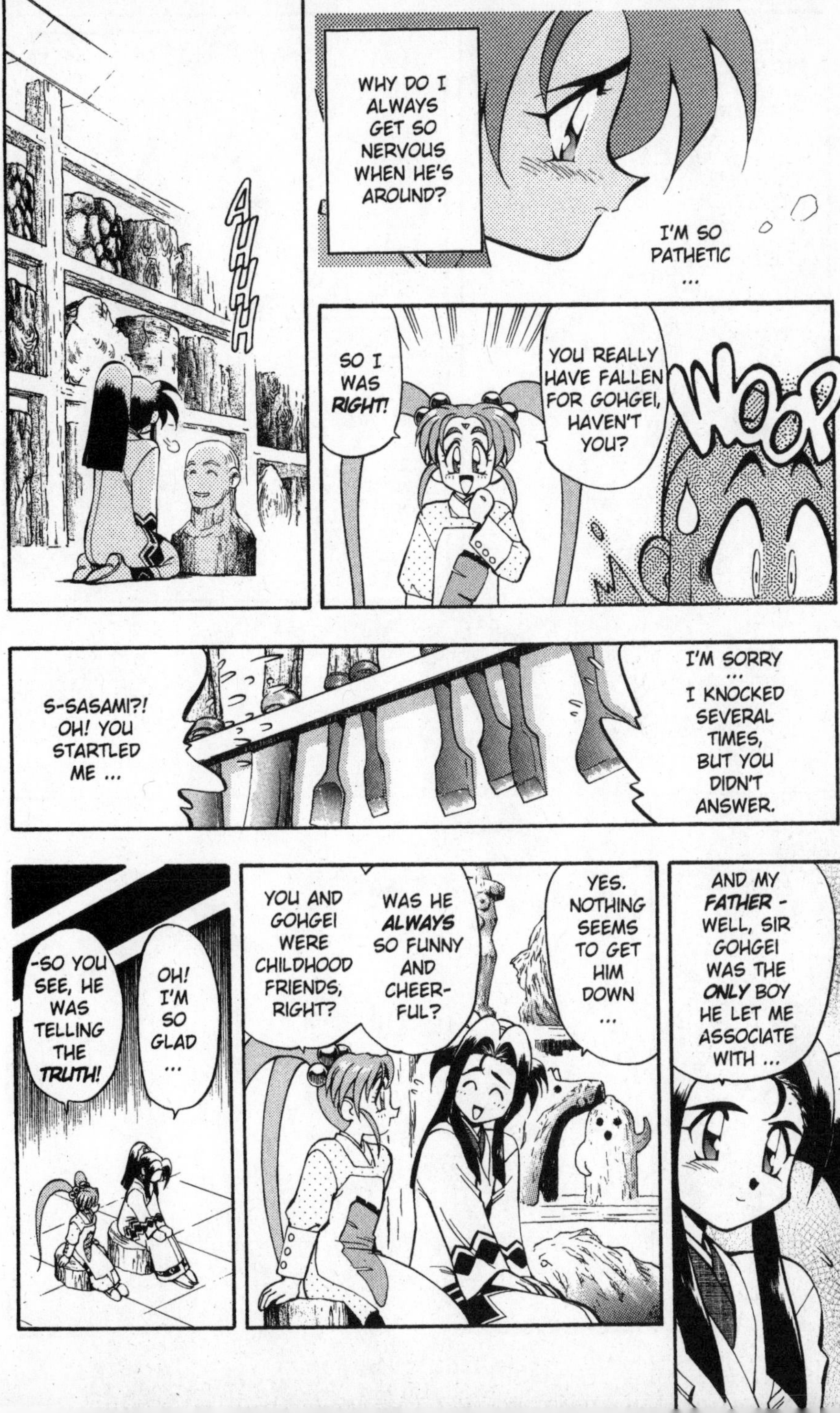
AHHHHH
WHY DO I ALWAYS GET SO NERVOUS WHEN HE'S AROUND?
I'M SO PATHETIC ...
SO I WAS RIGHT!
YOU REALLY HAVE FALLEN FOR GOHGEI, HAVEN'T YOU?
WOOP
S-SASAMI?! OH! YOU STARTLED ME ...
I'M SORRY ... I KNOCKED SEVERAL TIMES, BUT YOU DIDN'T ANSWER.
-SO YOU SEE, HE WAS TELLING THE TRUTH!
OH! I'M SO GLAD ...
YOU AND GOHGEI WERE CHILDHOOD FRIENDS, RIGHT?
WAS HE ALWAYS SO FUNNY AND CHEER-FUL?
YES. NOTHING SEEMS TO GET HIM DOWN ...
AND MY FATHER - WELL, SIR GOHGEI WAS THE ONLY BOY HE LET ME ASSOCIATE WITH ...

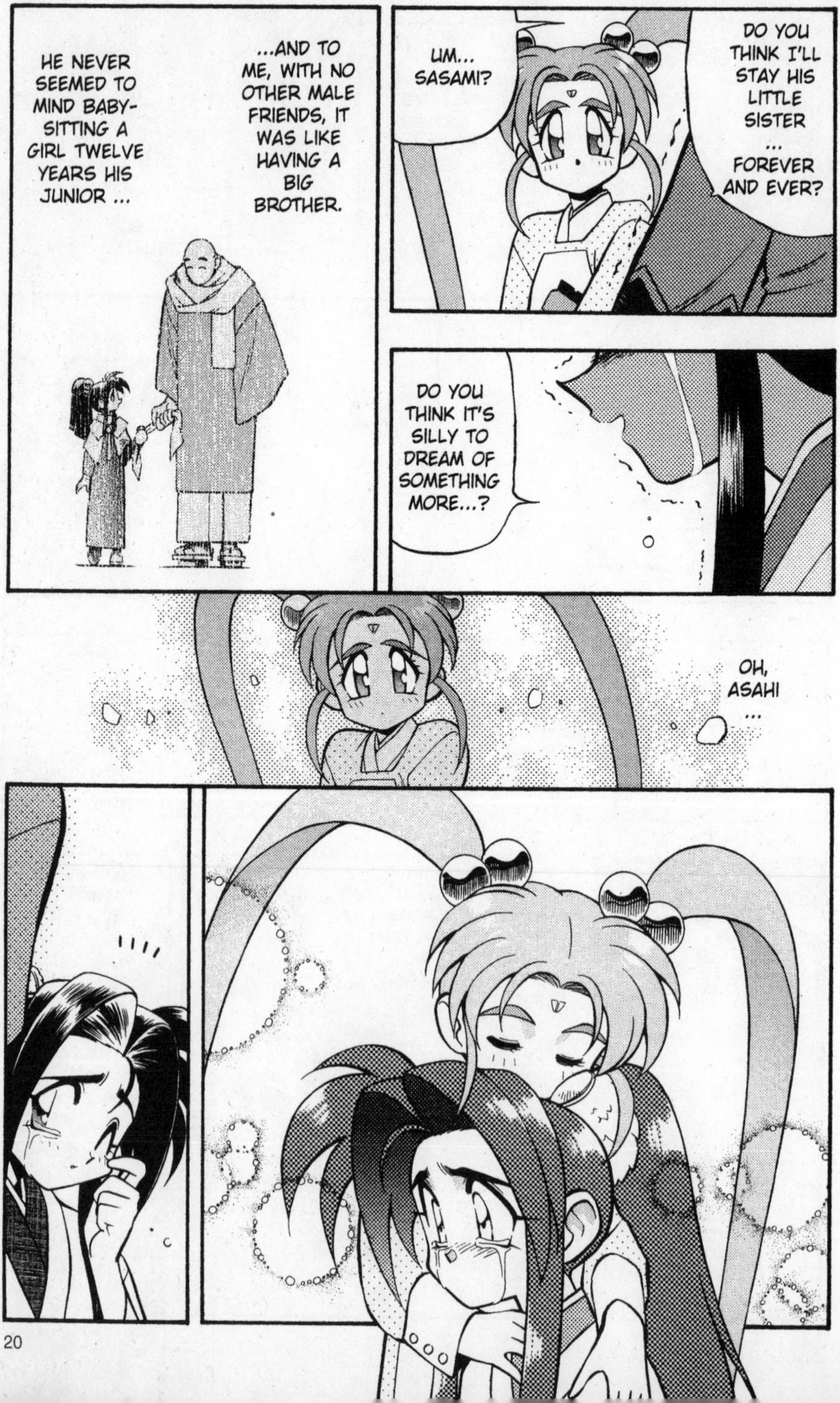
HE NEVER SEEMED TO MIND BABY-SITTING A GIRL TWELVE YEARS HIS JUNIOR ...
...AND TO ME, WITH NO OTHER MALE FRIENDS, IT WAS LIKE HAVING A BIG BROTHER.
UM... SASAMI?
DO YOU THINK I'LL STAY HIS LITTLE SISTER ... FOREVER AND EVER?
DO YOU THINK IT'S SILLY TO DREAM OF SOMETHING MORE...?
OH, ASAHI ...

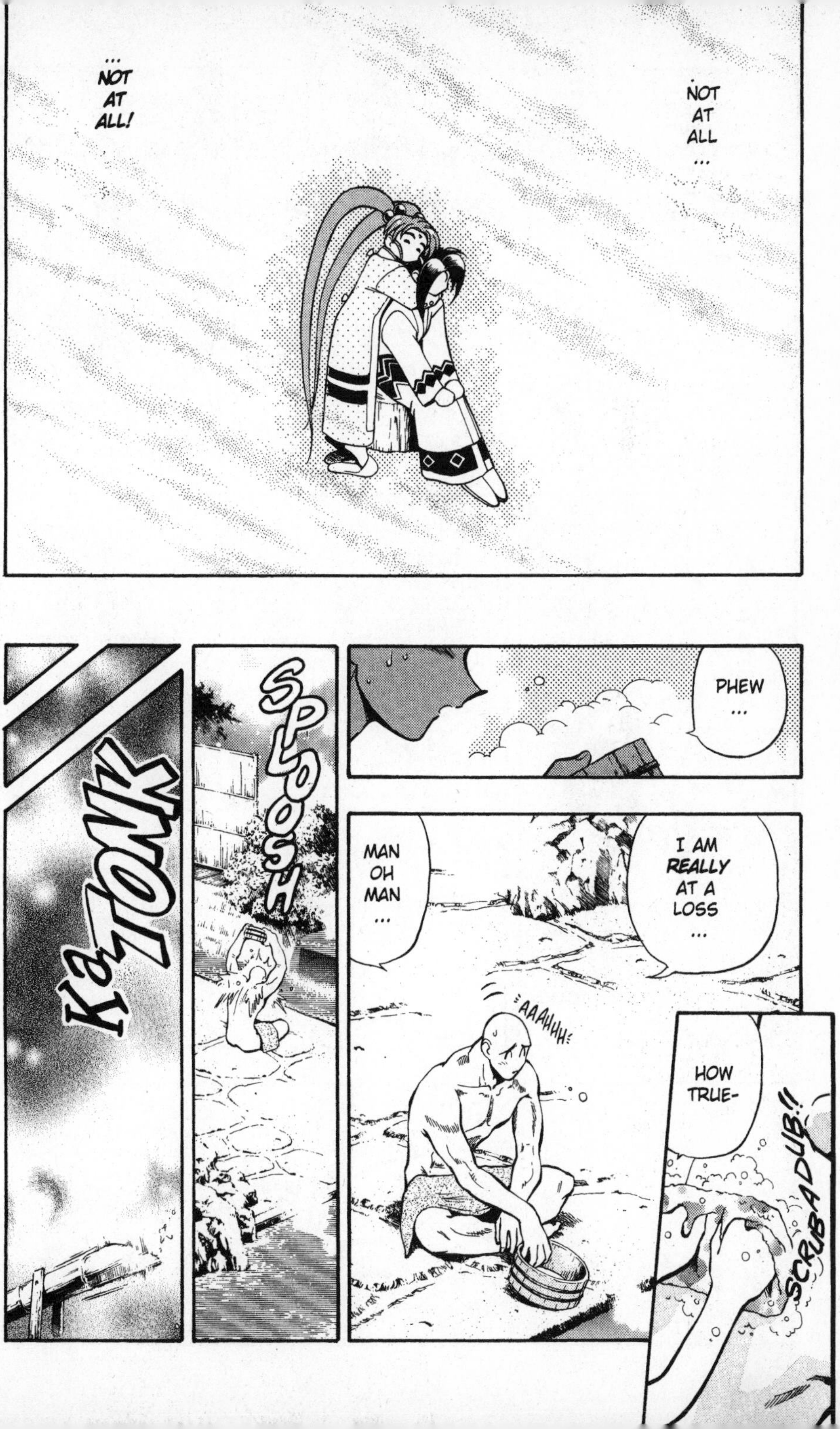
... NOT AT ALL!
NOT AT ALL ...
KaTONK
SPLOOSH
PHEW ...
MAN OH MAN ...
I AM REALLY AT A LOSS ...
AAAHHH
HOW TRUE-
SCRUBADUB!!

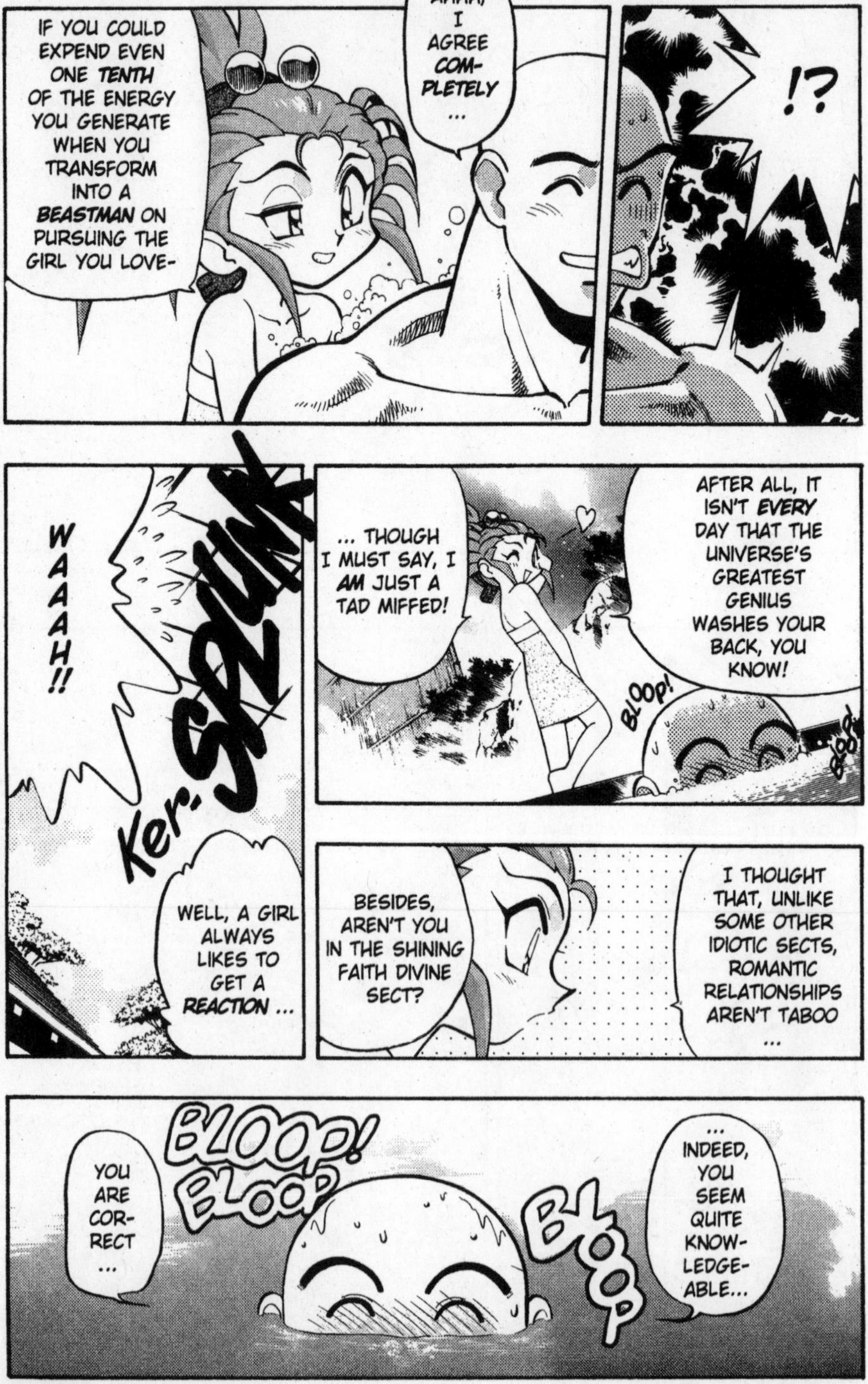
IF YOU COULD EXPEND EVEN ONE TENTH OF THE ENERGY YOU GENERATE WHEN YOU TRANSFORM INTO A BEASTMAN ON PURSUING THE GIRL YOU LOVE-
AHHH, I AGREE COMPLETELY ...
!?
WAAAAH!!
Ker-SPLUNK
WELL, A GIRL ALWAYS LIKES TO GET A REACTION ...
... THOUGH I MUST SAY, I AM JUST A TAD MIFFED!
AFTER ALL, IT ISN'T EVERY DAY THAT THE UNIVERSE'S GREATEST GENIUS WASHES YOUR BACK, YOU KNOW!
BLOOP!
bloop
BESIDES, AREN'T YOU IN THE SHINING FAITH DIVINE SECT?
I THOUGHT THAT, UNLIKE SOME OTHER IDIOTIC SECTS, ROMANTIC RELATIONSHIPS AREN'T TABOO ...
YOU ARE CORRECT ...
BLOOP! BLOOP
BLOOP
... INDEED, YOU SEEM QUITE KNOWLEDGEABLE...

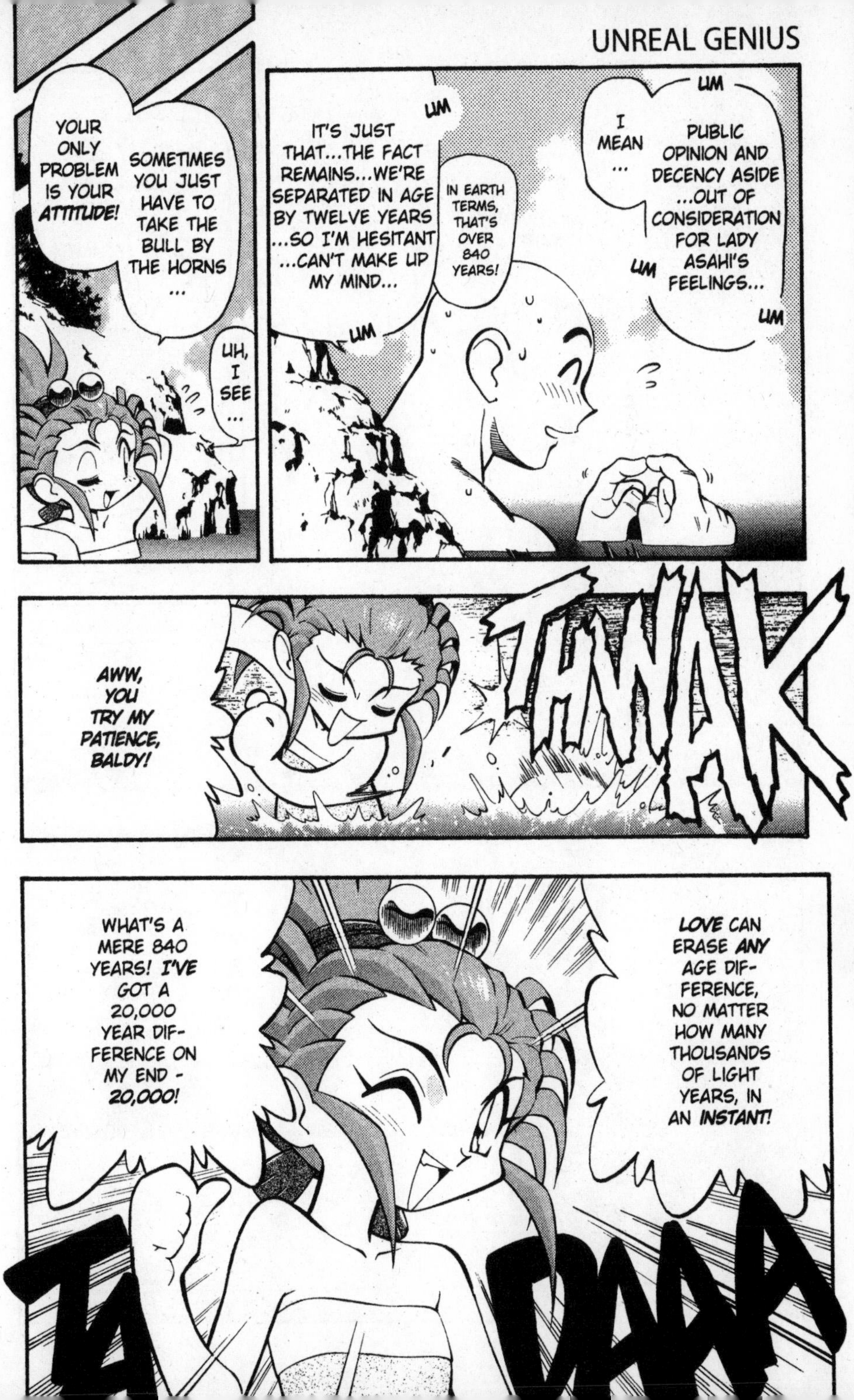
YOUR ONLY PROBLEM IS YOUR ATTITUDE!
SOMETIMES YOU JUST HAVE TO TAKE THE BULL BY THE HORNS ...
UH, I SEE ...
UM
IT'S JUST THAT...THE FACT REMAINS...WE'RE SEPARATED IN AGE BY TWELVE YEARS ...SO I'M HESITANT ...CAN'T MAKE UP MY MIND...
UM
IN EARTH TERMS, THAT'S OVER 840 YEARS!
I MEAN ...
UM
PUBLIC OPINION AND DECENCY ASIDE ...OUT OF CONSIDERATION FOR LADY ASAHI'S FEELINGS...
UM
UM
AWW, YOU TRY MY PATIENCE, BALDY!
THWAK
WHAT'S A MERE 840 YEARS! I'VE GOT A 20,000 YEAR DIF- FERENCE ON MY END - 20,000!
LOVE CAN ERASE ANY AGE DIF- FERENCE, NO MATTER HOW MANY THOUSANDS OF LIGHT YEARS, IN AN INSTANT!
TA DADA

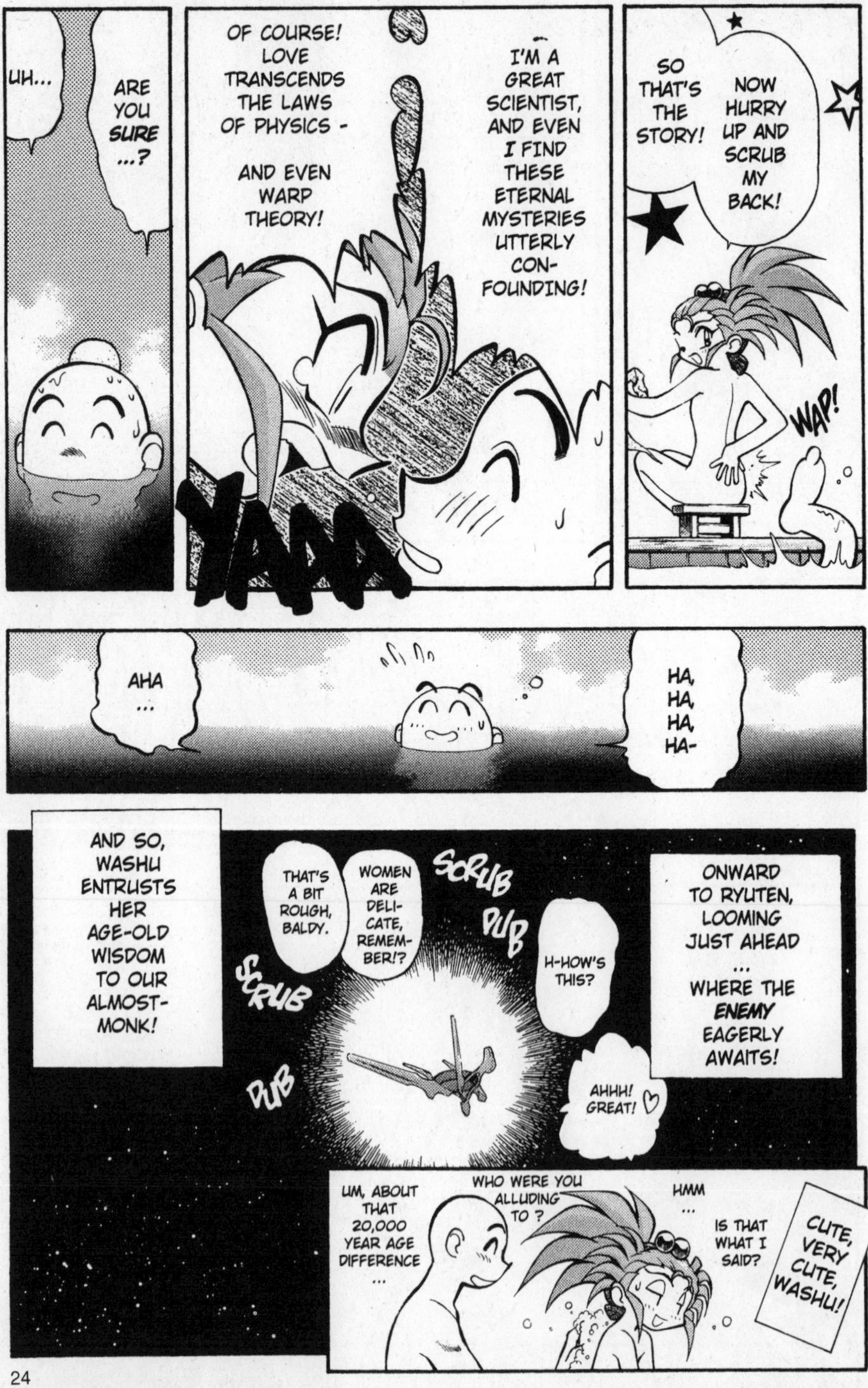
UH...
ARE YOU SURE ...?
OF COURSE! LOVE TRANSCENDS THE LAWS OF PHYSICS -
AND EVEN WARP THEORY!
I'M A GREAT SCIENTIST, AND EVEN I FIND THESE ETERNAL MYSTERIES UTTERLY CON-FOUNDING!
YAAA
SO THAT'S THE STORY!
NOW HURRY UP AND SCRUB MY BACK!
WAP!
AHA ...
HA, HA, HA, HA-
AND SO, WASHU ENTRUSTS HER AGE-OLD WISDOM TO OUR ALMOST-MONK!
THAT'S A BIT ROUGH, BALDY.
WOMEN ARE DELI-CATE, REMEM-BER!?
SCRUB
DUB
SCRUB
DUB
H-HOW'S THIS?
AHHH! GREAT! ♡
ONWARD TO RYUTEN, LOOMING JUST AHEAD ... WHERE THE ENEMY EAGERLY AWAITS!
UM, ABOUT THAT 20,000 YEAR AGE DIFFERENCE ...
WHO WERE YOU ALLUDING TO ?
HMM ...
IS THAT WHAT I SAID?
CUTE, VERY CUTE, WASHU!

Tales of Tenchi #2
CAPTIVE OF WAR

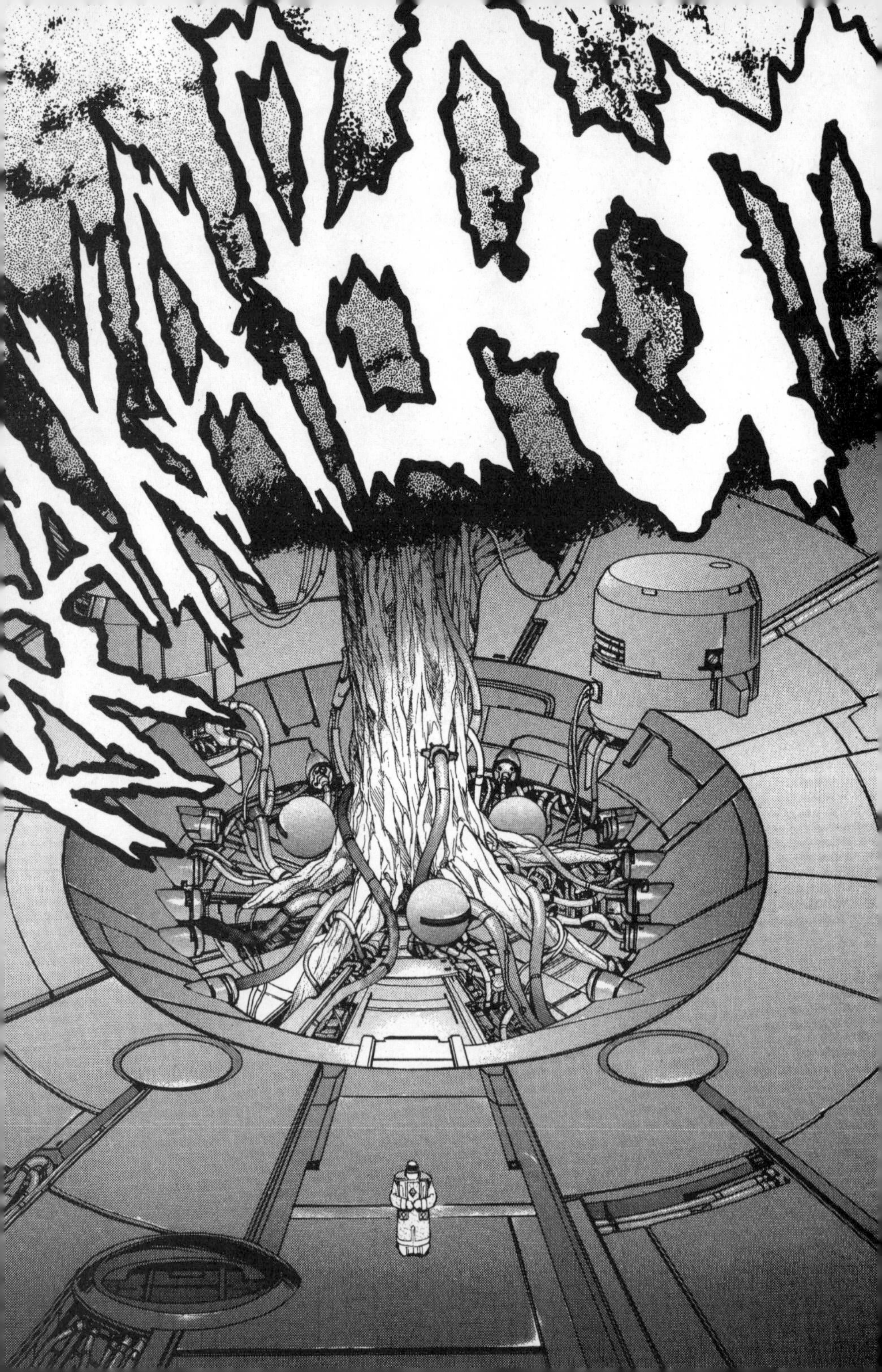

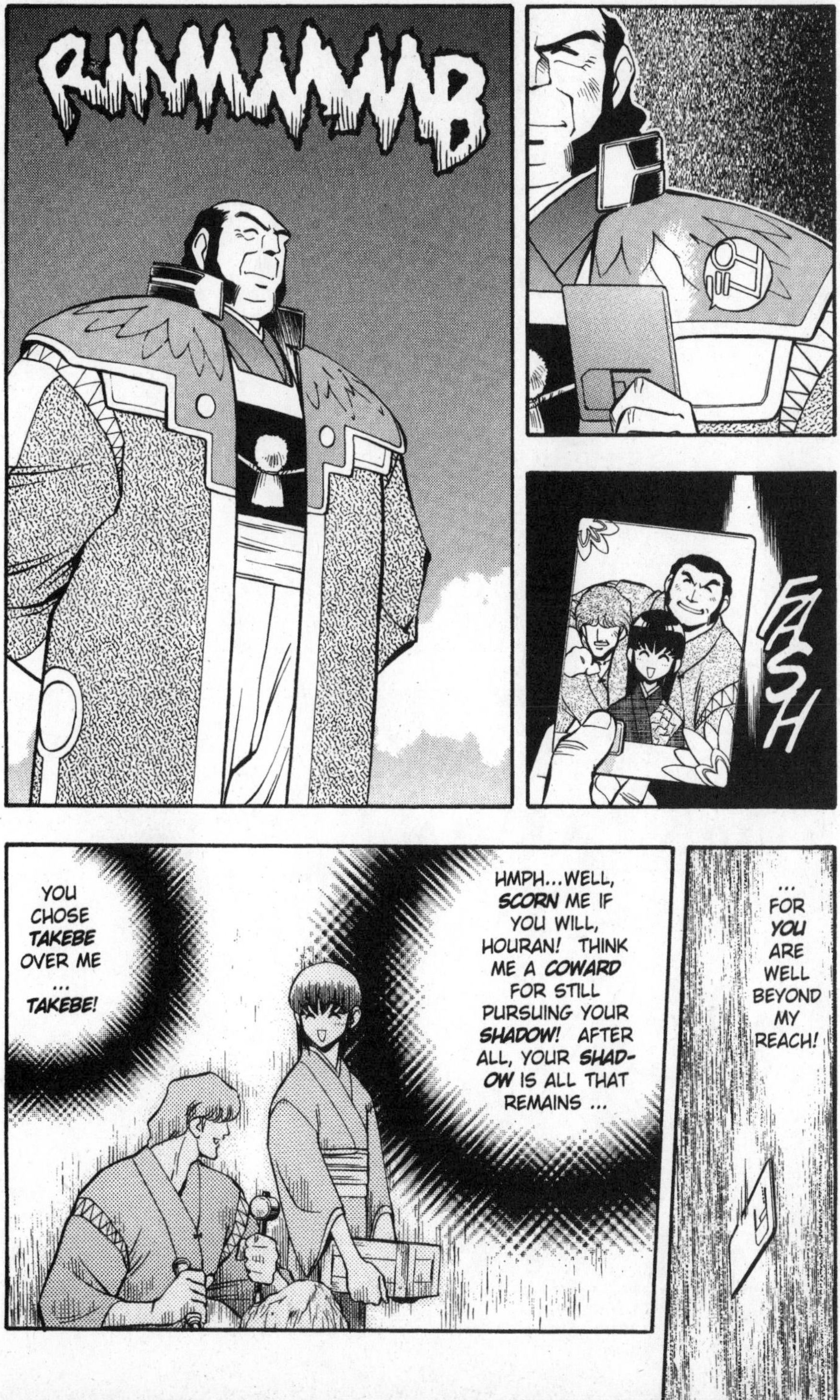
FASH
YOU CHOSE TAKEBE OVER ME ... TAKEBE!
HMPH...WELL, SCORN ME IF YOU WILL, HOURAN! THINK ME A COWARD FOR STILL PURSUING YOUR SHADOW! AFTER ALL, YOUR SHADOW IS ALL THAT REMAINS ...
... FOR YOU ARE WELL BEYOND MY REACH!

BUT YOU LEFT BEHIND THE ONES YOU LOVED... NOMORI AND ASAHI TAKEBE WILL *DIE* BY MY HAND! *THAT* SHALL BE THE TURNING POINT IN MY REBIRTH!

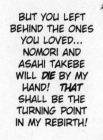

AND ONCE *THEY* ARE GONE, I WILL NEVER AGAIN SUFFER YOUR CONTEMPT!

AARRGH

GAH ... AAGH ... AAAH !

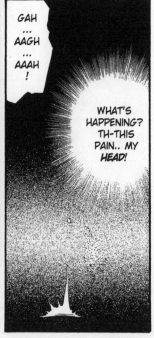

WHAT'S HAPPENING? TH-THIS PAIN.. MY *HEAD!*

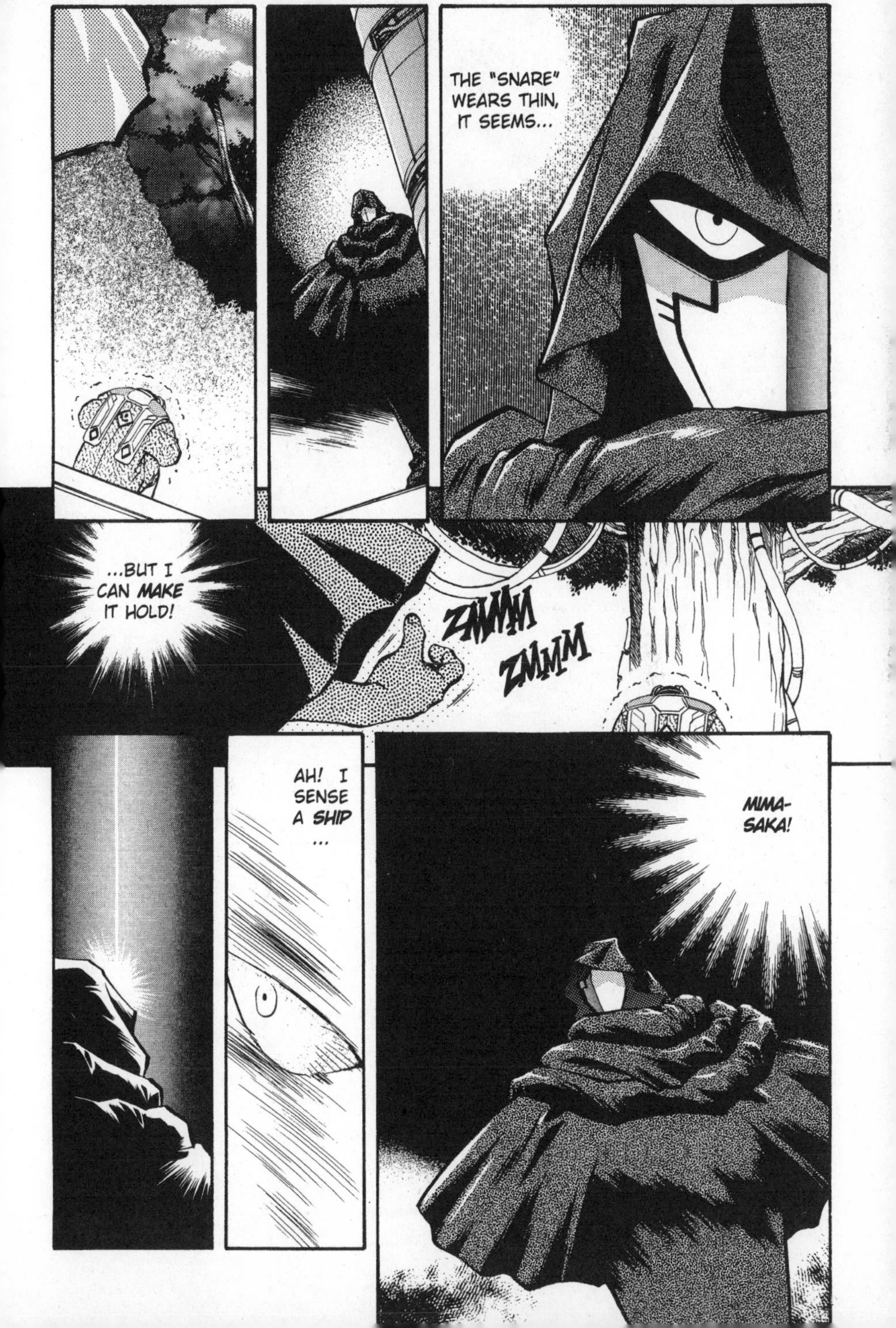
THE "SNARE" WEARS THIN, IT SEEMS...
...BUT I CAN MAKE IT HOLD!
ZMMM
ZMMM
AH! I SENSE A SHIP ...
MIMA-SAKA!

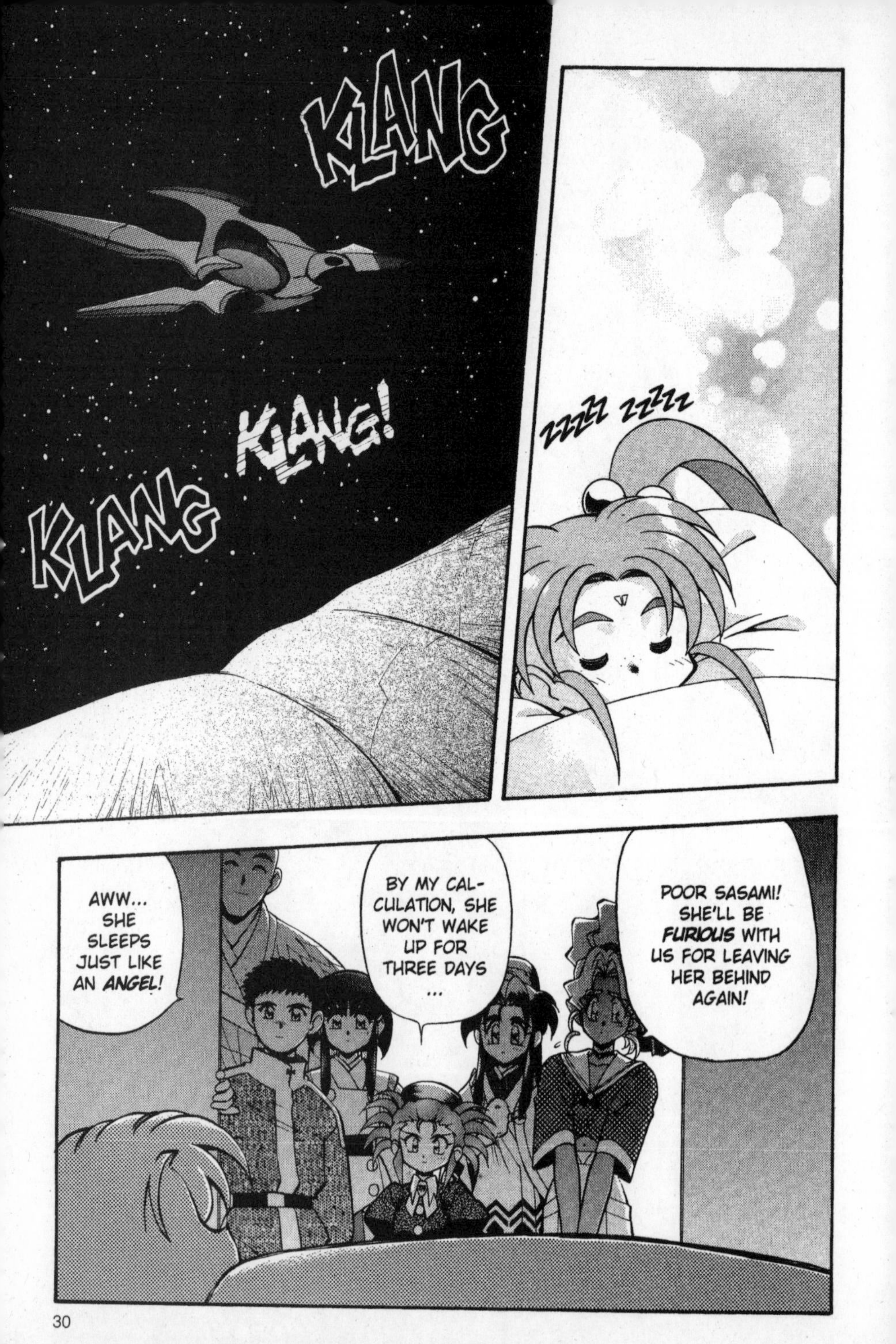
KLANG
KLANG
KLANG!
ZZZZZ ZZZZZ
AWW... SHE SLEEPS JUST LIKE AN ANGEL!
BY MY CAL-CULATION, SHE WON'T WAKE UP FOR THREE DAYS ...
POOR SASAMI! SHE'LL BE FURIOUS WITH US FOR LEAVING HER BEHIND AGAIN!

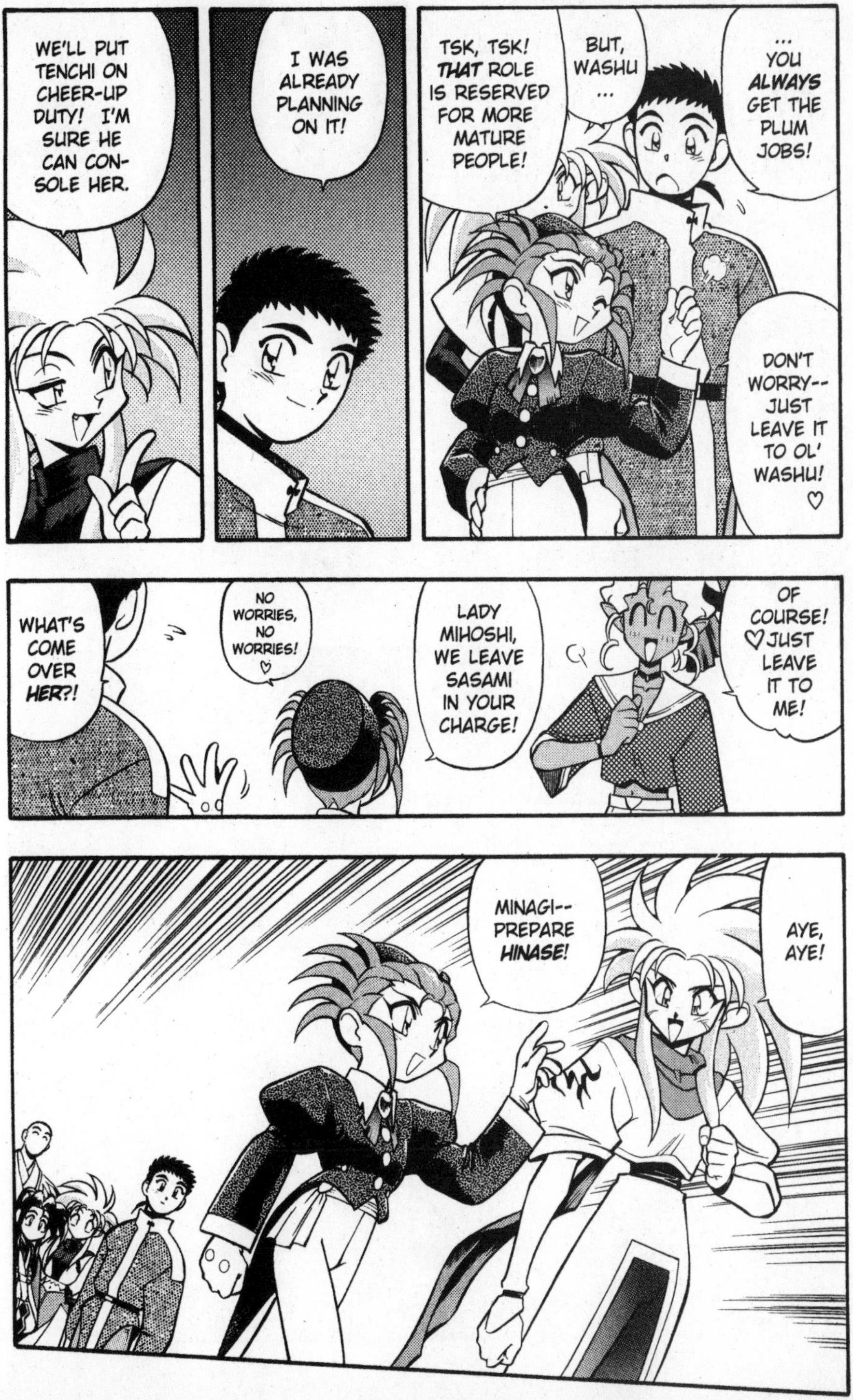
WE'LL PUT TENCHI ON CHEER-UP DUTY! I'M SURE HE CAN CONSOLE HER.
I WAS ALREADY PLANNING ON IT!
TSK, TSK! THAT ROLE IS RESERVED FOR MORE MATURE PEOPLE!
BUT, WASHU ...
... YOU ALWAYS GET THE PLUM JOBS!
DON'T WORRY--JUST LEAVE IT TO OL' WASHU! ♡
WHAT'S COME OVER HER?!
NO WORRIES, NO WORRIES! ♡
LADY MIHOSHI, WE LEAVE SASAMI IN YOUR CHARGE!
OF COURSE! ♡ JUST LEAVE IT TO ME!
MINAGI--PREPARE HINASE!
AYE, AYE!

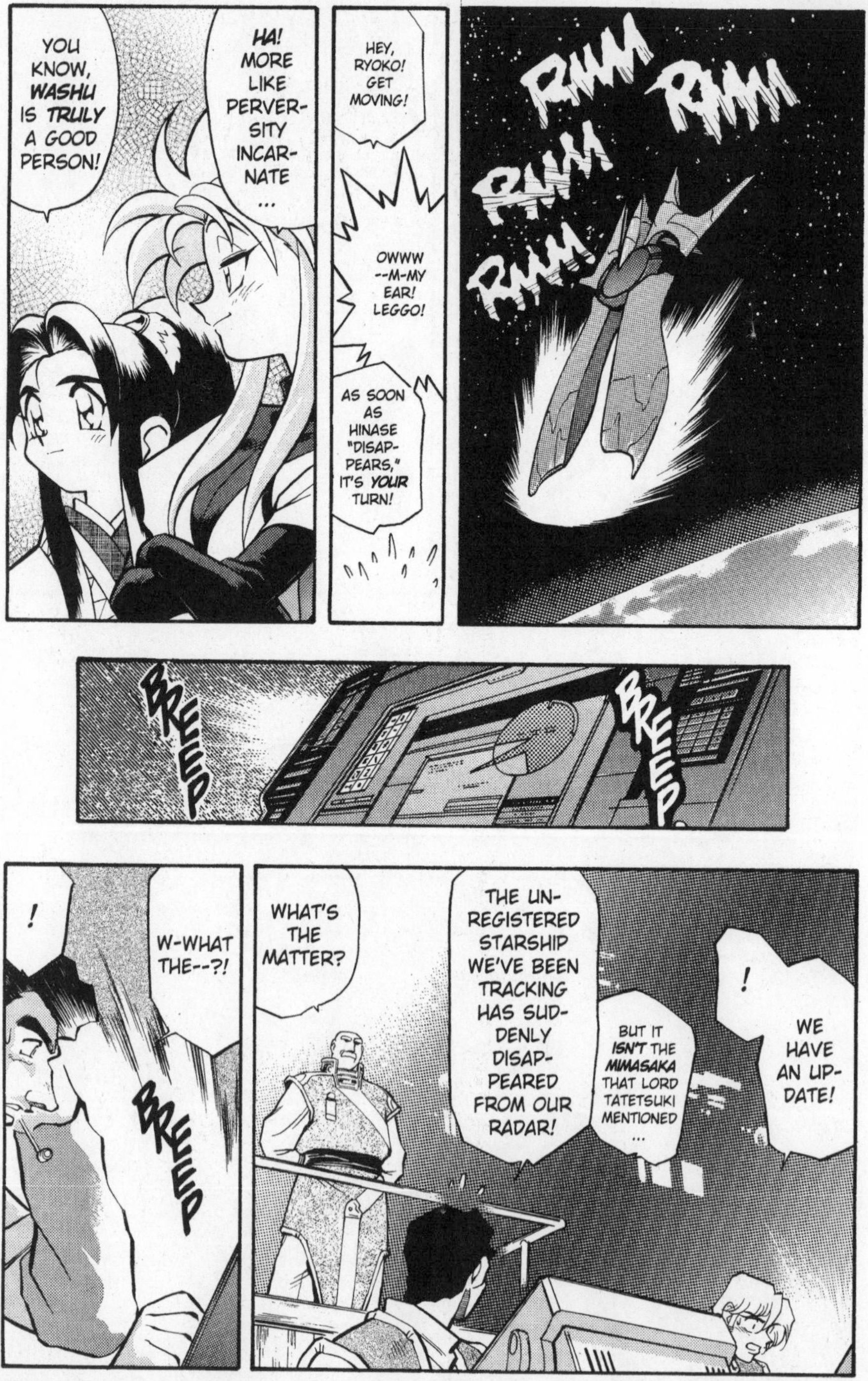
YOU KNOW, WASHU IS TRULY A GOOD PERSON!
HA! MORE LIKE PERVERSITY INCARNATE ...
HEY, RYOKO! GET MOVING!
OWWW --M-MY EAR! LEGGO!
AS SOON AS HINASE "DISAPPEARS," IT'S YOUR TURN!
RMM RMM RMM RMM
BREEP
BREEP
!
W-WHAT THE--?!
BREEP
WHAT'S THE MATTER?
THE UNREGISTERED STARSHIP WE'VE BEEN TRACKING HAS SUDDENLY DISAPPEARED FROM OUR RADAR!
BUT IT ISN'T THE MIMASAKA THAT LORD TATETSUKI MENTIONED ...
!
WE HAVE AN UPDATE!

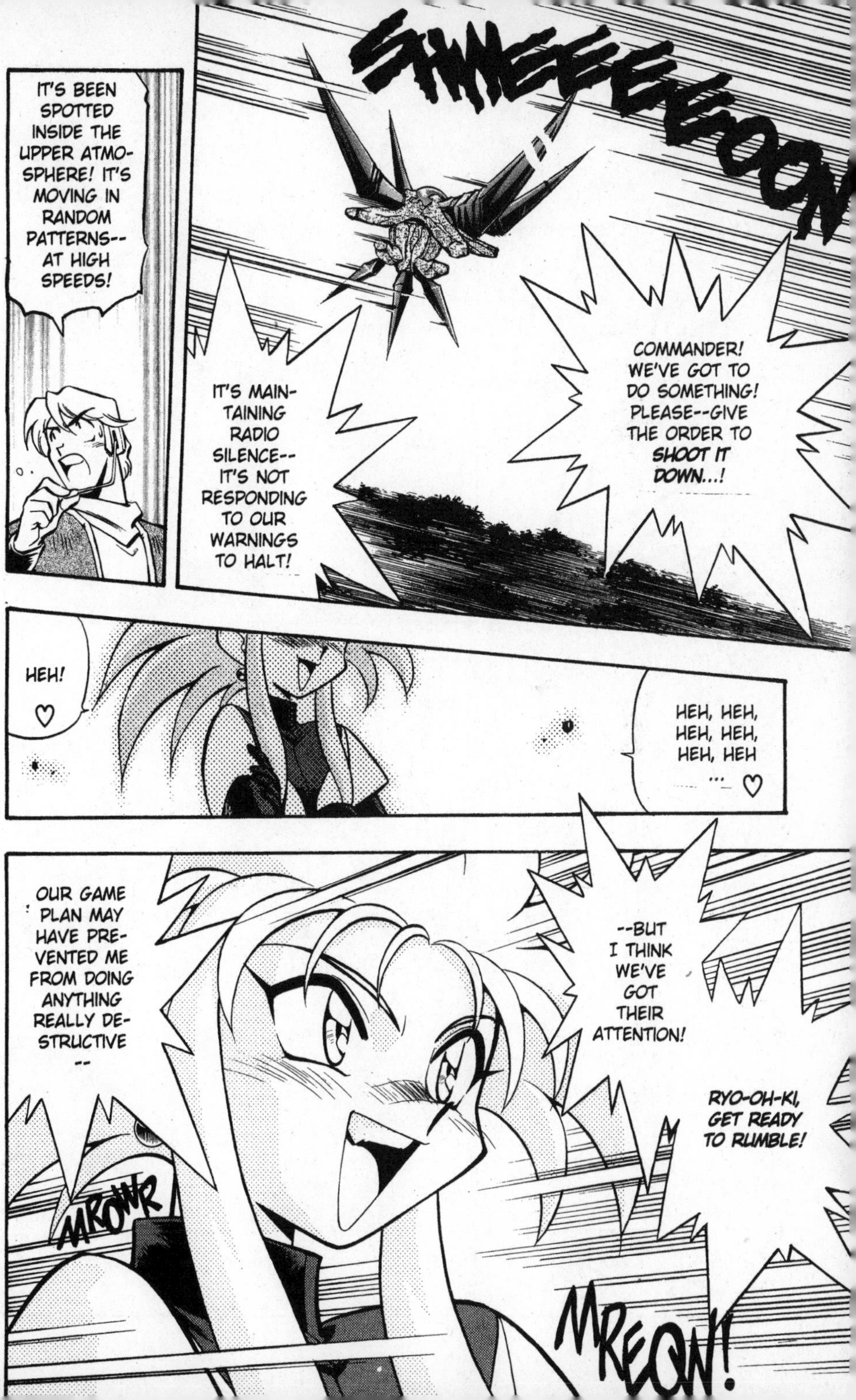
IT'S BEEN SPOTTED INSIDE THE UPPER ATMOSPHERE! IT'S MOVING IN RANDOM PATTERNS--AT HIGH SPEEDS!
SHWEEEEOOOM
IT'S MAINTAINING RADIO SILENCE--IT'S NOT RESPONDING TO OUR WARNINGS TO HALT!
COMMANDER! WE'VE GOT TO DO SOMETHING! PLEASE--GIVE THE ORDER TO SHOOT IT DOWN...!
HEH! ♡
HEH, HEH, HEH, HEH, HEH, HEH ... ♡
OUR GAME PLAN MAY HAVE PREVENTED ME FROM DOING ANYTHING REALLY DESTRUCTIVE --
--BUT I THINK WE'VE GOT THEIR ATTENTION!
RYO-OH-KI, GET READY TO RUMBLE!
MROWR
MREOW!

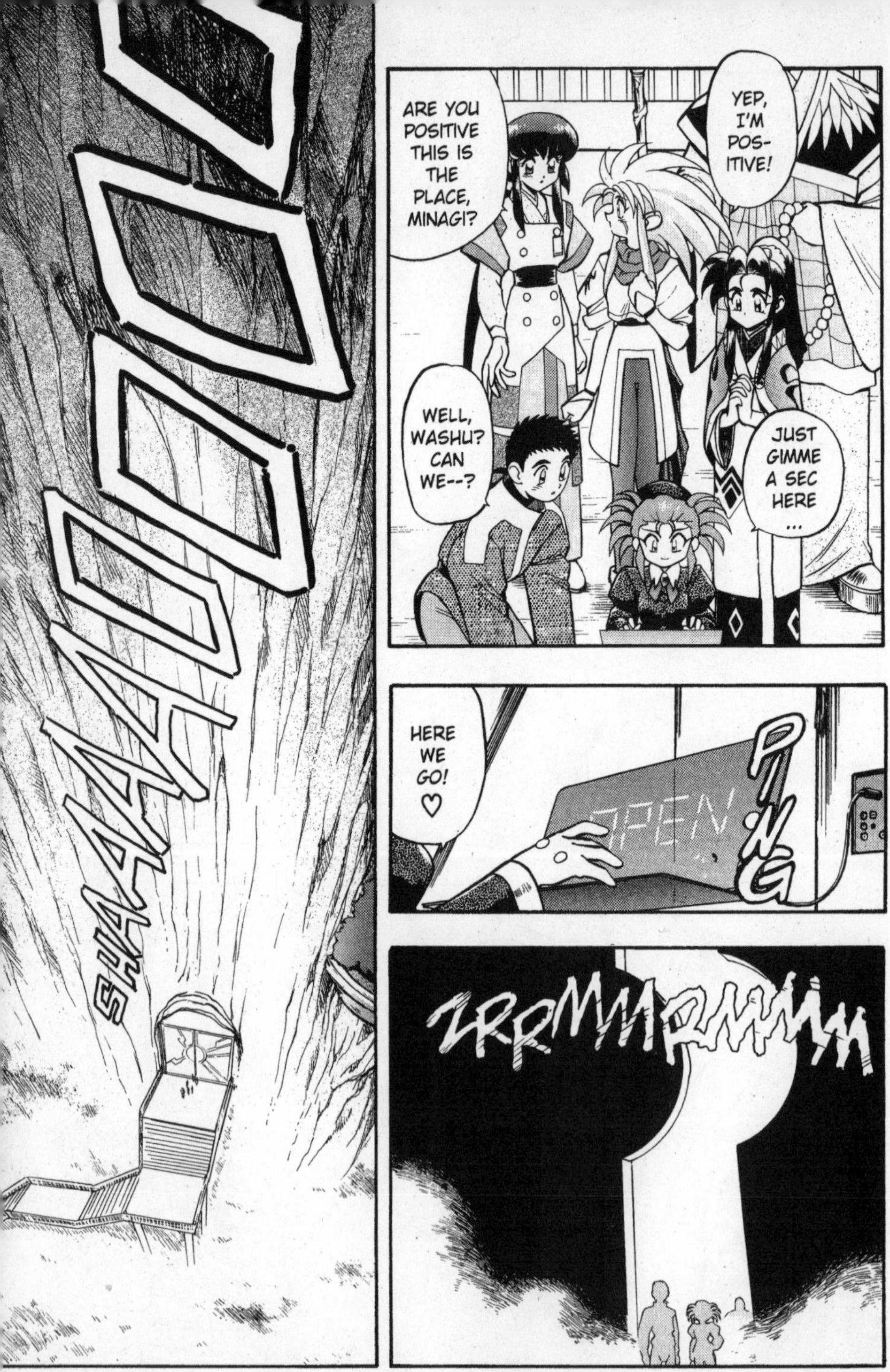
SHAAAHOOOO
ARE YOU POSITIVE THIS IS THE PLACE, MINAGI?
YEP, I'M POS-ITIVE!
WELL, WASHU? CAN WE--?
JUST GIMME A SEC HERE ...
HERE WE GO! ♡
OPEN
PING
ZRRMMMMMMMM

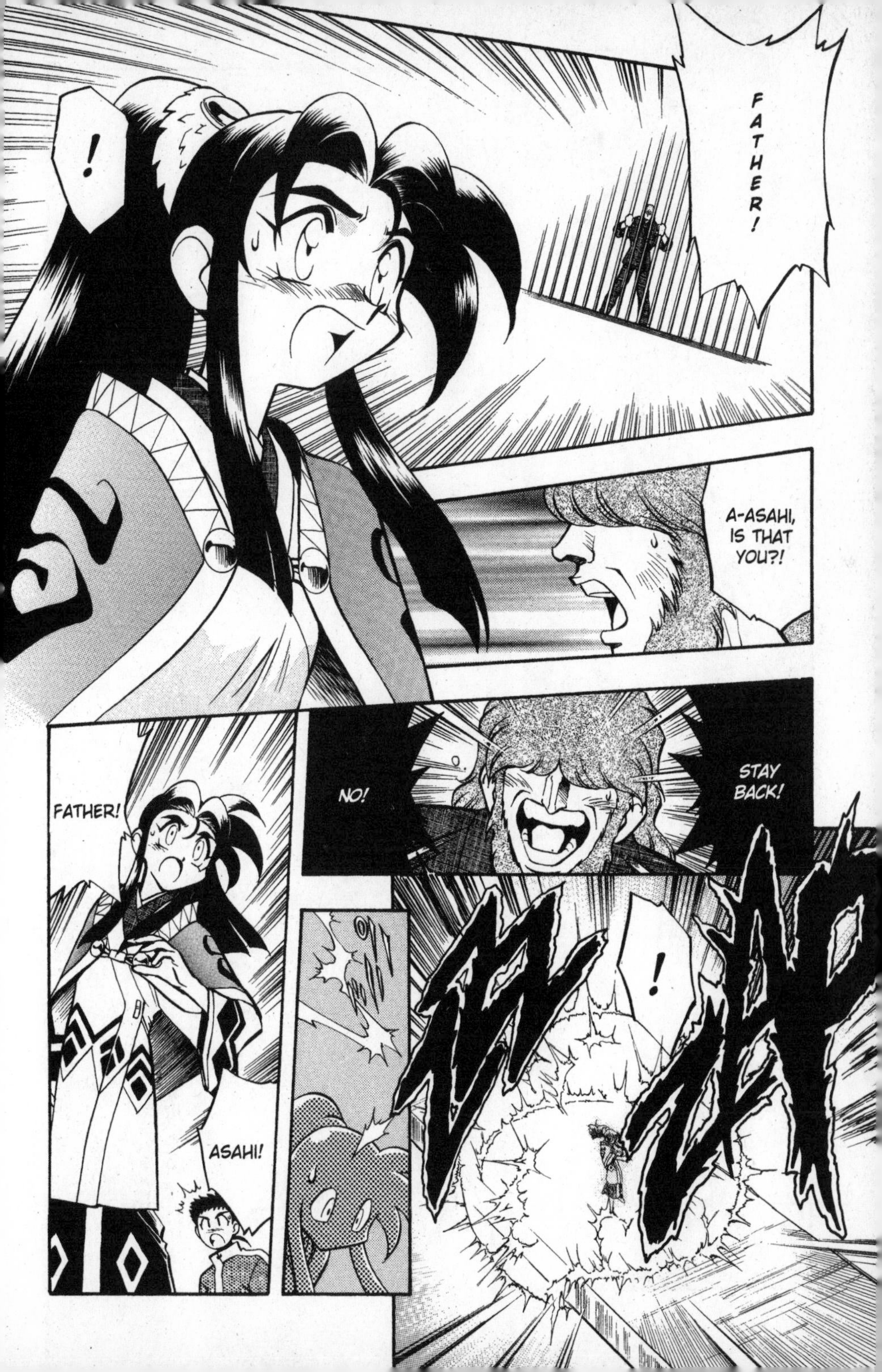
!
FATHER!
A-ASAHI, IS THAT YOU?!
FATHER!
ASAHI!
NO!
STAY BACK!
!

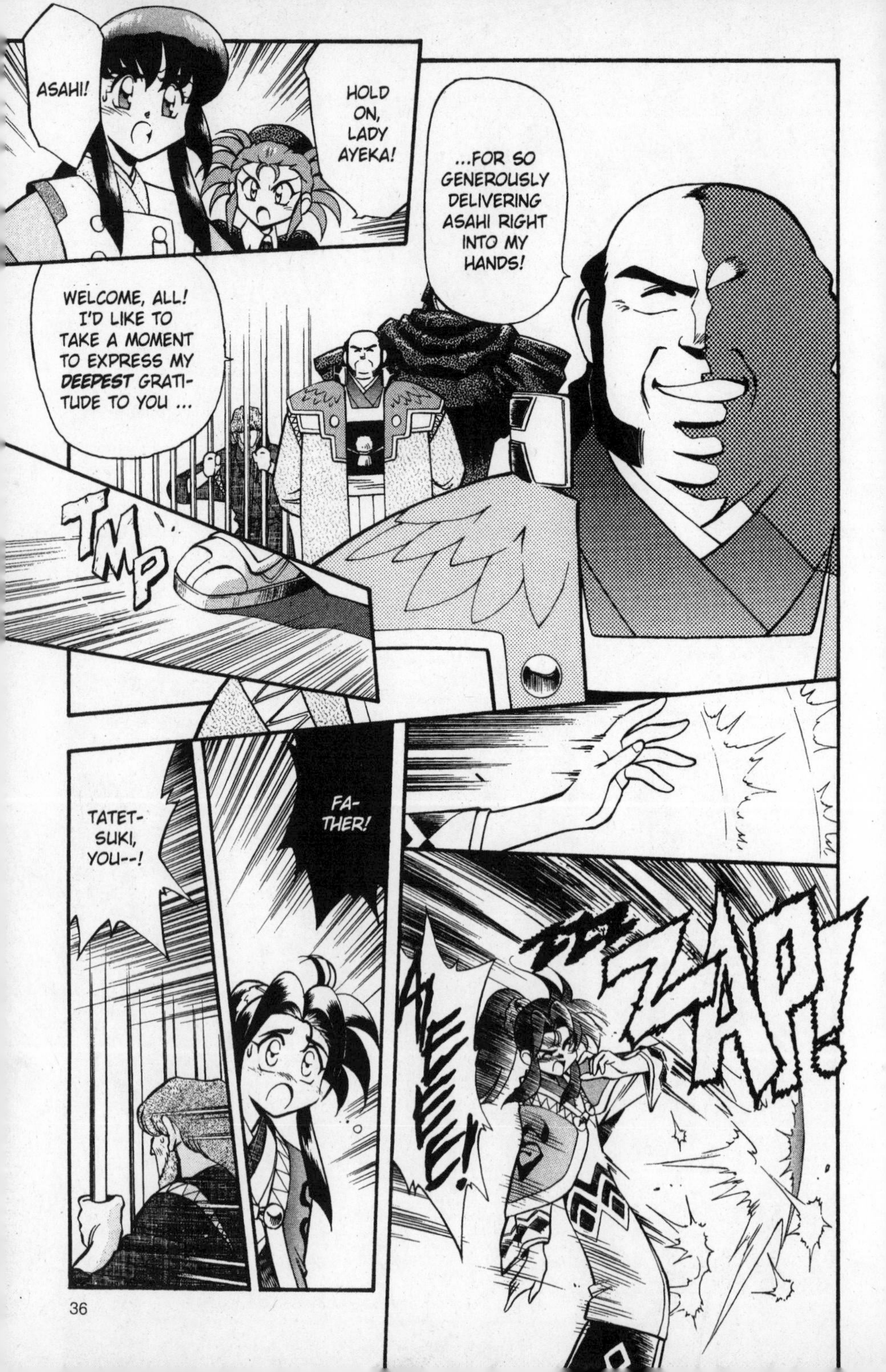
ASAHI!
HOLD ON, LADY AYEKA!
WELCOME, ALL! I'D LIKE TO TAKE A MOMENT TO EXPRESS MY DEEPEST GRATITUDE TO YOU ...
...FOR SO GENEROUSLY DELIVERING ASAHI RIGHT INTO MY HANDS!
TMP
TATET-SUKI, YOU--!
FA-THER!
AEEEE!
ZAP!

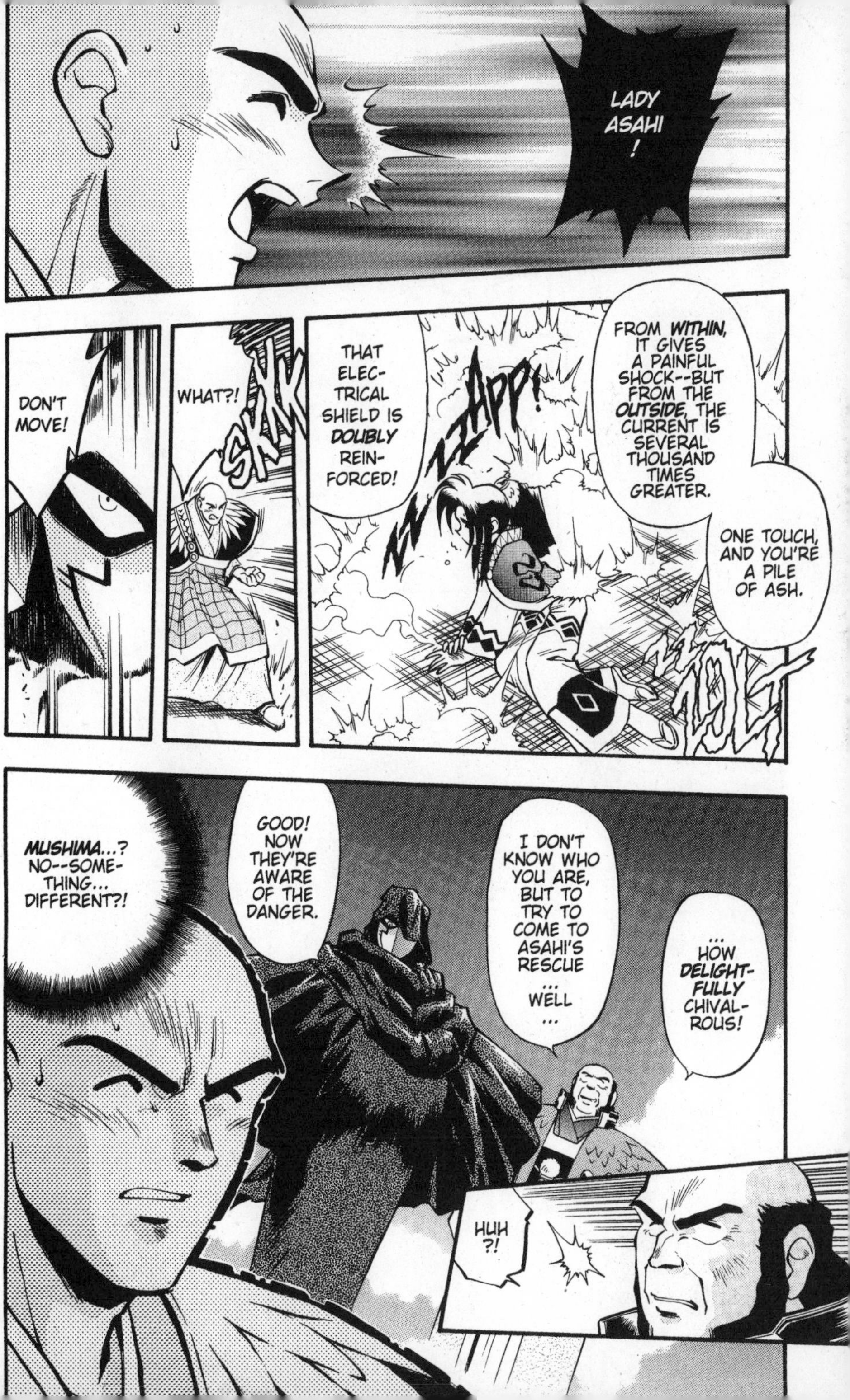
LADY ASAHI !
DON'T MOVE!
WHAT?!
THAT ELEC-TRICAL SHIELD IS DOUBLY REIN-FORCED!
FROM WITHIN, IT GIVES A PAINFUL SHOCK--BUT FROM THE OUTSIDE, THE CURRENT IS SEVERAL THOUSAND TIMES GREATER.
ONE TOUCH, AND YOU'RE A PILE OF ASH.
MUSHIMA...? NO--SOME-THING... DIFFERENT?!
GOOD! NOW THEY'RE AWARE OF THE DANGER.
I DON'T KNOW WHO YOU ARE, BUT TO TRY TO COME TO ASAHI'S RESCUE ... WELL ...
... HOW DELIGHT-FULLY CHIVAL-ROUS!
HUH ?!

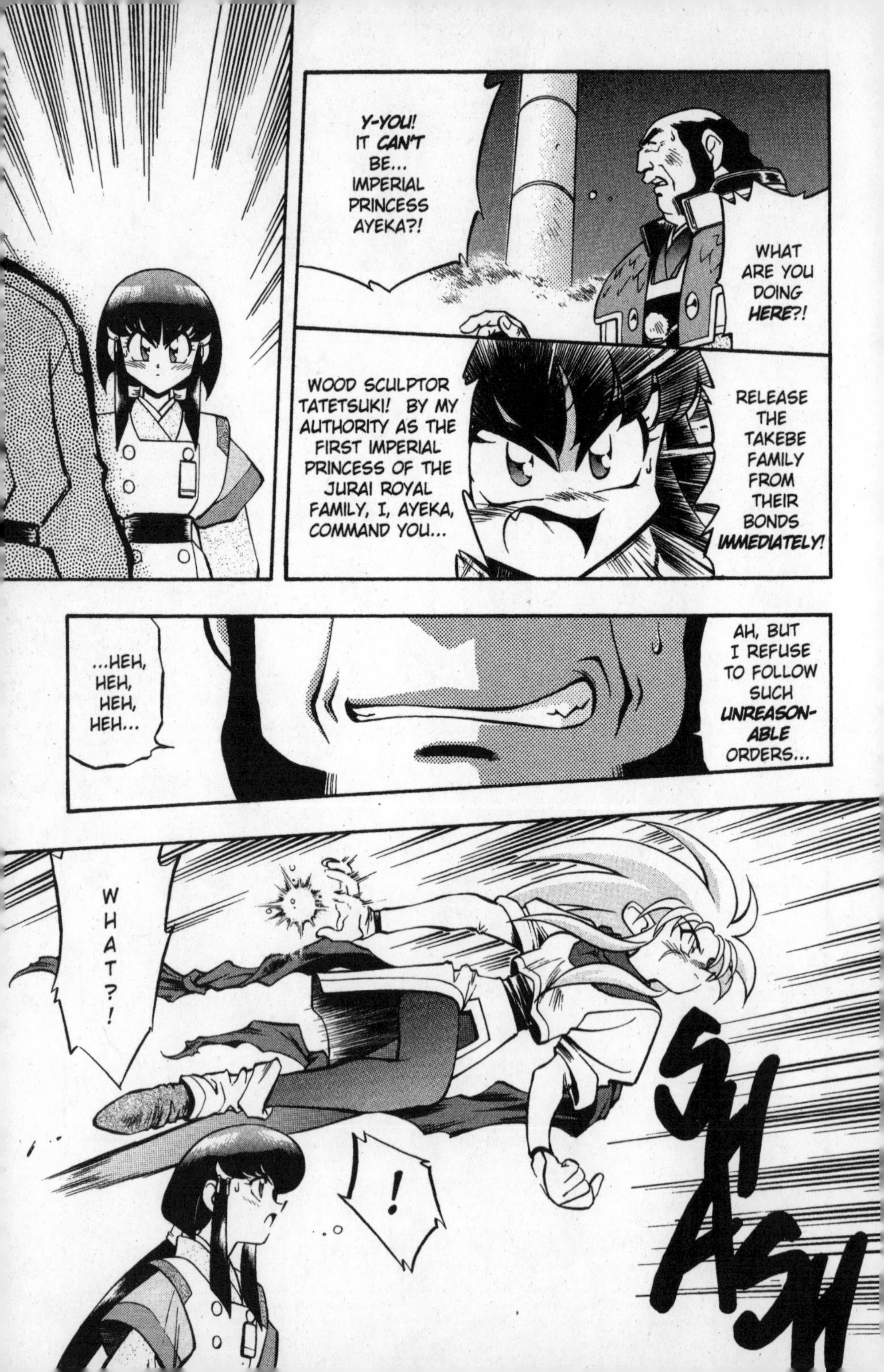
Y-YOU! IT CAN'T BE... IMPERIAL PRINCESS AYEKA?!
WHAT ARE YOU DOING HERE?!
WOOD SCULPTOR TATETSUKI! BY MY AUTHORITY AS THE FIRST IMPERIAL PRINCESS OF THE JURAI ROYAL FAMILY, I, AYEKA, COMMAND YOU...
RELEASE THE TAKEBE FAMILY FROM THEIR BONDS IMMEDIATELY!
...HEH, HEH, HEH, HEH...
AH, BUT I REFUSE TO FOLLOW SUCH UNREASONABLE ORDERS...
WHAT?!
!
SHASH

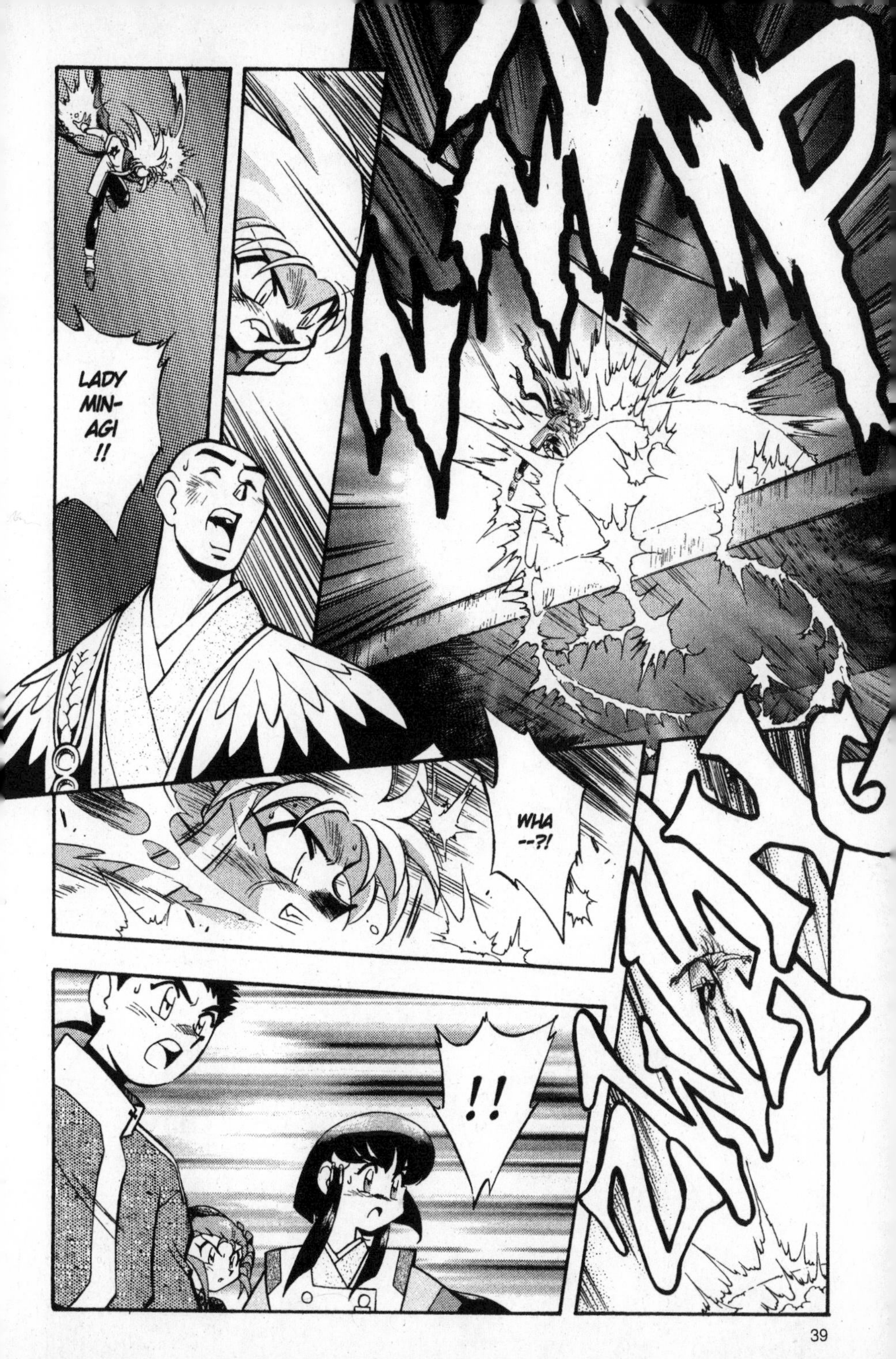
LADY MIN-AGI !!
WHA --?!
!!

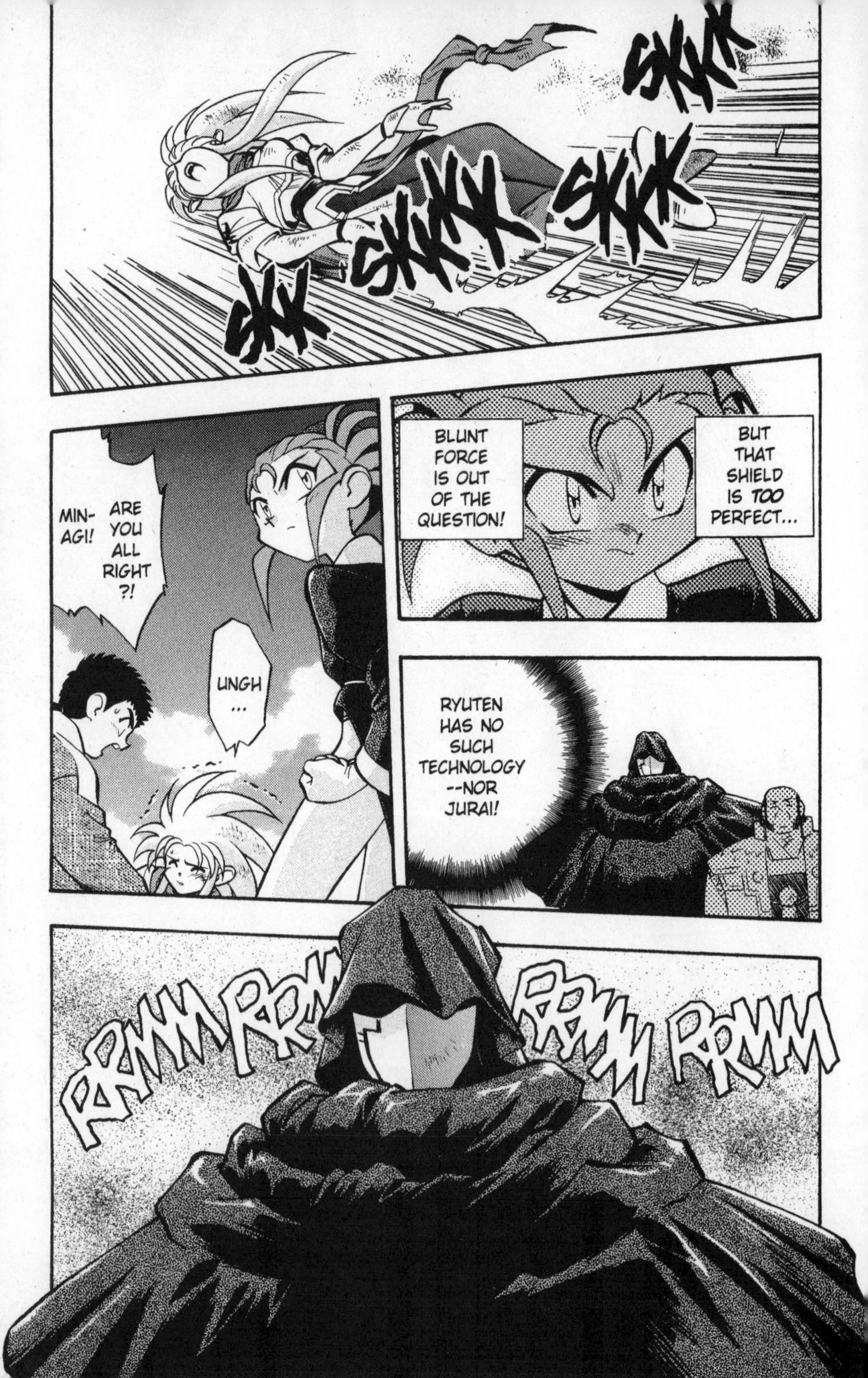

SKK
SKKK
SKKK
SKKK
MIN-AGI!
ARE YOU ALL RIGHT?!
UNGH ...
BLUNT FORCE IS OUT OF THE QUESTION!
BUT THAT SHIELD IS *TOO* PERFECT...
RYUTEN HAS NO SUCH TECHNOLOGY --NOR JURAI!
RRMM RRM
RRMM RRMM

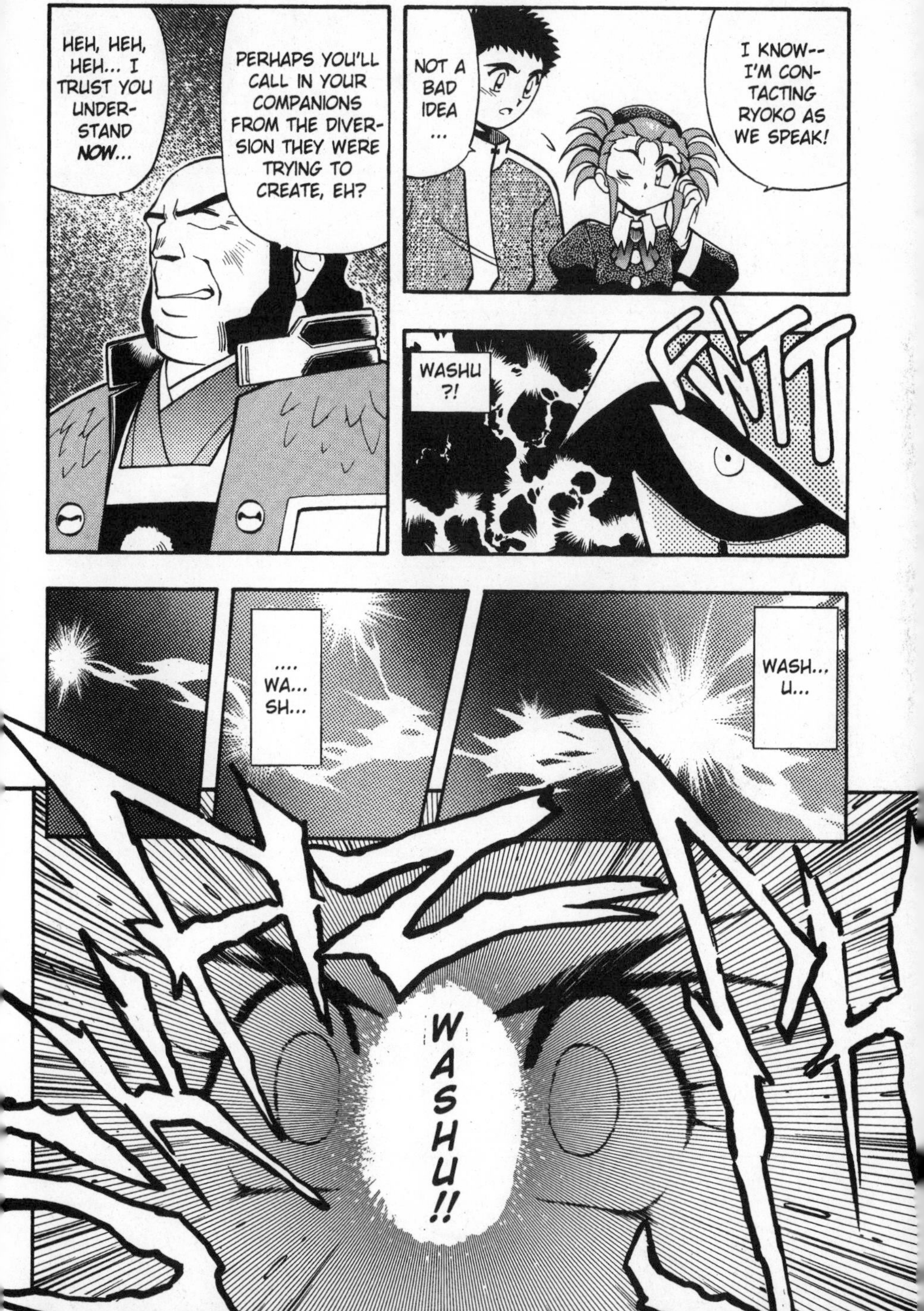
HEH, HEH, HEH... I TRUST YOU UNDERSTAND NOW...
PERHAPS YOU'LL CALL IN YOUR COMPANIONS FROM THE DIVERSION THEY WERE TRYING TO CREATE, EH?
NOT A BAD IDEA ...
I KNOW-- I'M CONTACTING RYOKO AS WE SPEAK!
WASHU ?!
FWTT
.... WA... SH...
WASH... U...
WASHU!!

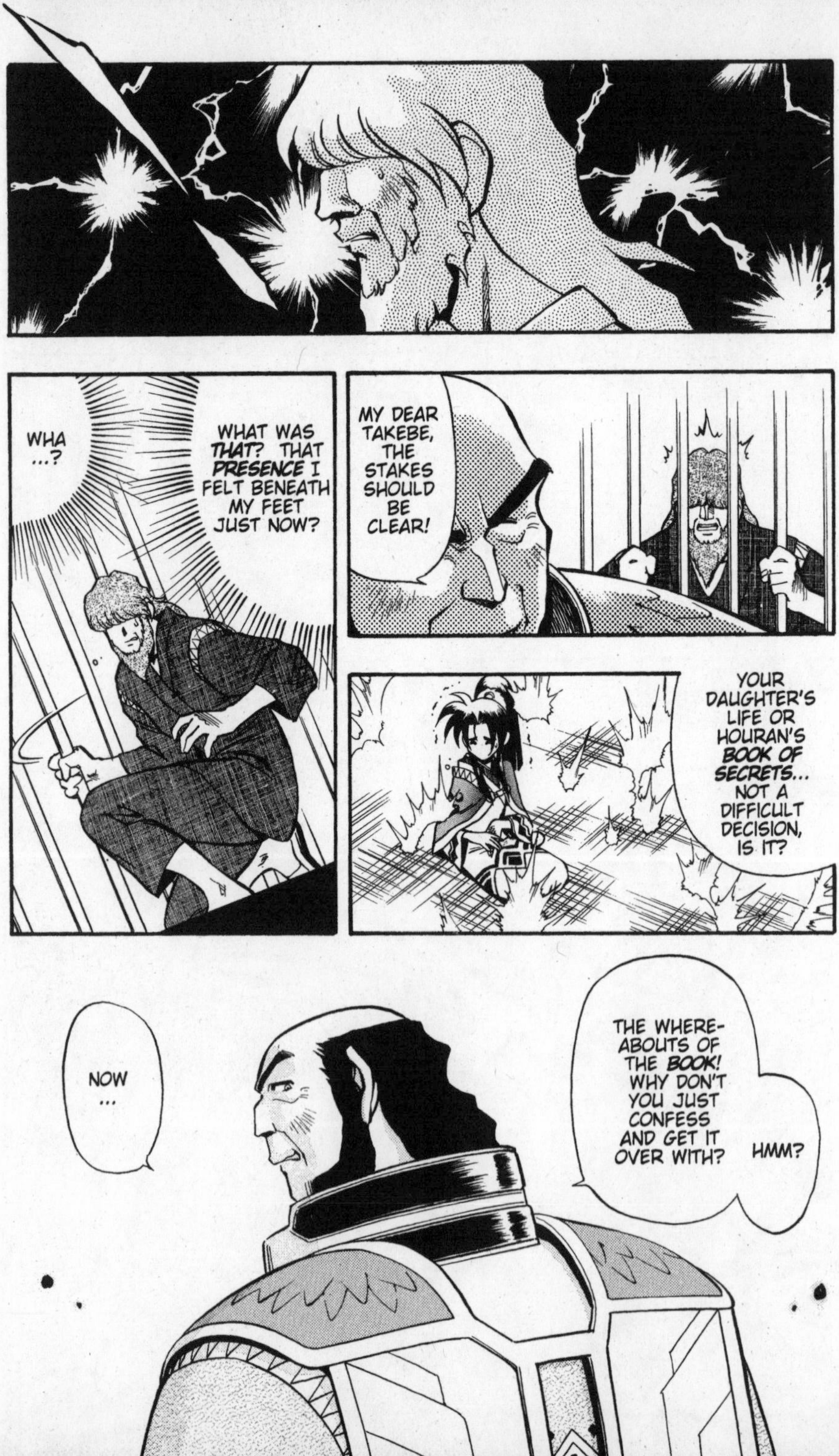
WHA ...?
WHAT WAS THAT? THAT PRESENCE I FELT BENEATH MY FEET JUST NOW?
MY DEAR TAKEBE, THE STAKES SHOULD BE CLEAR!
YOUR DAUGHTER'S LIFE OR HOURAN'S BOOK OF SECRETS... NOT A DIFFICULT DECISION, IS IT?
NOW ...
THE WHERE-ABOUTS OF THE BOOK! WHY DON'T YOU JUST CONFESS AND GET IT OVER WITH?
HMM?

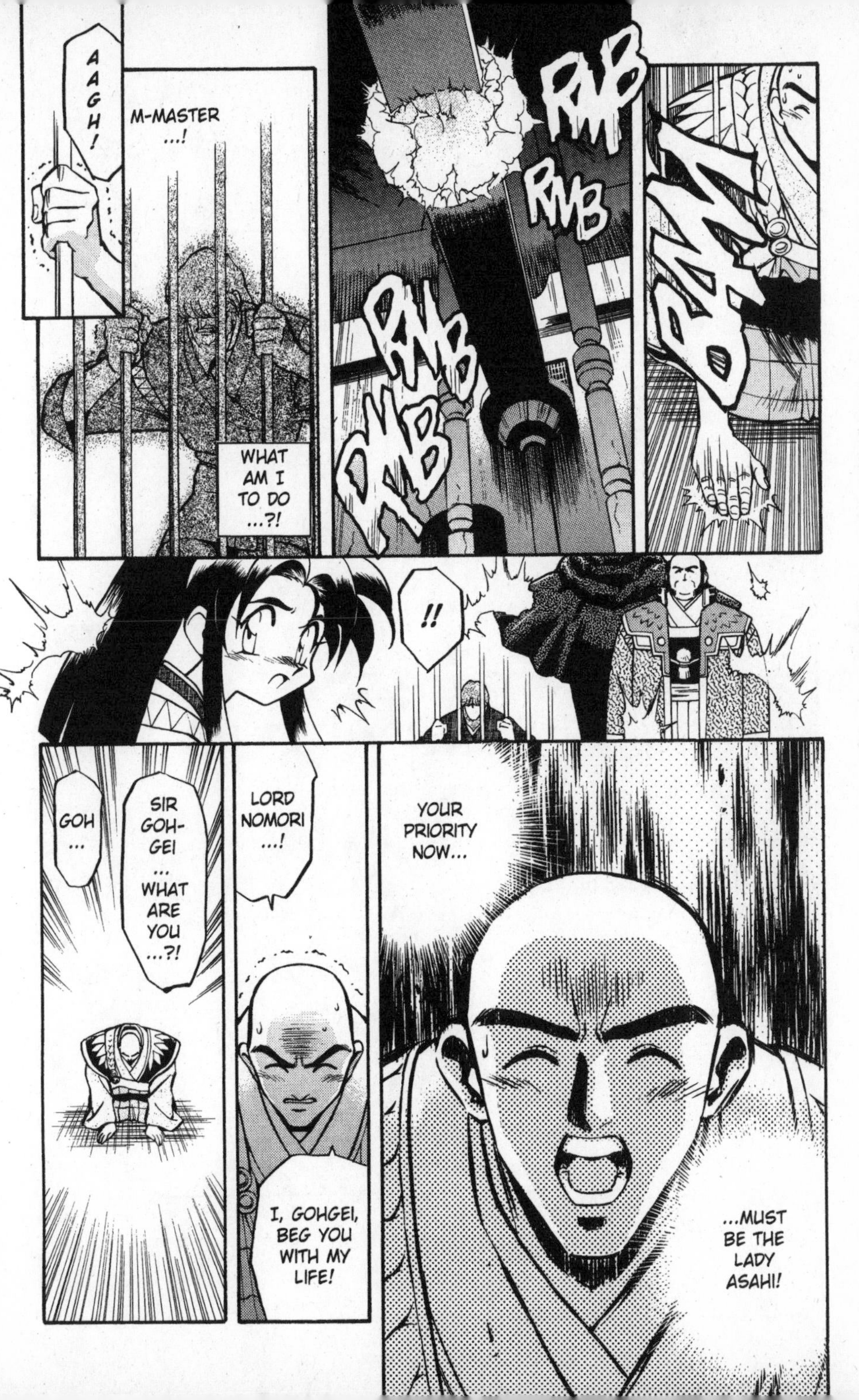
AAGH!
M-MASTER ...!
WHAT AM I TO DO ...?!
RMB
RMB
RMB
RMB
!!
GOH ...
SIR GOH-GEI ... WHAT ARE YOU ...?!
LORD NOMORI ...!
I, GOHGEI, BEG YOU WITH MY LIFE!
YOUR PRIORITY NOW...
...MUST BE THE LADY ASAHI!

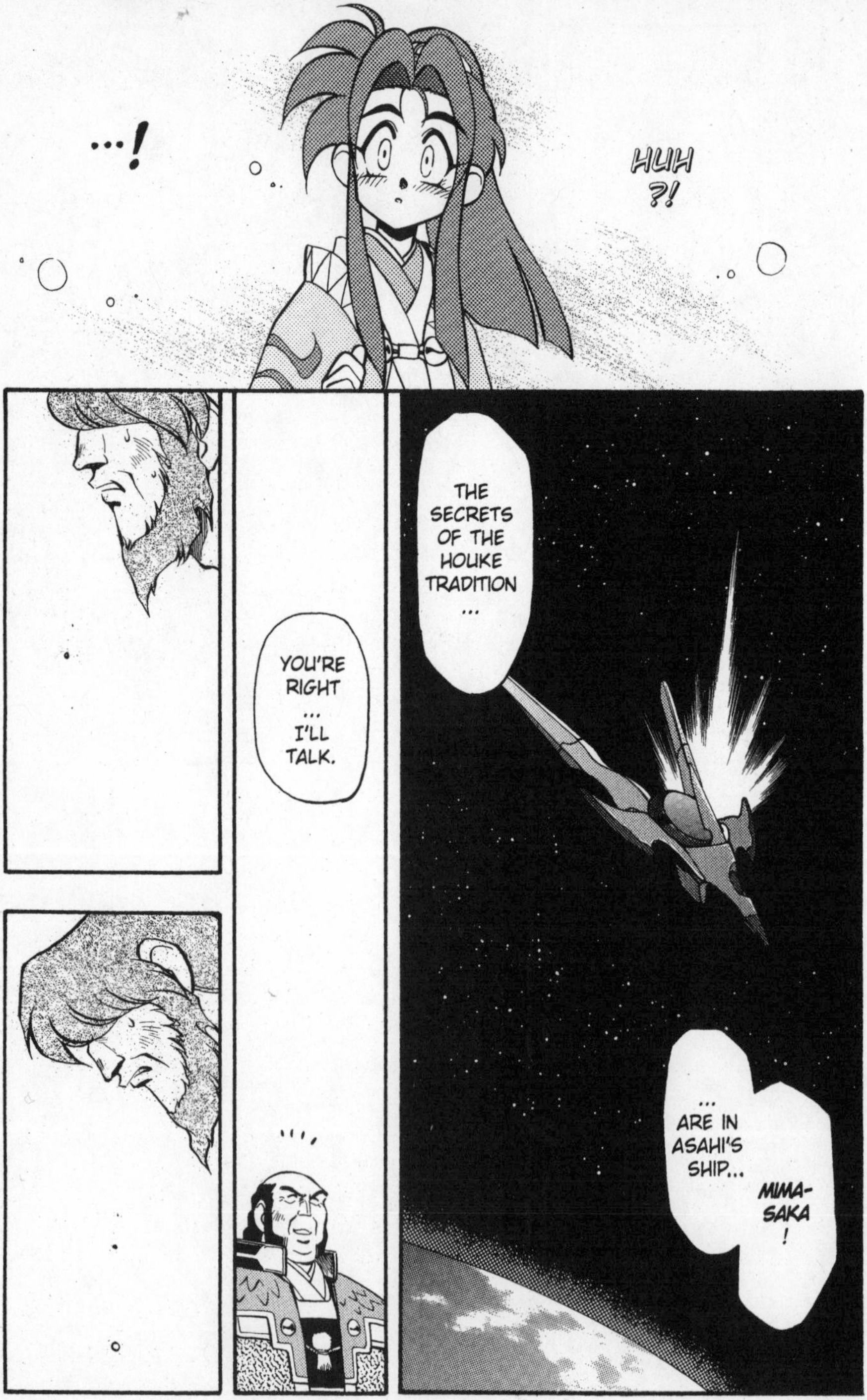

...!
HUH ?!
YOU'RE RIGHT ... I'LL TALK.
THE SECRETS OF THE HOUKE TRADITION ...
... ARE IN ASAHI'S SHIP...
MIMA-SAKA !

Tales of Tenchi #3

THE GREAT ESCAPE

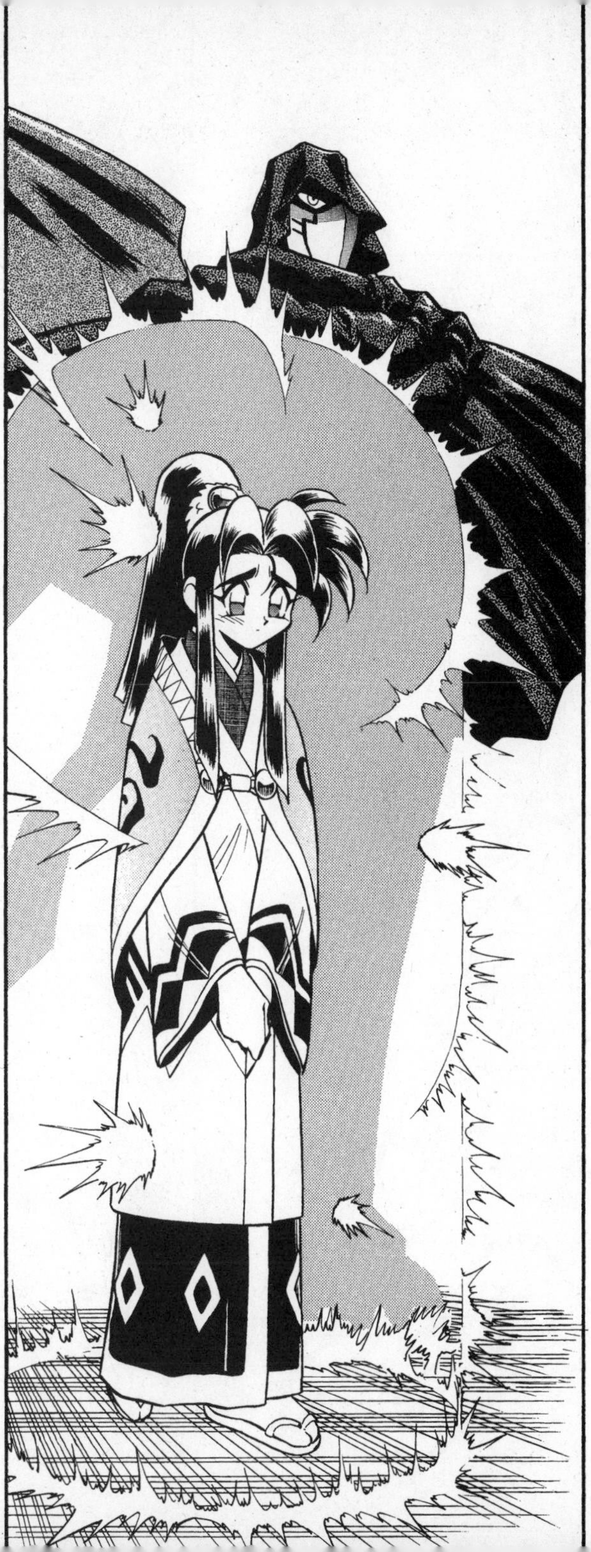

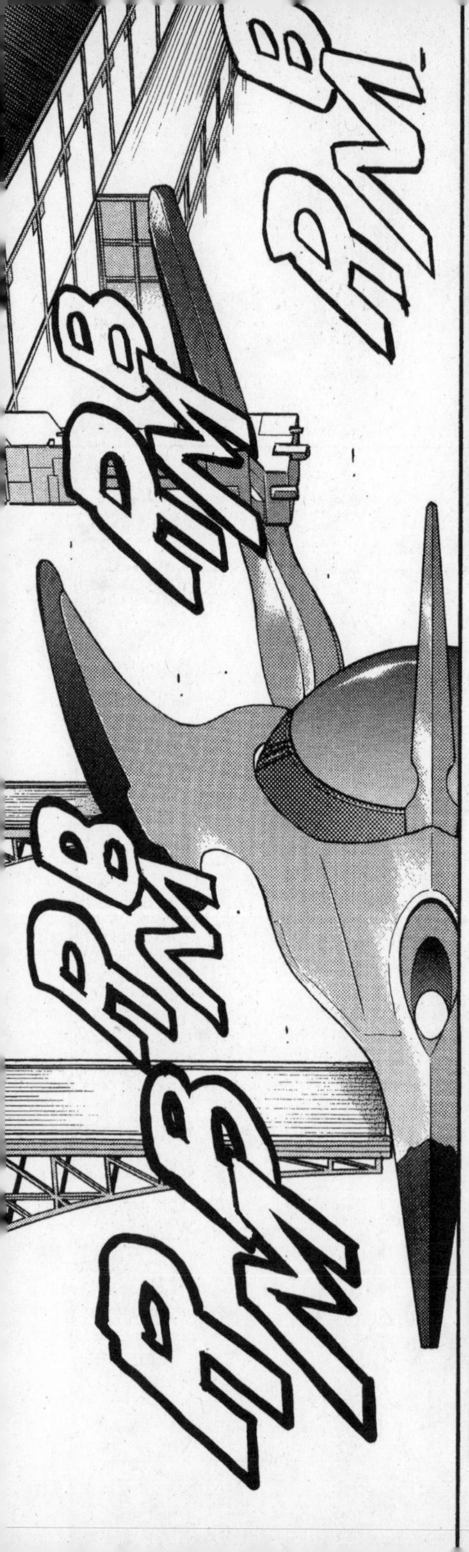

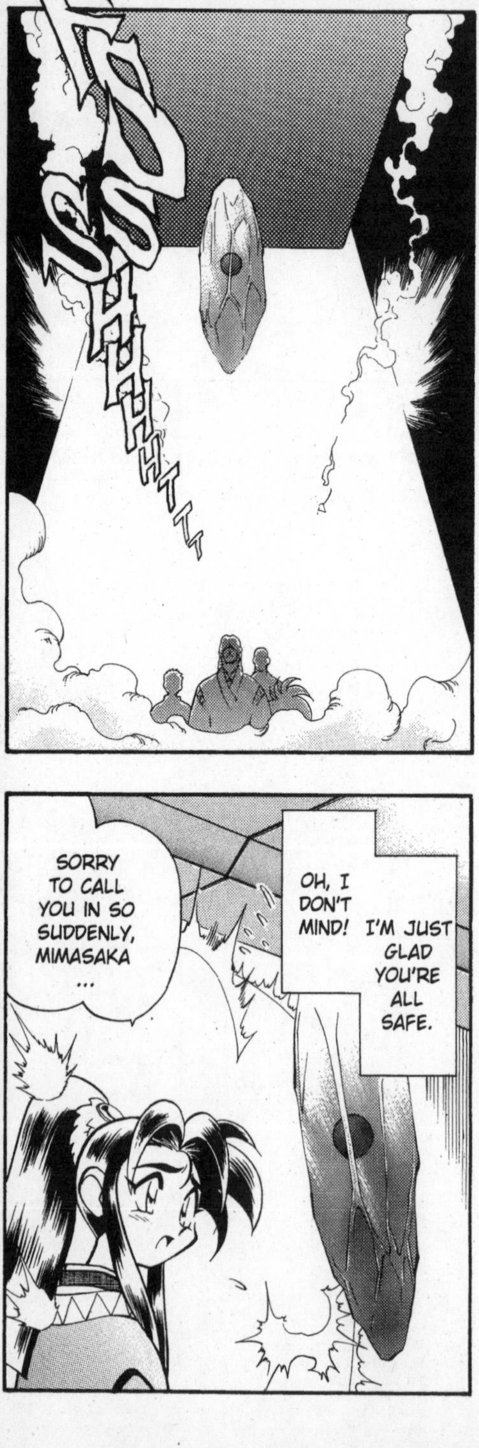
SORRY TO CALL YOU IN SO SUDDENLY, MIMASAKA ...
OH, I DON'T MIND!
I'M JUST GLAD YOU'RE ALL SAFE.

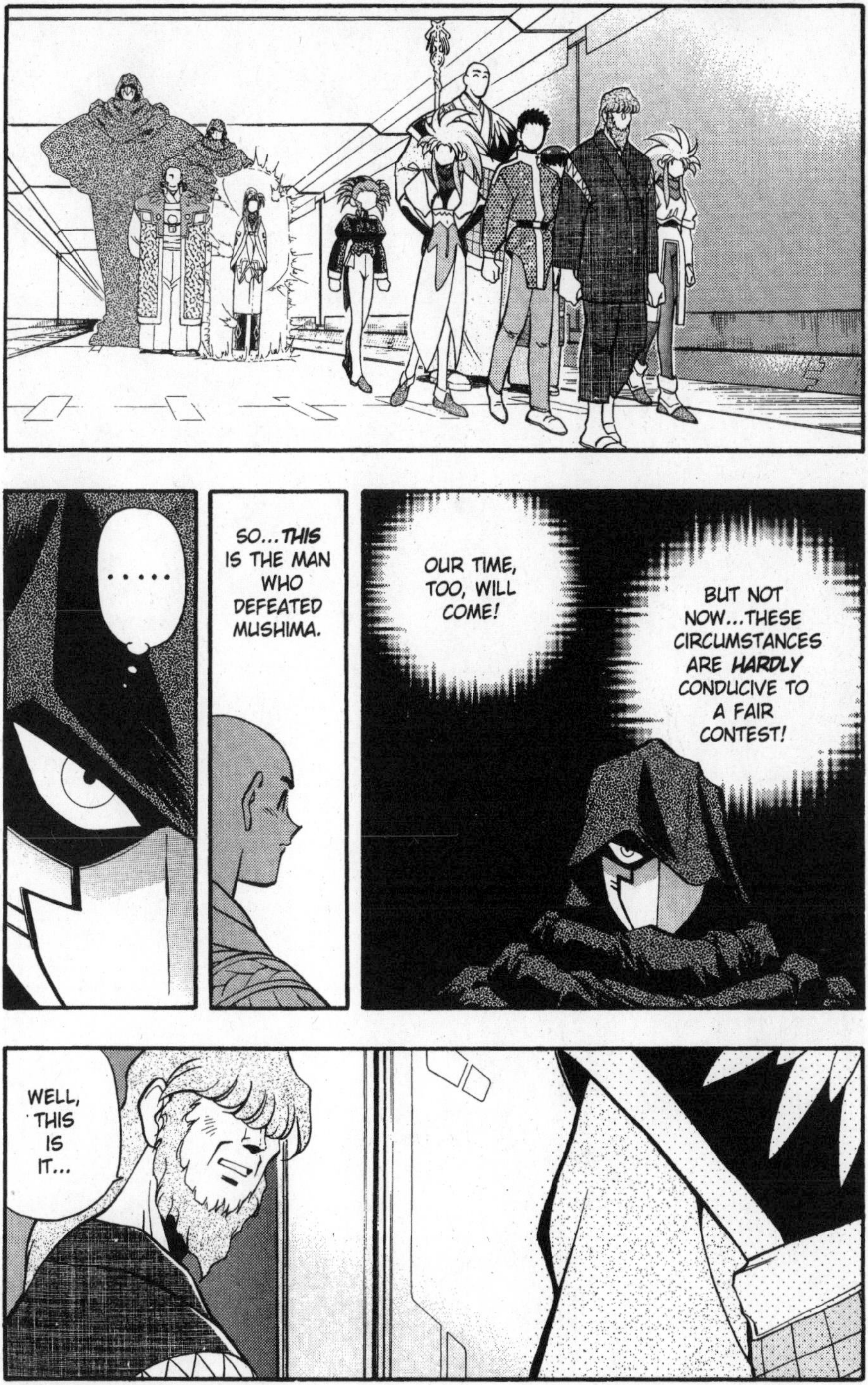
.....
SO...THIS IS THE MAN WHO DEFEATED MUSHIMA.
OUR TIME, TOO, WILL COME!
BUT NOT NOW...THESE CIRCUMSTANCES ARE HARDLY CONDUCIVE TO A FAIR CONTEST!
WELL, THIS IS IT...

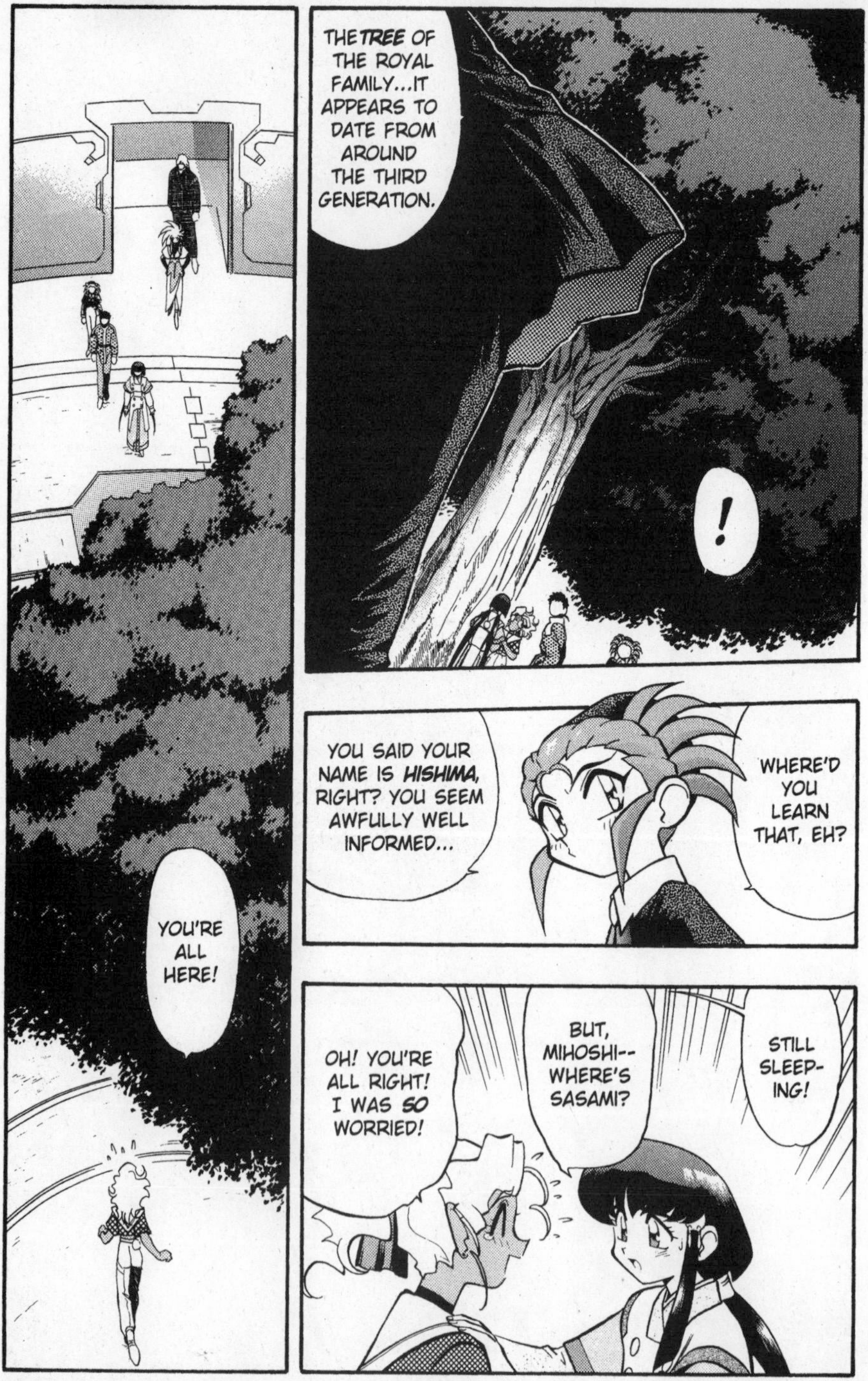
YOU'RE ALL HERE!
THE TREE OF THE ROYAL FAMILY...IT APPEARS TO DATE FROM AROUND THE THIRD GENERATION.
!
YOU SAID YOUR NAME IS HISHIMA, RIGHT? YOU SEEM AWFULLY WELL INFORMED...
WHERE'D YOU LEARN THAT, EH?
OH! YOU'RE ALL RIGHT! I WAS SO WORRIED!
BUT, MIHOSHI-- WHERE'S SASAMI?
STILL SLEEP-ING!

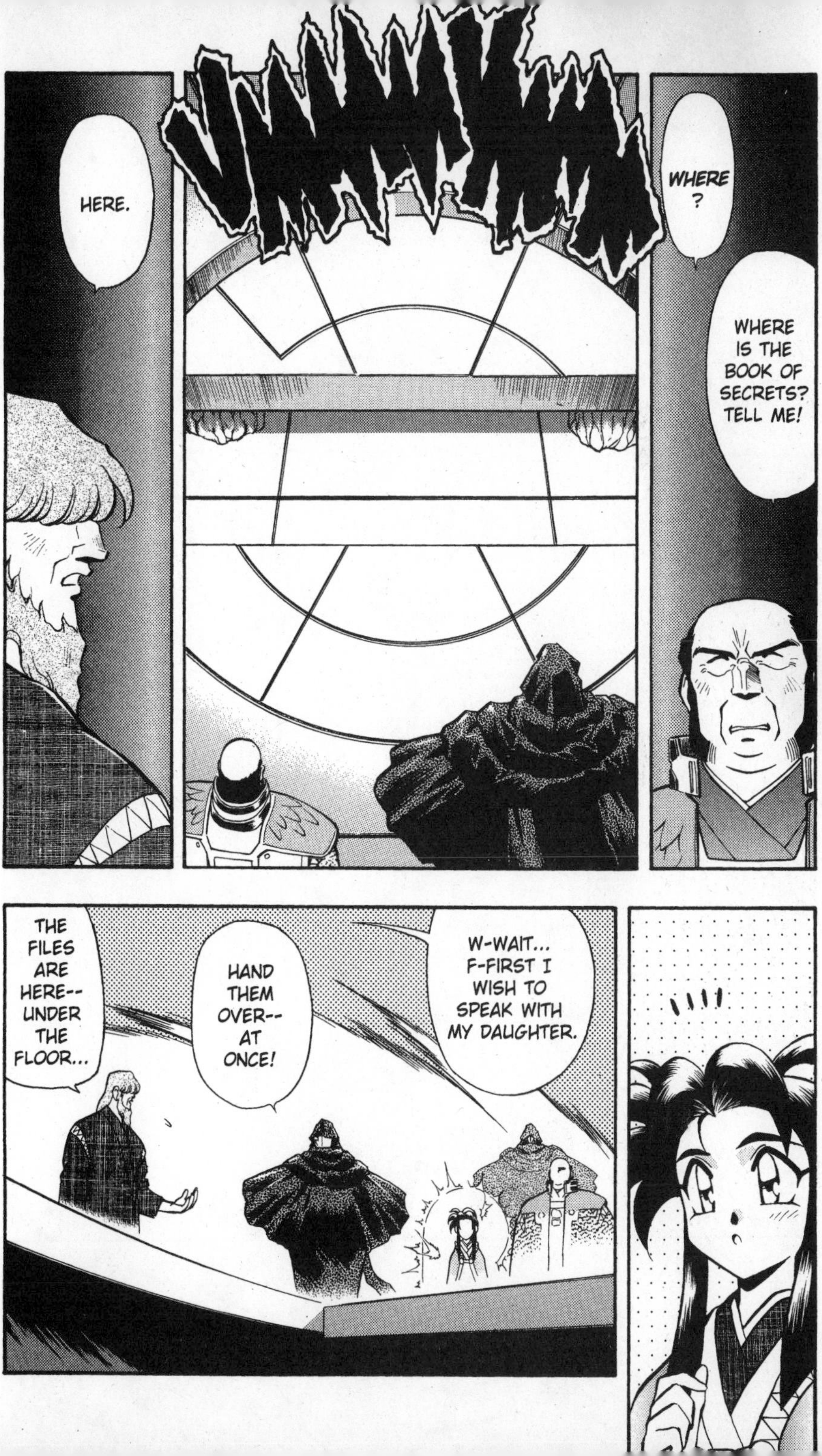
HERE.
WHERE ?
WHERE IS THE BOOK OF SECRETS? TELL ME!
THE FILES ARE HERE-- UNDER THE FLOOR...
HAND THEM OVER-- AT ONCE!
W-WAIT... F-FIRST I WISH TO SPEAK WITH MY DAUGHTER.

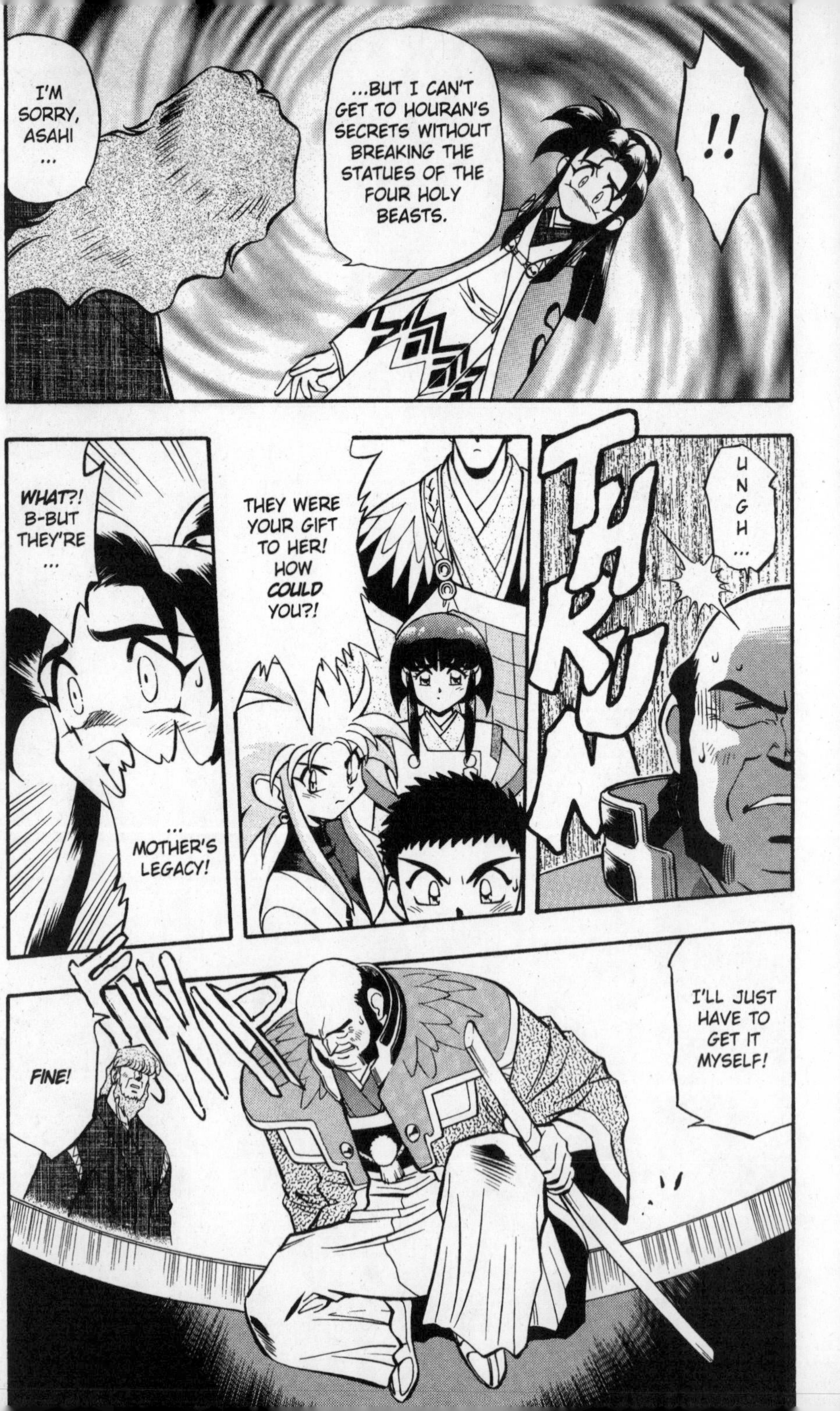
I'M SORRY, ASAHI ...
...BUT I CAN'T GET TO HOURAN'S SECRETS WITHOUT BREAKING THE STATUES OF THE FOUR HOLY BEASTS.
!!
WHAT?! B-BUT THEY'RE ...
... MOTHER'S LEGACY!
THEY WERE YOUR GIFT TO HER! HOW COULD YOU?!
THKU
UNGH ...
FINE!
I'LL JUST HAVE TO GET IT MYSELF!

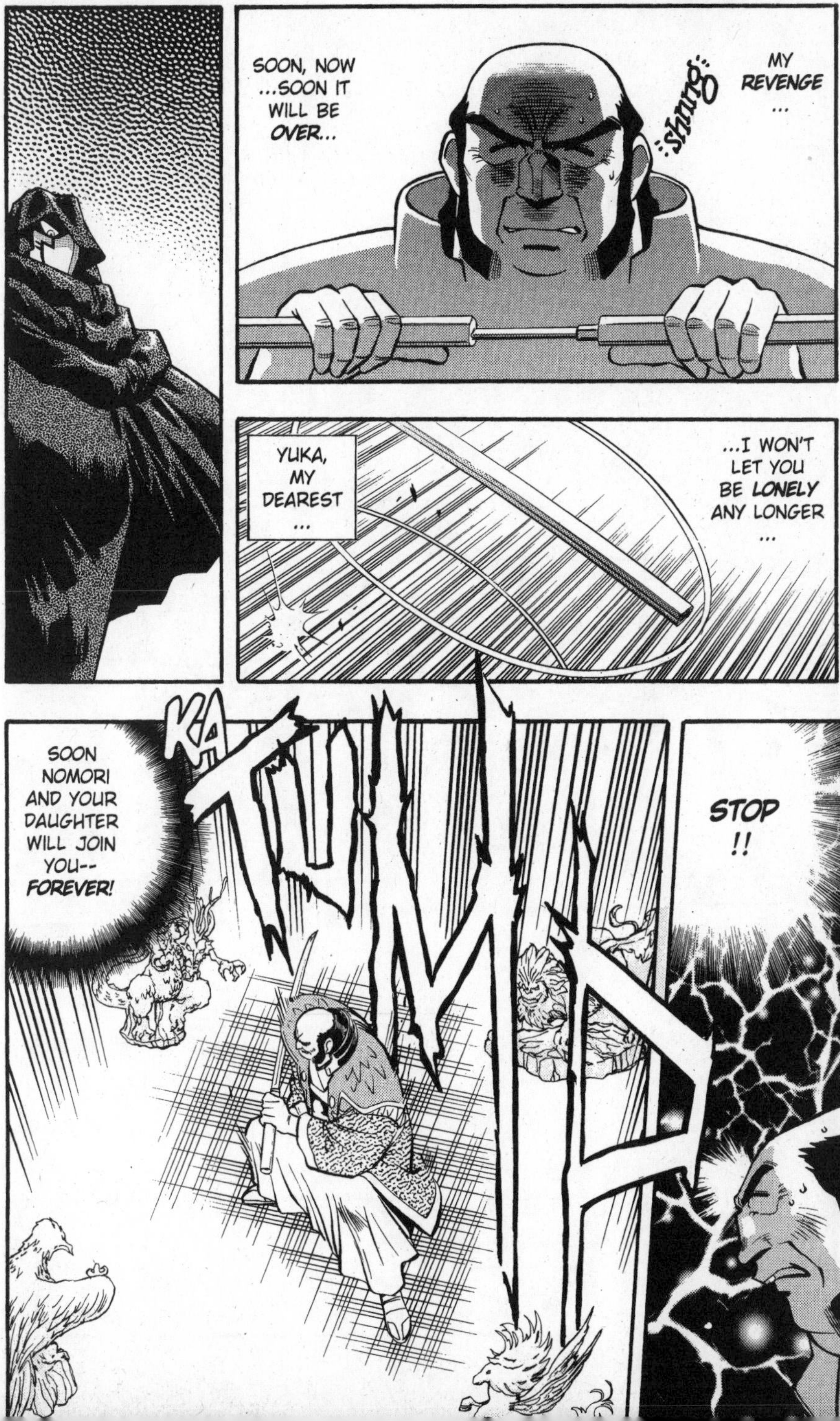
SOON, NOW ...SOON IT WILL BE OVER...
shhng
MY REVENGE ...
YUKA, MY DEAREST ...
...I WON'T LET YOU BE LONELY ANY LONGER ...
KA
TUMP
SOON NOMORI AND YOUR DAUGHTER WILL JOIN YOU-- FOREVER!
STOP !!

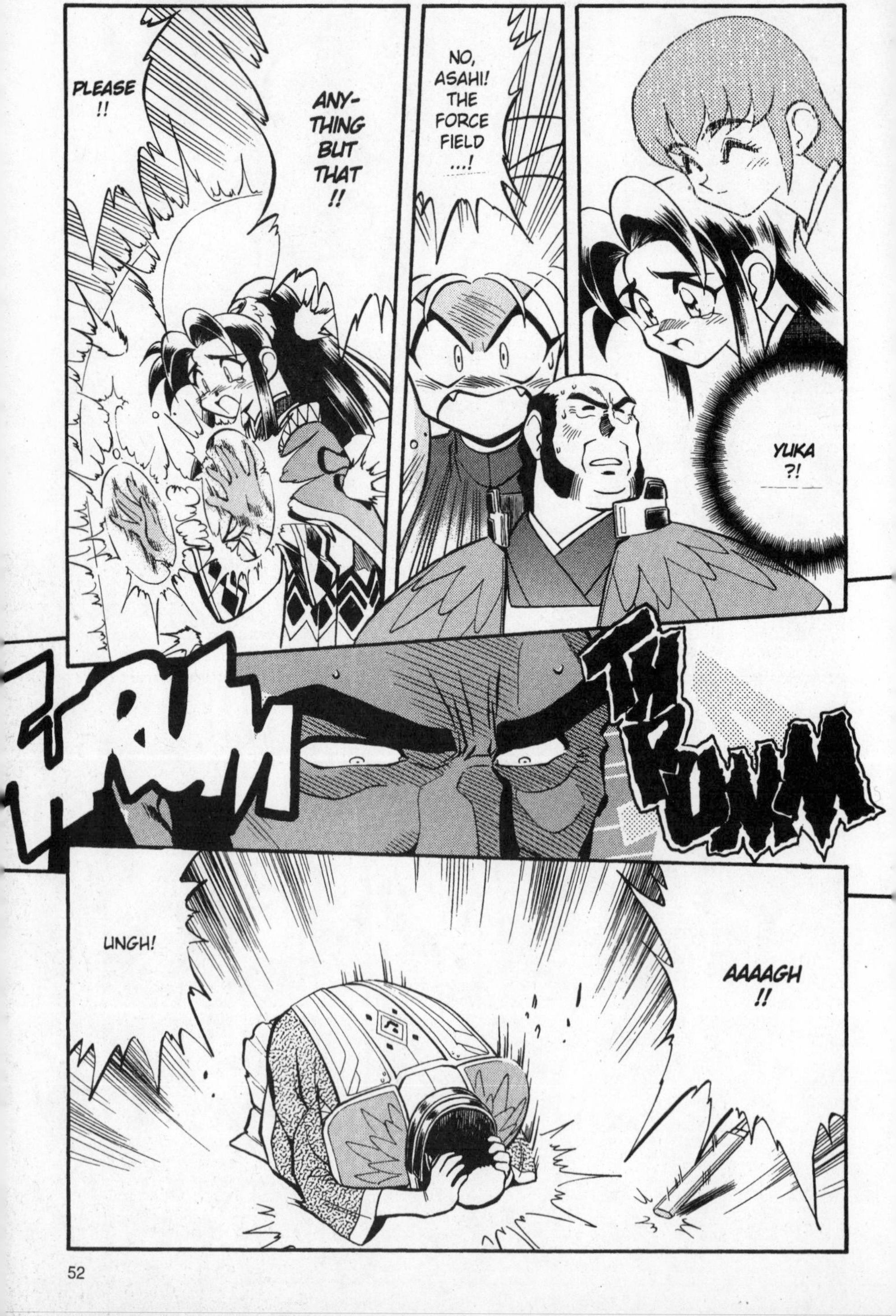
YUKA ?!
NO, ASAHI! THE FORCE FIELD ...!
PLEASE !!
ANYTHING BUT THAT !!
AAAAGH !!
UNGH!

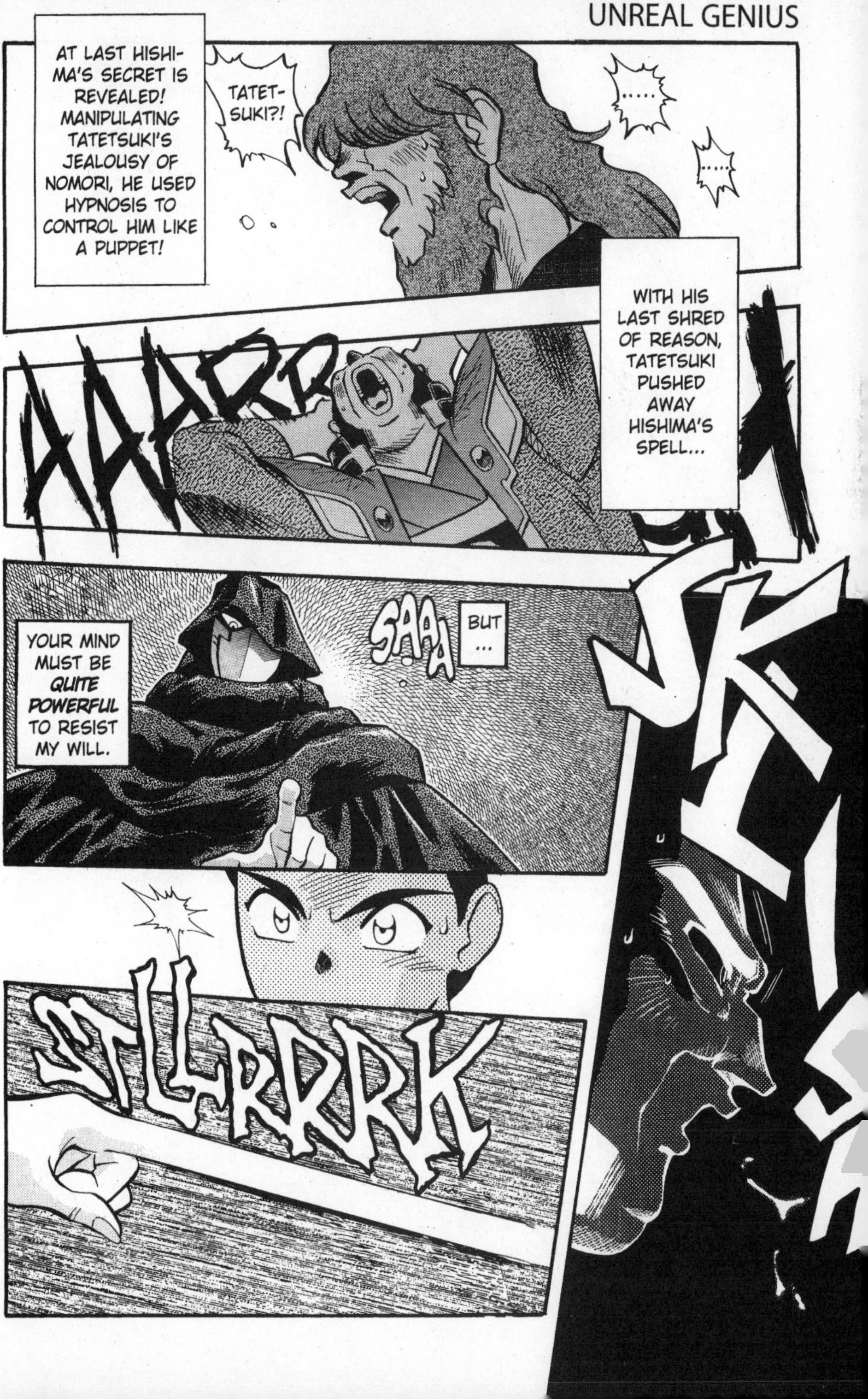
AT LAST HISHIMA'S SECRET IS REVEALED! MANIPULATING TATETSUKI'S JEALOUSY OF NOMORI, HE USED HYPNOSIS TO CONTROL HIM LIKE A PUPPET!
TATETSUKI?!
.....
.....
AAARR
WITH HIS LAST SHRED OF REASON, TATETSUKI PUSHED AWAY HISHIMA'S SPELL...
YOUR MIND MUST BE ***QUITE POWERFUL*** TO RESIST MY WILL.
SAAAA
BUT ...
STLLRRRK

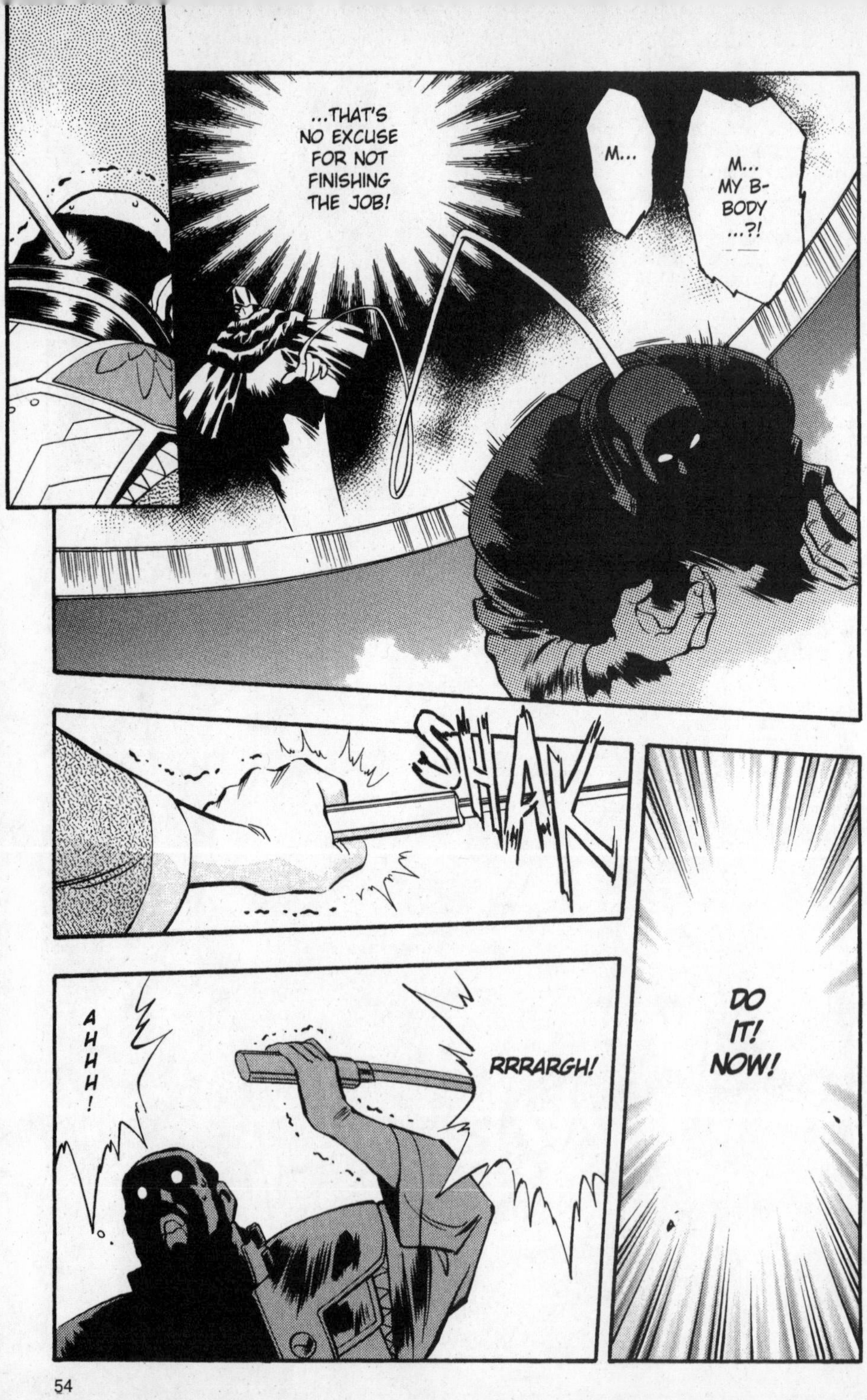

...THAT'S NO EXCUSE FOR NOT FINISHING THE JOB!
M...
M... MY B-BODY ...?!
SHAK
A H H H !
RRRARGH!
DO IT! NOW!

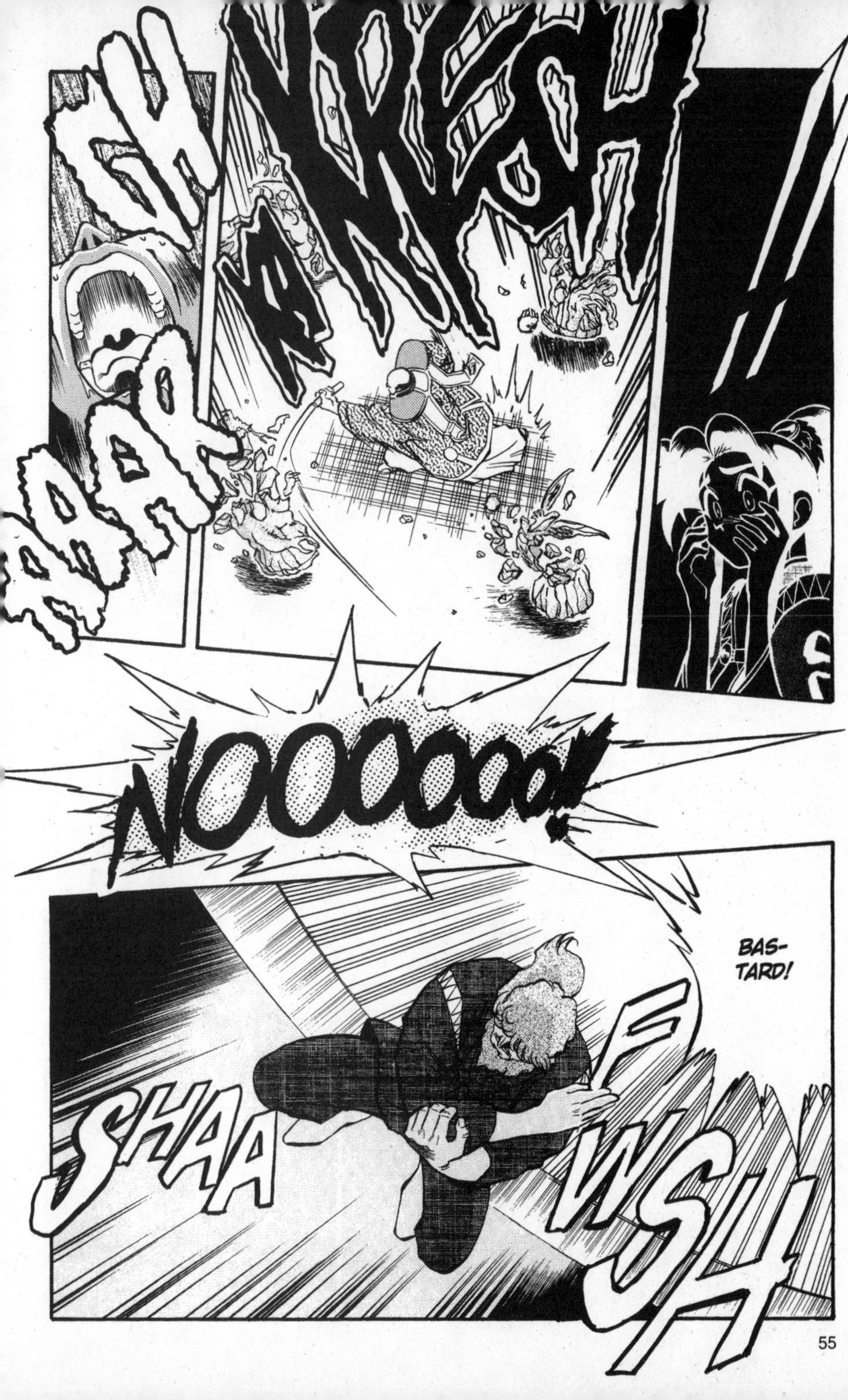
NOOOOOO!
BAS-
TARD!
SHAA
WSH

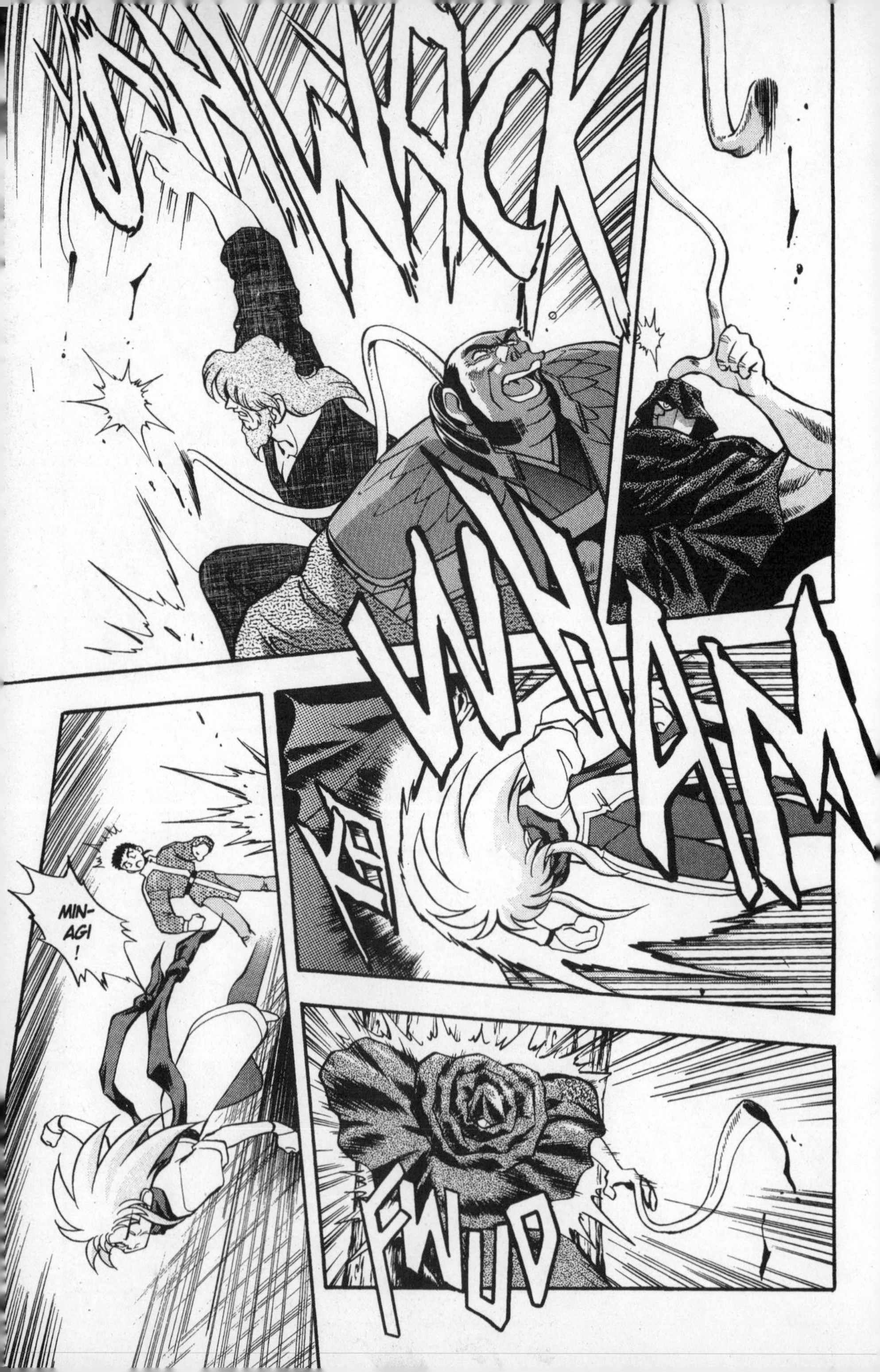
WHACK
WHAM
MIN-AGI!
FWUD

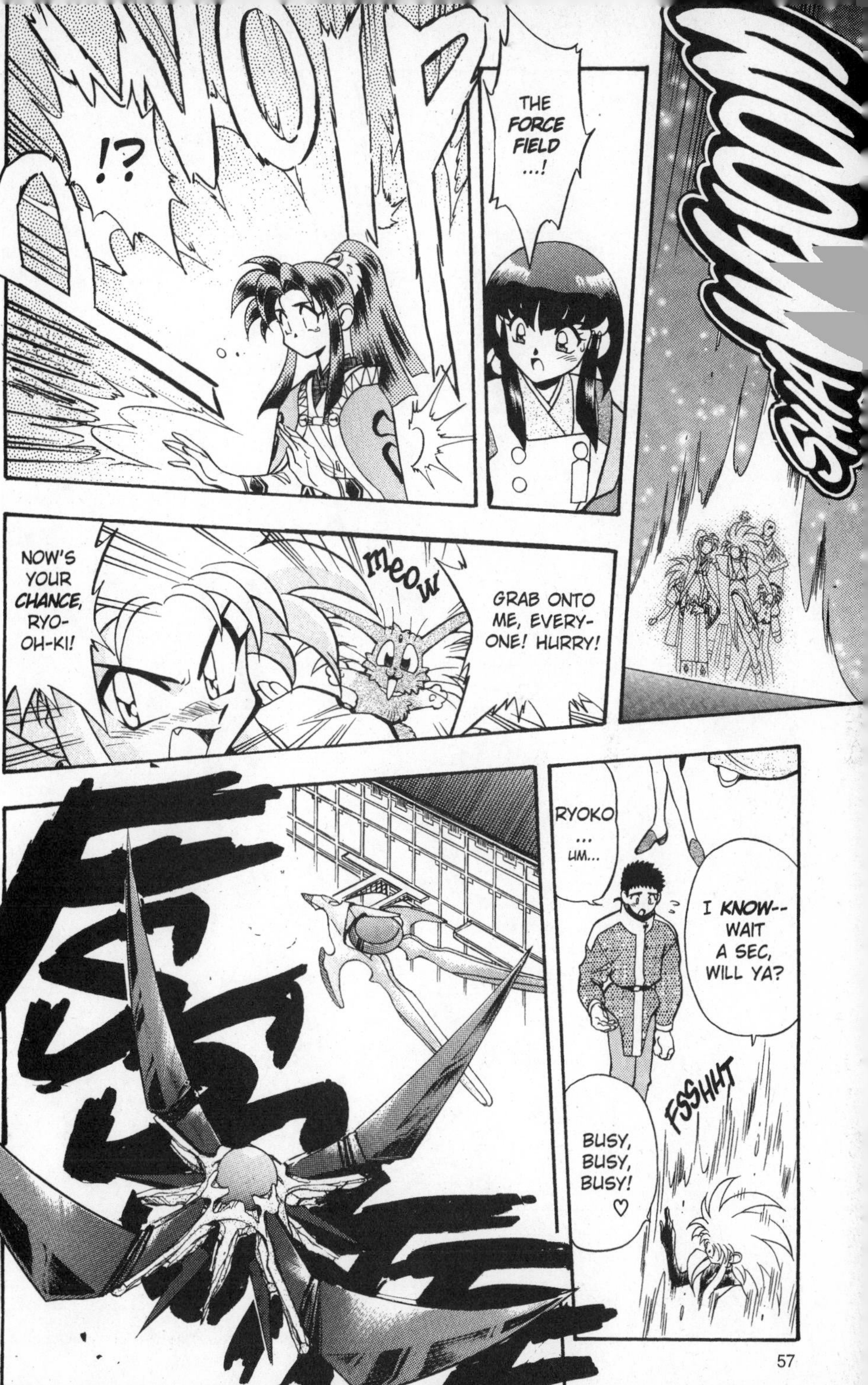
!?
THE FORCE FIELD ...!
NOW'S YOUR CHANCE, RYO-OH-KI!
meow
GRAB ONTO ME, EVERY-ONE! HURRY!
RYOKO ... UM...
I KNOW-- WAIT A SEC, WILL YA?
FSSHHT
BUSY, BUSY, BUSY! ♡

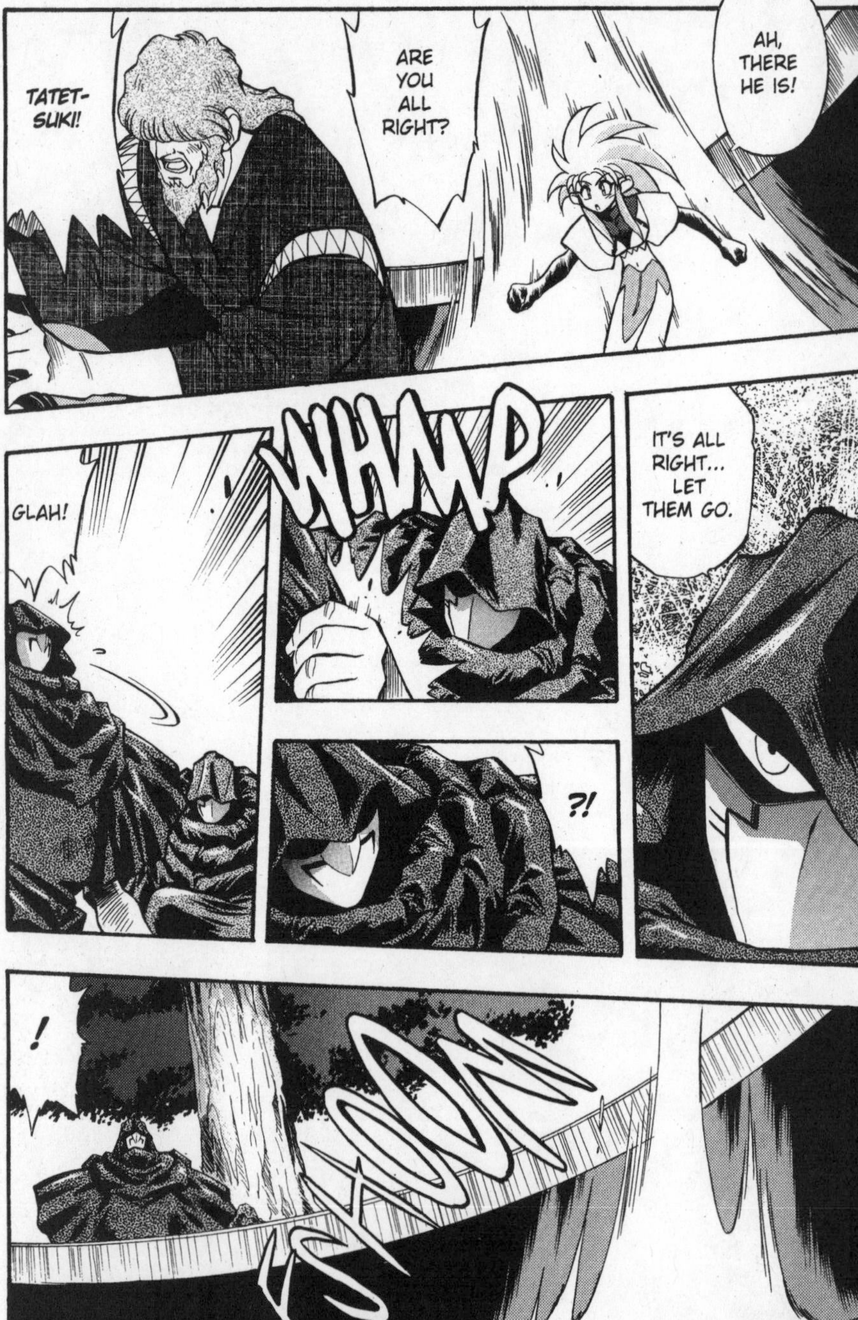
TATET-SUKI!
ARE YOU ALL RIGHT?
AH, THERE HE IS!
GLAH!
WHAMP
?!
IT'S ALL RIGHT... LET THEM GO.
!
SHOOM

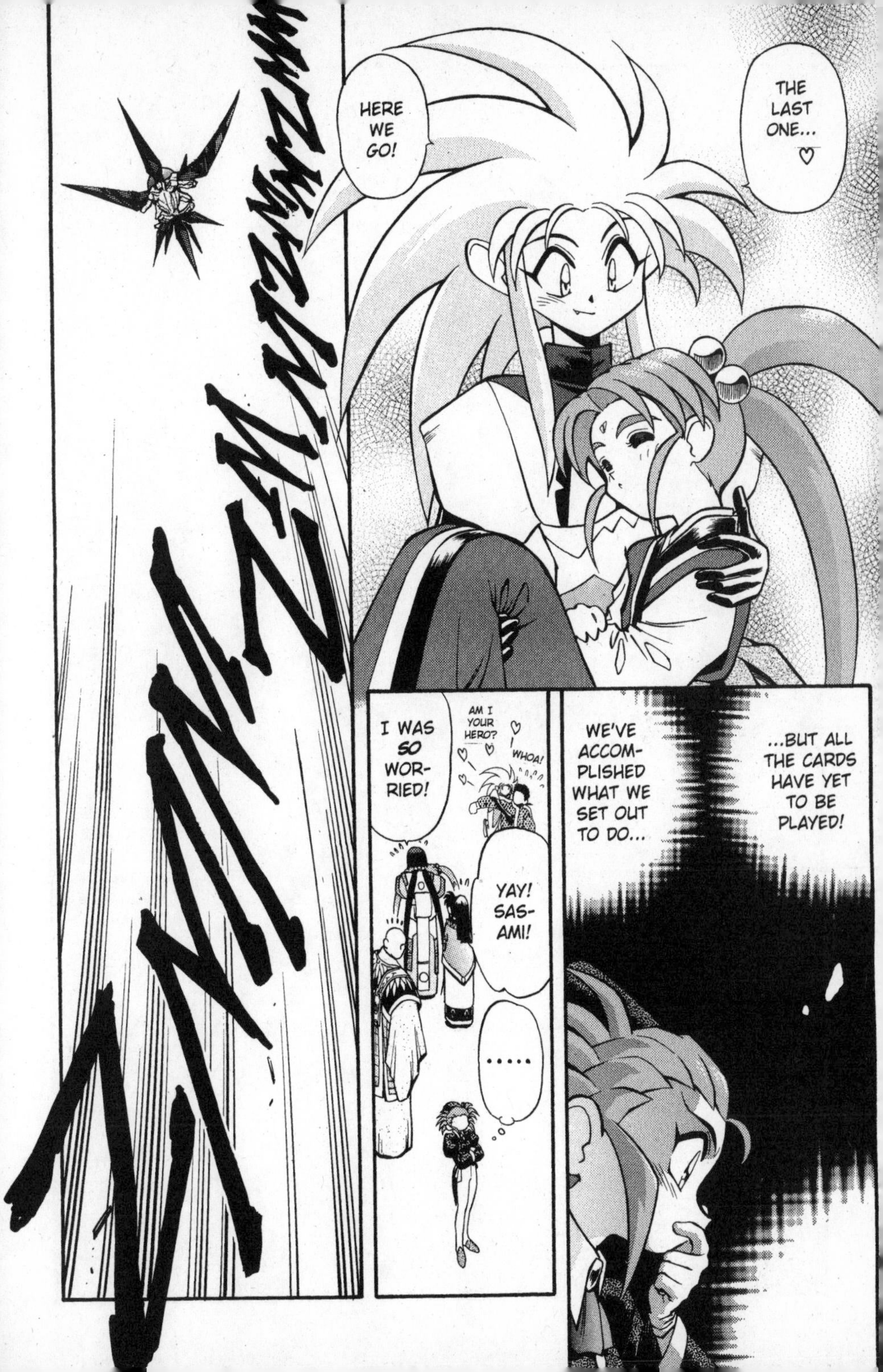
HERE WE GO!
THE LAST ONE... ♡
I WAS SO WORRIED!
AM I YOUR HERO?
WHOA!
YAY! SASAMI!
.....
WE'VE ACCOMPLISHED WHAT WE SET OUT TO DO...
...BUT ALL THE CARDS HAVE YET TO BE PLAYED!

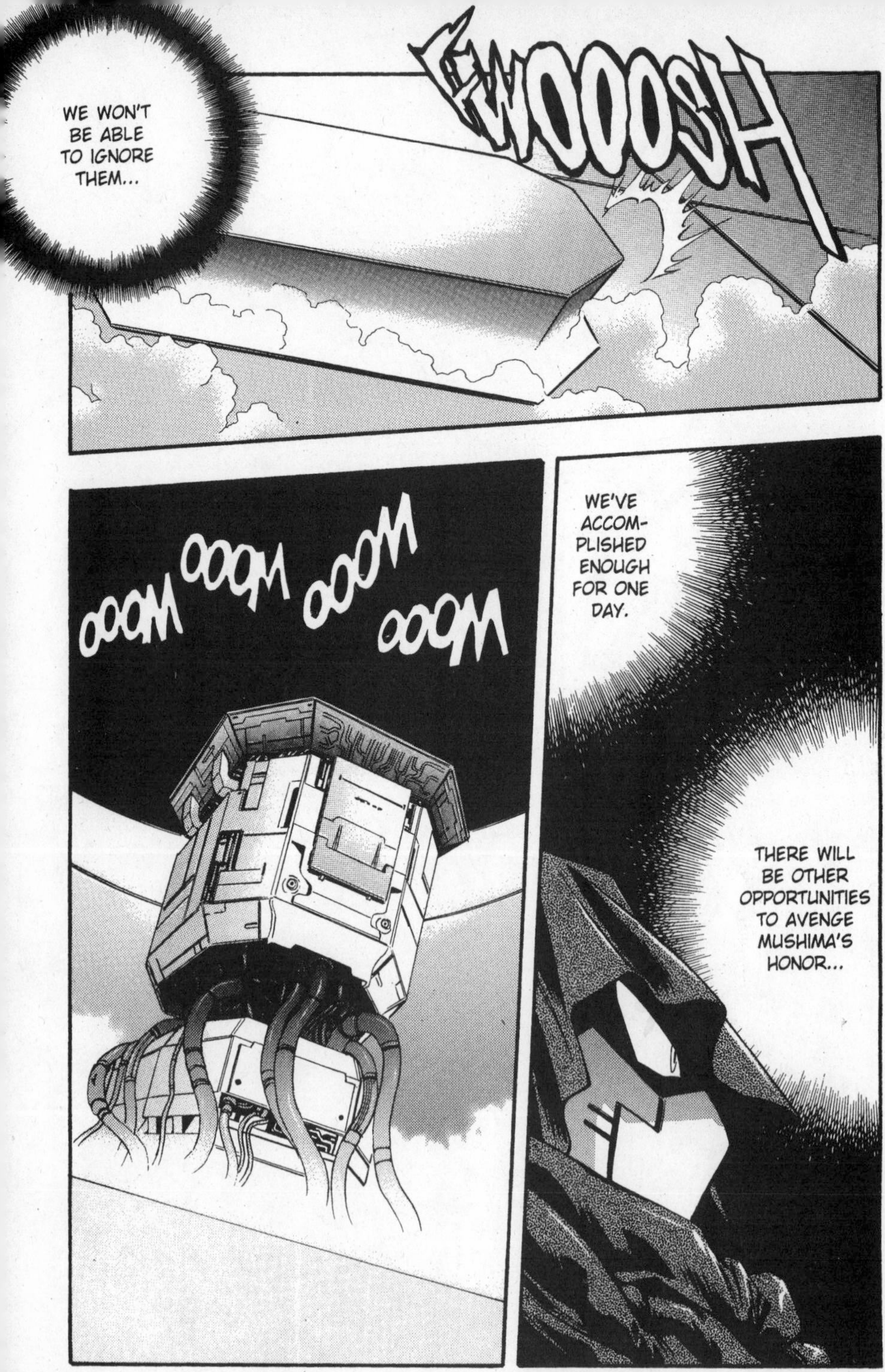
WE WON'T BE ABLE TO IGNORE THEM...
WOOOSH
OOOM OOOM OOOM OOOM
WE'VE ACCOM-PLISHED ENOUGH FOR ONE DAY.
THERE WILL BE OTHER OPPORTUNITIES TO AVENGE MUSHIMA'S HONOR...

Tales of Tenchi #4

IT'S A GUY THING

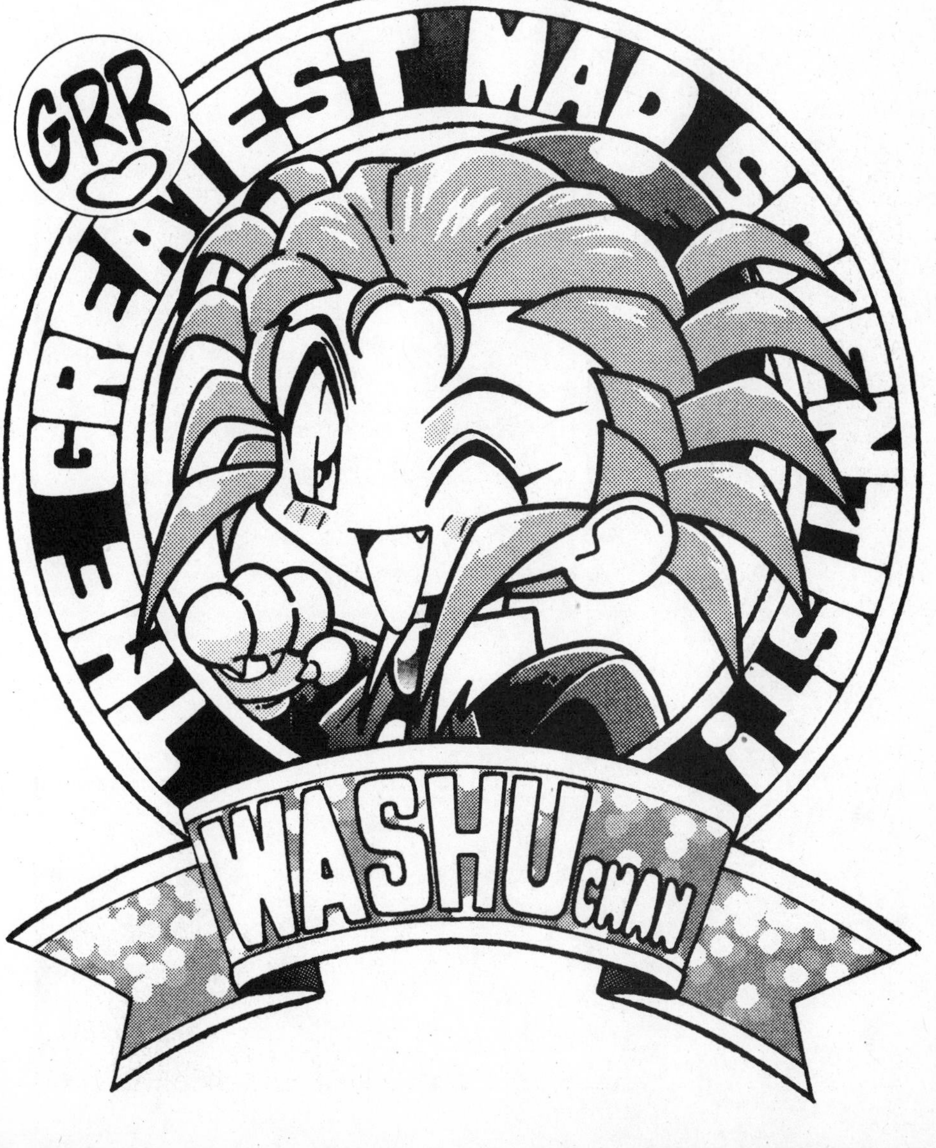
GRR
WASHU CHAN

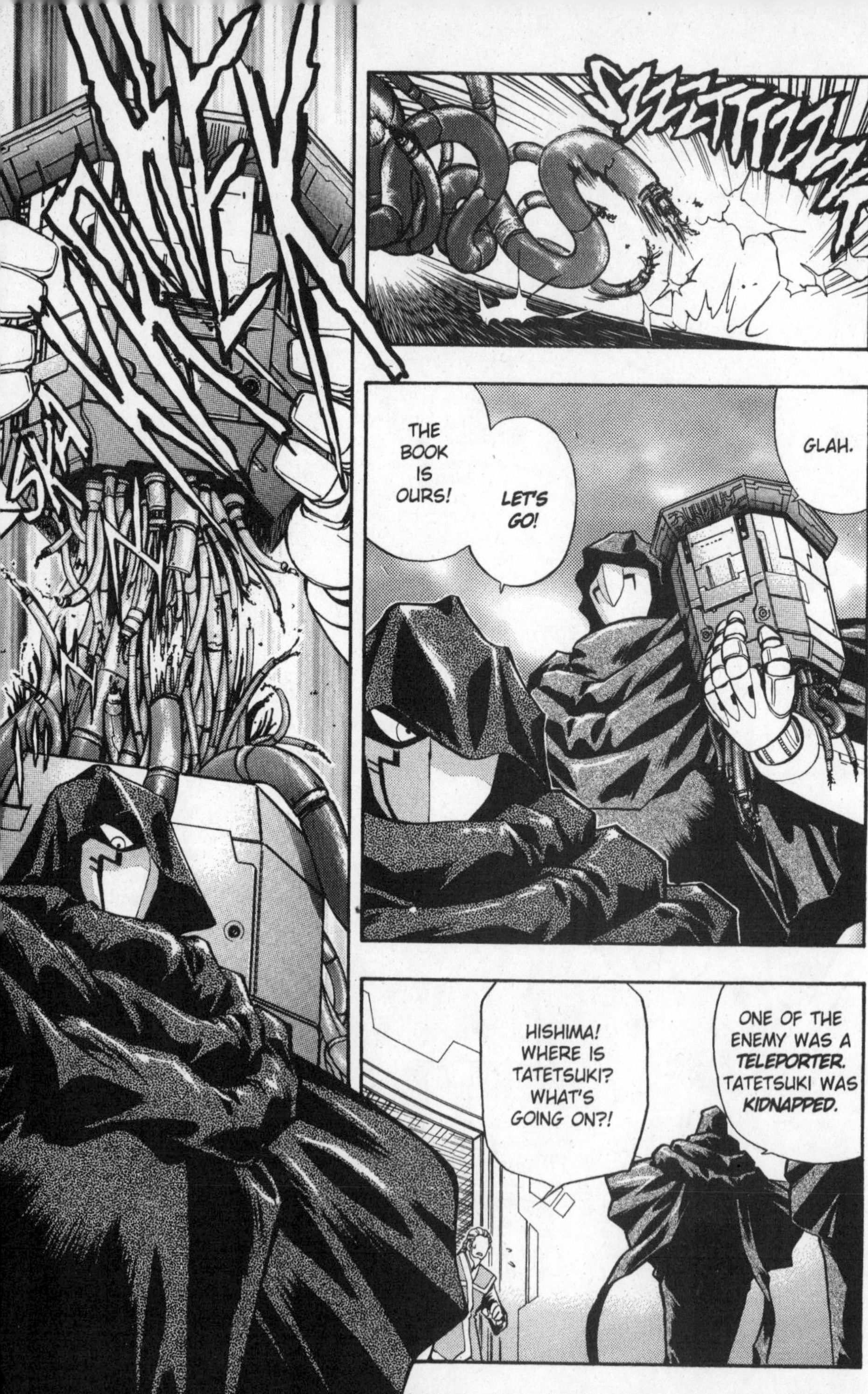
THE BOOK IS OURS!
LET'S GO!
GLAH.
HISHIMA! WHERE IS TATETSUKI? WHAT'S GOING ON?!
ONE OF THE ENEMY WAS A TELEPORTER. TATETSUKI WAS KIDNAPPED.

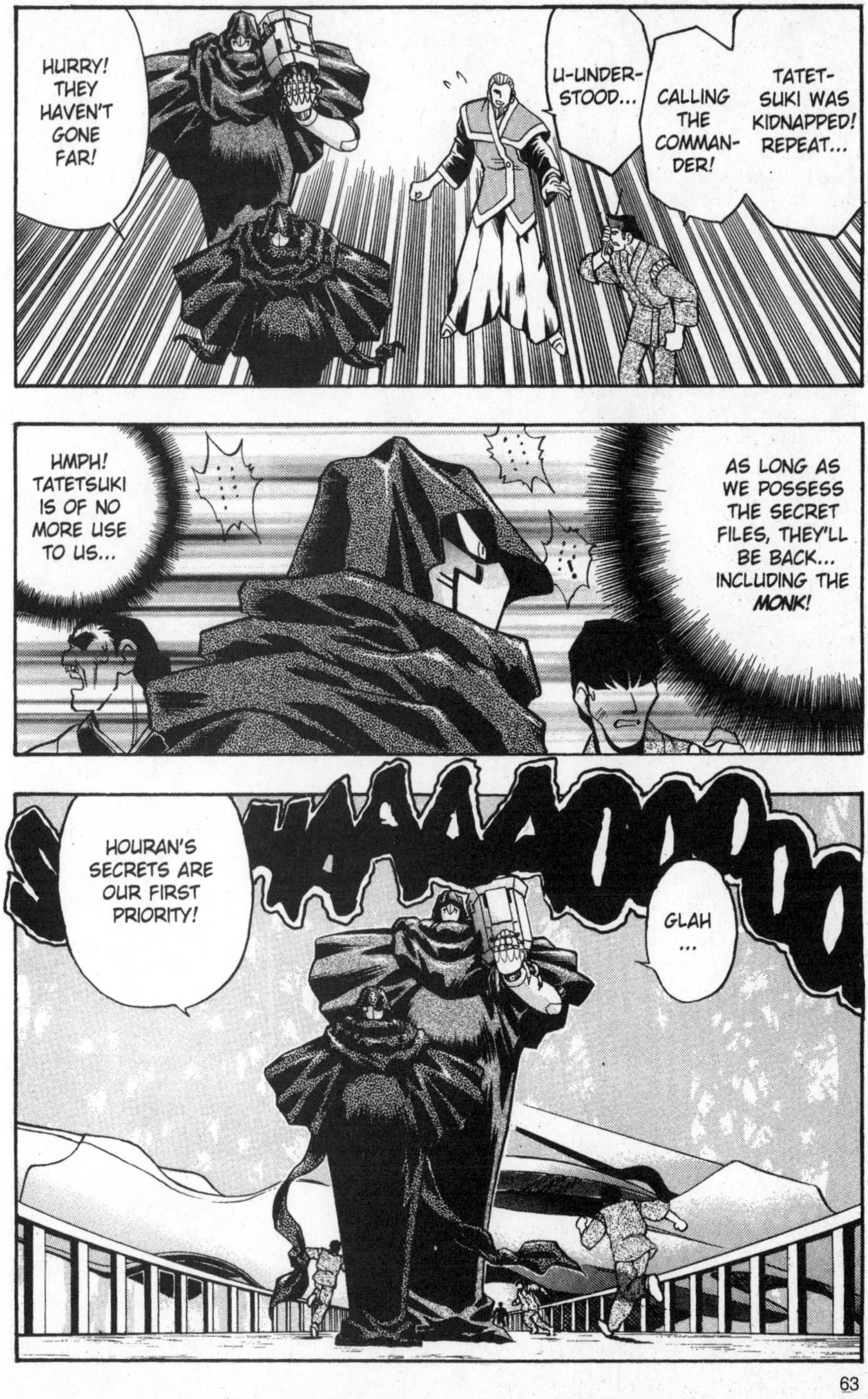
HURRY! THEY HAVEN'T GONE FAR!
U-UNDER-STOOD...
CALLING THE COMMAN-DER!
TATET-SUKI WAS KIDNAPPED! REPEAT...
HMPH! TATETSUKI IS OF NO MORE USE TO US...
AS LONG AS WE POSSESS THE SECRET FILES, THEY'LL BE BACK... INCLUDING THE *MONK*!
HOURAN'S SECRETS ARE OUR FIRST PRIORITY!
GLAH ...

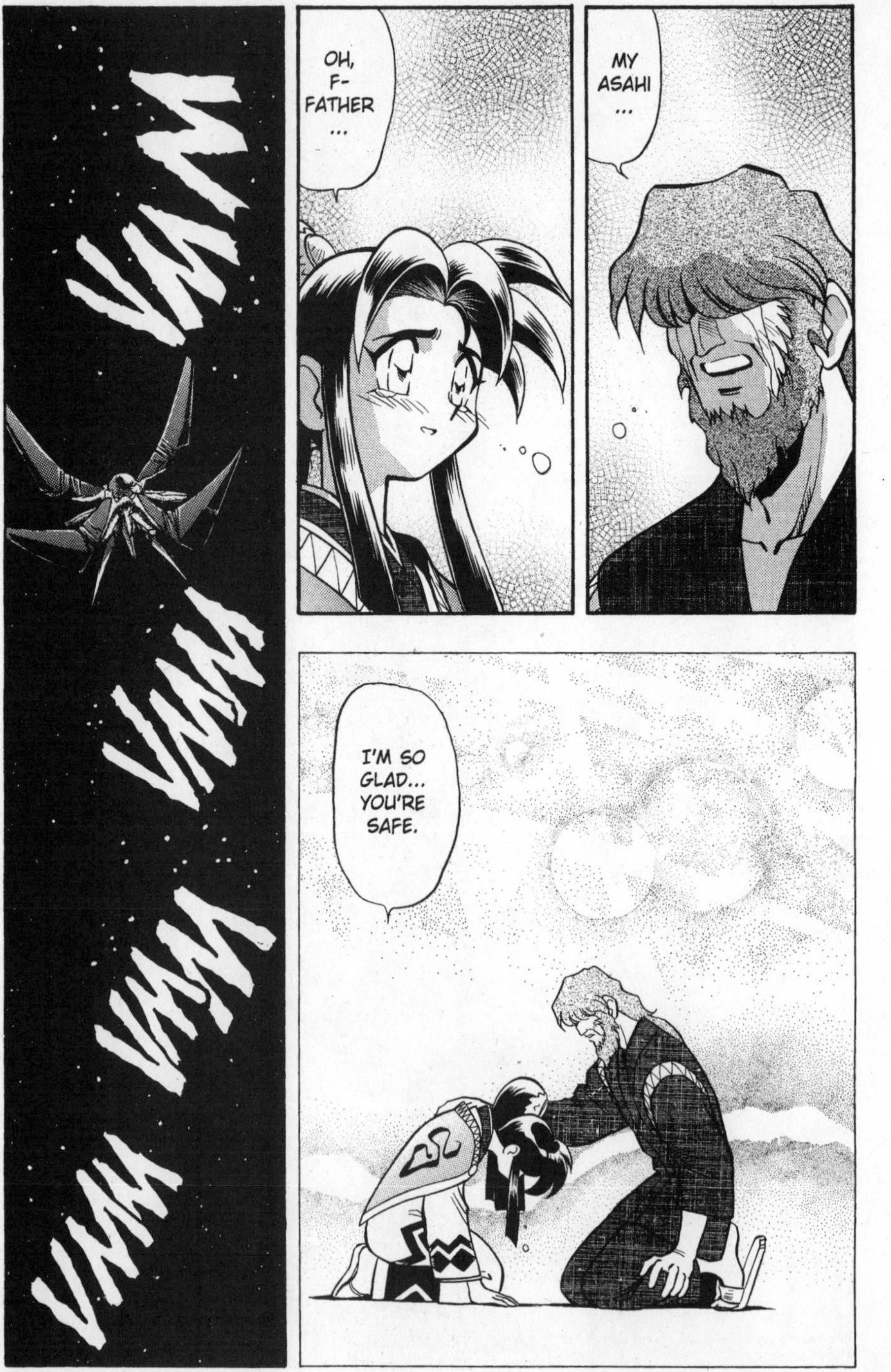
OH, F-FATHER ...
MY ASAHI ...
I'M SO GLAD... YOU'RE SAFE.

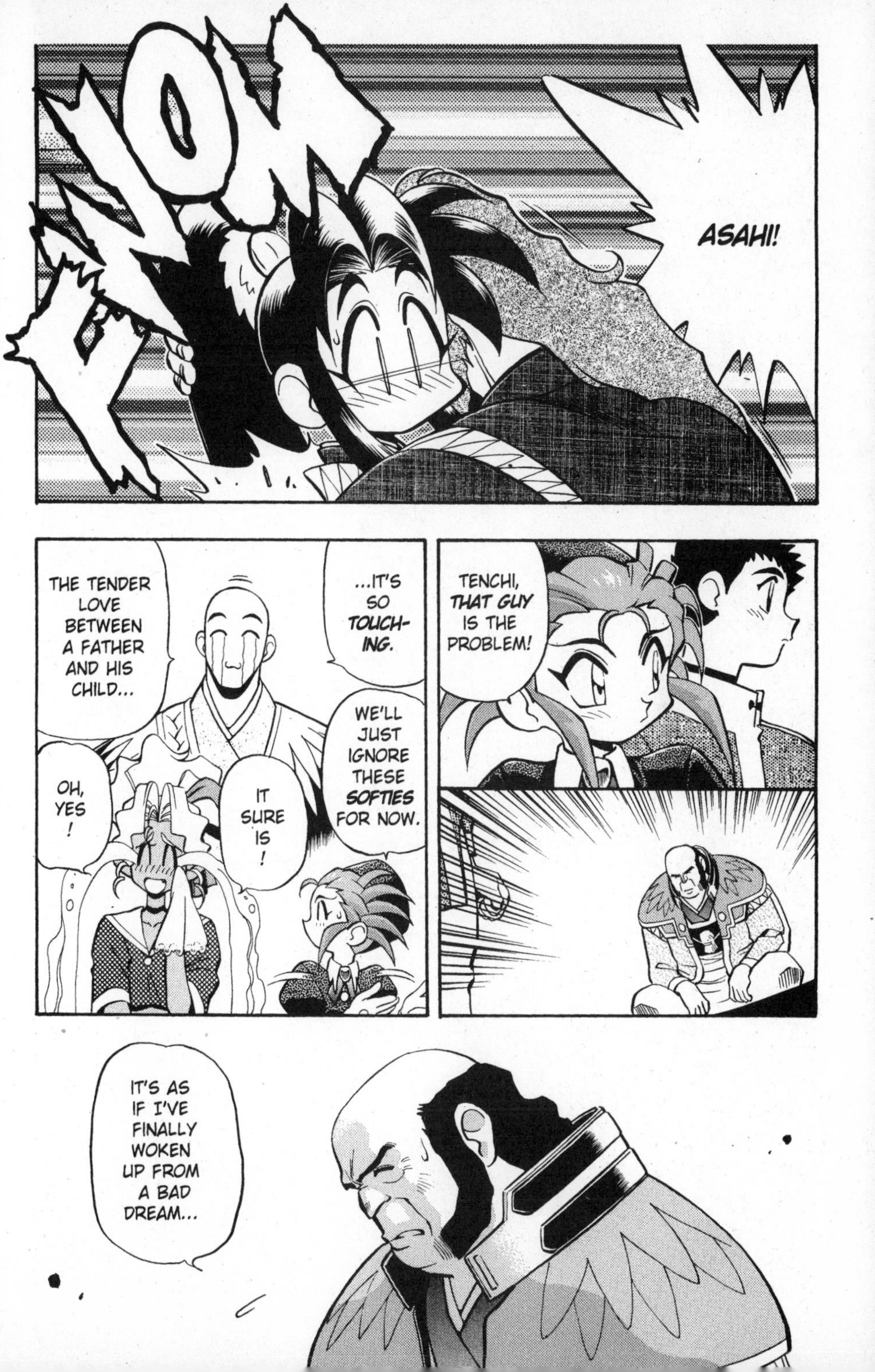
ASAHI!
THE TENDER LOVE BETWEEN A FATHER AND HIS CHILD...
...IT'S SO *TOUCHING.*
WE'LL JUST IGNORE THESE *SOFTIES* FOR NOW.
OH, YES!
IT SURE IS!
TENCHI, *THAT GUY* IS THE PROBLEM!
IT'S AS IF I'VE FINALLY WOKEN UP FROM A BAD DREAM...

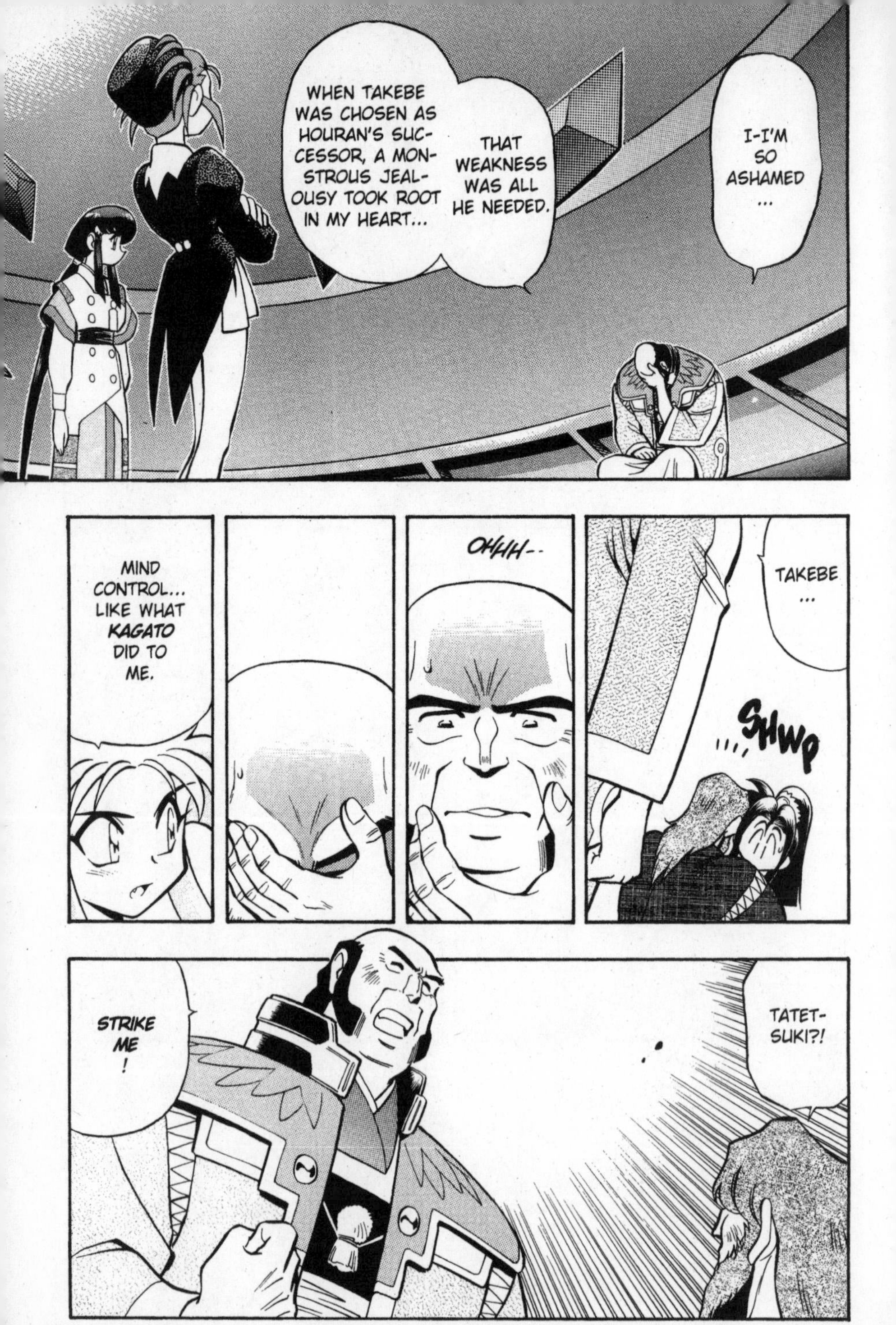
WHEN TAKEBE WAS CHOSEN AS HOURAN'S SUCCESSOR, A MONSTROUS JEALOUSY TOOK ROOT IN MY HEART...
THAT WEAKNESS WAS ALL HE NEEDED.
I-I'M SO ASHAMED ...
MIND CONTROL... LIKE WHAT **KAGATO** DID TO ME.
OHHH--
TAKEBE ...
SHWP
STRIKE ME !
TATET-SUKI?!

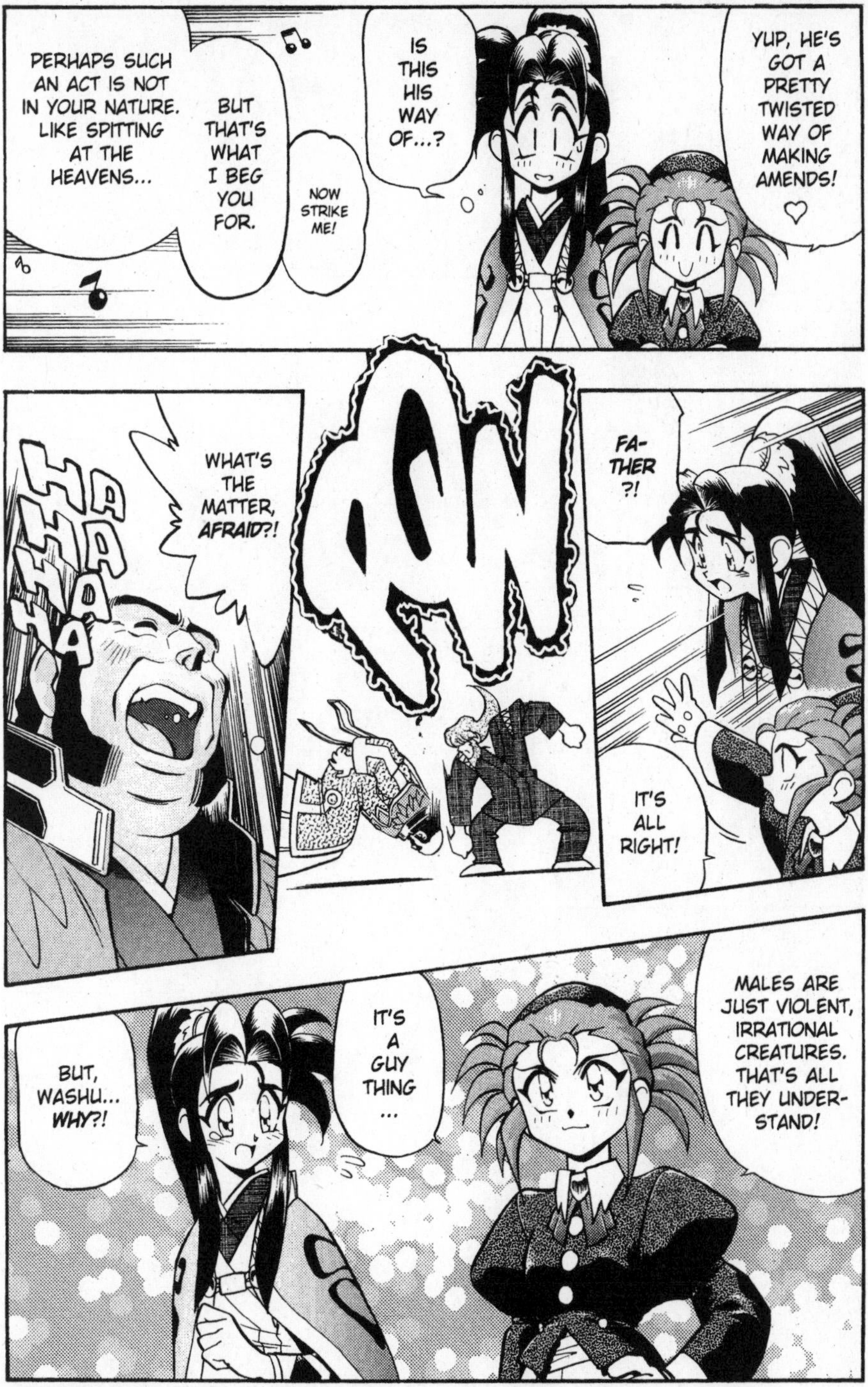
PERHAPS SUCH AN ACT IS NOT IN YOUR NATURE. LIKE SPITTING AT THE HEAVENS...
BUT THAT'S WHAT I BEG YOU FOR.
NOW STRIKE ME!
IS THIS HIS WAY OF...?
YUP, HE'S GOT A PRETTY TWISTED WAY OF MAKING AMENDS!
HA HA HA HA HA
WHAT'S THE MATTER, AFRAID?!
FA-THER?!
IT'S ALL RIGHT!
BUT, WASHU... WHY?!
IT'S A GUY THING ...
MALES ARE JUST VIOLENT, IRRATIONAL CREATURES. THAT'S ALL THEY UNDER-STAND!

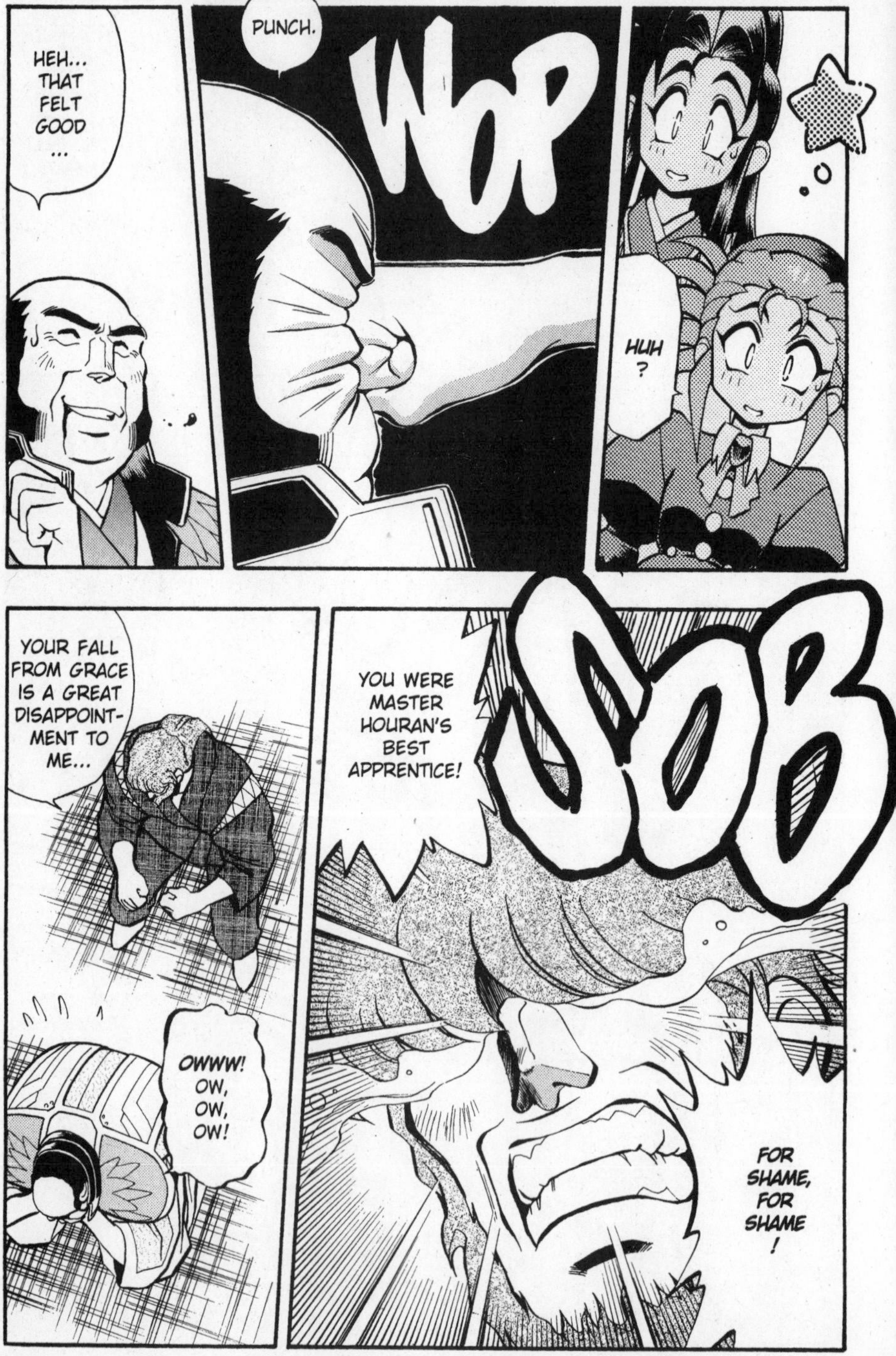
HEH... THAT FELT GOOD ...
PUNCH.
WOP
HUH ?
YOUR FALL FROM GRACE IS A GREAT DISAPPOINT-MENT TO ME...
OWWW! OW, OW, OW!
YOU WERE MASTER HOURAN'S BEST APPRENTICE!
SOB
FOR SHAME, FOR SHAME !

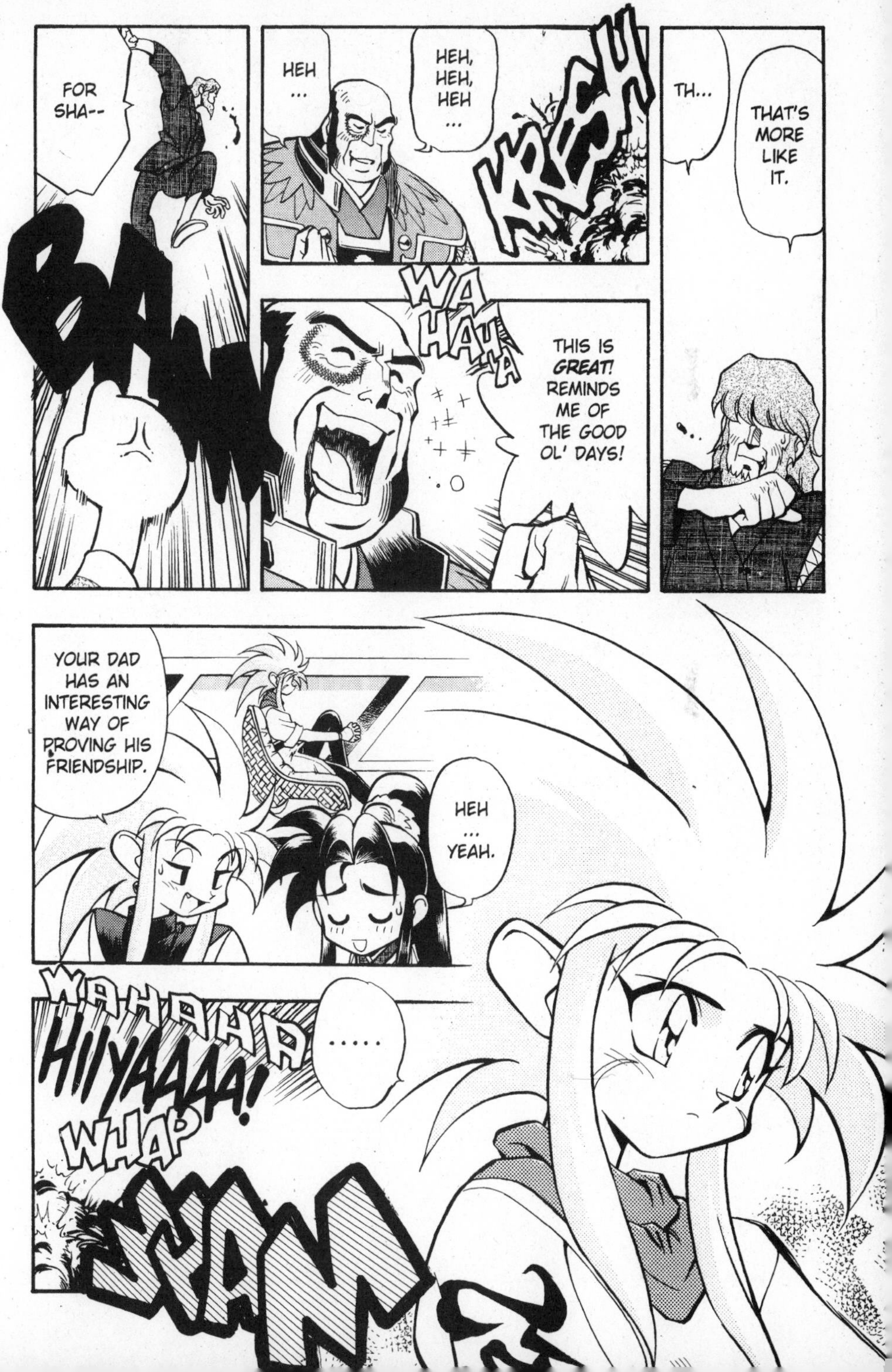
FOR SHA--
BAM
HEH ...
HEH, HEH, HEH ...
KRESH
WA HAHAHA
THIS IS GREAT! REMINDS ME OF THE GOOD OL' DAYS!
TH...
THAT'S MORE LIKE IT.
...
YOUR DAD HAS AN INTERESTING WAY OF PROVING HIS FRIENDSHIP.
HEH ... YEAH.
WAHAHAHA
HIIYAAAA!
WHAP
......

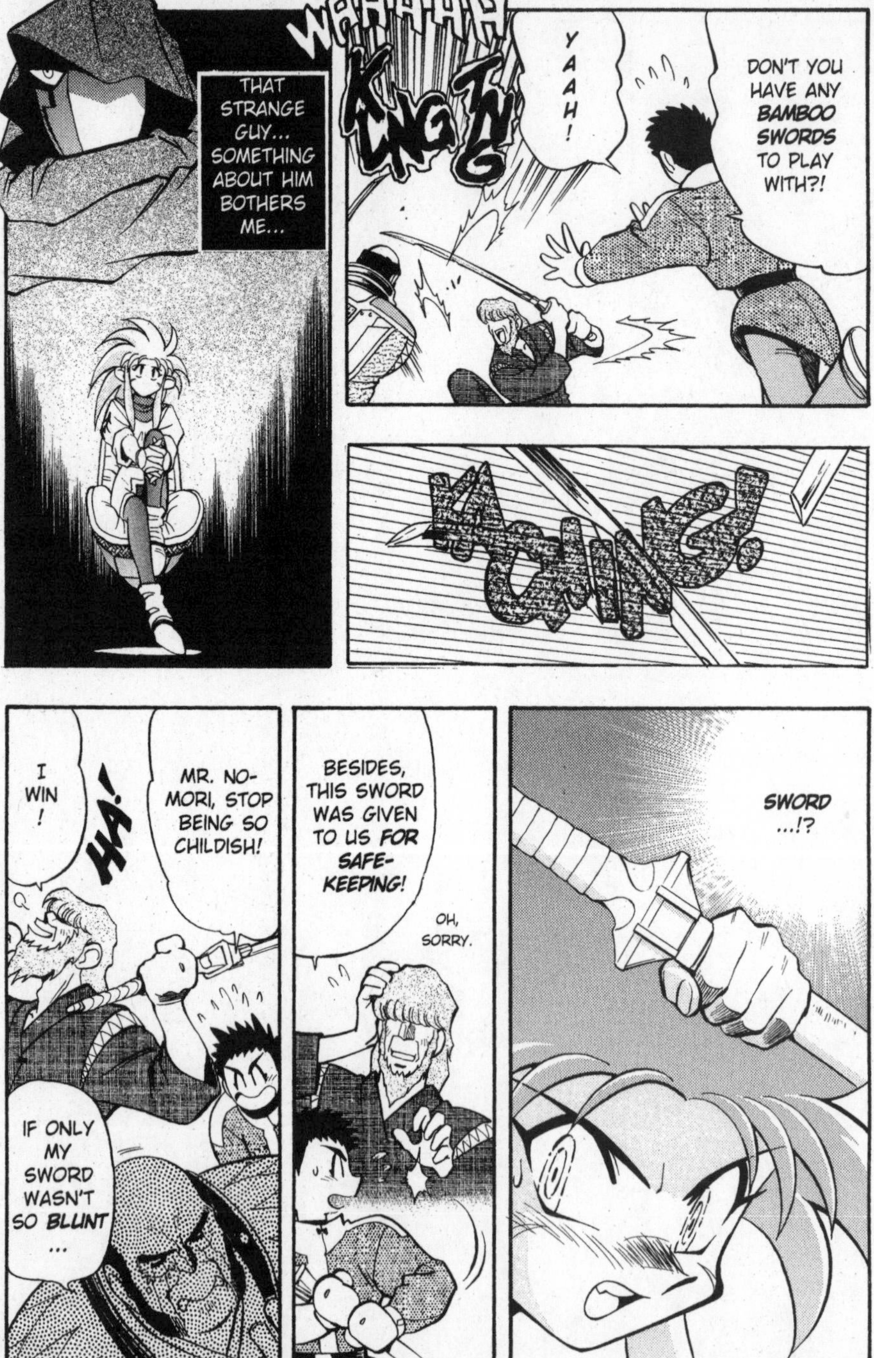
THAT STRANGE GUY... SOMETHING ABOUT HIM BOTHERS ME...
WAHAHA
KLANG
YAAAH!
DON'T YOU HAVE ANY BAMBOO SWORDS TO PLAY WITH?!
KA CHING!
I WIN!
HA!
MR. NO-MORI, STOP BEING SO CHILDISH!
IF ONLY MY SWORD WASN'T SO BLUNT...
BESIDES, THIS SWORD WAS GIVEN TO US FOR SAFE-KEEPING!
OH, SORRY.
SWORD...!?

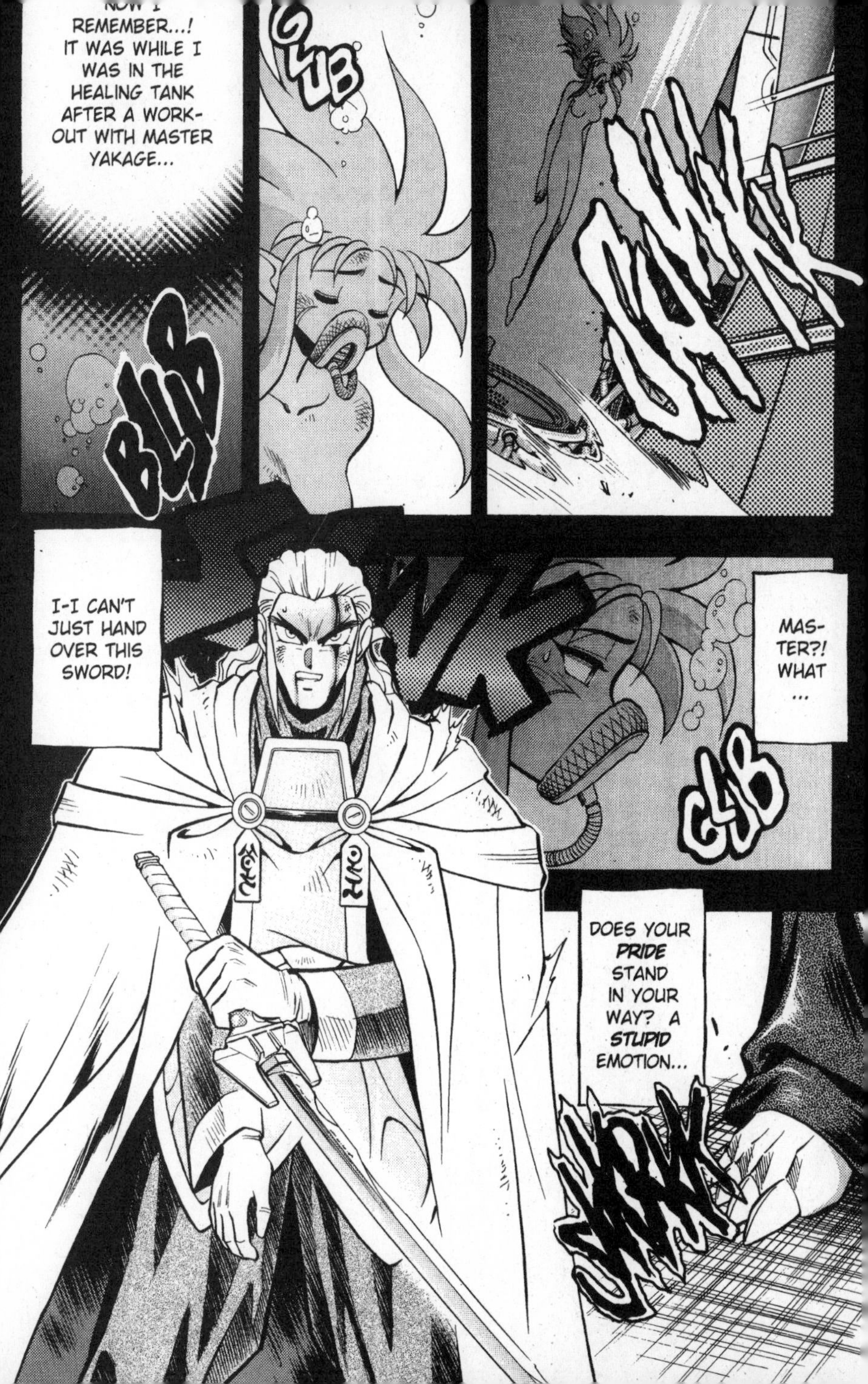
NOW I REMEMBER...! IT WAS WHILE I WAS IN THE HEALING TANK AFTER A WORK-OUT WITH MASTER YAKAGE...
BLUB
GLUB
I-I CAN'T JUST HAND OVER THIS SWORD!
MASTER?! WHAT...
GLUB
DOES YOUR PRIDE STAND IN YOUR WAY? A STUPID EMOTION...

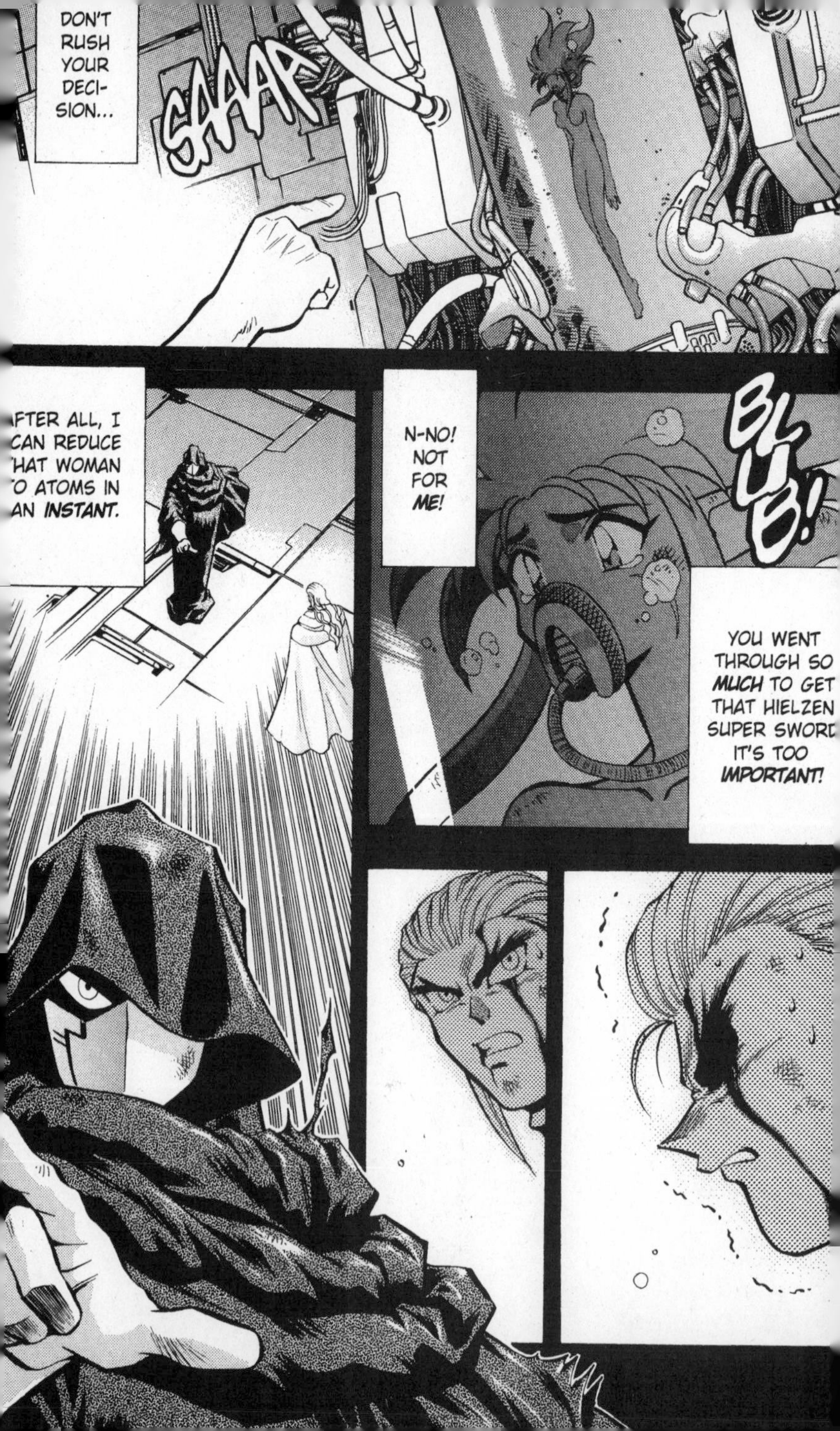
DON'T RUSH YOUR DECI-SION...
SAAAP
AFTER ALL, I CAN REDUCE THAT WOMAN TO ATOMS IN AN *INSTANT.*
N-NO! NOT FOR *ME!*
BLUB!
YOU WENT THROUGH SO *MUCH* TO GET THAT HIELZEN SUPER SWORD IT'S TOO *IMPORTANT!*

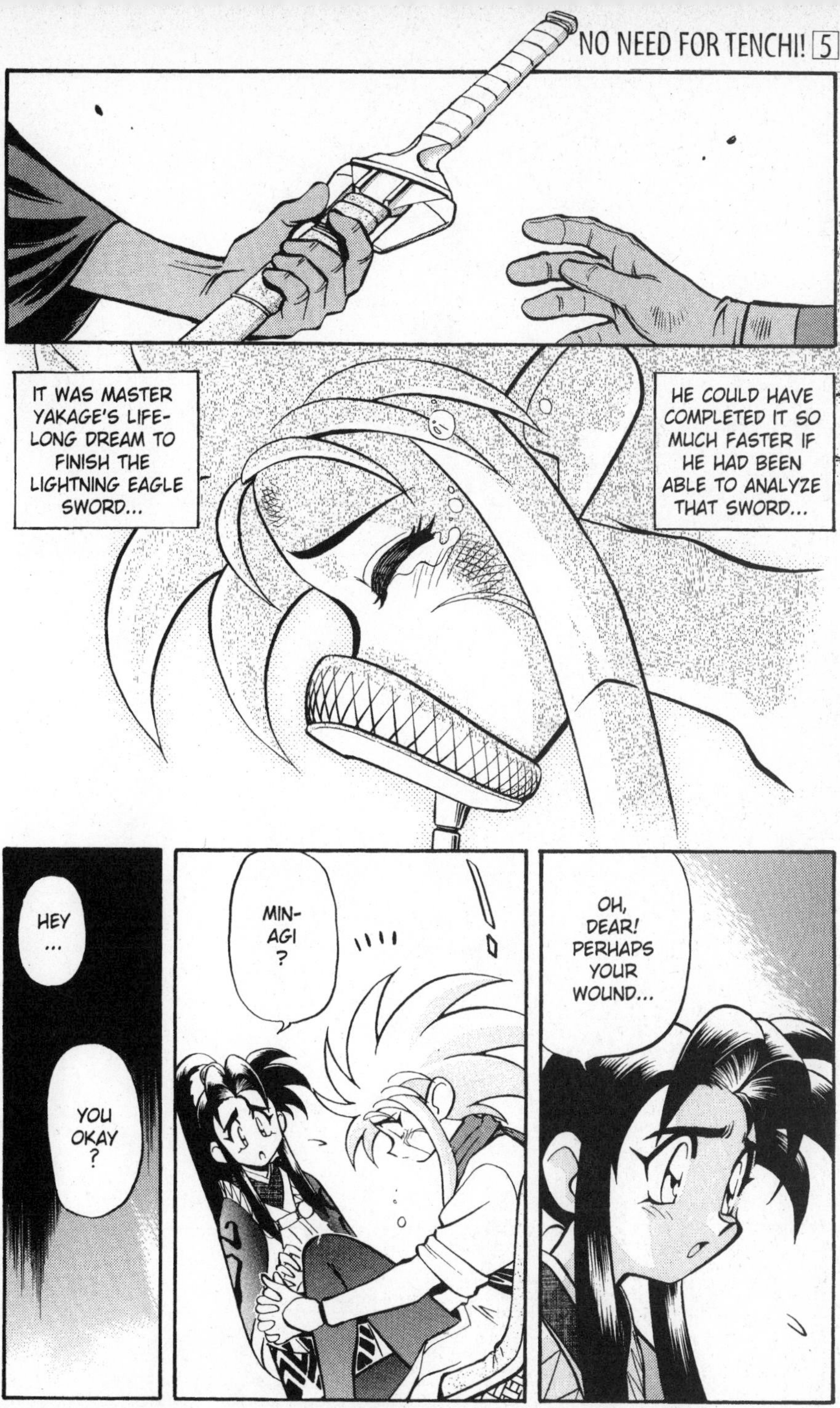
IT WAS MASTER YAKAGE'S LIFE-LONG DREAM TO FINISH THE LIGHTNING EAGLE SWORD...
HE COULD HAVE COMPLETED IT SO MUCH FASTER IF HE HAD BEEN ABLE TO ANALYZE THAT SWORD...
HEY ...
YOU OKAY ?
MIN-AGI ?
!
OH, DEAR! PERHAPS YOUR WOUND...

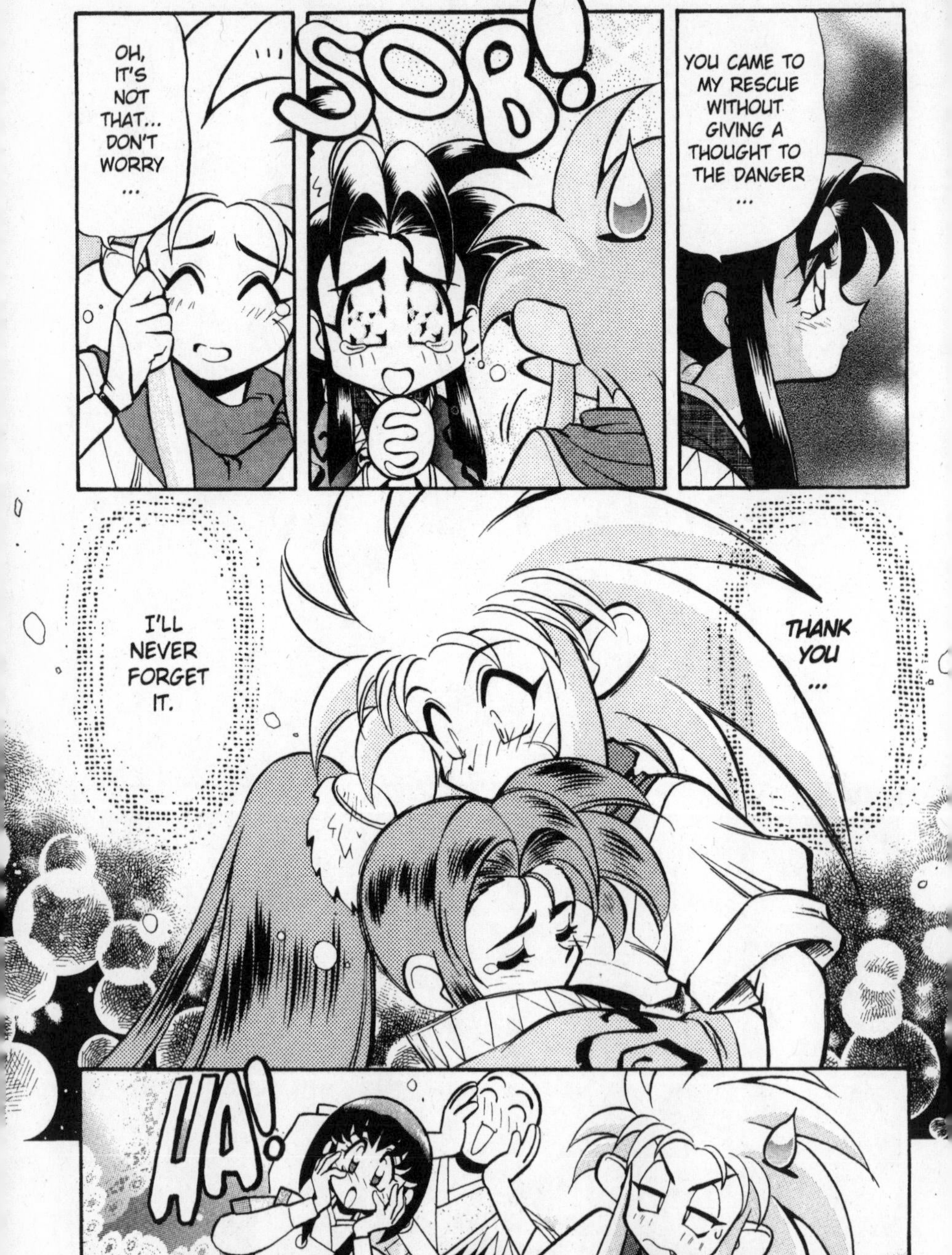

OH, IT'S NOT THAT... DON'T WORRY ...
SOB!
YOU CAME TO MY RESCUE WITHOUT GIVING A THOUGHT TO THE DANGER ...
I'LL NEVER FORGET IT.
THANK YOU ...
HA!

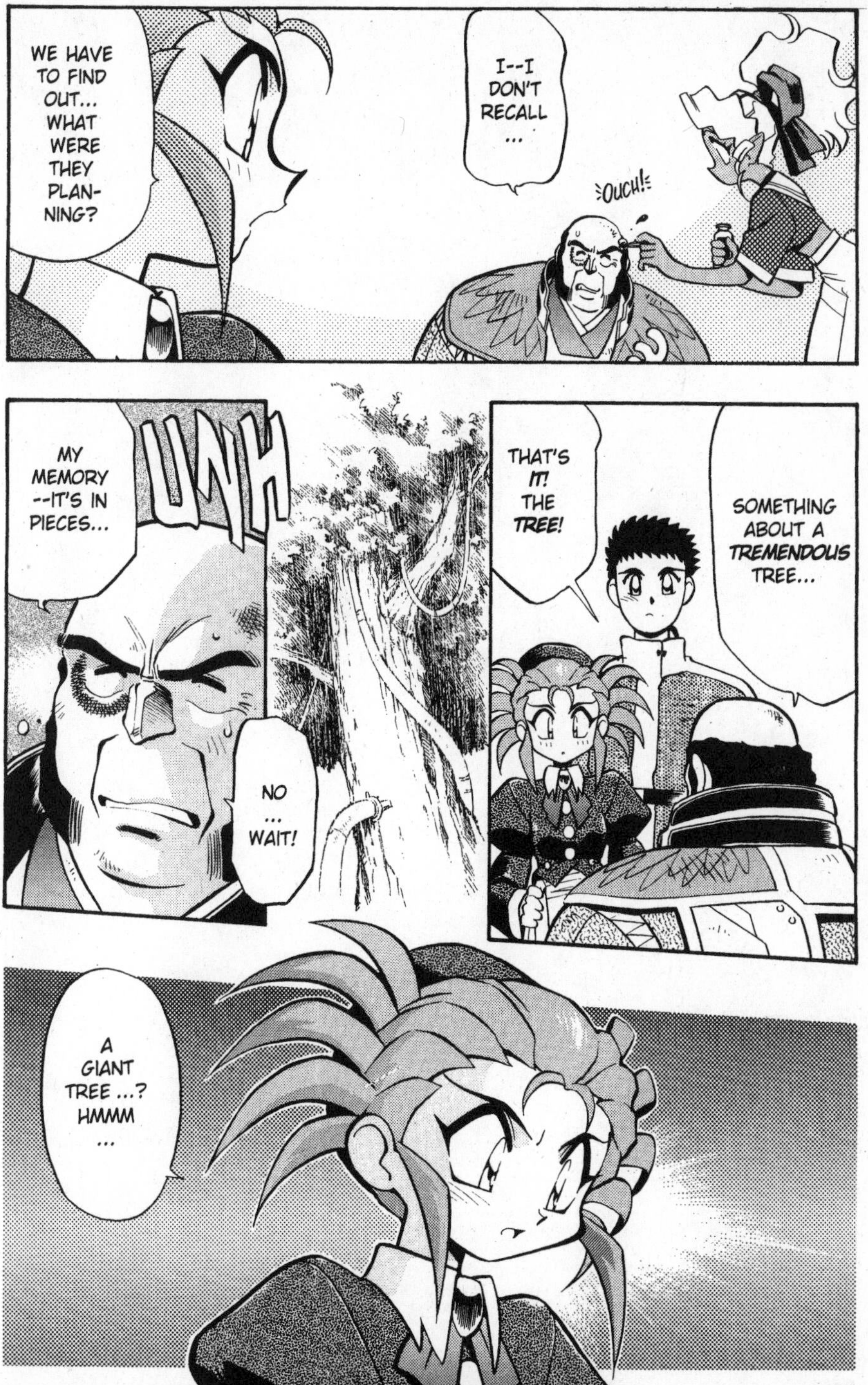
WE HAVE TO FIND OUT... WHAT WERE THEY PLAN-NING?
I--I DON'T RECALL ...
OUCH!
UNH
MY MEMORY --IT'S IN PIECES...
NO ... WAIT!
THAT'S IT! THE TREE!
SOMETHING ABOUT A TREMENDOUS TREE...
A GIANT TREE ...? HMMM ...

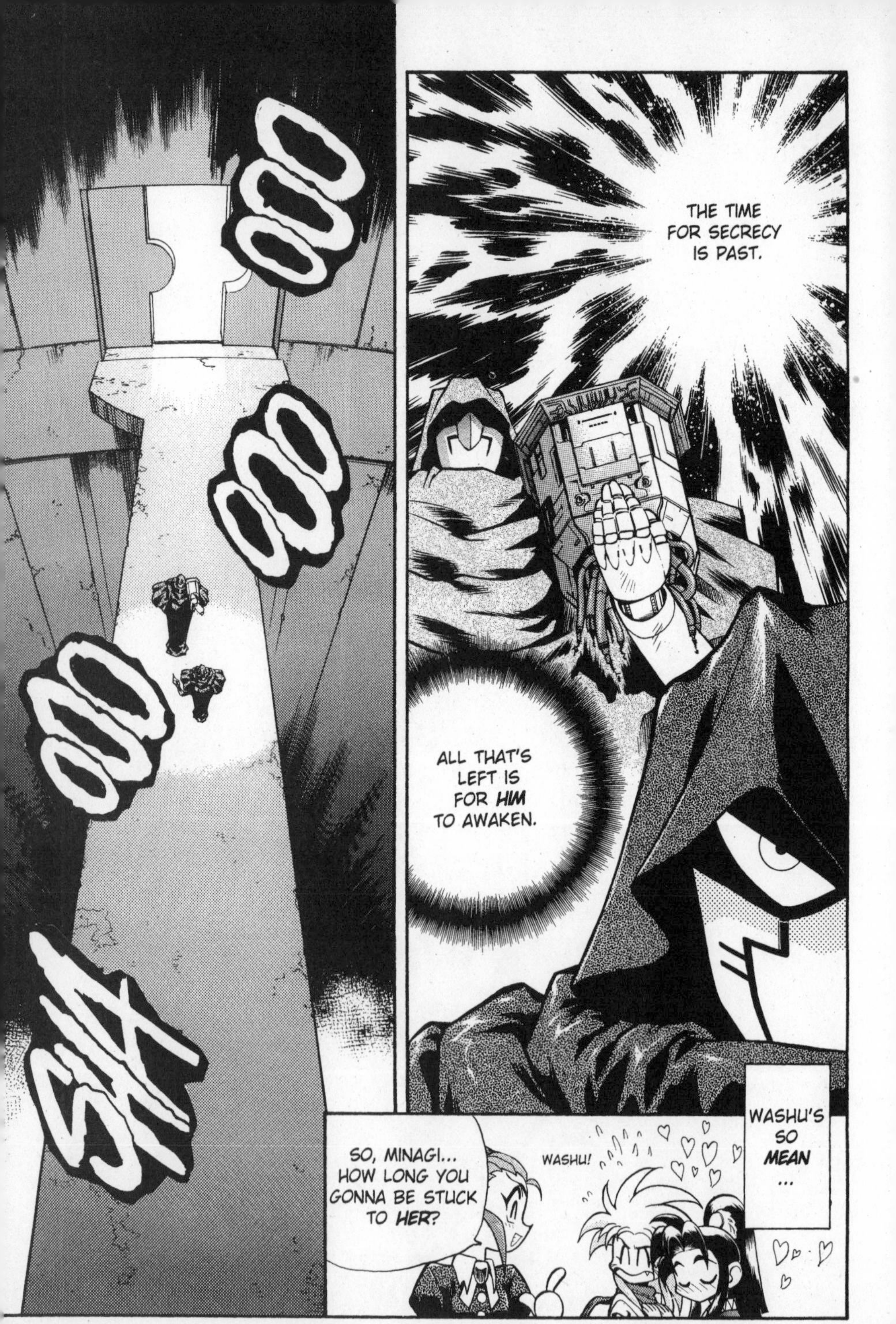
OOO
OOO
OOO
SHA
THE TIME FOR SECRECY IS PAST.
ALL THAT'S LEFT IS FOR **HIM** TO AWAKEN.
SO, MINAGI... HOW LONG YOU GONNA BE STUCK TO **HER**?
WASHU!
WASHU'S SO **MEAN** ...

Tales of Tenchi #5
NO ABSENCE OF MALICE

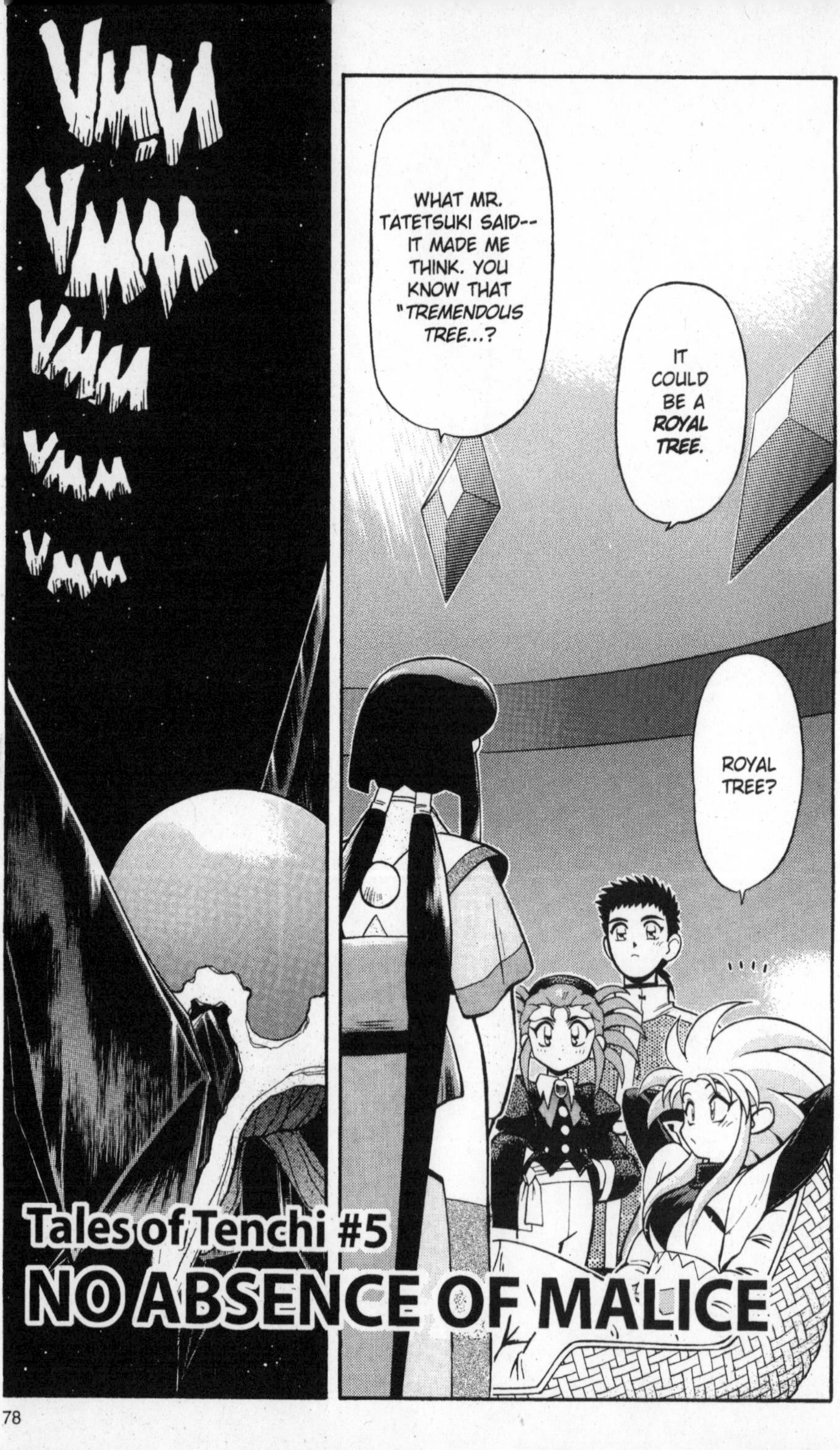
VMM
VMM
VMM
VMM
VMM
WHAT MR. TATETSUKI SAID-- IT MADE ME THINK. YOU KNOW THAT "*TREMENDOUS TREE*...?
IT COULD BE A **ROYAL TREE.**
ROYAL TREE?
...
Tales of Tenchi #5
NO ABSENCE OF MALICE

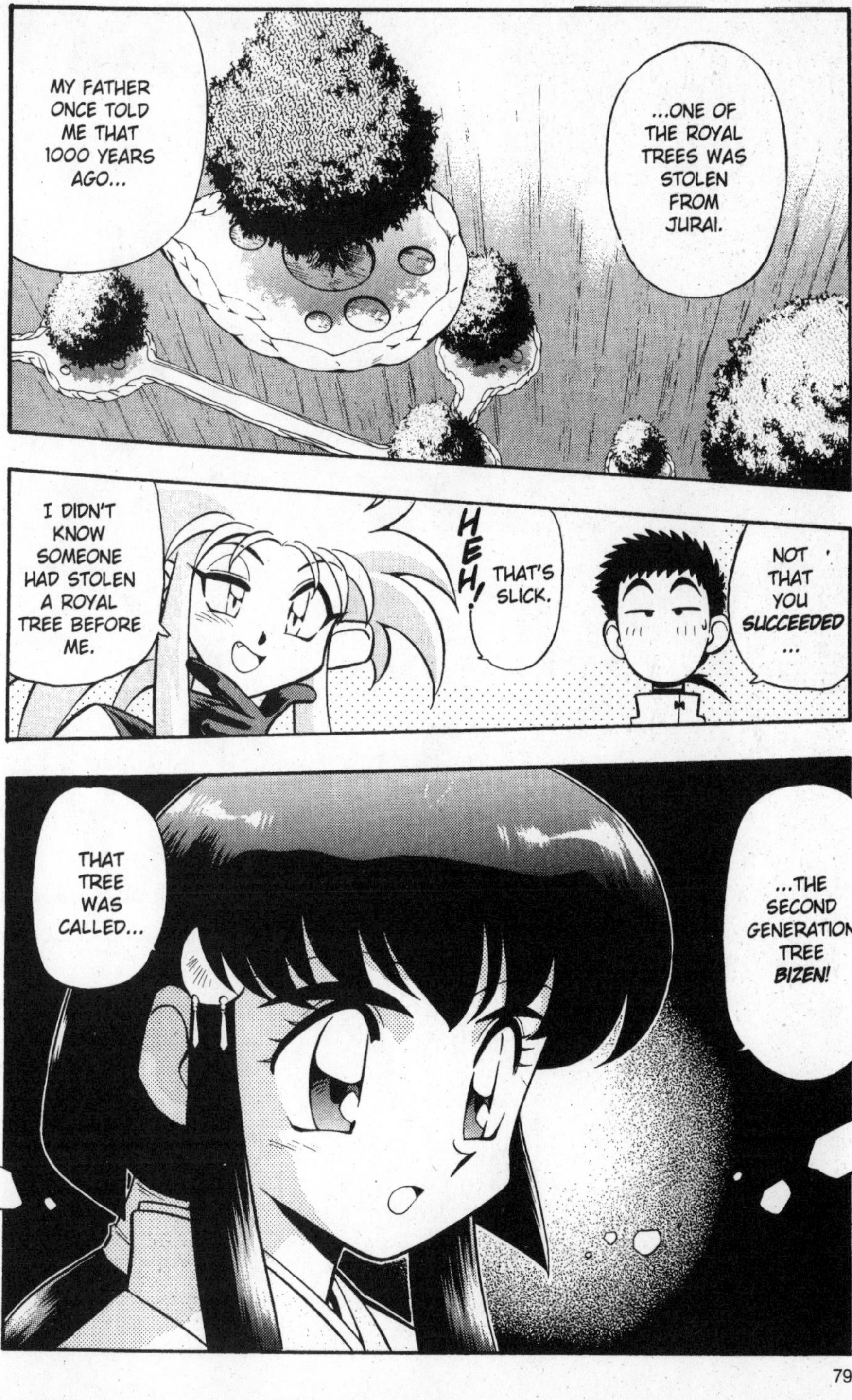
MY FATHER ONCE TOLD ME THAT 1000 YEARS AGO...
...ONE OF THE ROYAL TREES WAS STOLEN FROM JURAI.
I DIDN'T KNOW SOMEONE HAD STOLEN A ROYAL TREE BEFORE ME.
HEH!
THAT'S SLICK.
NOT THAT YOU SUCCEEDED ...
THAT TREE WAS CALLED...
...THE SECOND GENERATION TREE BIZEN!

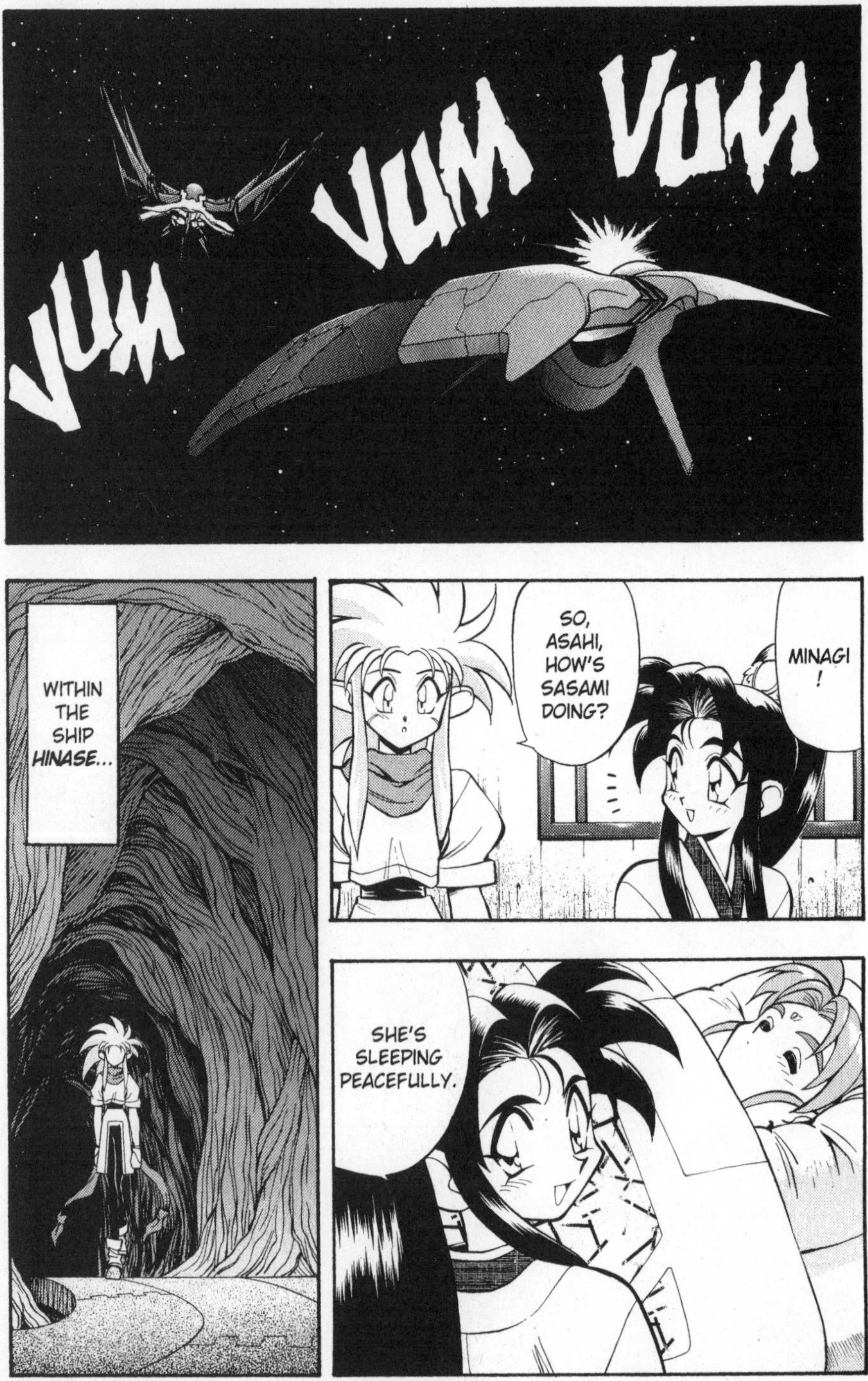
VUM
VUM
VUM
WITHIN THE SHIP HINASE...
SO, ASAHI, HOW'S SASAMI DOING?
MINAGI!
SHE'S SLEEPING PEACEFULLY.

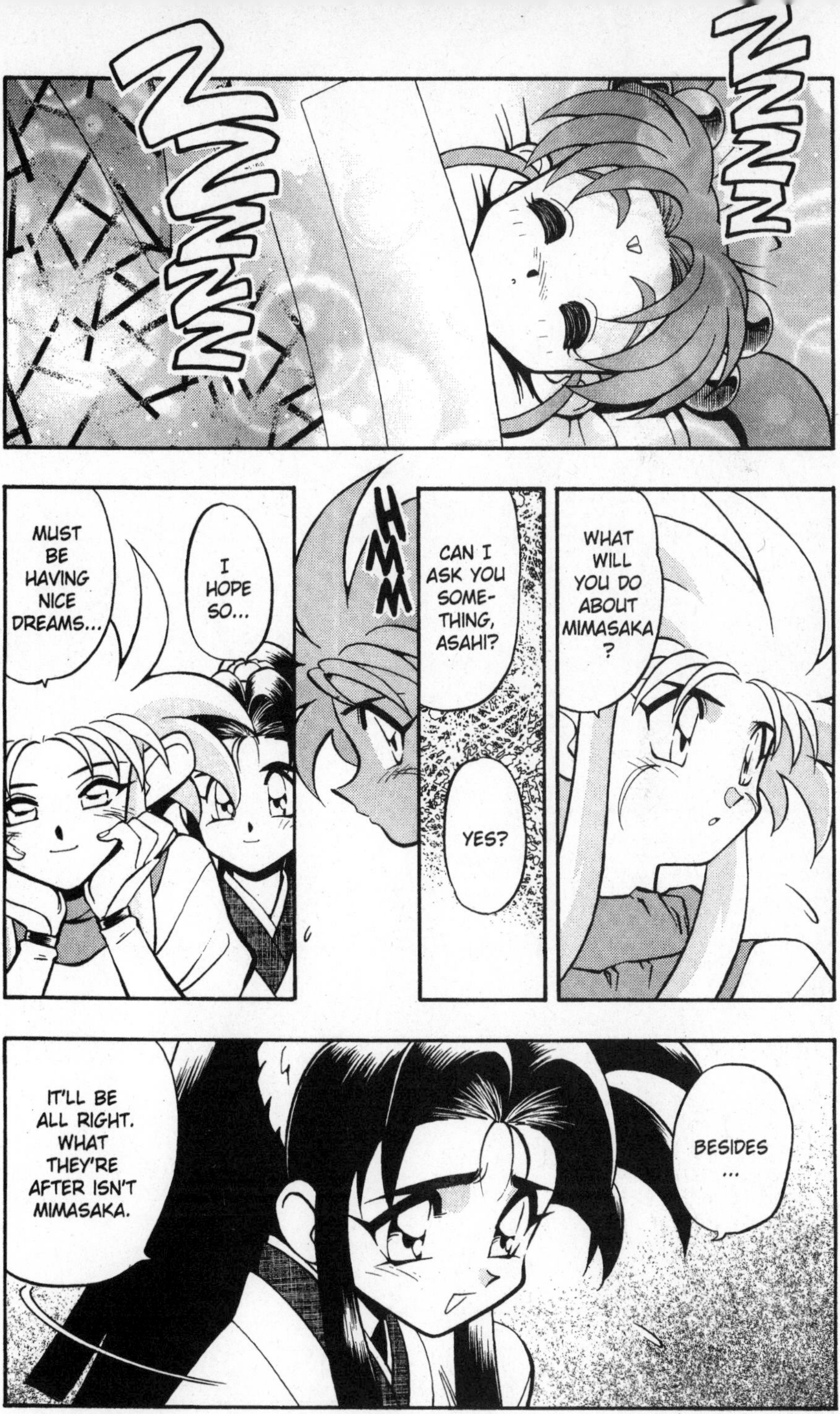
MUST BE HAVING NICE DREAMS...
I HOPE SO...
HMMM
CAN I ASK YOU SOME-THING, ASAHI?
YES?
WHAT WILL YOU DO ABOUT MIMASAKA?
IT'LL BE ALL RIGHT. WHAT THEY'RE AFTER ISN'T MIMASAKA.
BESIDES...

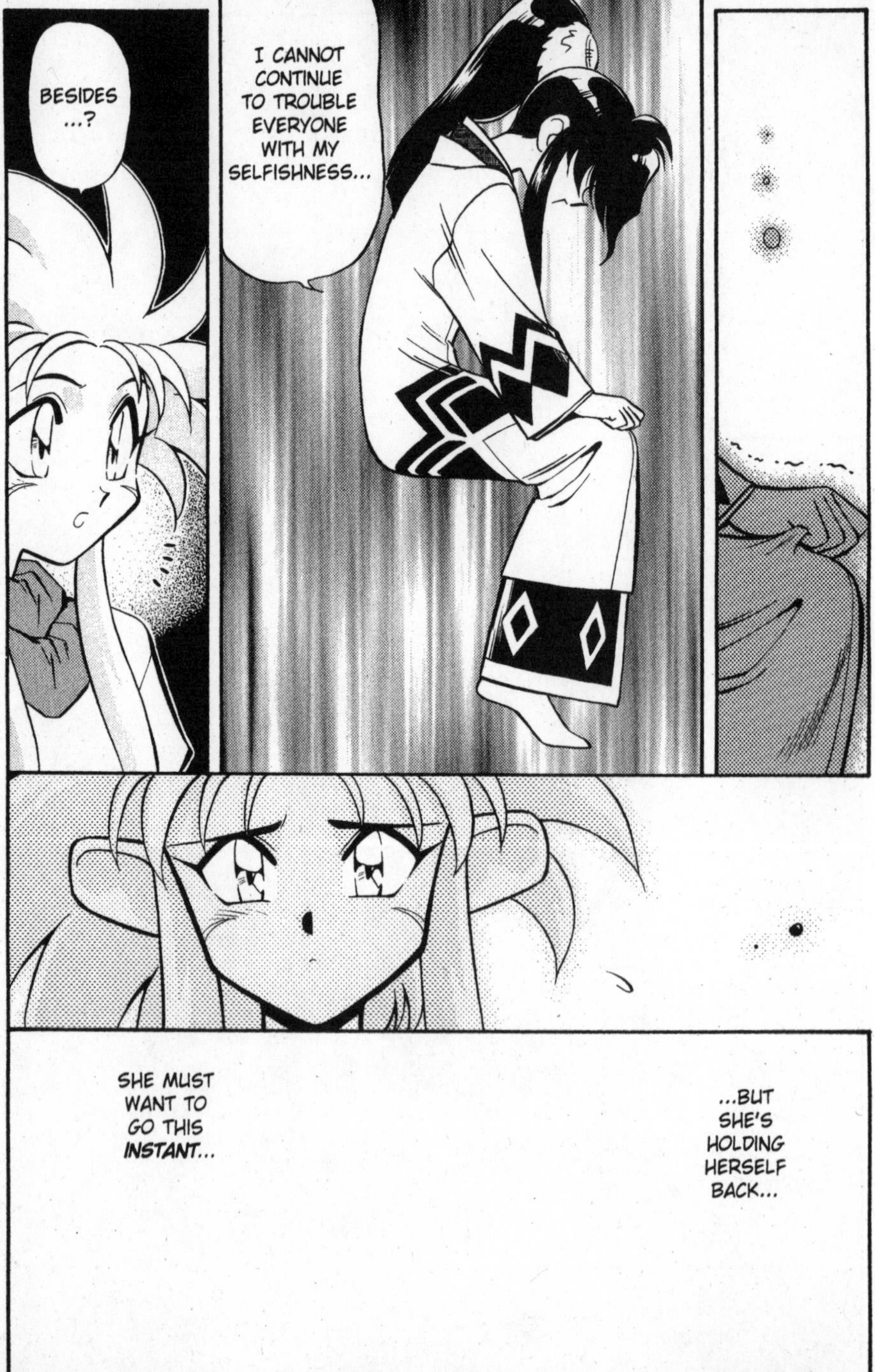
BESIDES ...?
I CANNOT CONTINUE TO TROUBLE EVERYONE WITH MY SELFISHNESS...
SHE MUST WANT TO GO THIS INSTANT...
...BUT SHE'S HOLDING HERSELF BACK...

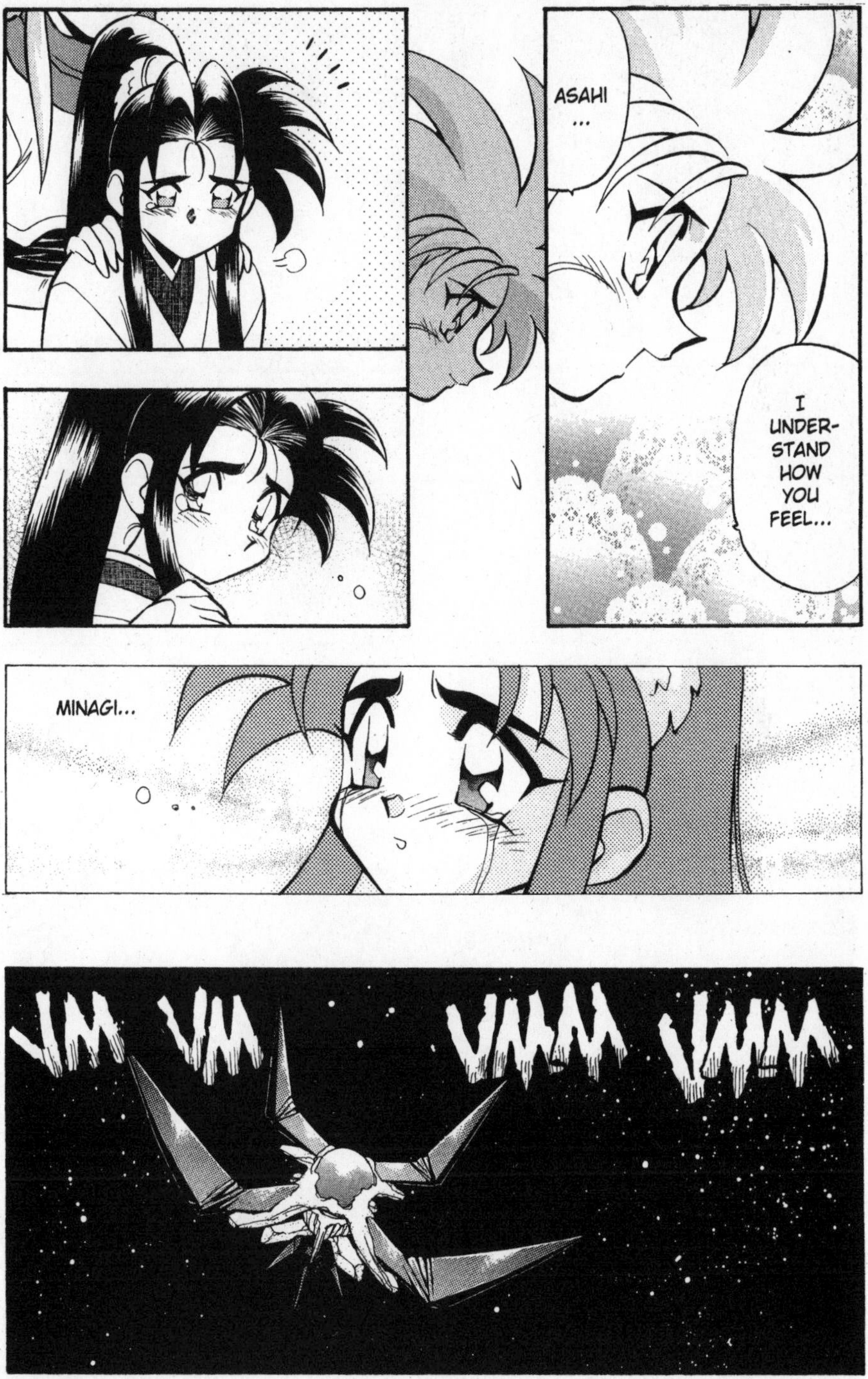
ASAHI ...
I UNDER-STAND HOW YOU FEEL...
MINAGI...

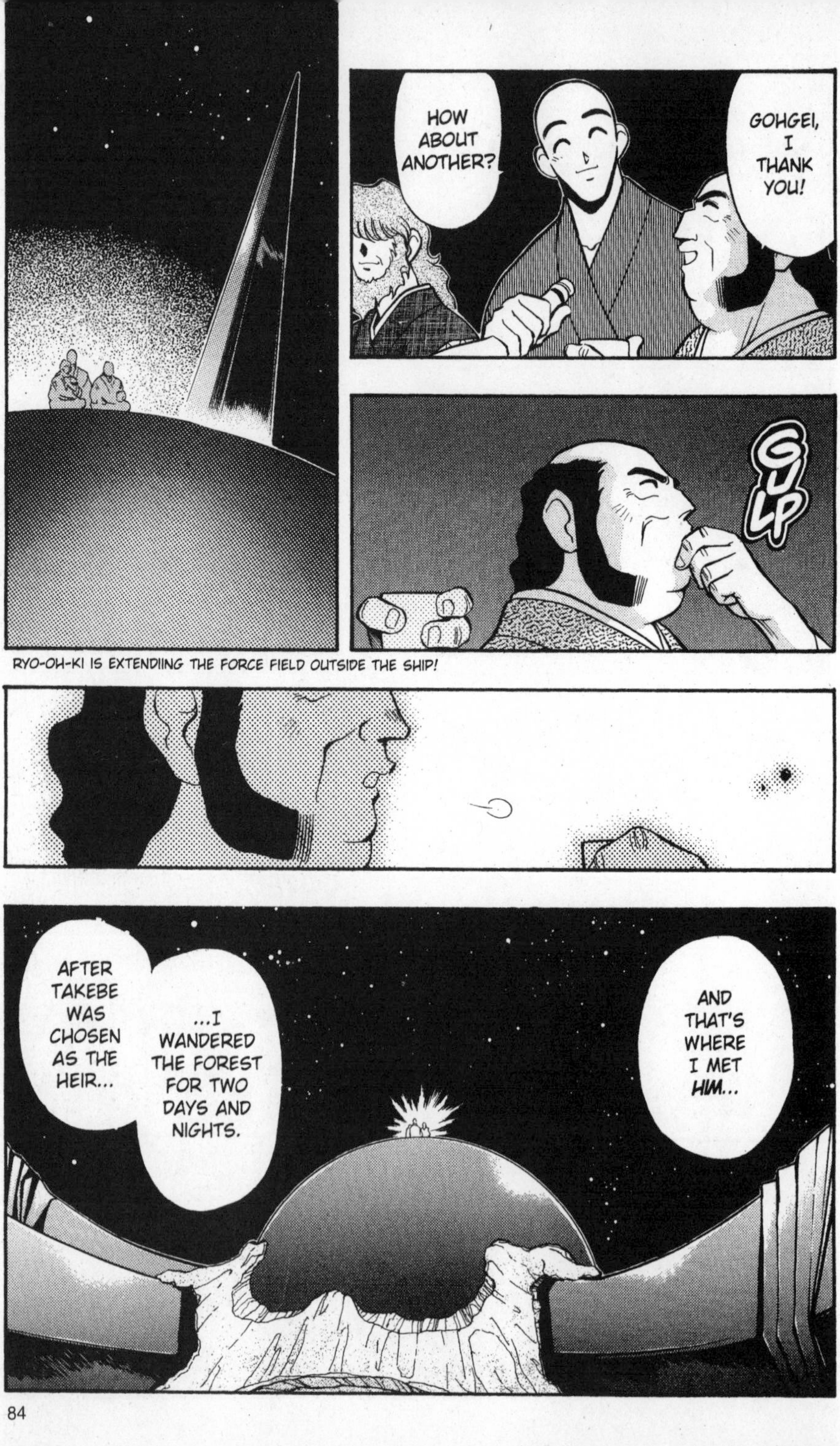
HOW ABOUT ANOTHER?
GOHGEI, I THANK YOU!
GULP
RYO-OH-KI IS EXTENDIING THE FORCE FIELD OUTSIDE THE SHIP!
AFTER TAKEBE WAS CHOSEN AS THE HEIR...
...I WANDERED THE FOREST FOR TWO DAYS AND NIGHTS.
AND THAT'S WHERE I MET *HIM*...

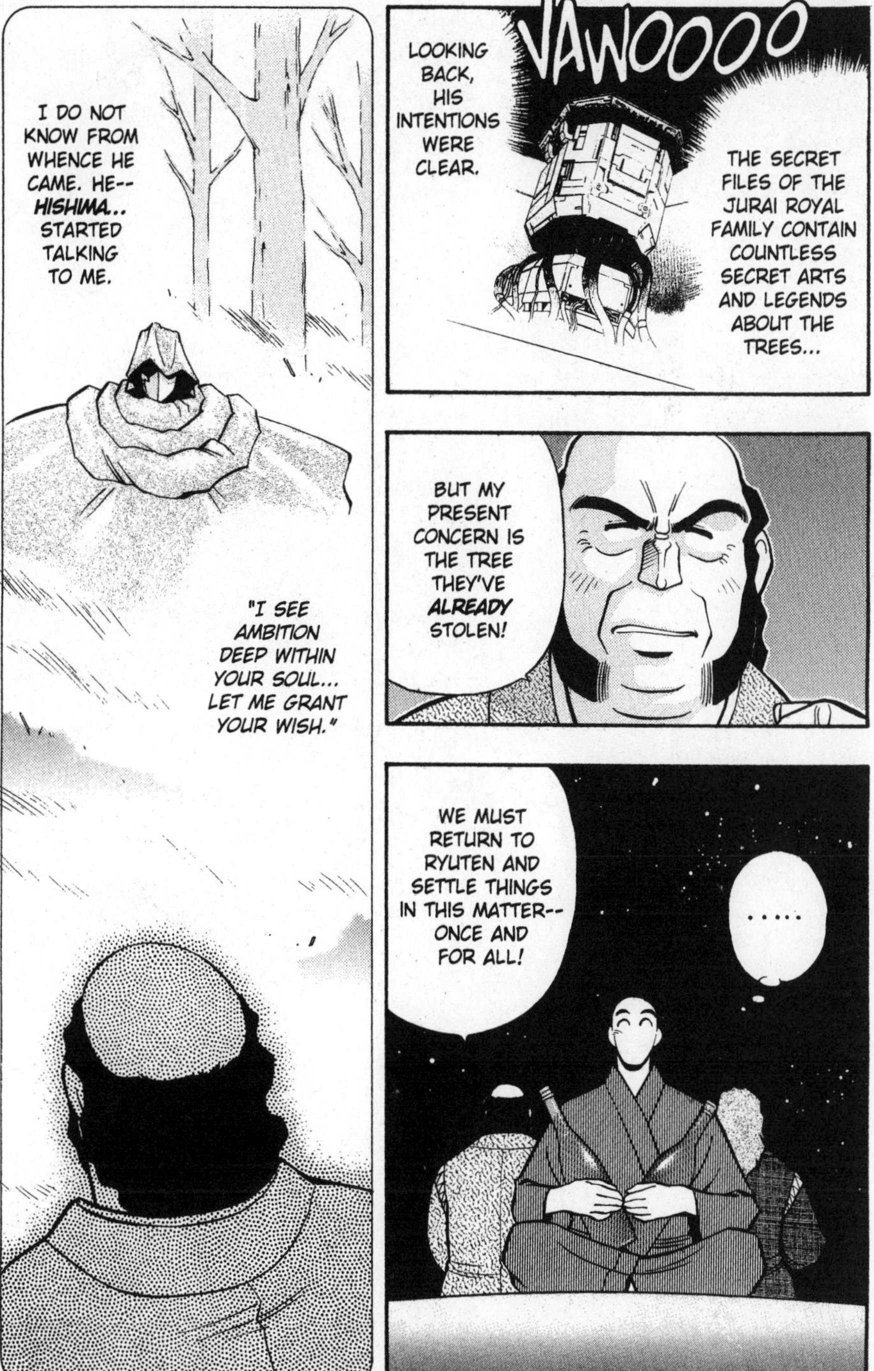
I DO NOT KNOW FROM WHENCE HE CAME. HE-- **HISHIMA...** STARTED TALKING TO ME.
"I SEE AMBITION DEEP WITHIN YOUR SOUL... LET ME GRANT YOUR WISH."
LOOKING BACK, HIS INTENTIONS WERE CLEAR.
VAWOOOO
THE SECRET FILES OF THE JURAI ROYAL FAMILY CONTAIN COUNTLESS SECRET ARTS AND LEGENDS ABOUT THE TREES...
BUT MY PRESENT CONCERN IS THE TREE THEY'VE ***ALREADY*** STOLEN!
WE MUST RETURN TO RYUTEN AND SETTLE THINGS IN THIS MATTER-- ONCE AND FOR ALL!
.....

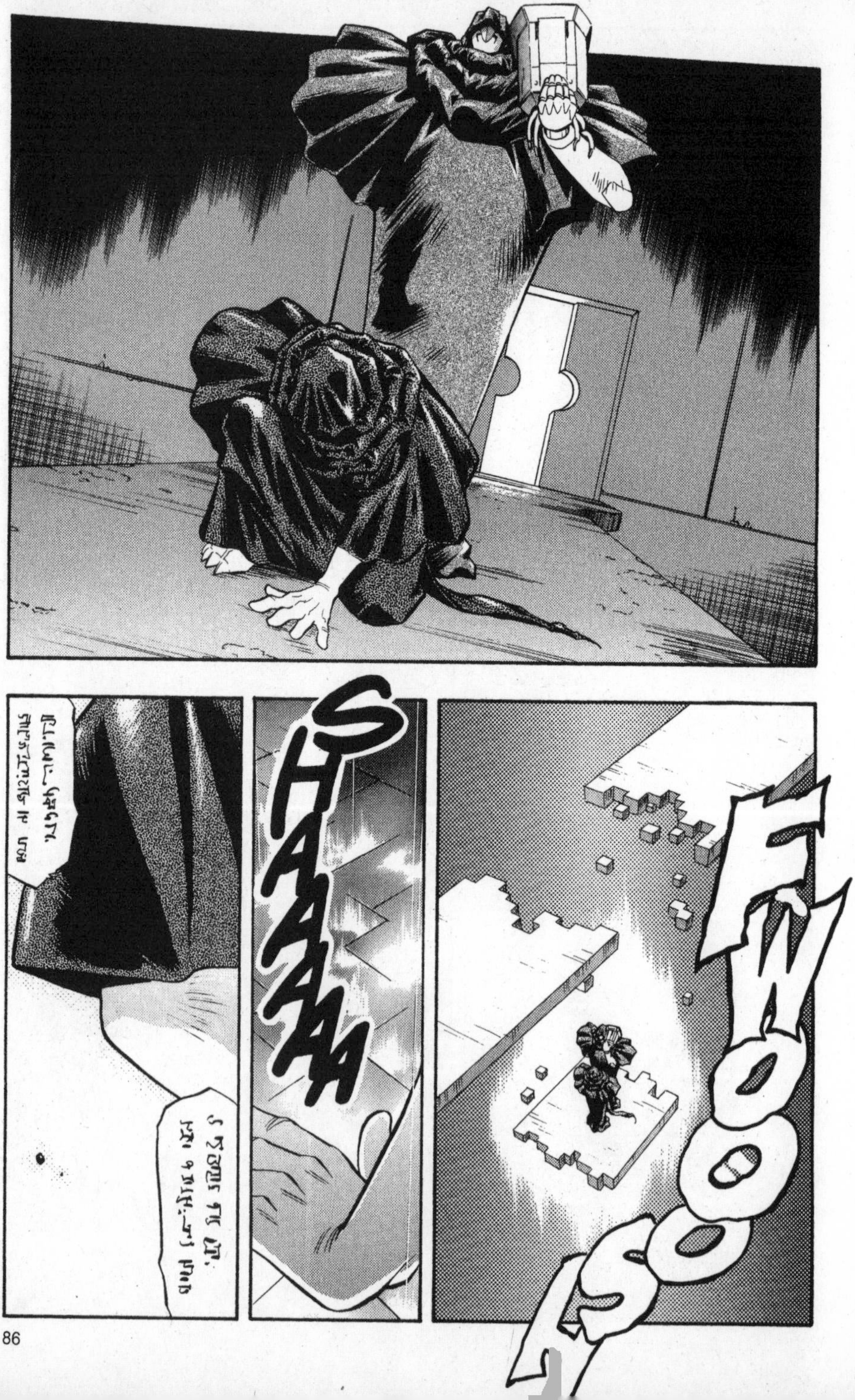
SHAAAAA
WHOOOSH

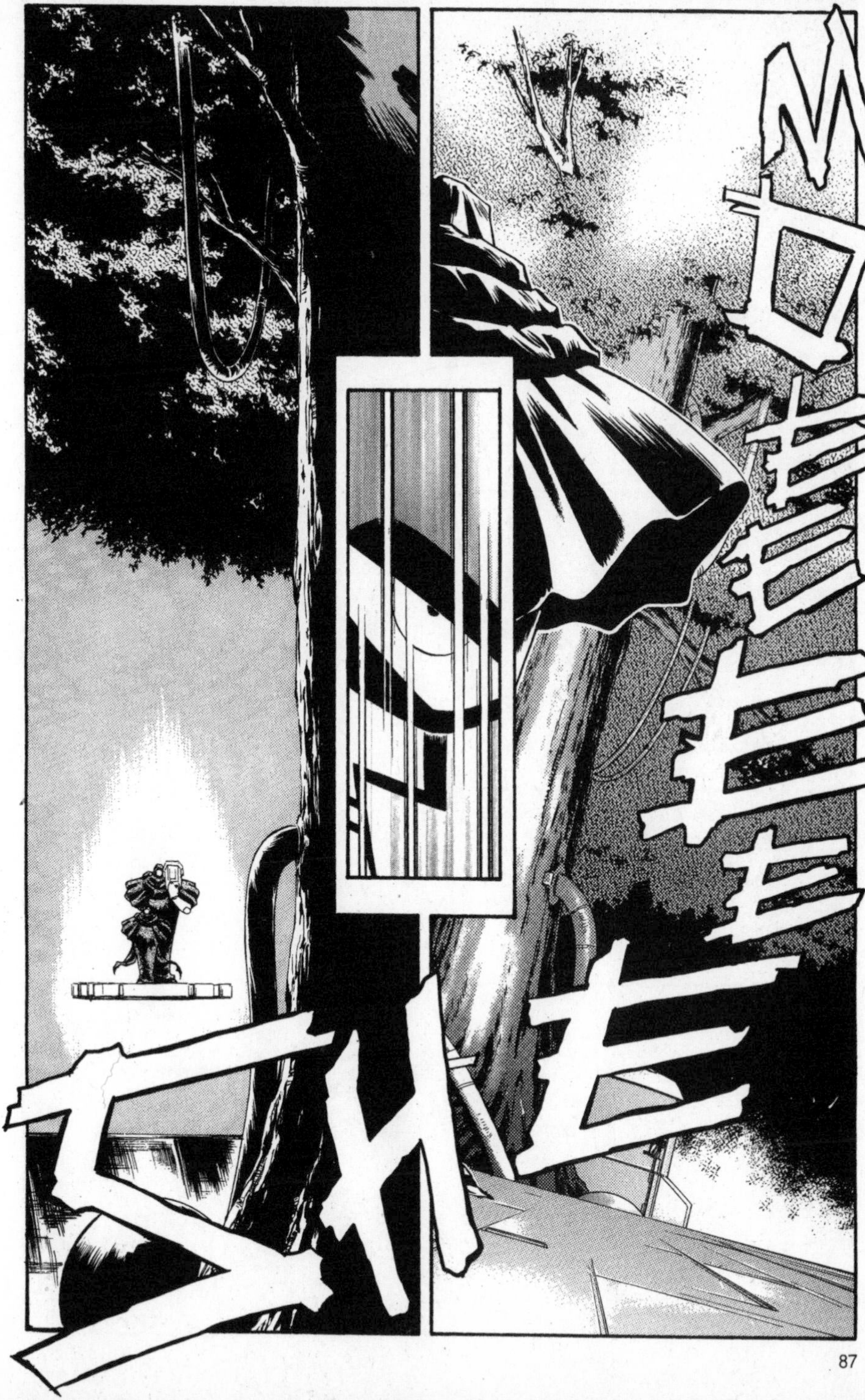

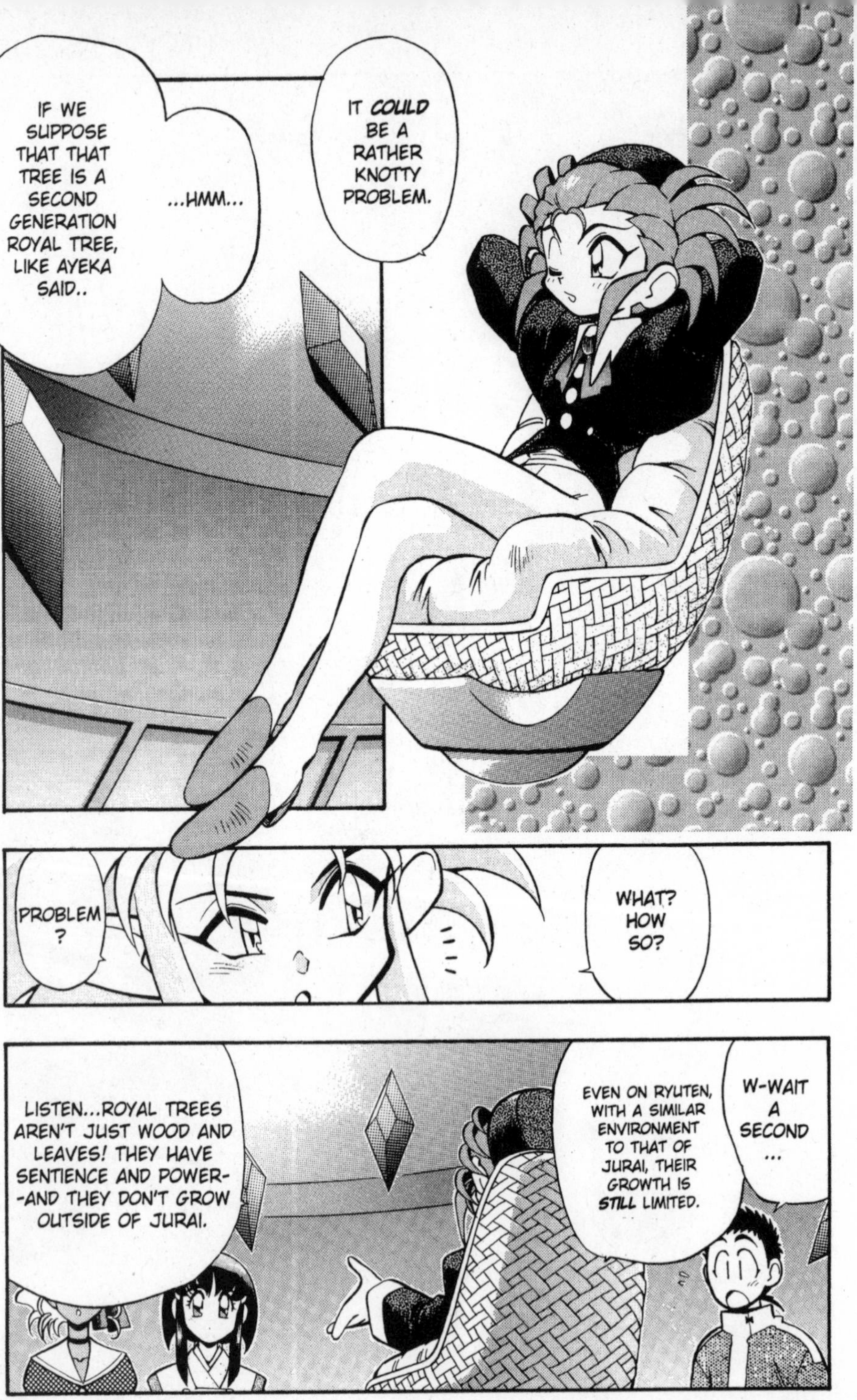
IF WE SUPPOSE THAT THAT TREE IS A SECOND GENERATION ROYAL TREE, LIKE AYEKA SAID..
...HMM...
IT **COULD** BE A RATHER KNOTTY PROBLEM.
PROBLEM ?
WHAT? HOW SO?
LISTEN...ROYAL TREES AREN'T JUST WOOD AND LEAVES! THEY HAVE SENTIENCE AND POWER--AND THEY DON'T GROW OUTSIDE OF JURAI.
EVEN ON RYUTEN, WITH A SIMILAR ENVIRONMENT TO THAT OF JURAI, THEIR GROWTH IS **STILL** LIMITED.
W-WAIT A SECOND ...

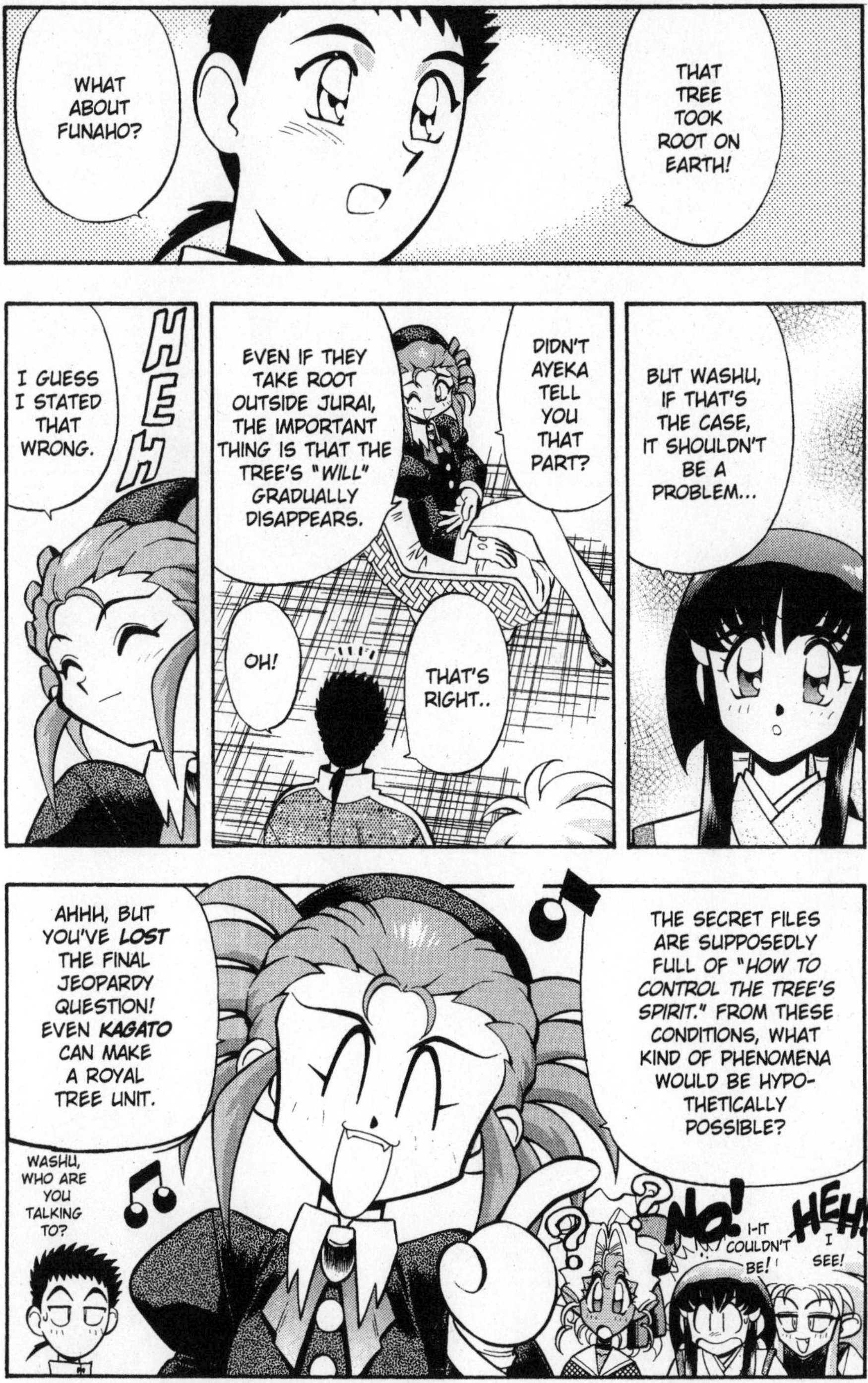
WHAT ABOUT FUNAHO?
THAT TREE TOOK ROOT ON EARTH!
I GUESS I STATED THAT WRONG.
HEH HEH
EVEN IF THEY TAKE ROOT OUTSIDE JURAI, THE IMPORTANT THING IS THAT THE TREE'S "WILL" GRADUALLY DISAPPEARS.
DIDN'T AYEKA TELL YOU THAT PART?
OH!
THAT'S RIGHT..
BUT WASHU, IF THAT'S THE CASE, IT SHOULDN'T BE A PROBLEM...
AHHH, BUT YOU'VE ***LOST*** THE FINAL JEOPARDY QUESTION! EVEN ***KAGATO*** CAN MAKE A ROYAL TREE UNIT.
THE SECRET FILES ARE SUPPOSEDLY FULL OF "*HOW TO CONTROL THE TREE'S SPIRIT.*" FROM THESE CONDITIONS, WHAT KIND OF PHENOMENA WOULD BE HYPO-THETICALLY POSSIBLE?
WASHU, WHO ARE YOU TALKING TO?
NA!
I-IT COULDN'T BE!
HEH!
I SEE!

THE PRESENT RYUOH UNIT WAS MADE BY KAGATO FOR THE PURPOSE OF TAKING TSUMANI AWAY (AS SHOWN IN OAV EP.7)

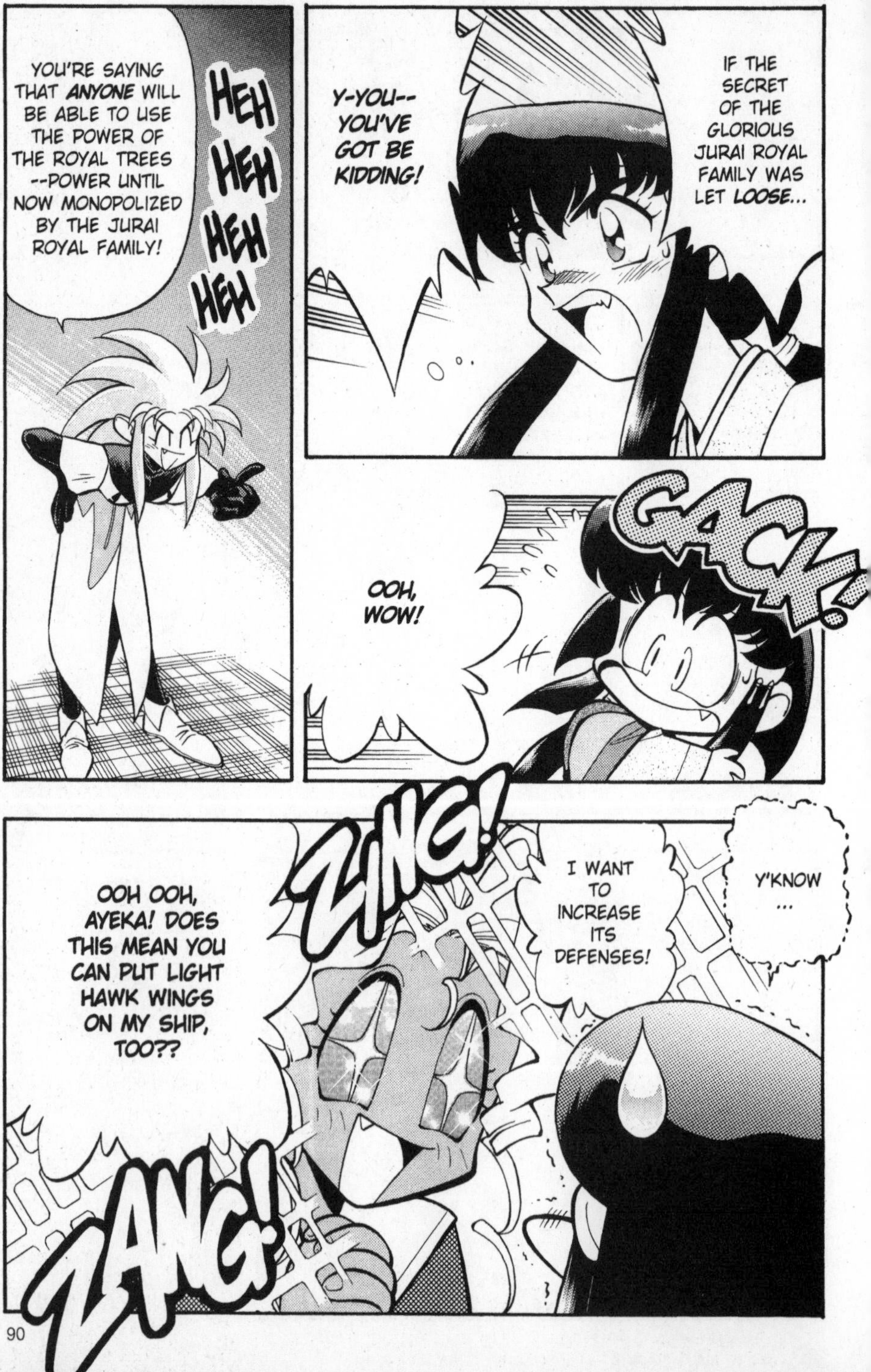
YOU'RE SAYING THAT ANYONE WILL BE ABLE TO USE THE POWER OF THE ROYAL TREES --POWER UNTIL NOW MONOPOLIZED BY THE JURAI ROYAL FAMILY!
HEH HEH HEH HEH
Y-YOU-- YOU'VE GOT BE KIDDING!
IF THE SECRET OF THE GLORIOUS JURAI ROYAL FAMILY WAS LET LOOSE...
OOH, WOW!
GACK!
OOH OOH, AYEKA! DOES THIS MEAN YOU CAN PUT LIGHT HAWK WINGS ON MY SHIP, TOO??
ZING!
I WANT TO INCREASE ITS DEFENSES!
Y'KNOW ...
ZANG!

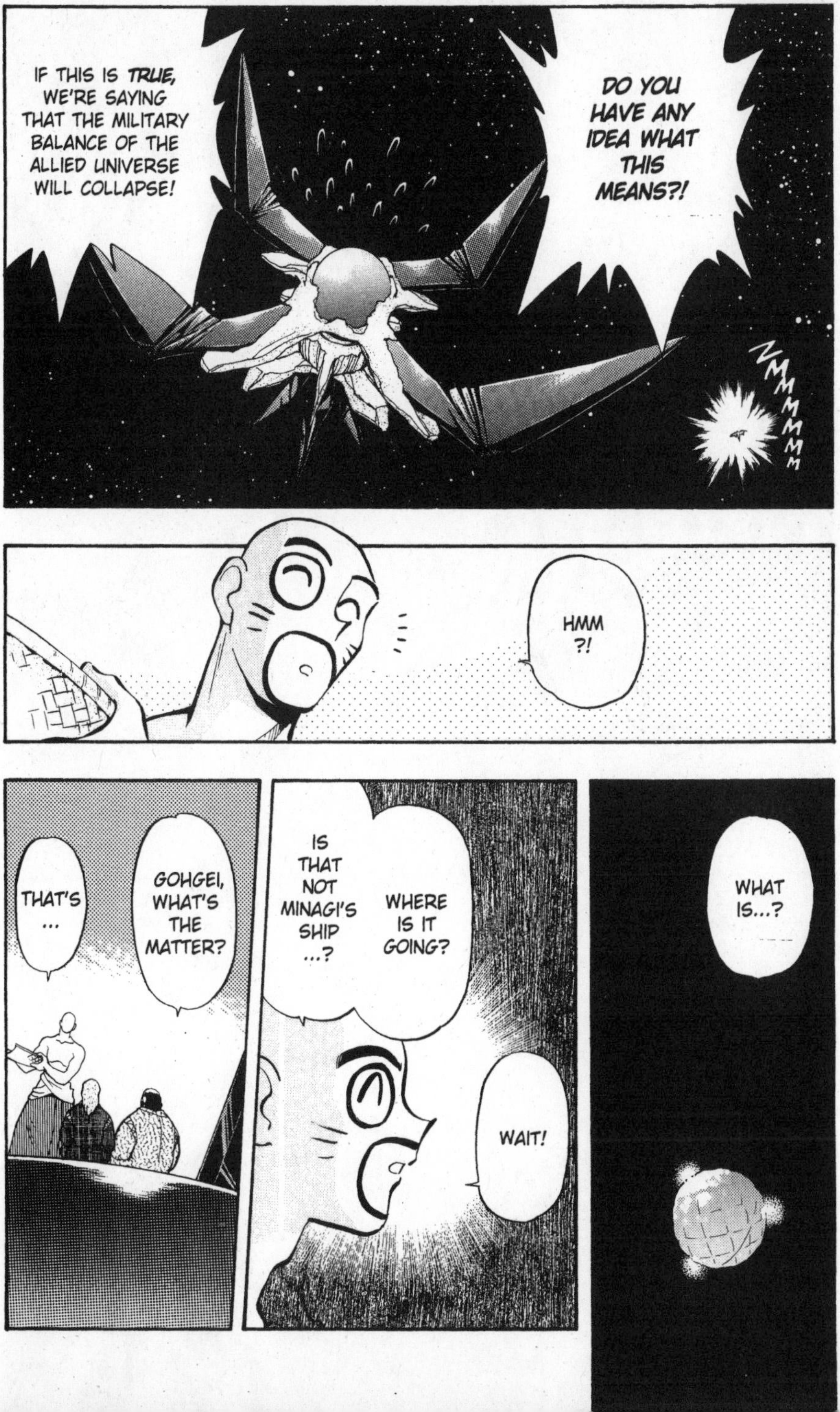
IF THIS IS *TRUE*, WE'RE SAYING THAT THE MILITARY BALANCE OF THE ALLIED UNIVERSE WILL COLLAPSE!
DO YOU HAVE ANY IDEA WHAT THIS MEANS?!
ZMMMMMMM
HMM ?!
THAT'S ...
GOHGEI, WHAT'S THE MATTER?
IS THAT NOT MINAGI'S SHIP ...?
WHERE IS IT GOING?
WAIT!
WHAT IS...?

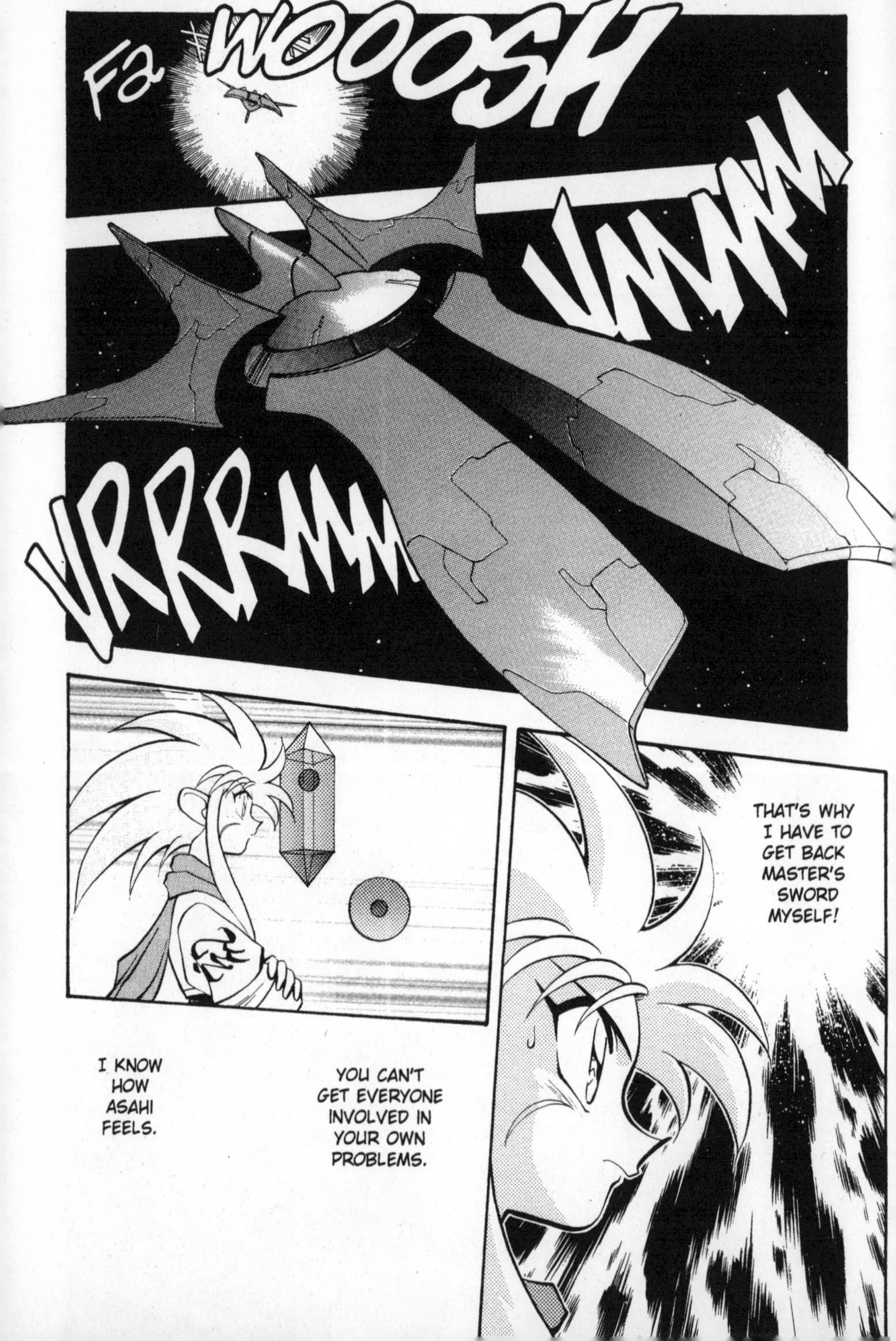
Fa WOOOSH
VRRRMMM
I KNOW HOW ASAHI FEELS.
YOU CAN'T GET EVERYONE INVOLVED IN YOUR OWN PROBLEMS.
THAT'S WHY I HAVE TO GET BACK MASTER'S SWORD MYSELF!

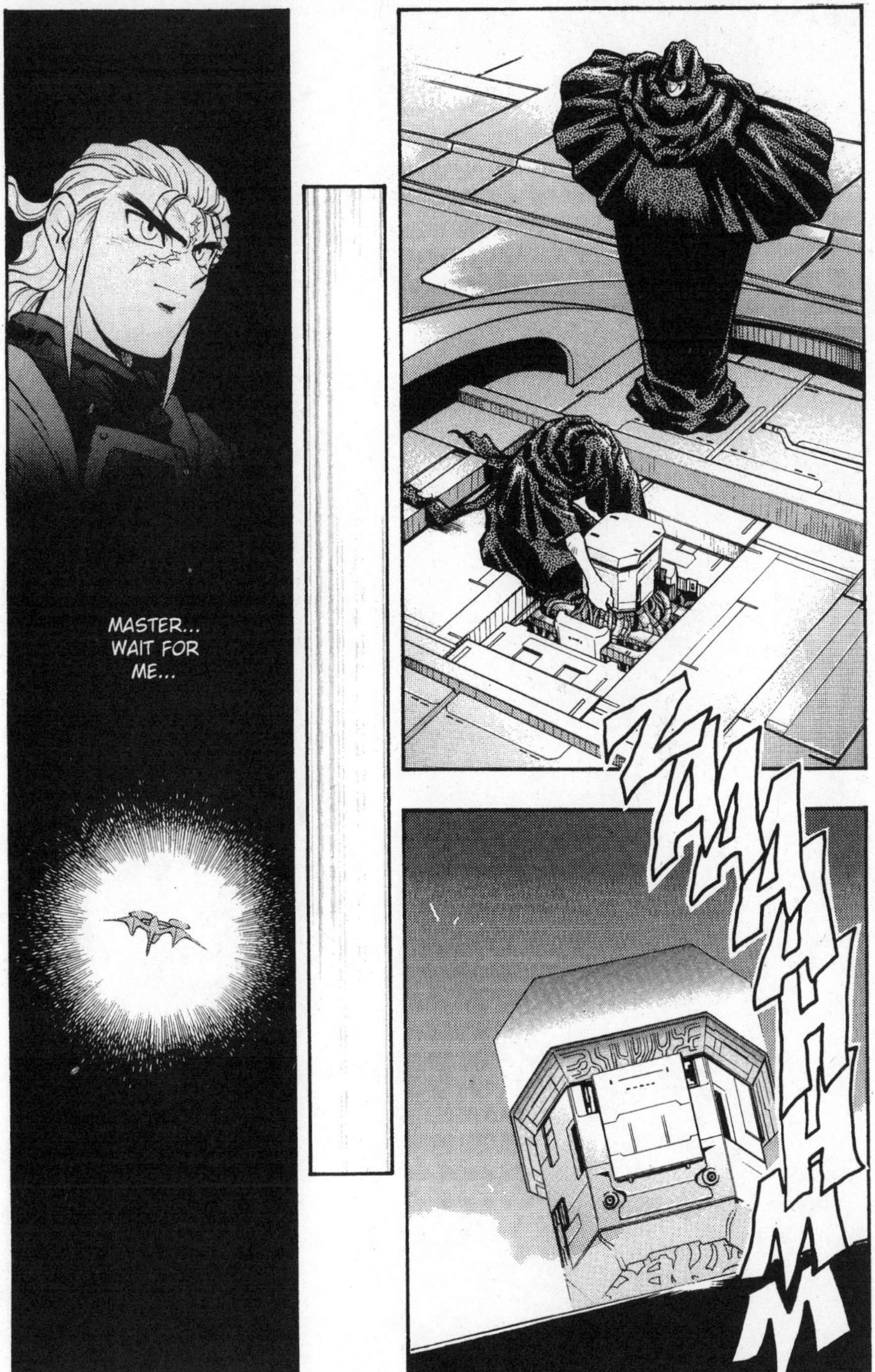
MASTER... WAIT FOR ME...
ZAAAHHHMM

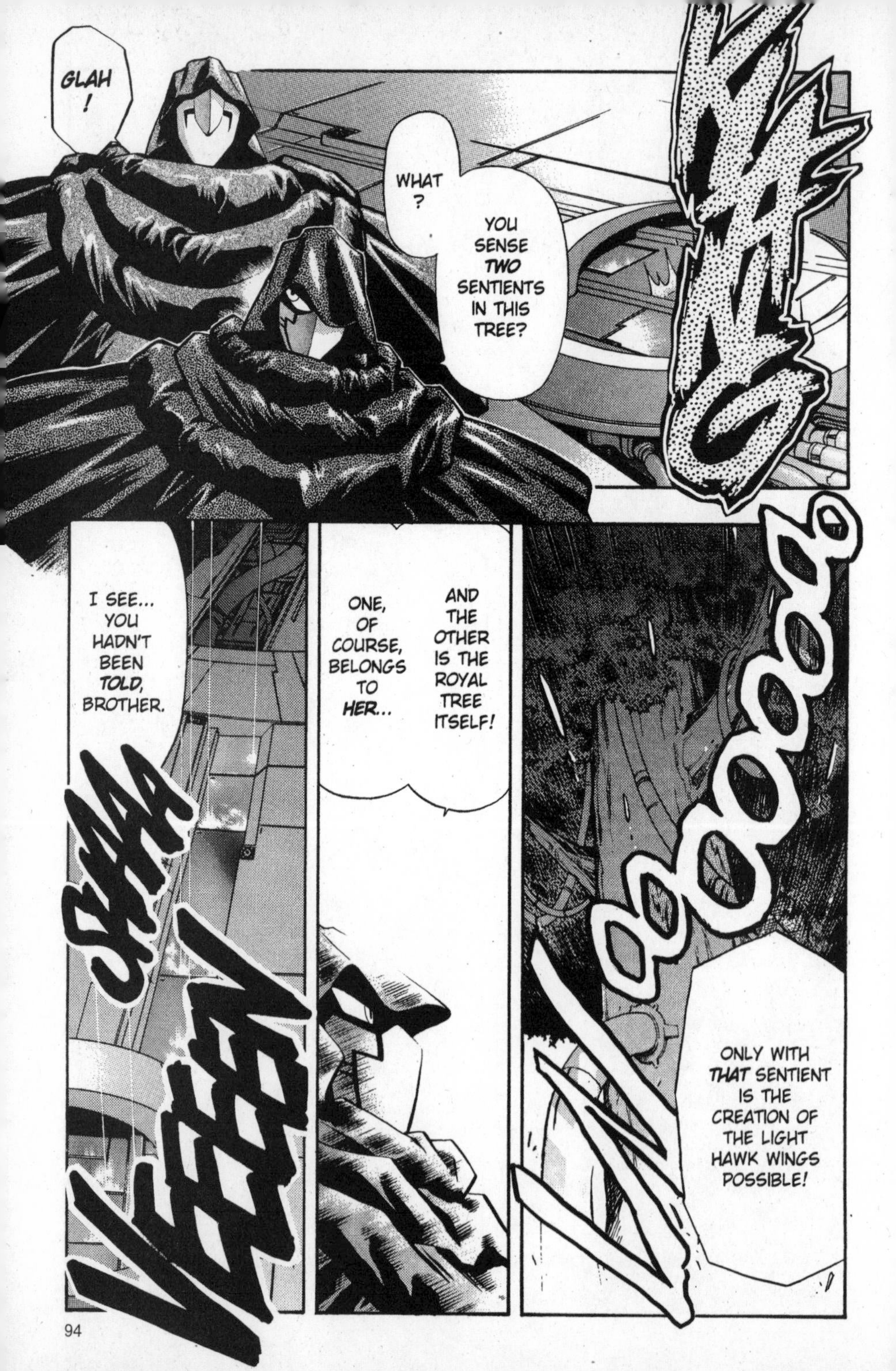
GLAH!
WHAT?
YOU SENSE TWO SENTIENTS IN THIS TREE?
I SEE... YOU HADN'T BEEN TOLD, BROTHER.
ONE, OF COURSE, BELONGS TO HER...
AND THE OTHER IS THE ROYAL TREE ITSELF!
ONLY WITH THAT SENTIENT IS THE CREATION OF THE LIGHT HAWK WINGS POSSIBLE!

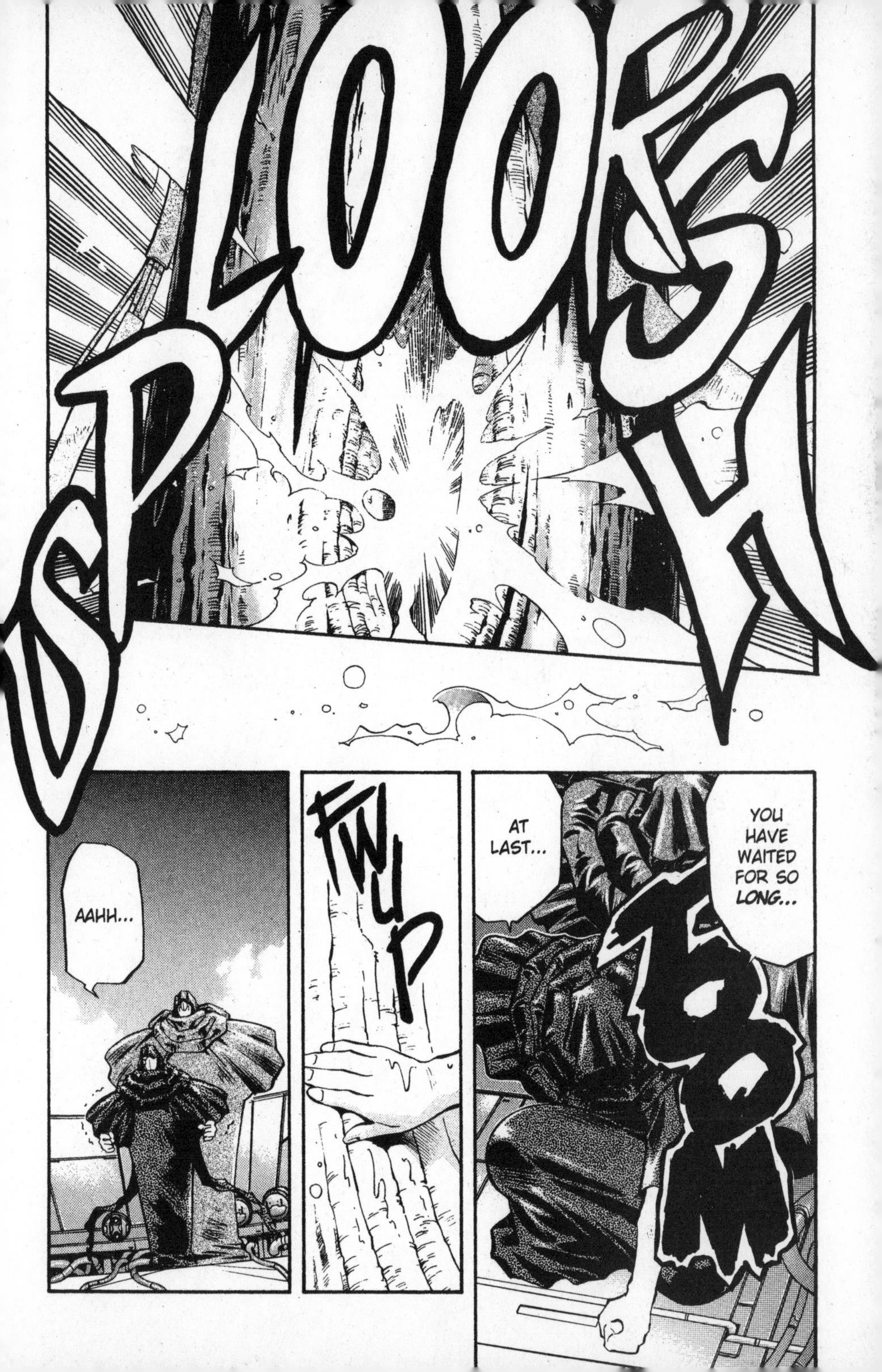
SPLOOOSH
AAHH...
FWUP
AT LAST...
YOU HAVE WAITED FOR SO LONG...

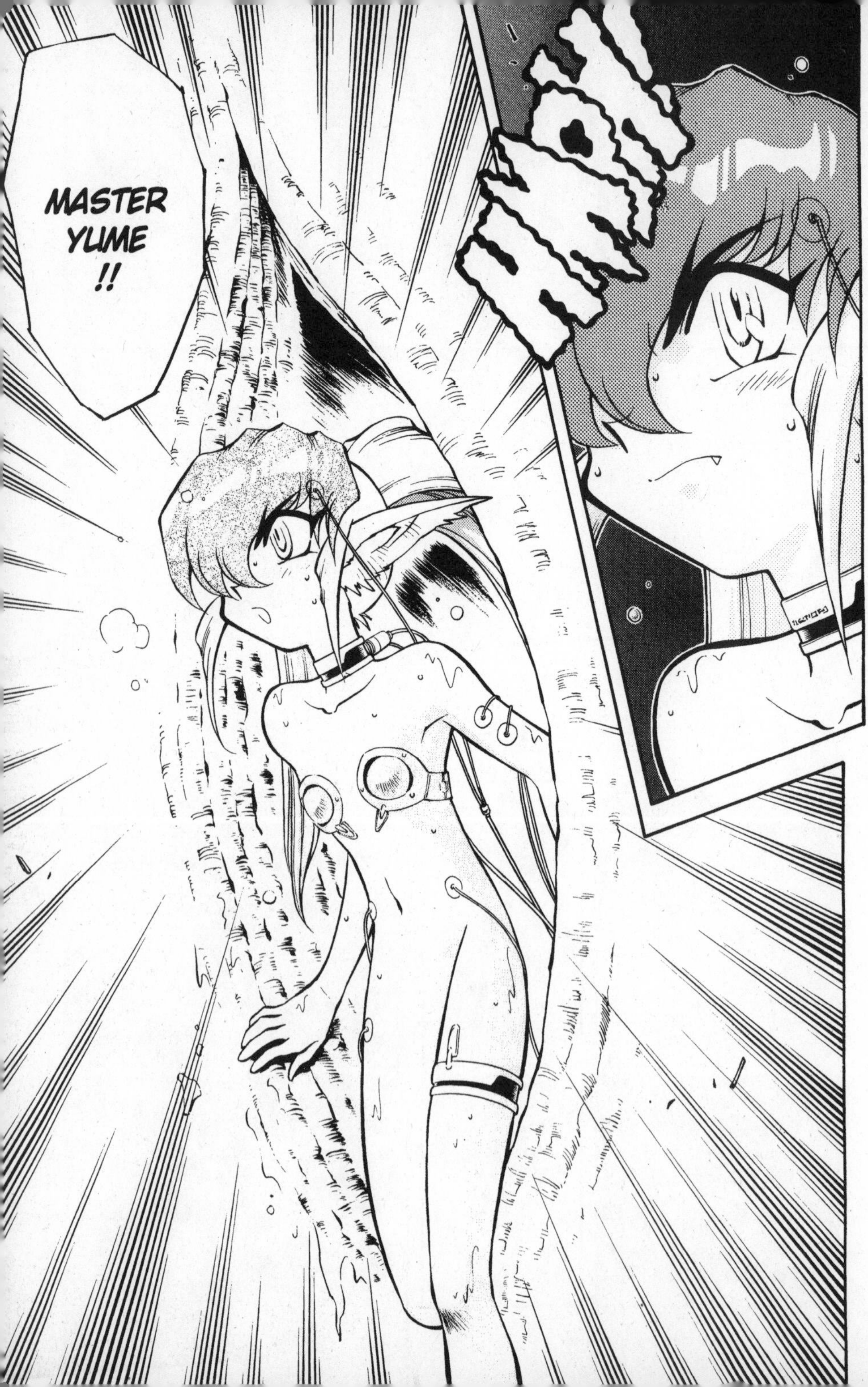
MASTER YUME !!

YOU'LL CATCH COLD.

PLEASE ...

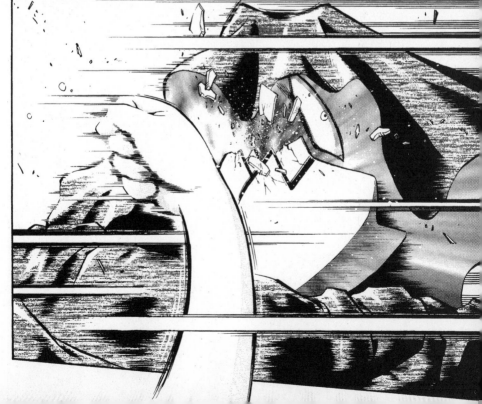

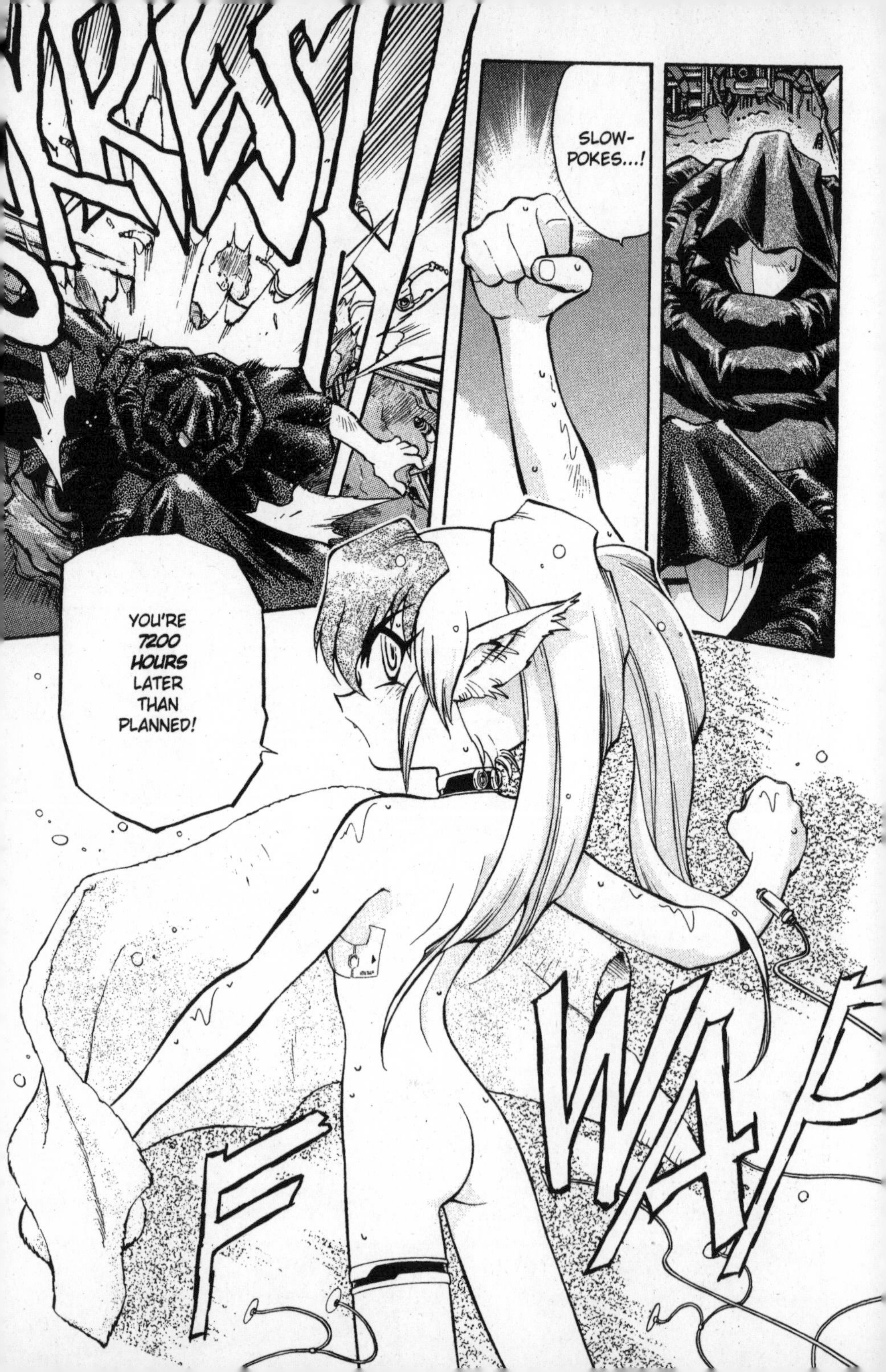
SLOW-POKES...!
YOU'RE 7200 HOURS LATER THAN PLANNED!
FWAP

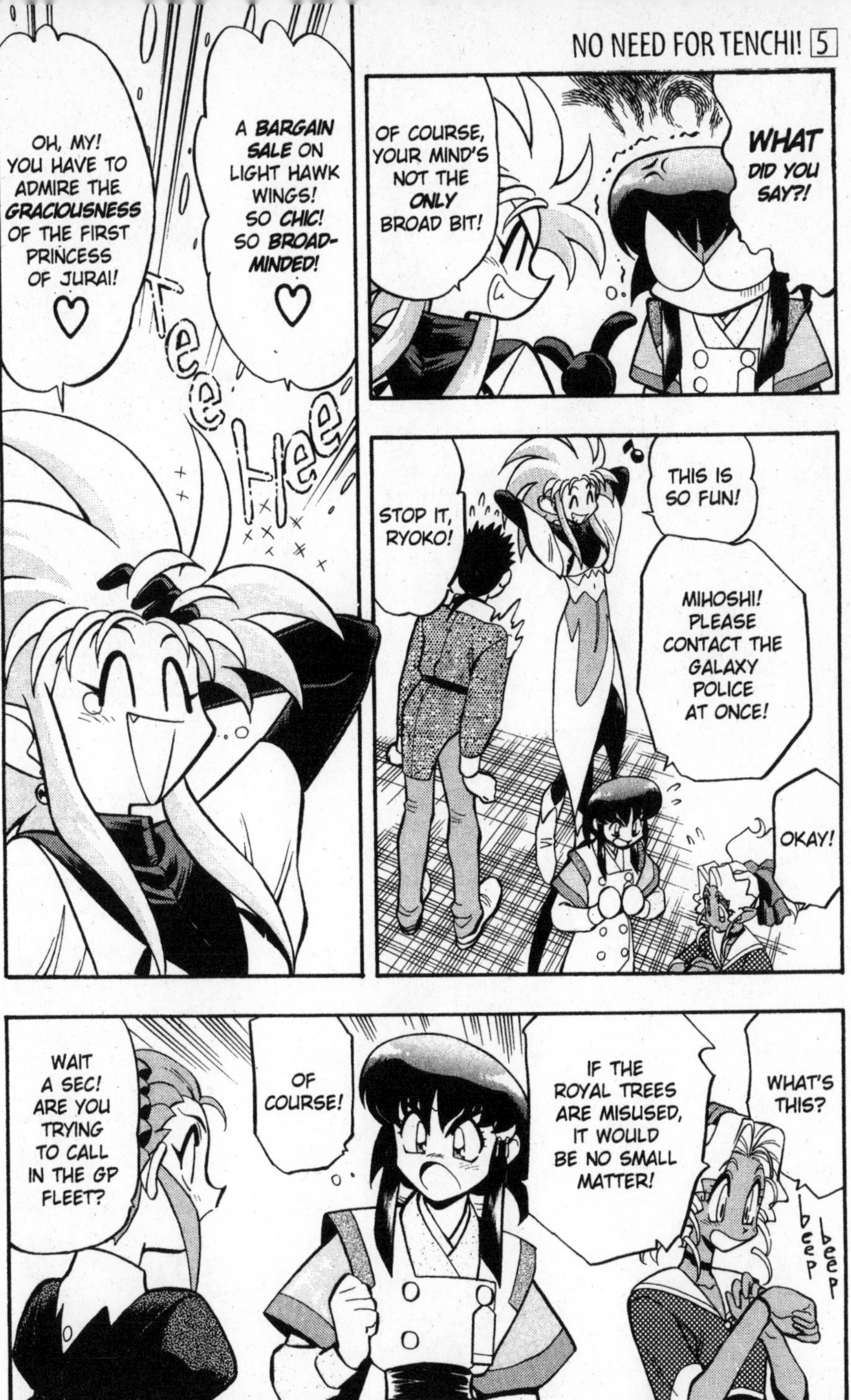
OH, MY! YOU HAVE TO ADMIRE THE **GRACIOUSNESS** OF THE FIRST PRINCESS OF JURAI! ♡
A **BARGAIN SALE** ON LIGHT HAWK WINGS! SO **CHIC!** SO **BROAD-MINDED!** ♡
Tee Hee
OF COURSE, YOUR MIND'S NOT THE **ONLY** BROAD BIT!
WHAT DID YOU SAY?!
STOP IT, RYOKO!
THIS IS SO FUN!
MIHOSHI! PLEASE CONTACT THE GALAXY POLICE AT ONCE!
OKAY!
WAIT A SEC! ARE YOU TRYING TO CALL IN THE GP FLEET?
OF COURSE!
IF THE ROYAL TREES ARE MISUSED, IT WOULD BE NO SMALL MATTER!
WHAT'S THIS?
beep beep

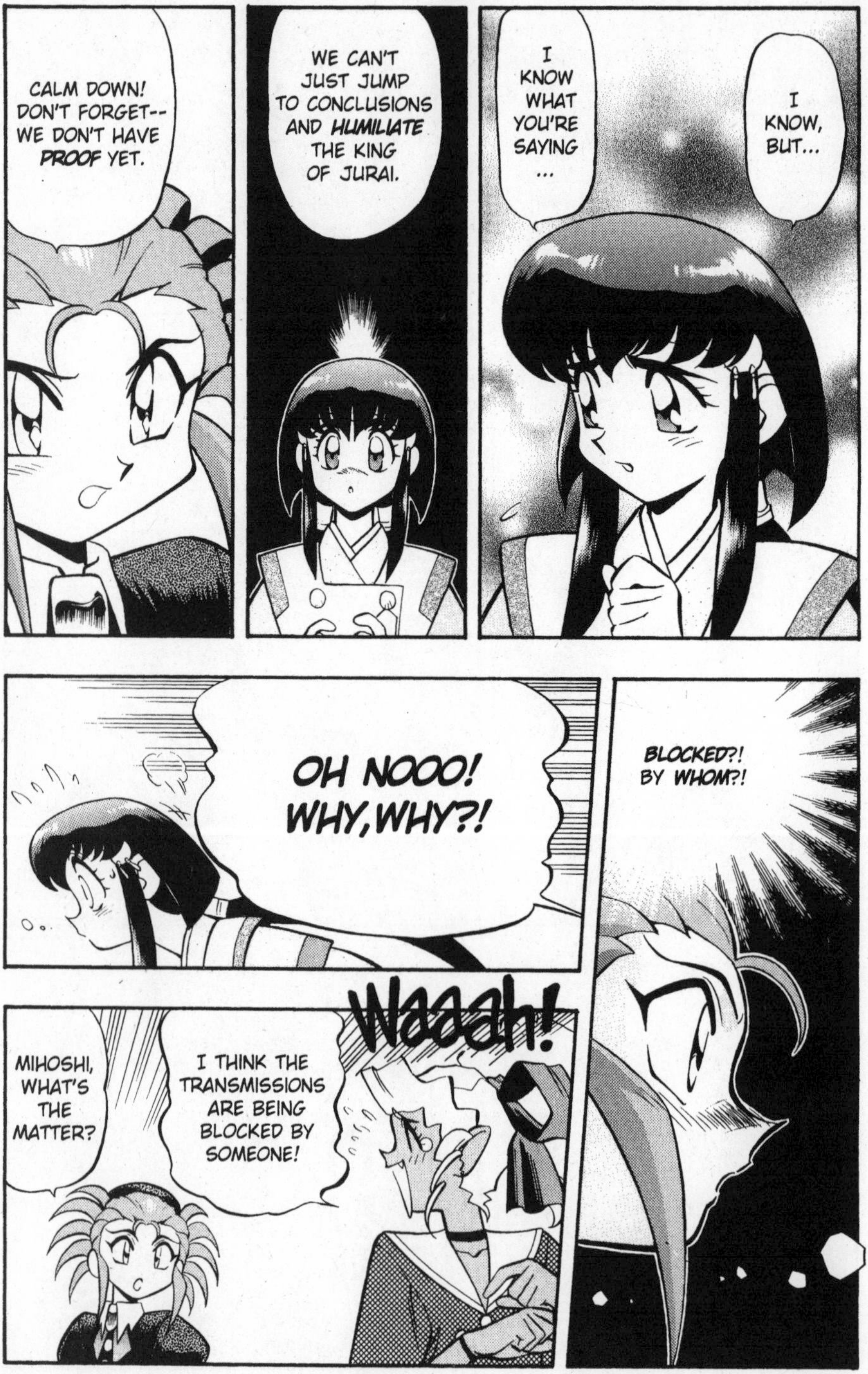
CALM DOWN! DON'T FORGET-- WE DON'T HAVE PROOF YET.
WE CAN'T JUST JUMP TO CONCLUSIONS AND HUMILIATE THE KING OF JURAI.
I KNOW WHAT YOU'RE SAYING ...
I KNOW, BUT...
OH NOOO! WHY,WHY?!
Waaah!
MIHOSHI, WHAT'S THE MATTER?
I THINK THE TRANSMISSIONS ARE BEING BLOCKED BY SOMEONE!
BLOCKED?! BY WHOM?!

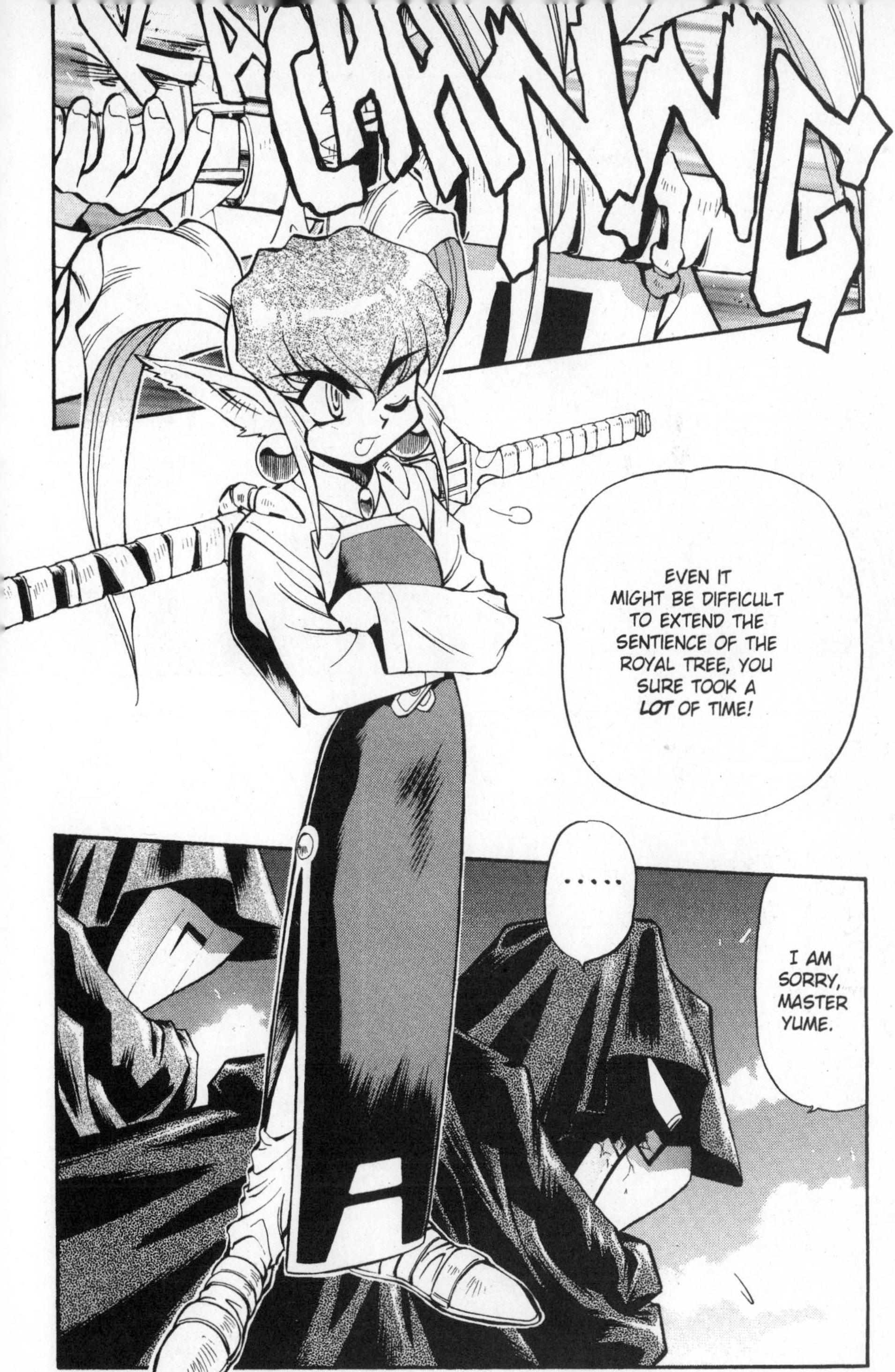
KA-CHANNNG!
EVEN IT MIGHT BE DIFFICULT TO EXTEND THE SENTIENCE OF THE ROYAL TREE, YOU SURE TOOK A LOT OF TIME!
.....
I AM SORRY, MASTER YUME.

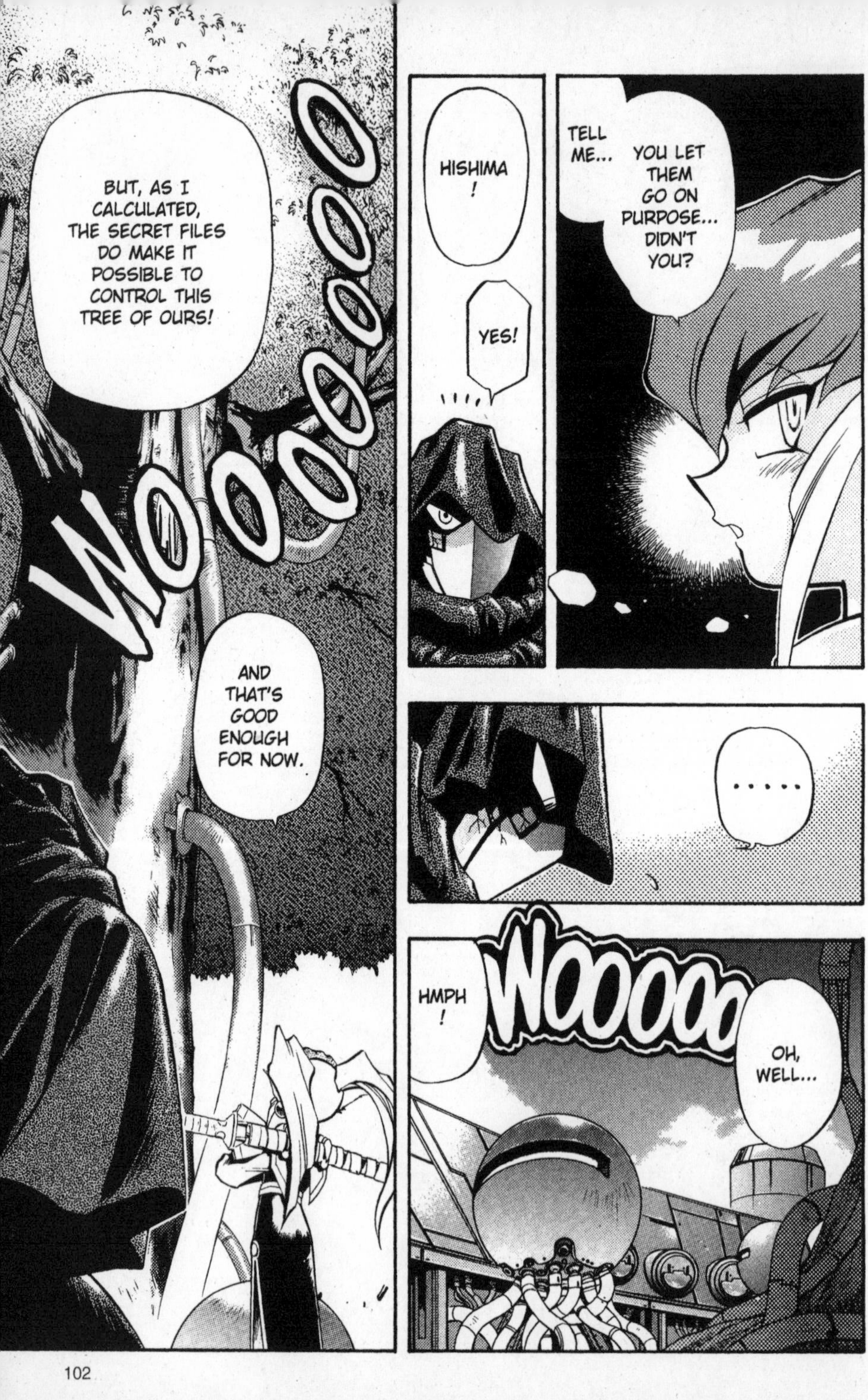
BUT, AS I CALCULATED, THE SECRET FILES DO MAKE IT POSSIBLE TO CONTROL THIS TREE OF OURS!
WOOOOOOOO
AND THAT'S GOOD ENOUGH FOR NOW.
HISHIMA!
YES!
TELL ME...
YOU LET THEM GO ON PURPOSE... DIDN'T YOU?
.....
HMPH!
WOOOOO
OH, WELL...

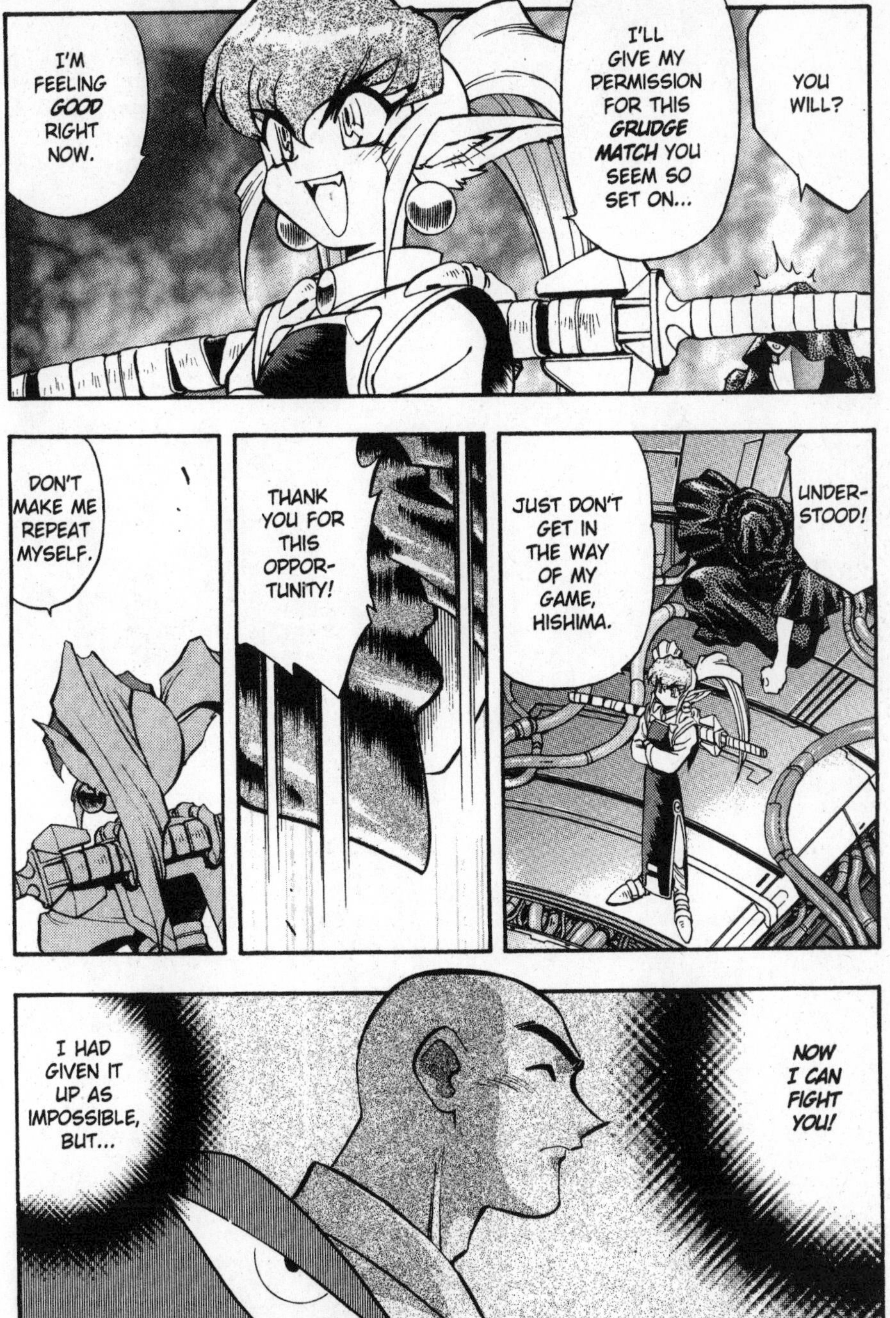
I'M FEELING **GOOD** RIGHT NOW.
I'LL GIVE MY PERMISSION FOR THIS **GRUDGE MATCH** YOU SEEM SO SET ON...
YOU WILL?
DON'T MAKE ME REPEAT MYSELF.
THANK YOU FOR THIS OPPORTUNITY!
JUST DON'T GET IN THE WAY OF MY GAME, HISHIMA.
UNDERSTOOD!
I HAD GIVEN IT UP AS IMPOSSIBLE, BUT...
NOW I CAN FIGHT YOU!

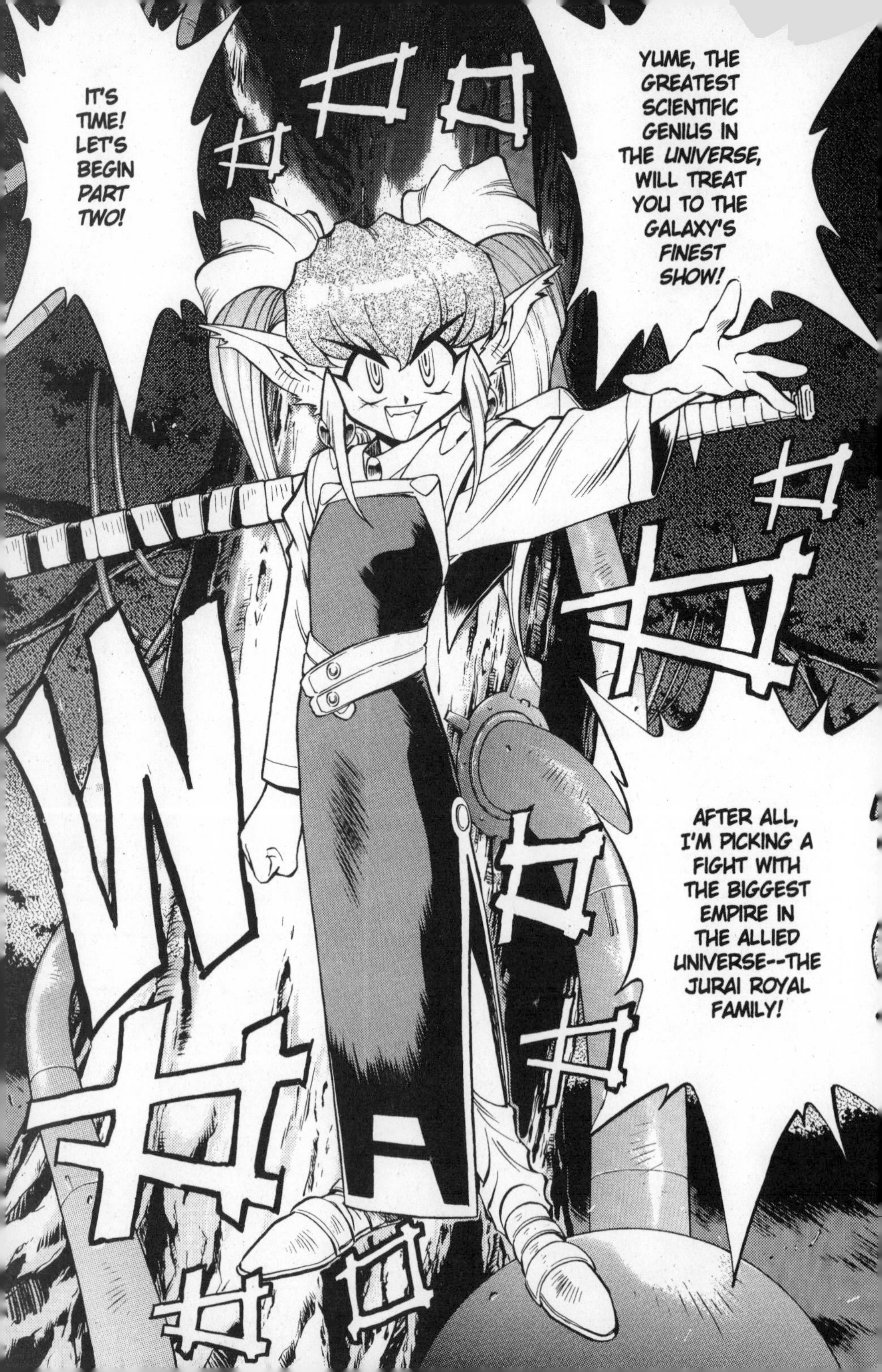
IT'S TIME! LET'S BEGIN PART TWO!
YUME, THE GREATEST SCIENTIFIC GENIUS IN THE *UNIVERSE*, WILL TREAT YOU TO THE GALAXY'S FINEST SHOW!
AFTER ALL, I'M PICKING A FIGHT WITH THE BIGGEST EMPIRE IN THE ALLIED UNIVERSE--THE JURAI ROYAL FAMILY!

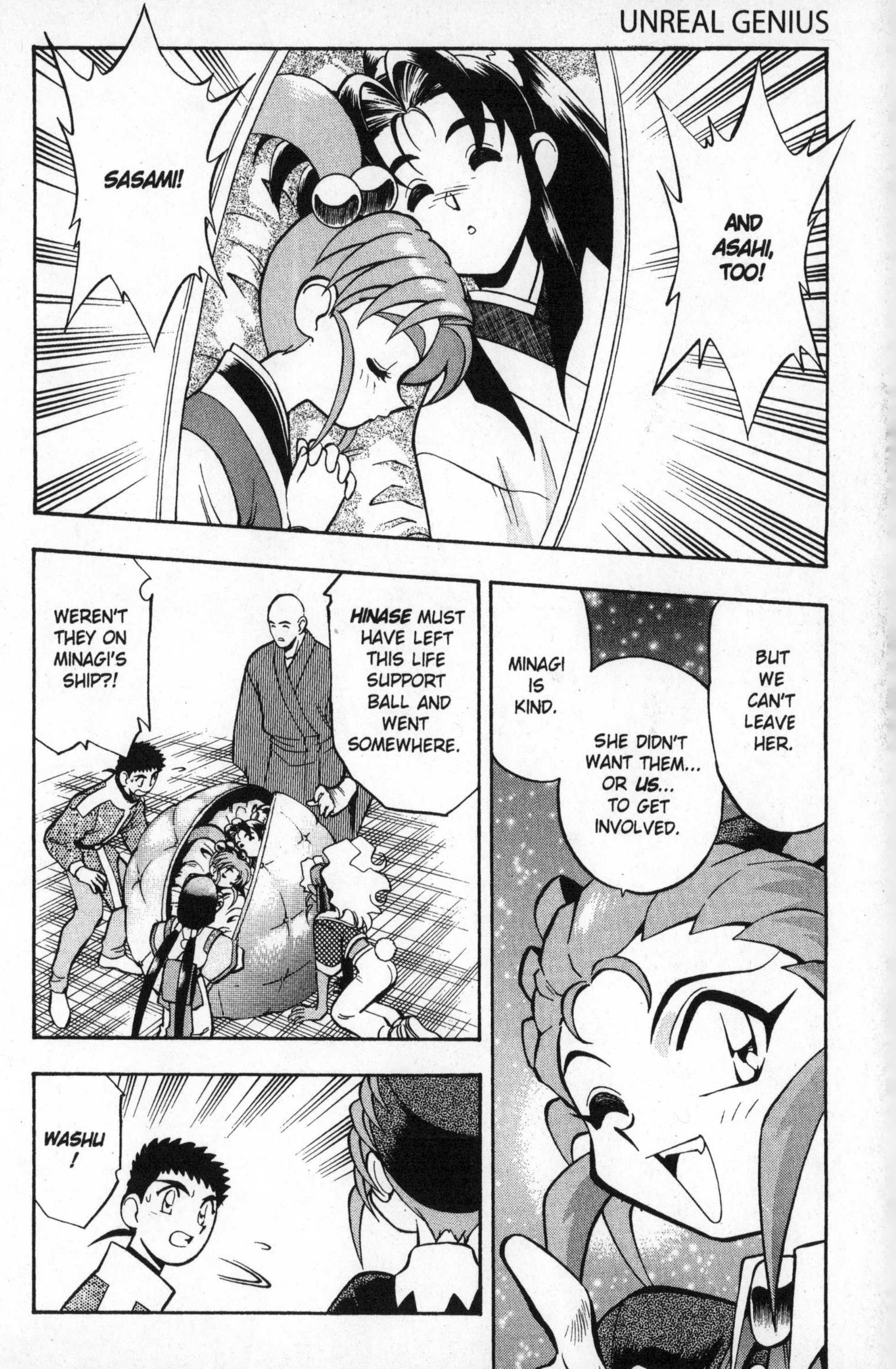
SASAMI!
AND ASAHI, TOO!
WEREN'T THEY ON MINAGI'S SHIP?!
HINASE MUST HAVE LEFT THIS LIFE SUPPORT BALL AND WENT SOMEWHERE.
MINAGI IS KIND.
SHE DIDN'T WANT THEM... OR US... TO GET INVOLVED.
BUT WE CAN'T LEAVE HER.
WASHU!

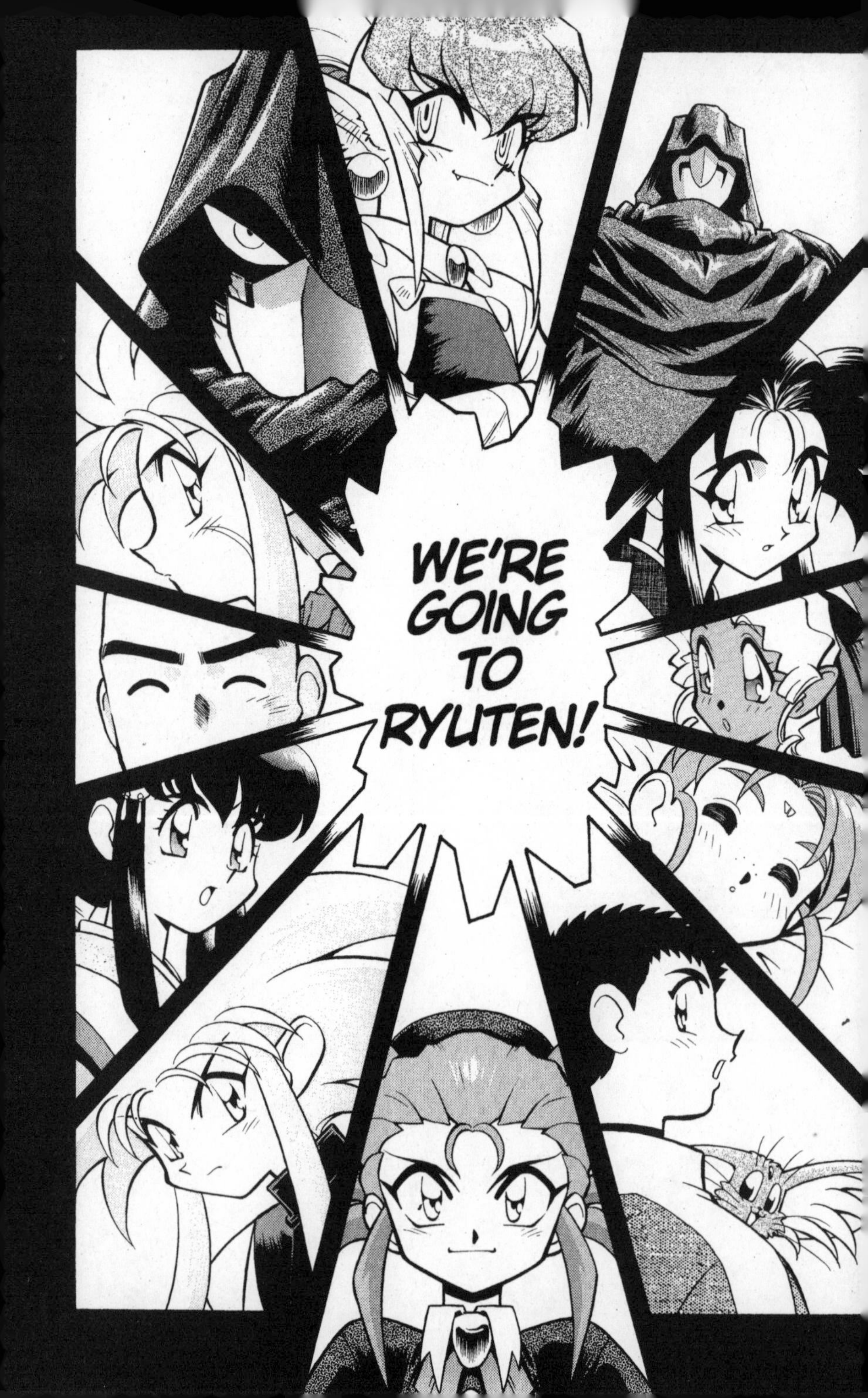
WE'RE GOING TO RYUTEN!

Tales of Tenchi #6

ADORABLE YOU

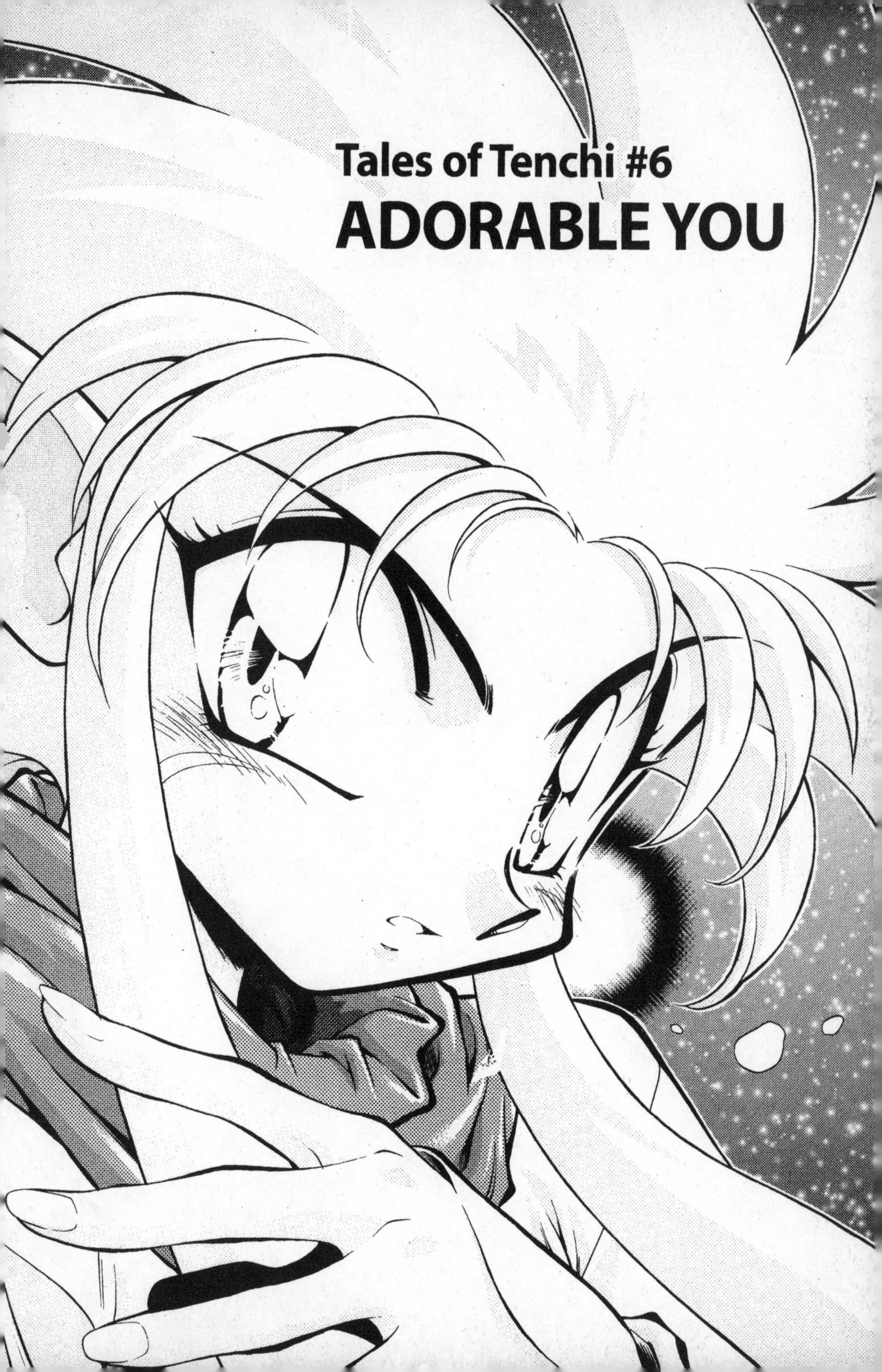

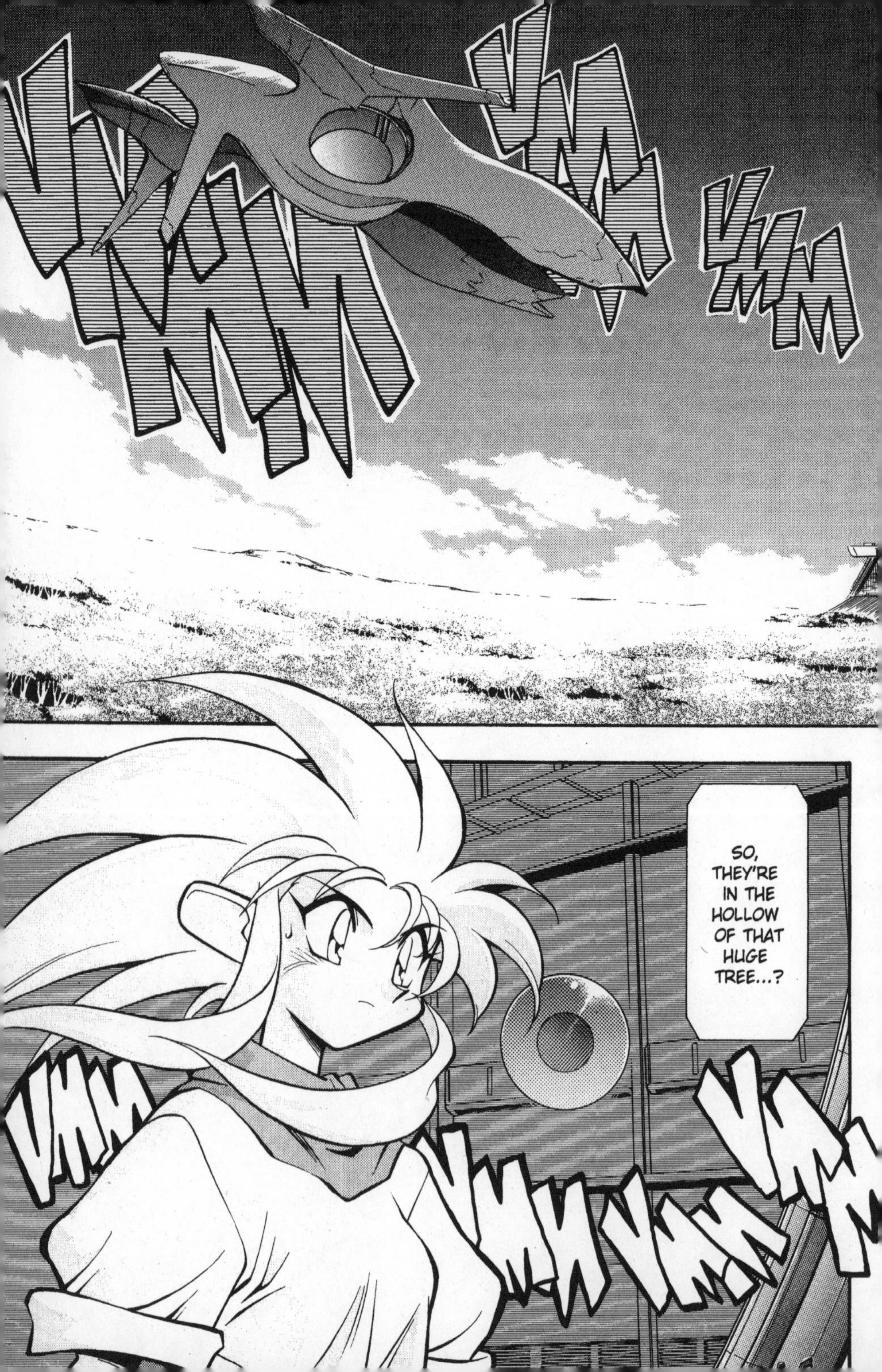
SO, THEY'RE IN THE HOLLOW OF THAT HUGE TREE...?

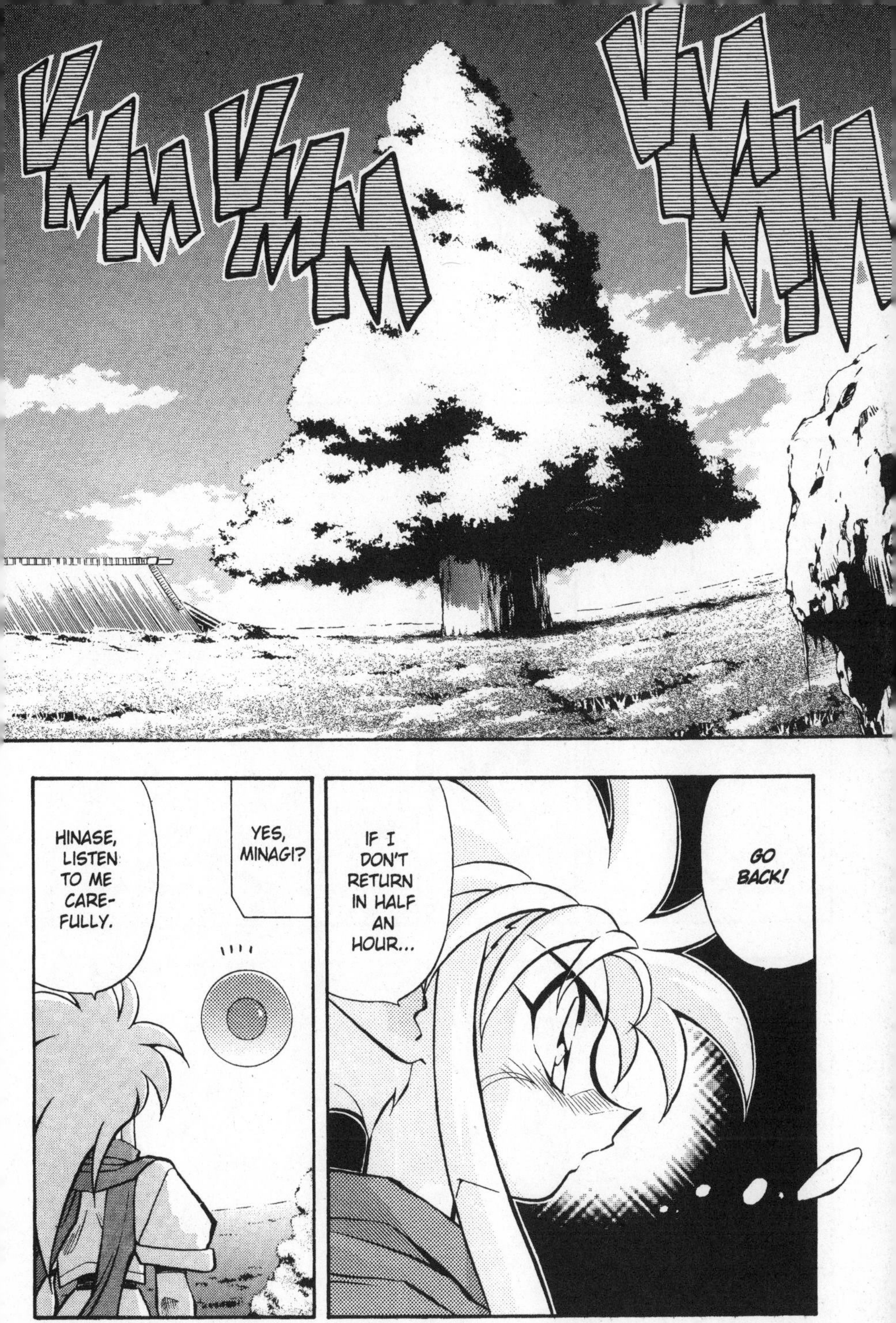
VMM VMM
VMMM
HINASE, LISTEN TO ME CARE-FULLY.
YES, MINAGI?
IF I DON'T RETURN IN HALF AN HOUR...
GO BACK!
...

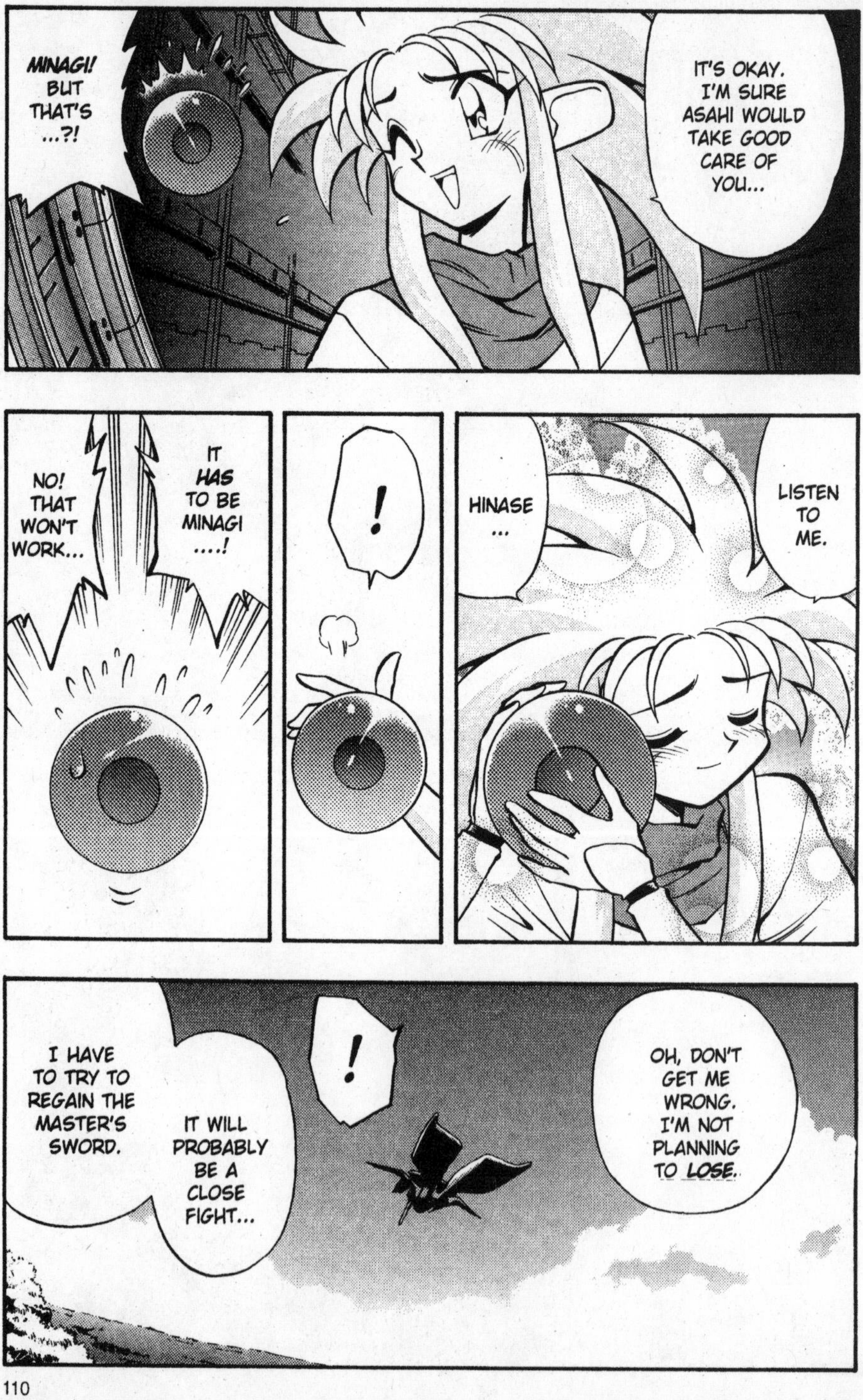
MINAGI! BUT THAT'S ...?!
IT'S OKAY. I'M SURE ASAHI WOULD TAKE GOOD CARE OF YOU...
NO! THAT WON'T WORK...
IT HAS TO BE MINAGI ....!
!
HINASE ...
LISTEN TO ME.
I HAVE TO TRY TO REGAIN THE MASTER'S SWORD.
IT WILL PROBABLY BE A CLOSE FIGHT...
!
OH, DON'T GET ME WRONG. I'M NOT PLANNING TO LOSE.

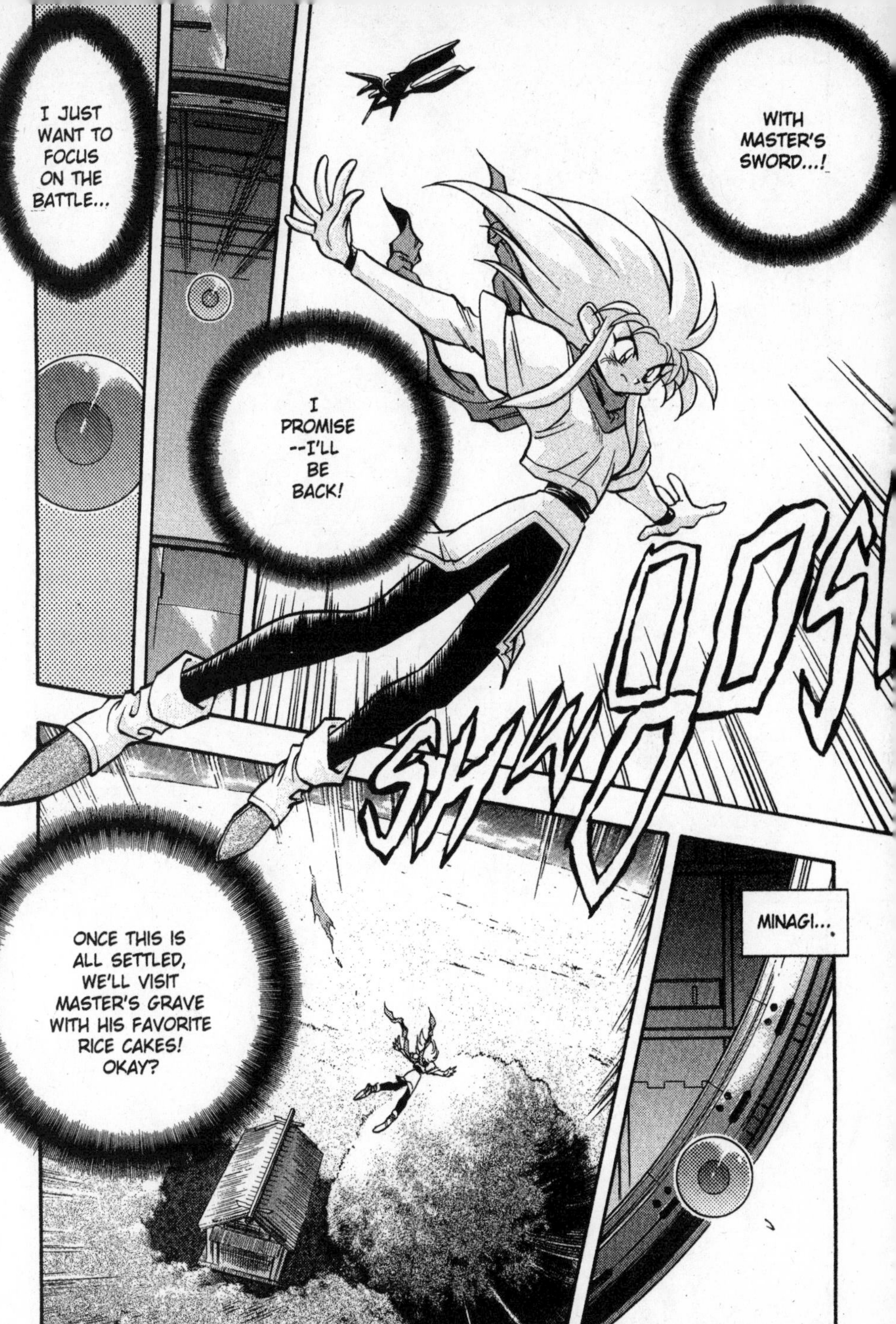
I JUST WANT TO FOCUS ON THE BATTLE...
WITH MASTER'S SWORD...!
I PROMISE --I'LL BE BACK!
SHWOOS
ONCE THIS IS ALL SETTLED, WE'LL VISIT MASTER'S GRAVE WITH HIS FAVORITE RICE CAKES! OKAY?
MINAGI...

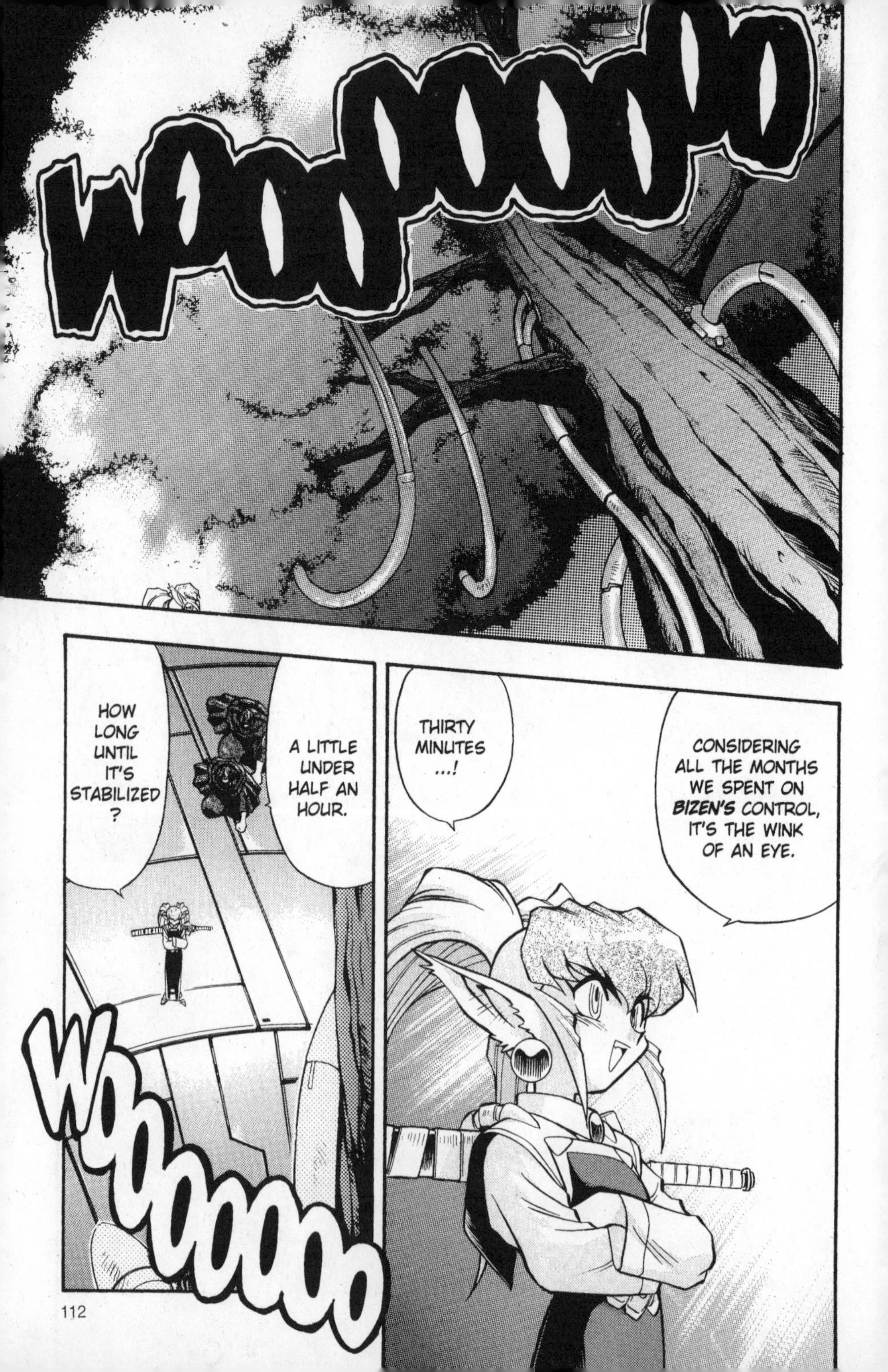

WOOOOOOO
HOW LONG UNTIL IT'S STABILIZED?
A LITTLE UNDER HALF AN HOUR.
WOOOOOO
THIRTY MINUTES ...!
CONSIDERING ALL THE MONTHS WE SPENT ON **BIZEN'S** CONTROL, IT'S THE WINK OF AN EYE.

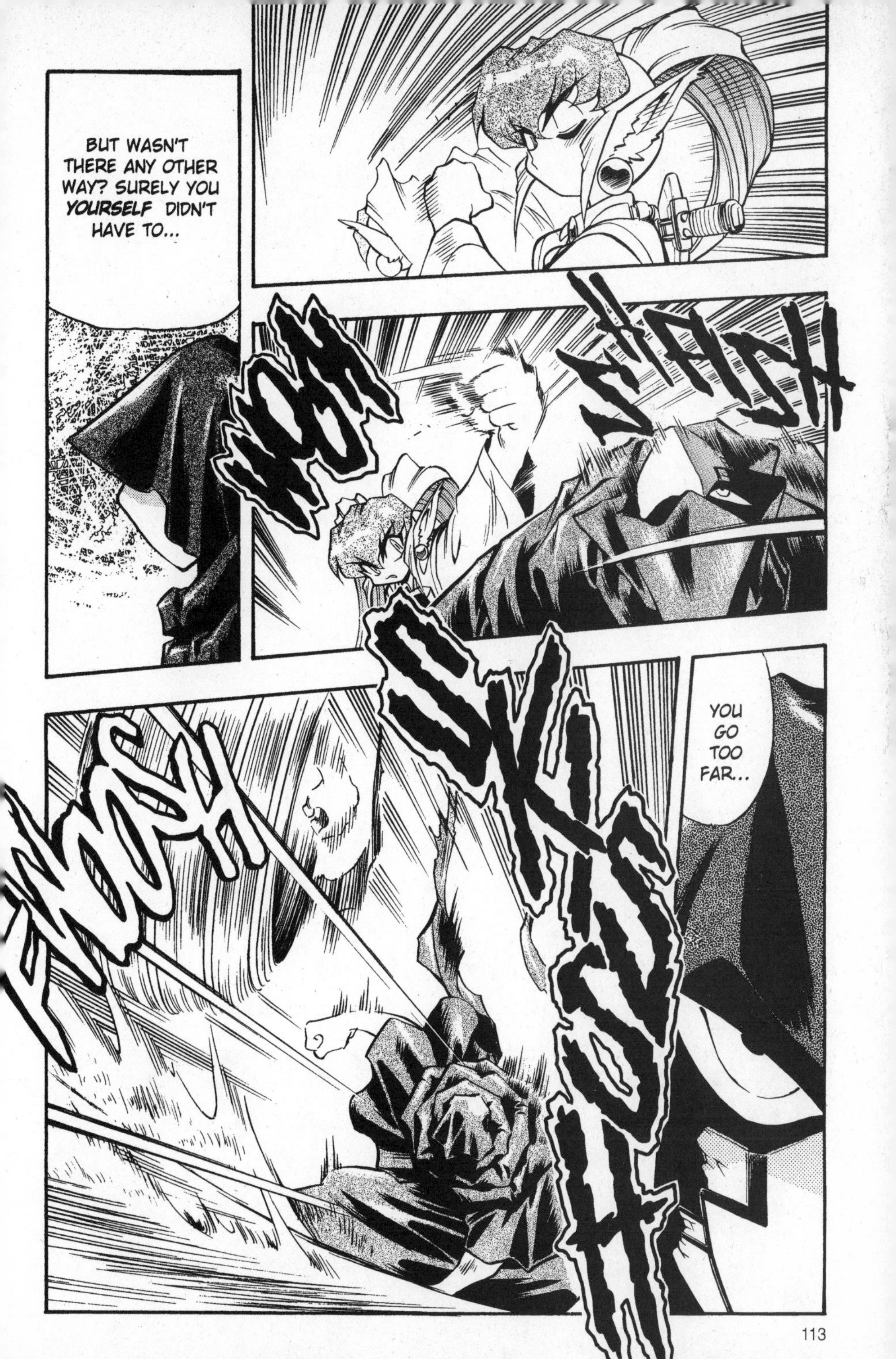
BUT WASN'T THERE ANY OTHER WAY? SURELY YOU *YOURSELF* DIDN'T HAVE TO...
YOU GO TOO FAR...

HMPH... SO HE *DID* LET ME HIT HIM THE LAST TIME.

PERHAPS THERE WERE OTHER WAYS... BUT WE DIDN'T HAVE THE TIME.

AS YOU KNOW, ALL ROYAL TREES ARE CONNECTED TO *TSUNAMI*, THE ORIGINAL TREE.

I HAD TO PUT BIZEN DIRECTLY UNDER MY CONTROL --A *TOTAL* LOSS OF WILL WOULD HAVE BEEN NOTICED BY TSUNAMI.

I GAMBLED EVERYTHING ON THE THE THE EXISTENCE OF THOSE SECRET FILES--AND NOW *I* CAN CONTROL THE ROYAL TREES.

DIDN'T YOU CONSIDER THAT WE MIGHT NOT OBTAIN THE SECRET FILES?

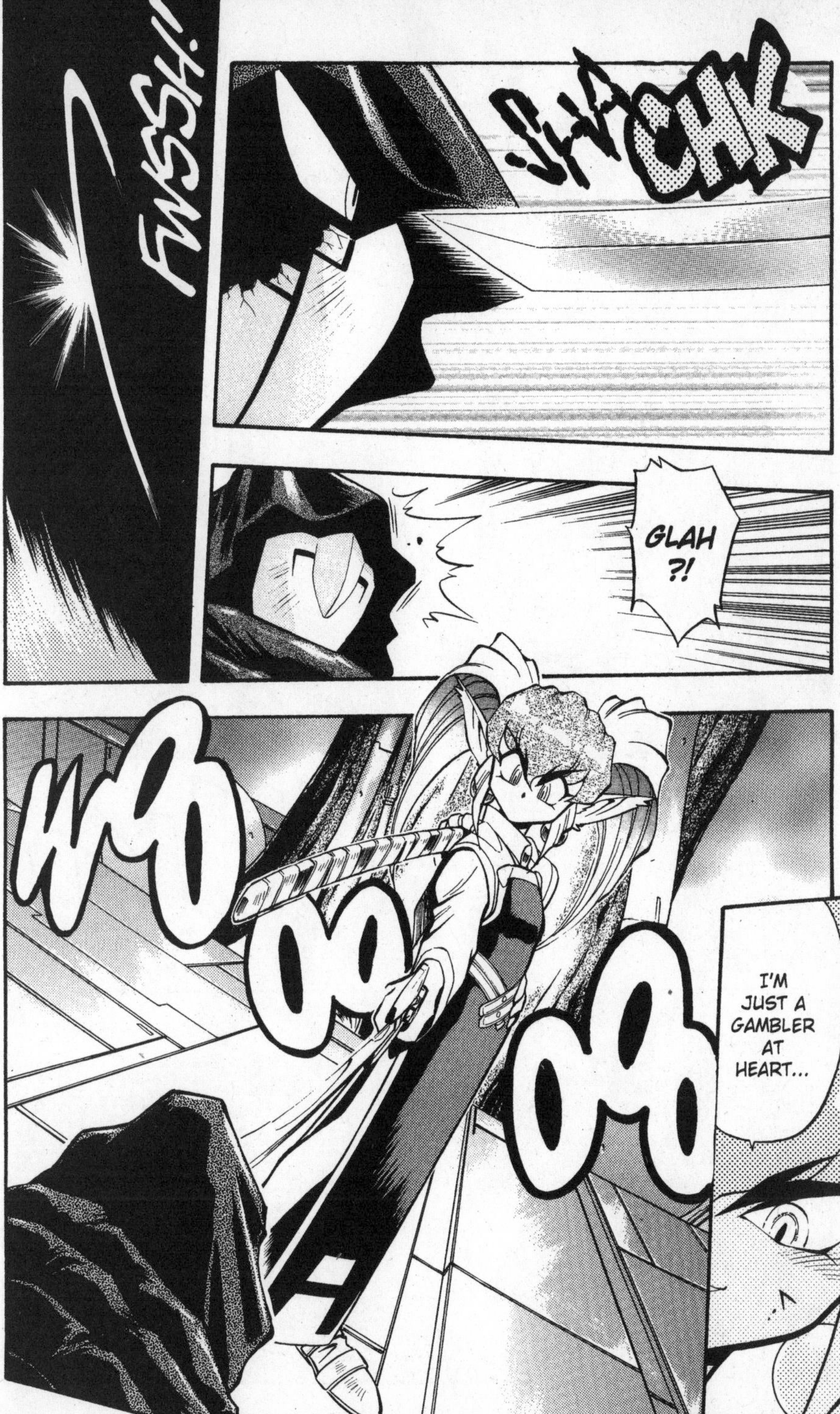
FWSSH!
CHK
GLAH ?!
I'M JUST A GAMBLER AT HEART...

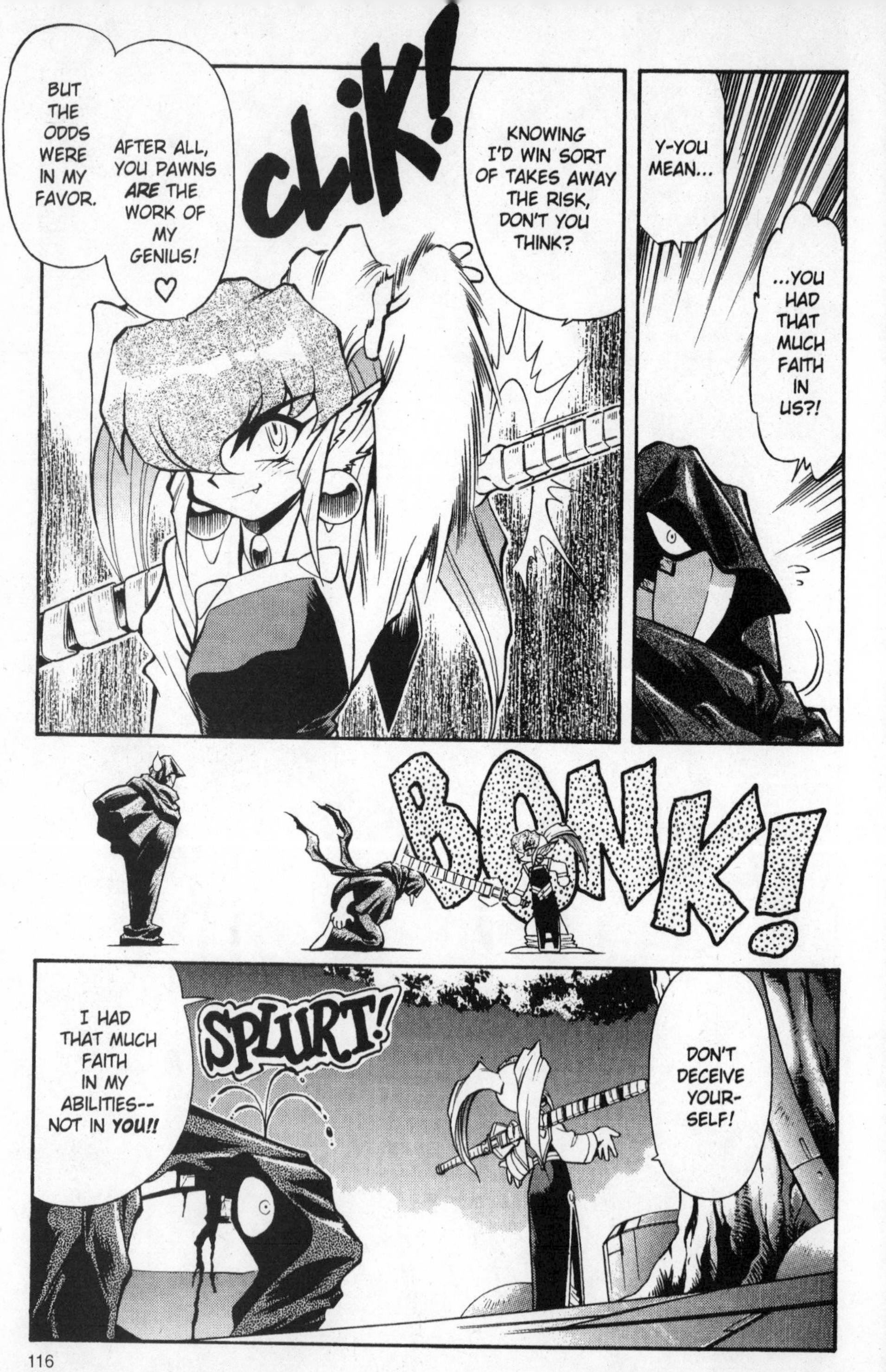
BUT THE ODDS WERE IN MY FAVOR.
AFTER ALL, YOU PAWNS ARE THE WORK OF MY GENIUS! ♡
CLIK!
KNOWING I'D WIN SORT OF TAKES AWAY THE RISK, DON'T YOU THINK?
Y-YOU MEAN...
...YOU HAD THAT MUCH FAITH IN US?!
BONK!
I HAD THAT MUCH FAITH IN MY ABILITIES-- NOT IN YOU!!
SPLURT!
DON'T DECEIVE YOUR-SELF!

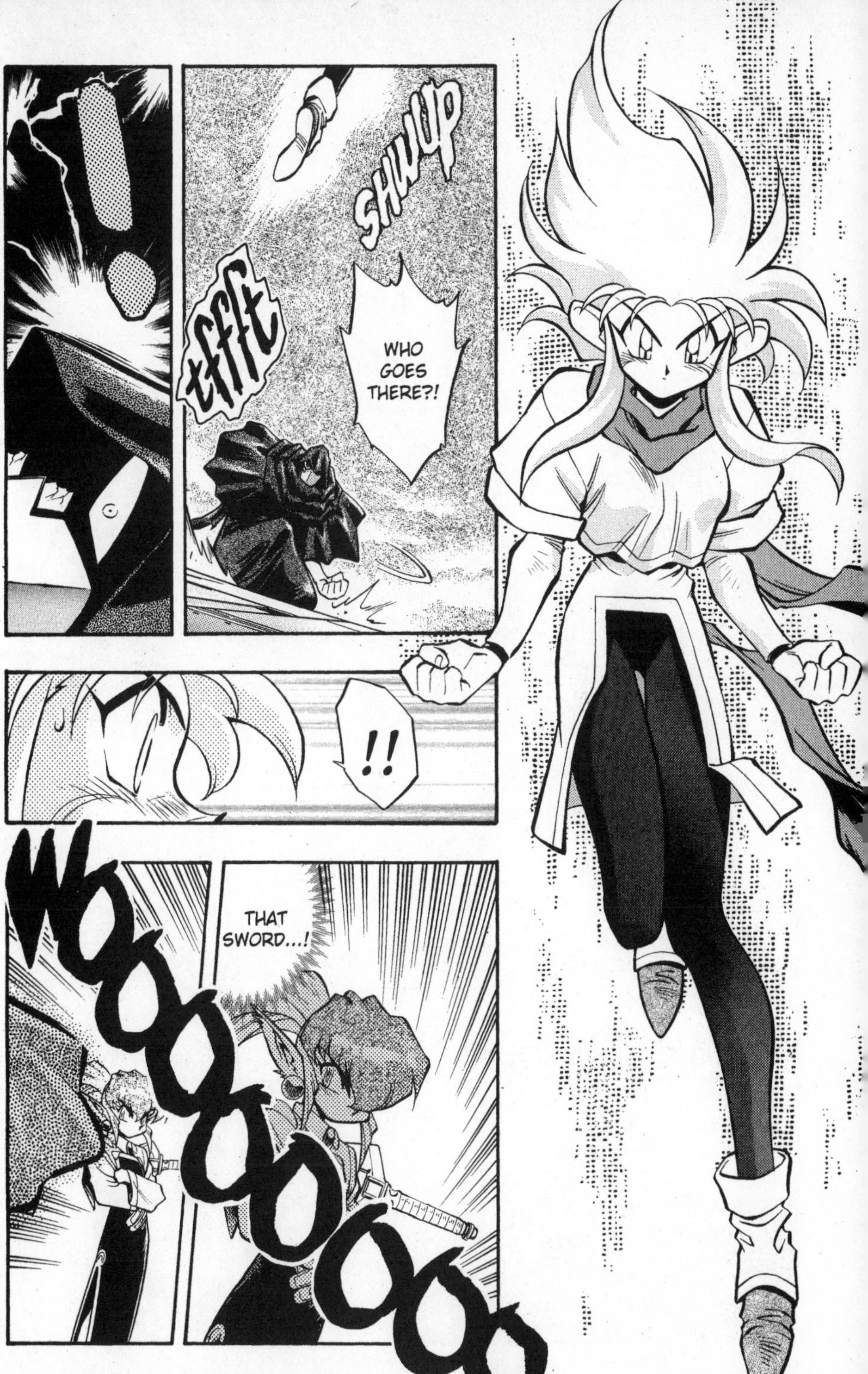
!
SHWUP
tfft
WHO GOES THERE?!
!!
WOOOOOOOOO
THAT SWORD...!

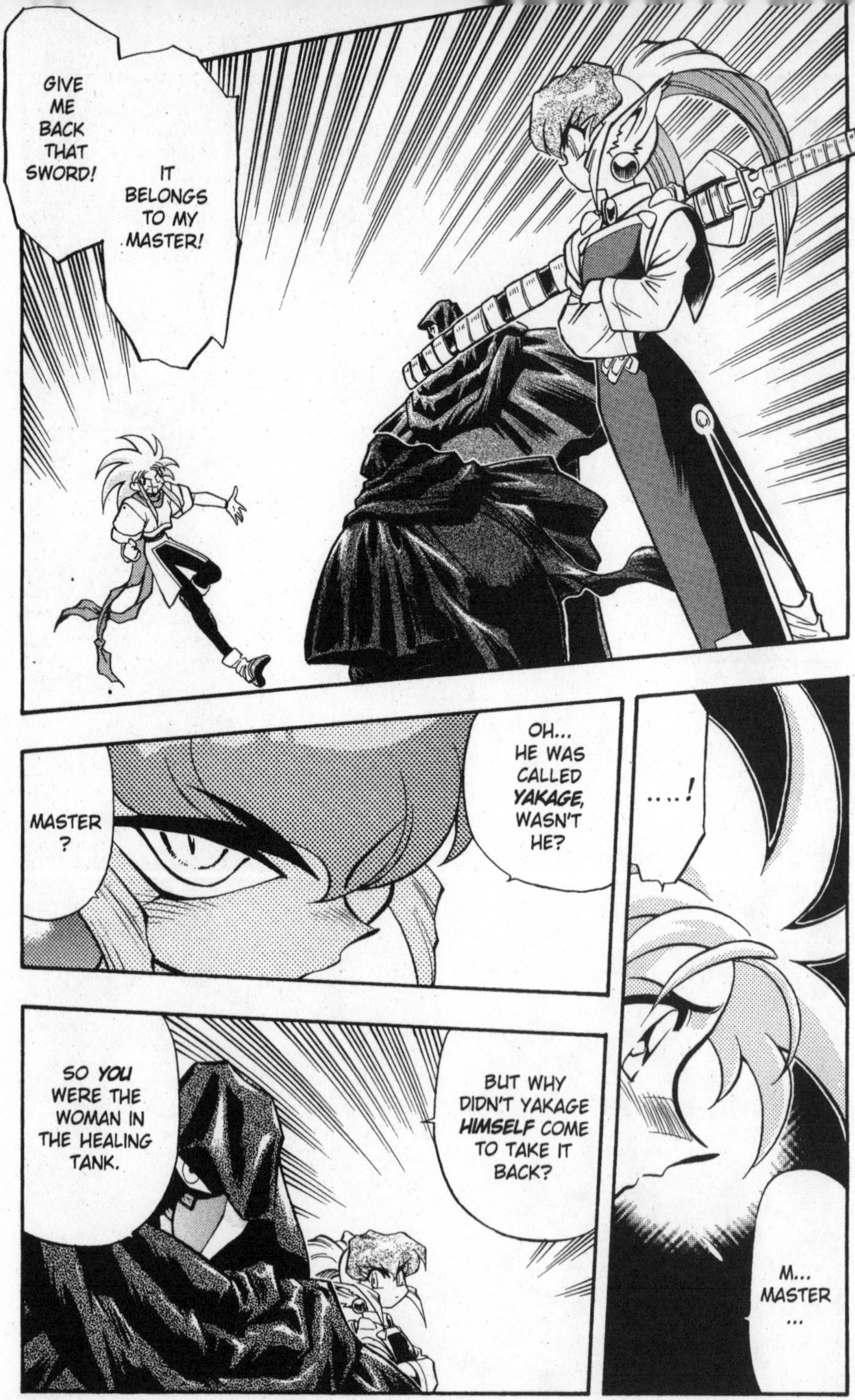
GIVE ME BACK THAT SWORD!
IT BELONGS TO MY MASTER!
MASTER ?
OH... HE WAS CALLED *YAKAGE,* WASN'T HE?
SO *YOU* WERE THE WOMAN IN THE HEALING TANK.
BUT WHY DIDN'T YAKAGE *HIMSELF* COME TO TAKE IT BACK?
....!
M... MASTER ...

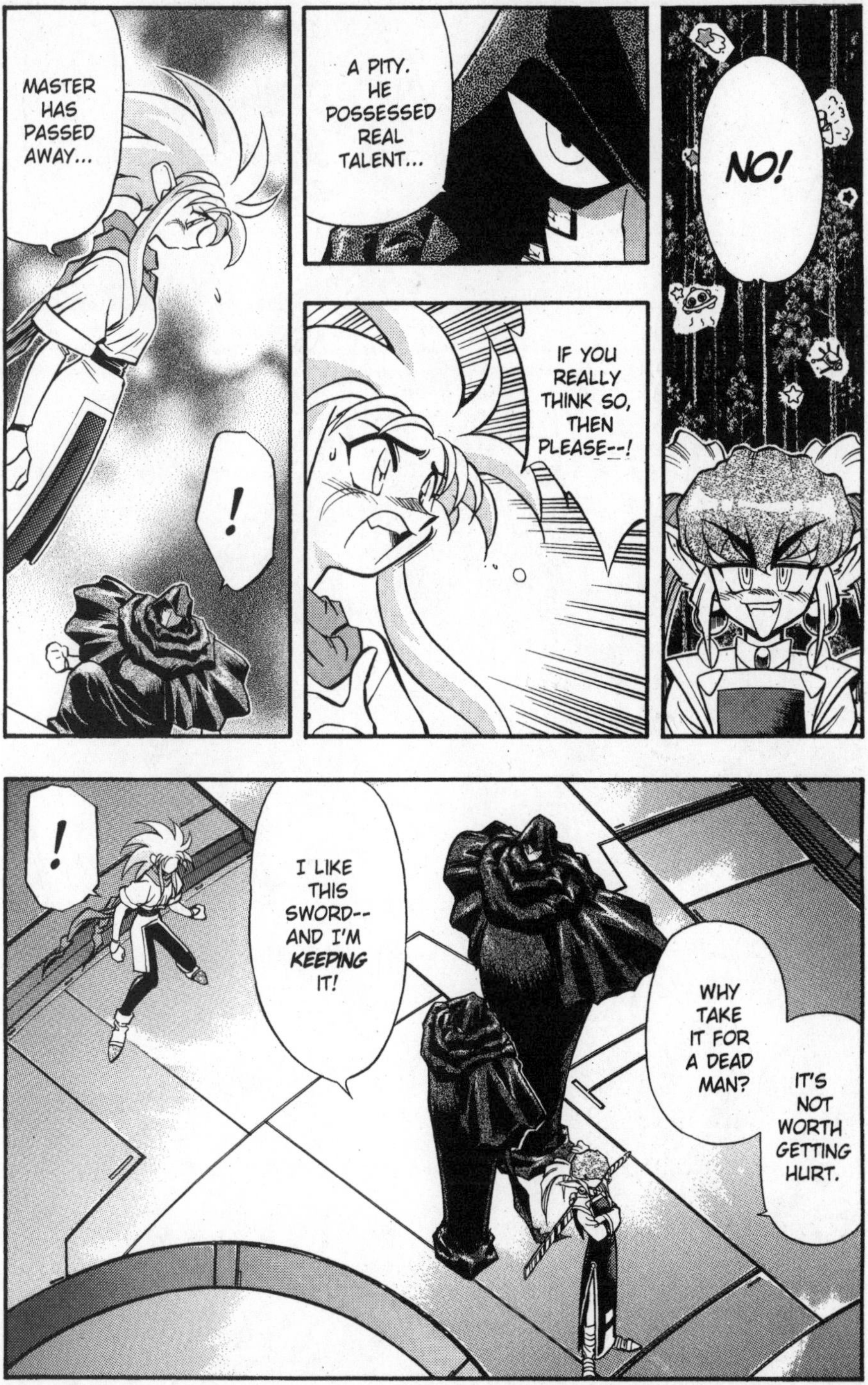
MASTER HAS PASSED AWAY...
!
A PITY. HE POSSESSED REAL TALENT...
IF YOU REALLY THINK SO, THEN PLEASE--!
NO!
!
I LIKE THIS SWORD--AND I'M *KEEPING* IT!
WHY TAKE IT FOR A DEAD MAN?
IT'S NOT WORTH GETTING HURT.

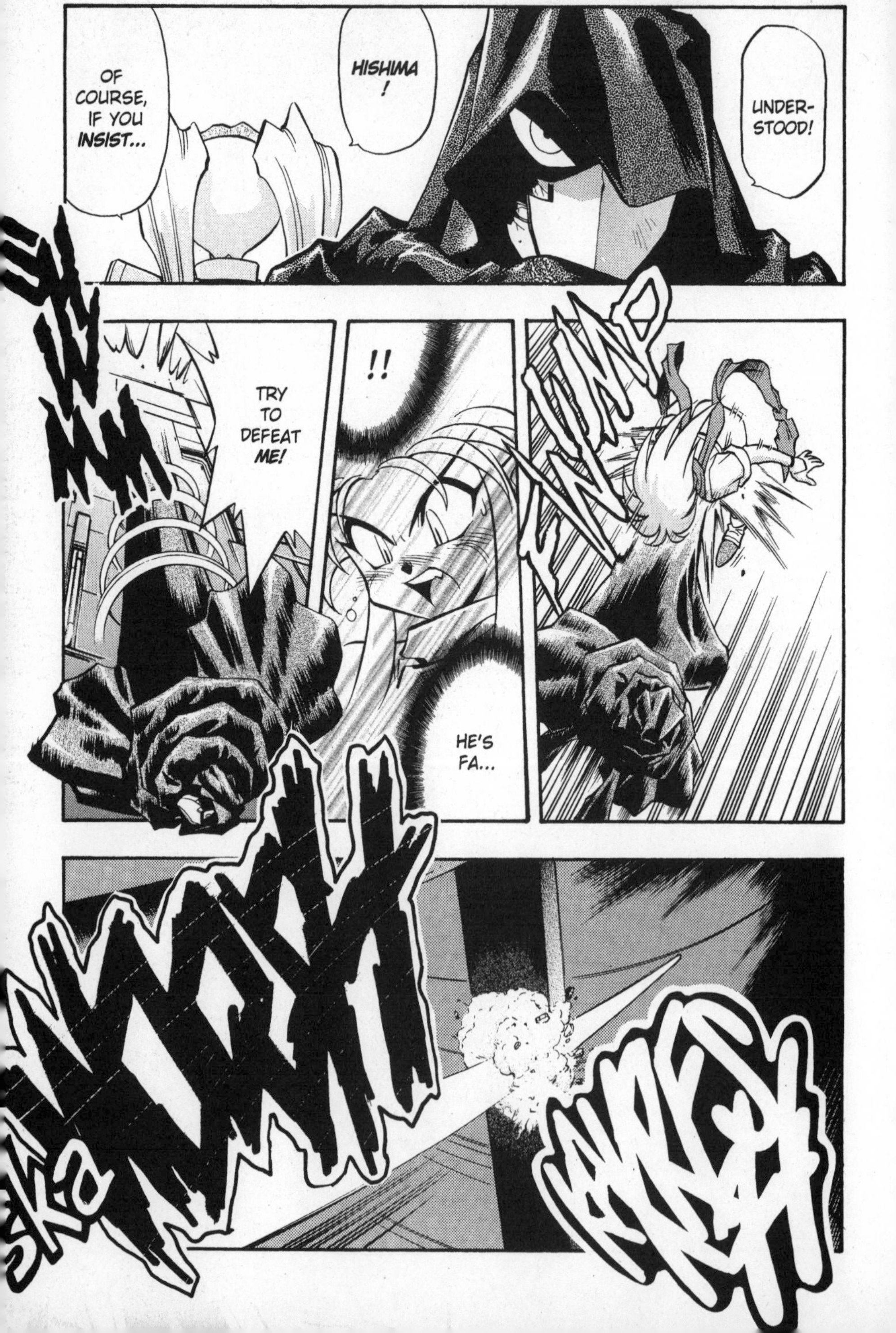
OF COURSE, IF YOU INSIST...
HISHIMA!
UNDER-STOOD!
TRY TO DEFEAT ME!
!!
HE'S FA...

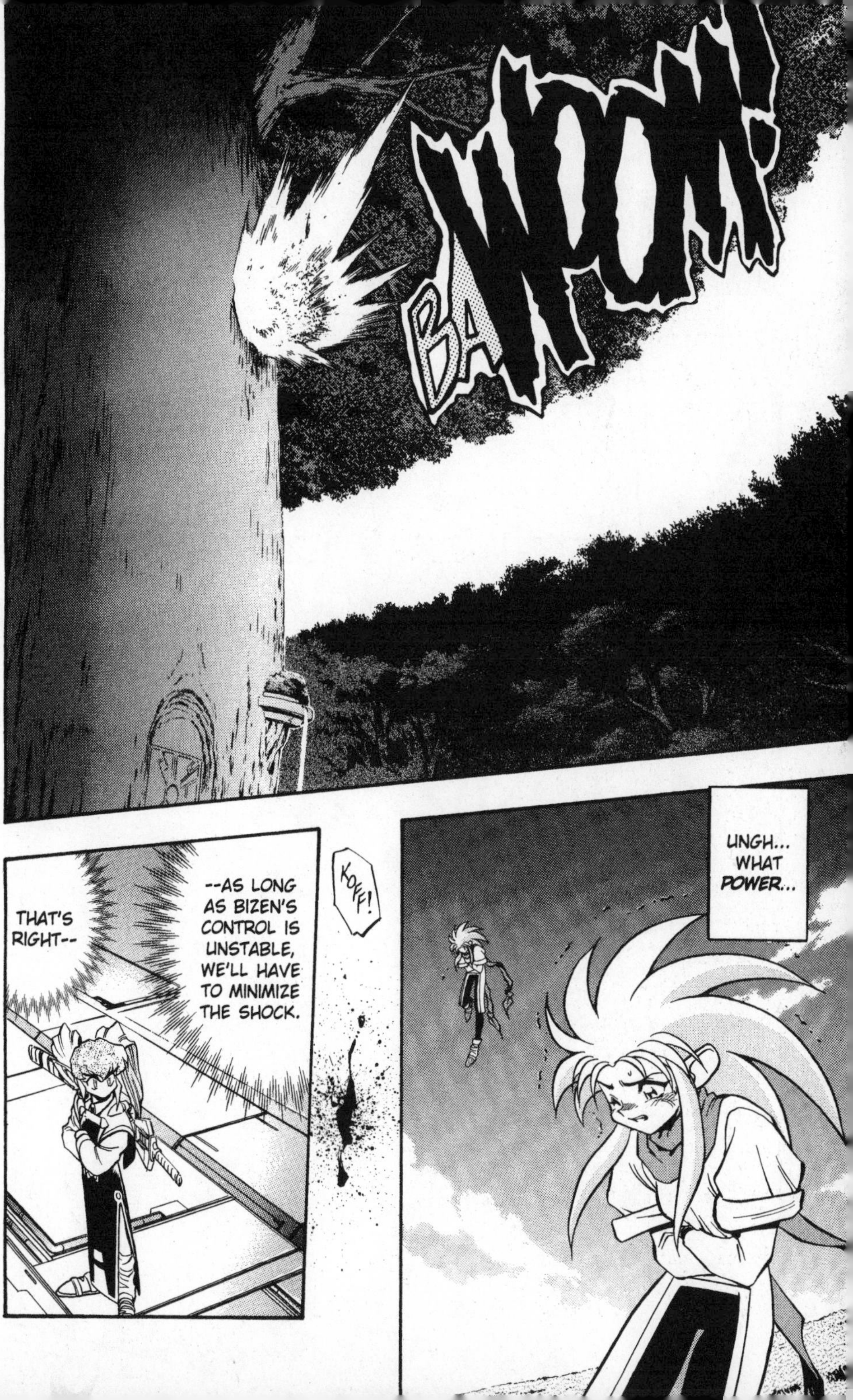
BAPOW!
THAT'S RIGHT--
--AS LONG AS BIZEN'S CONTROL IS UNSTABLE, WE'LL HAVE TO MINIMIZE THE SHOCK.
KOFF!
UNGH... WHAT POWER...

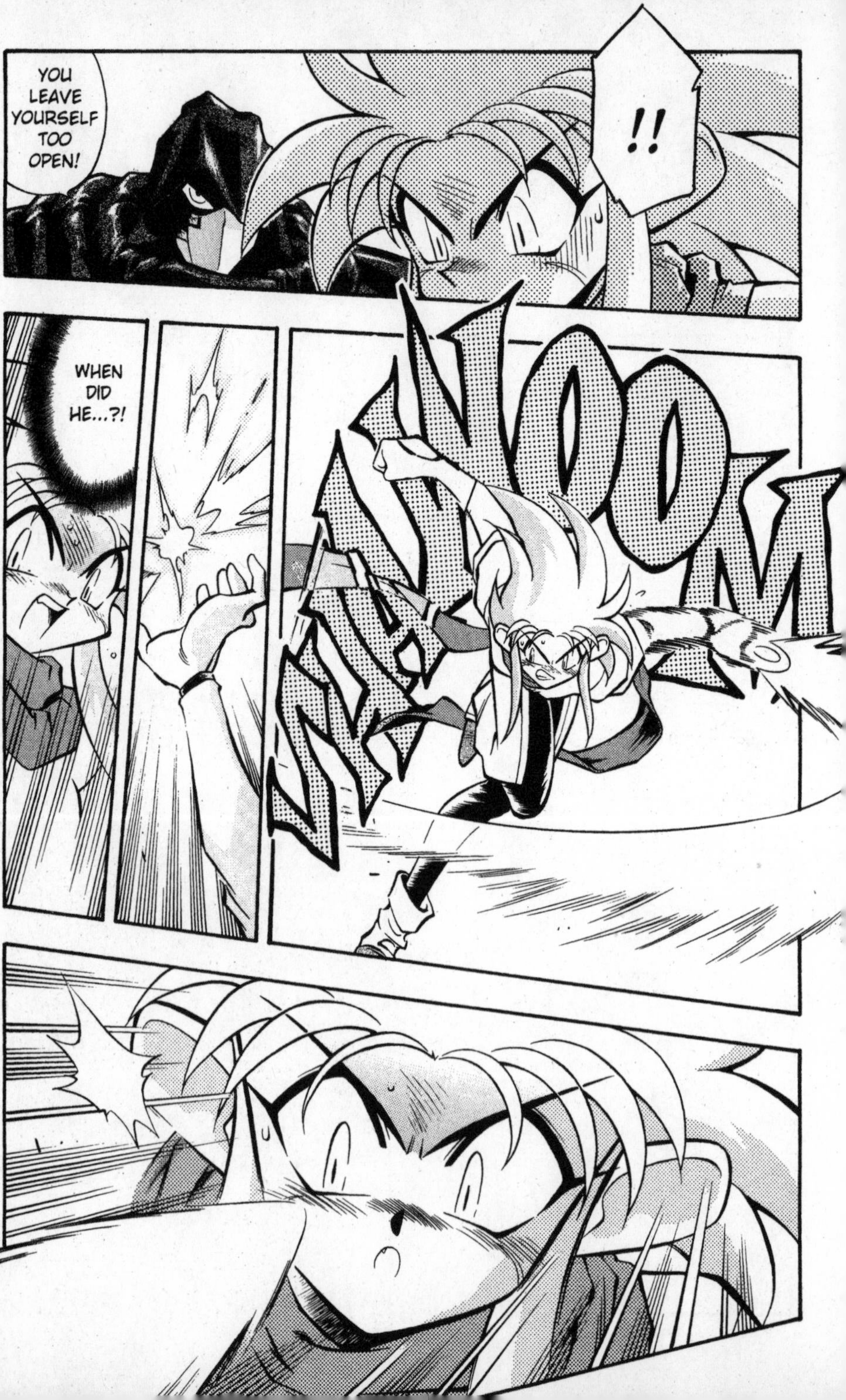
YOU LEAVE YOURSELF TOO OPEN!
!!
WHEN DID HE...?!
SHWOOM

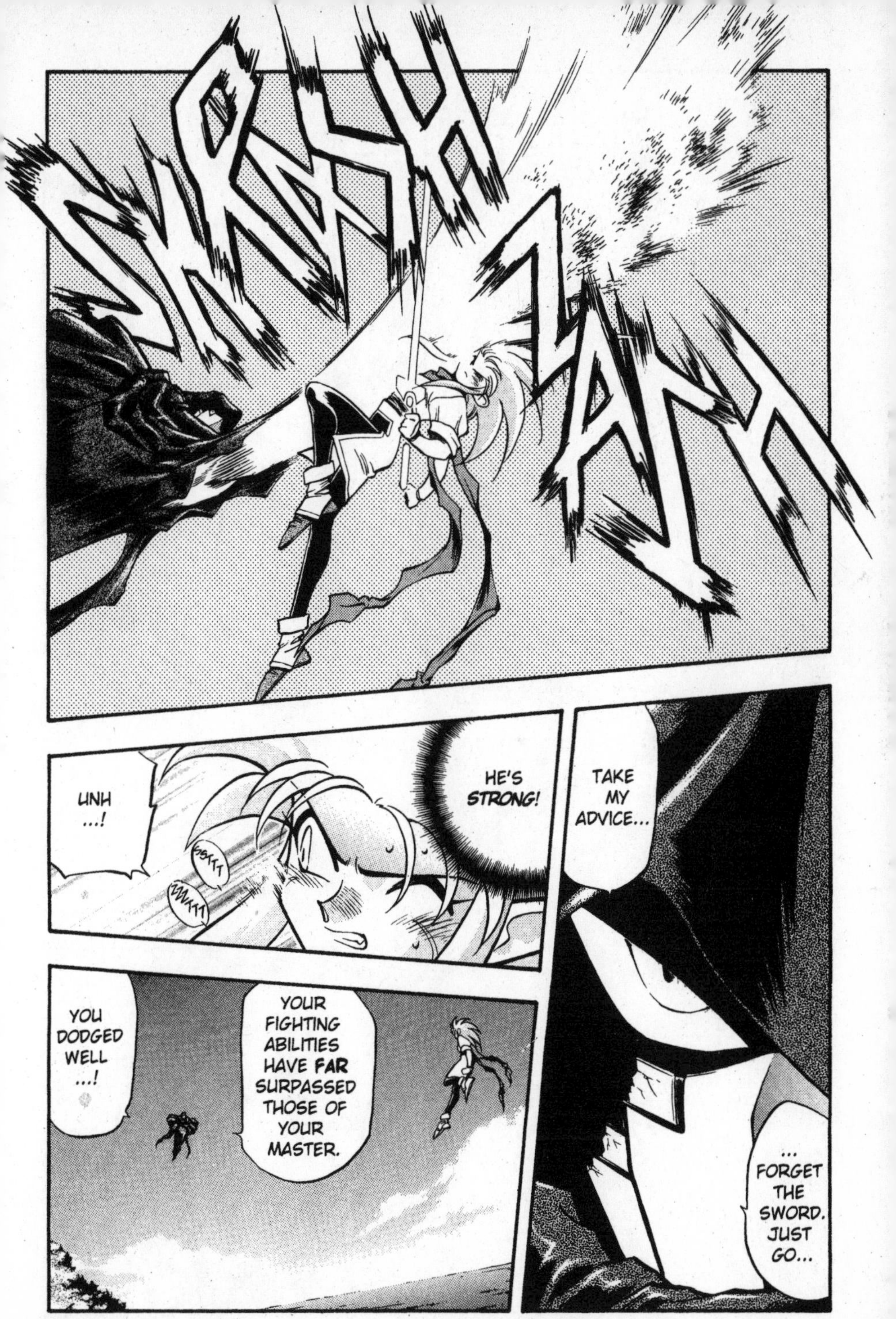
UNH ...!
HE'S **STRONG**!
YOU DODGED WELL ...!
YOUR FIGHTING ABILITIES HAVE **FAR** SURPASSED THOSE OF YOUR MASTER.
TAKE MY ADVICE...
... FORGET THE SWORD. JUST GO...

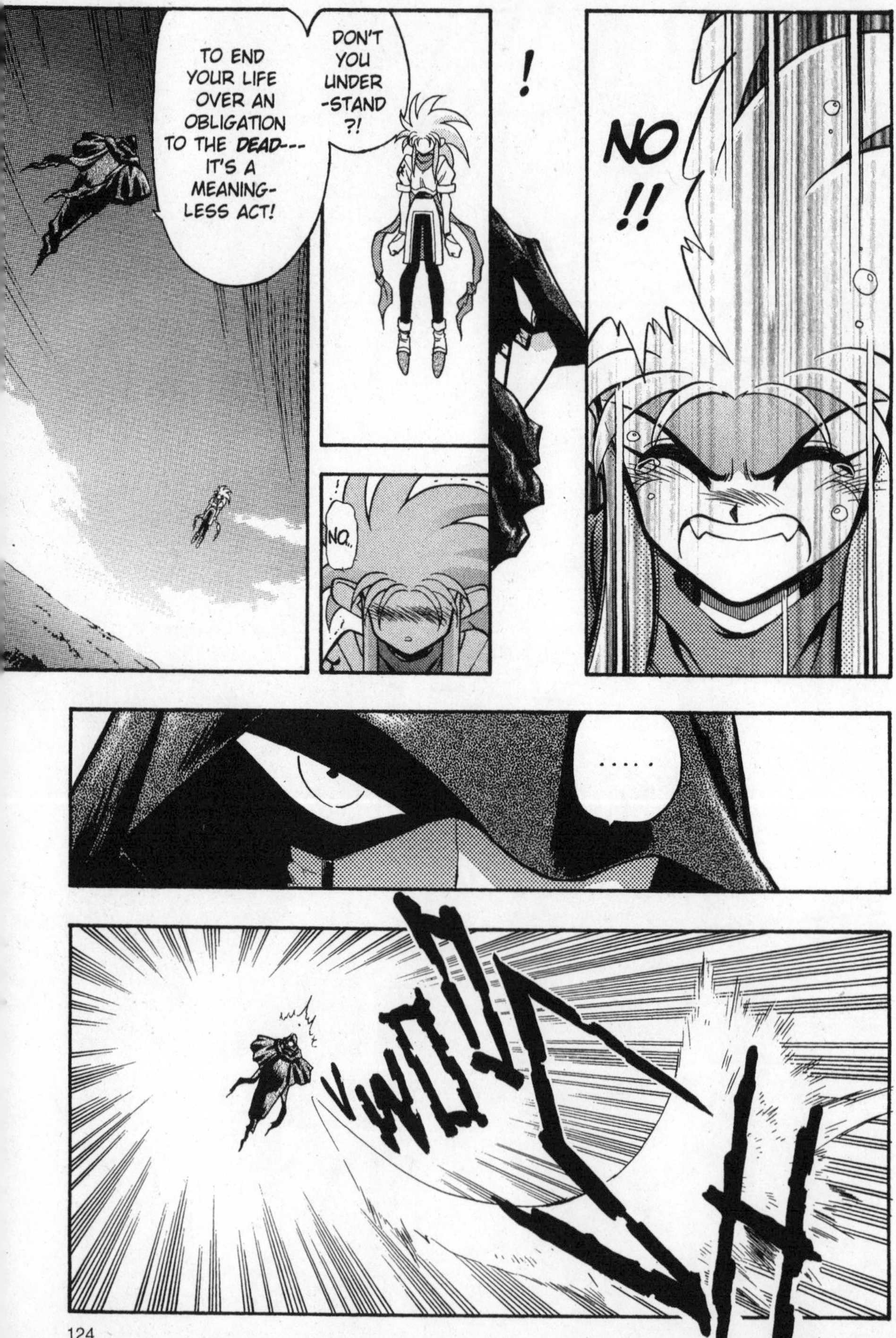
TO END YOUR LIFE OVER AN OBLIGATION TO THE DEAD--- IT'S A MEANING-LESS ACT!
DON'T YOU UNDER-STAND?!
!
NO..
NO!!
.....

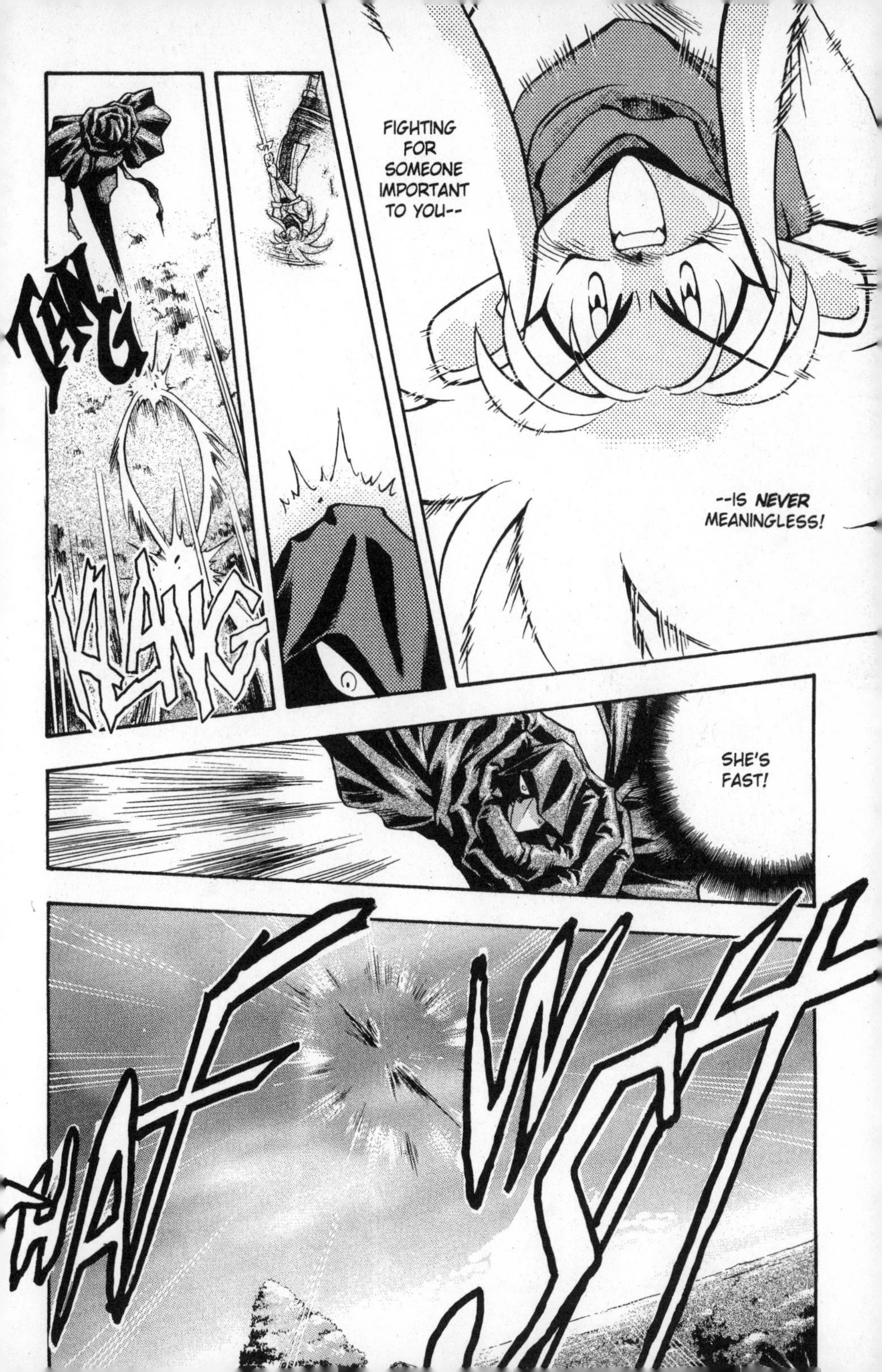
TANG
KLANG
FIGHTING FOR SOMEONE IMPORTANT TO YOU--
--IS **NEVER** MEANINGLESS!
SHE'S FAST!

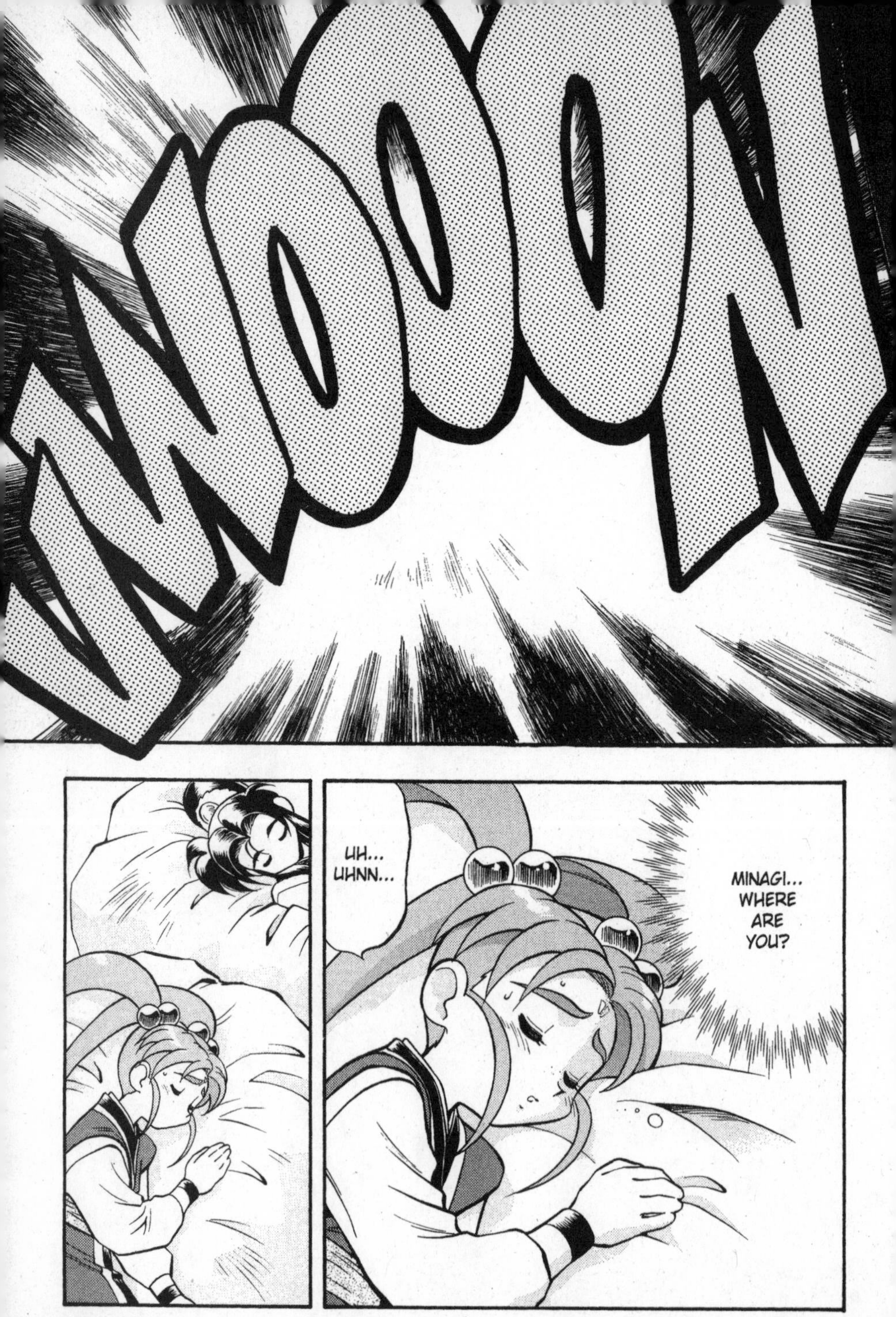
UH...
UHNN...
MINAGI... WHERE ARE YOU?

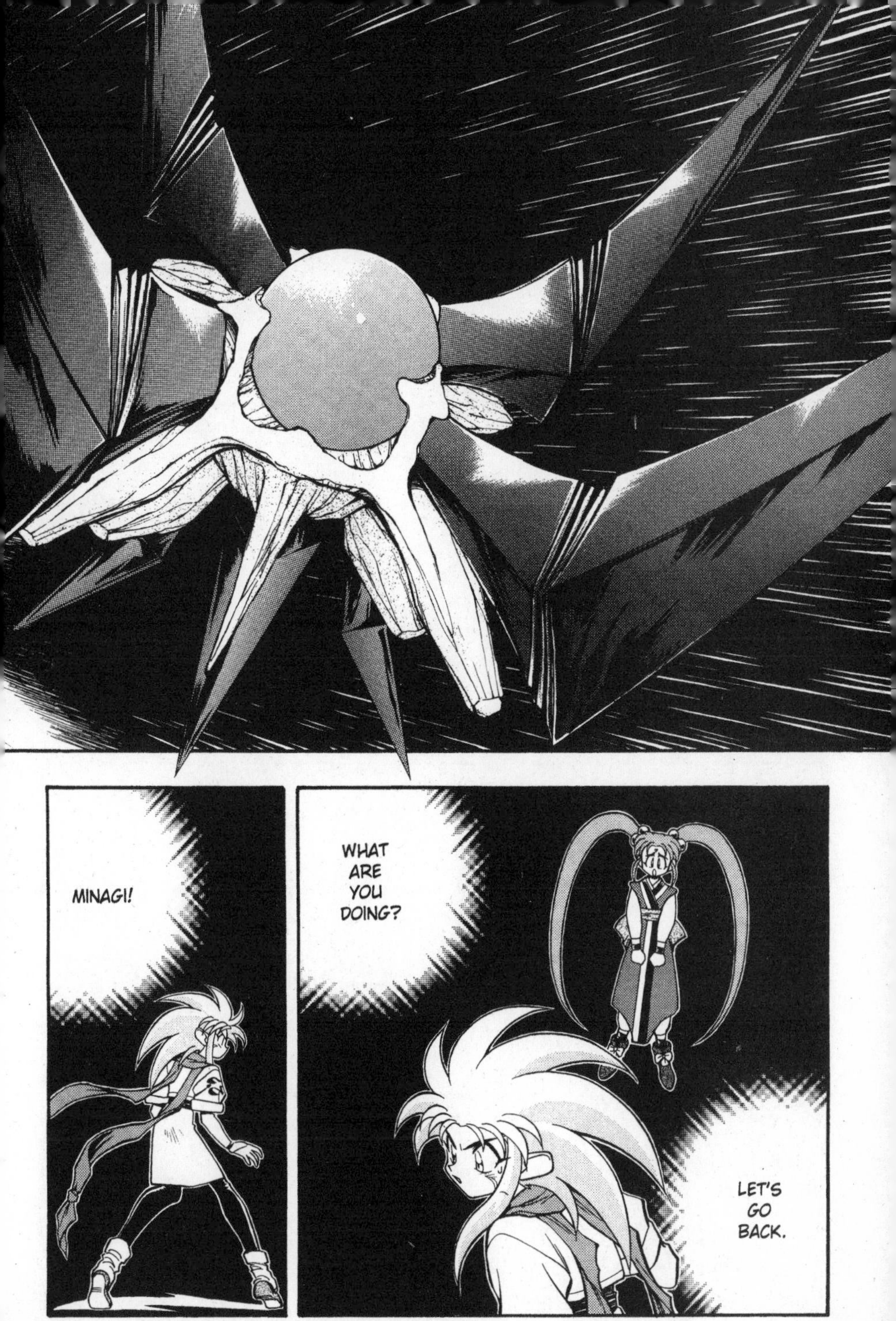
MINAGI!
WHAT ARE YOU DOING?
LET'S GO BACK.

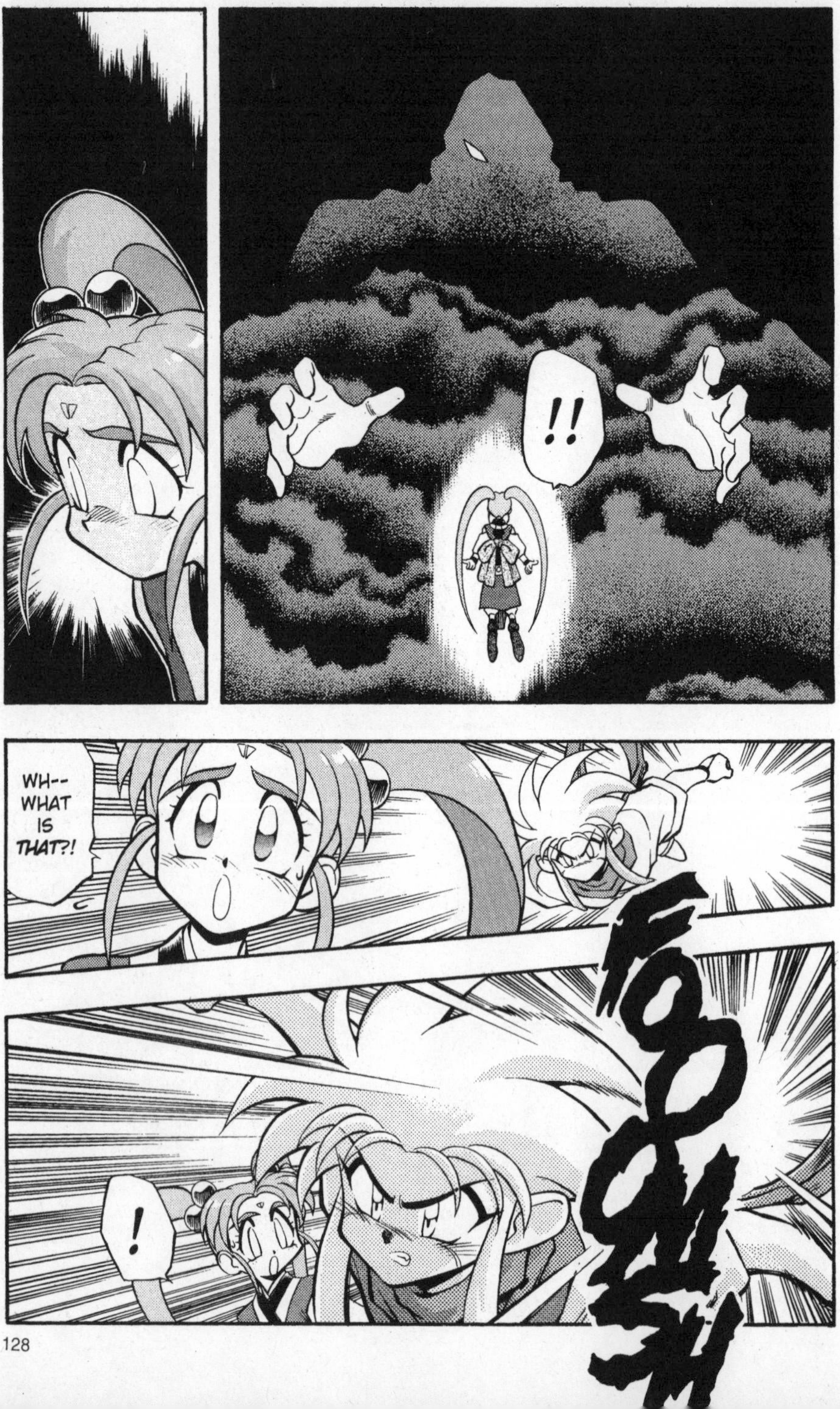
!!
WH-- WHAT IS THAT?!
!
FOOSH!

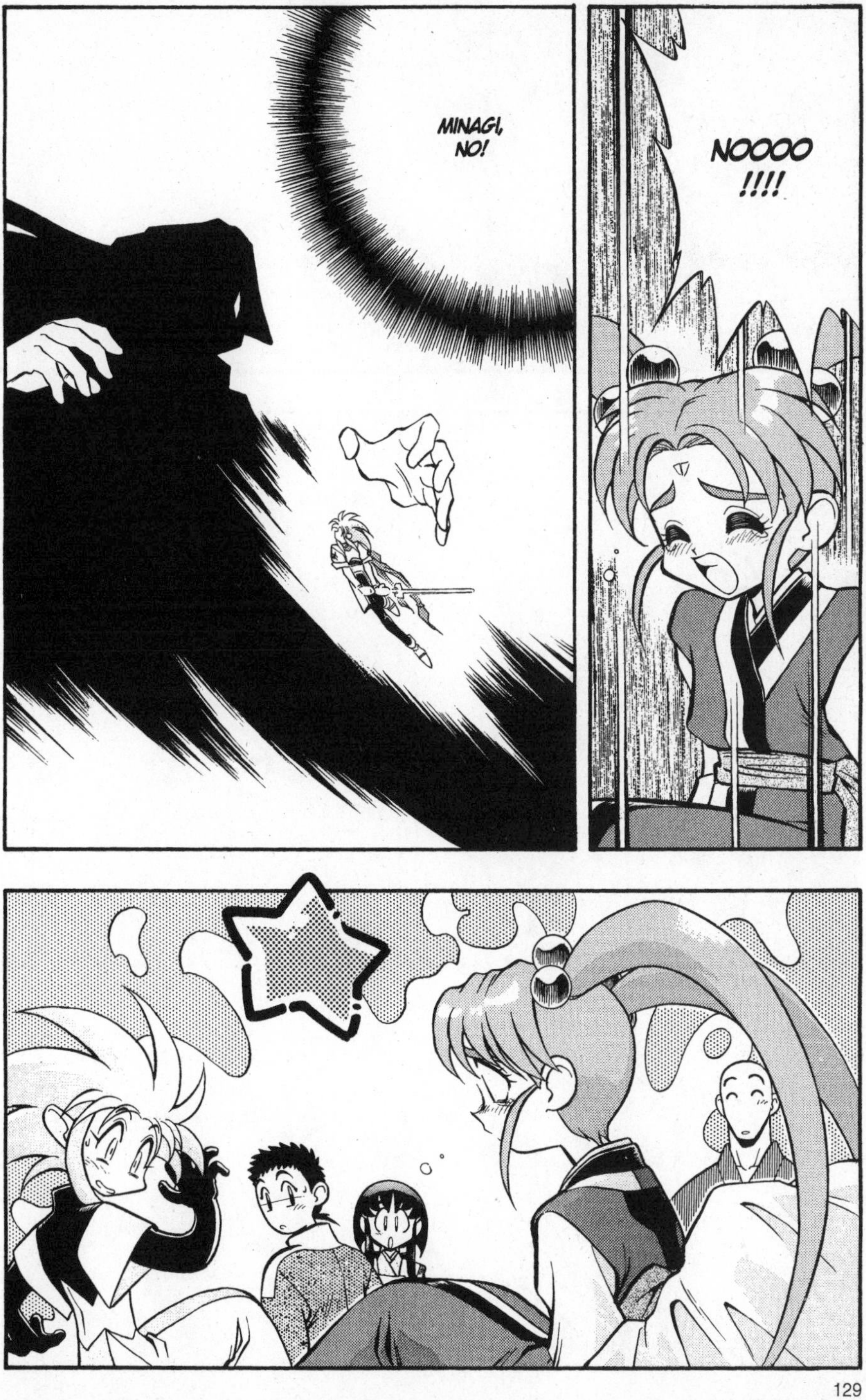
MINAGI, NO!
NOOOO !!!!

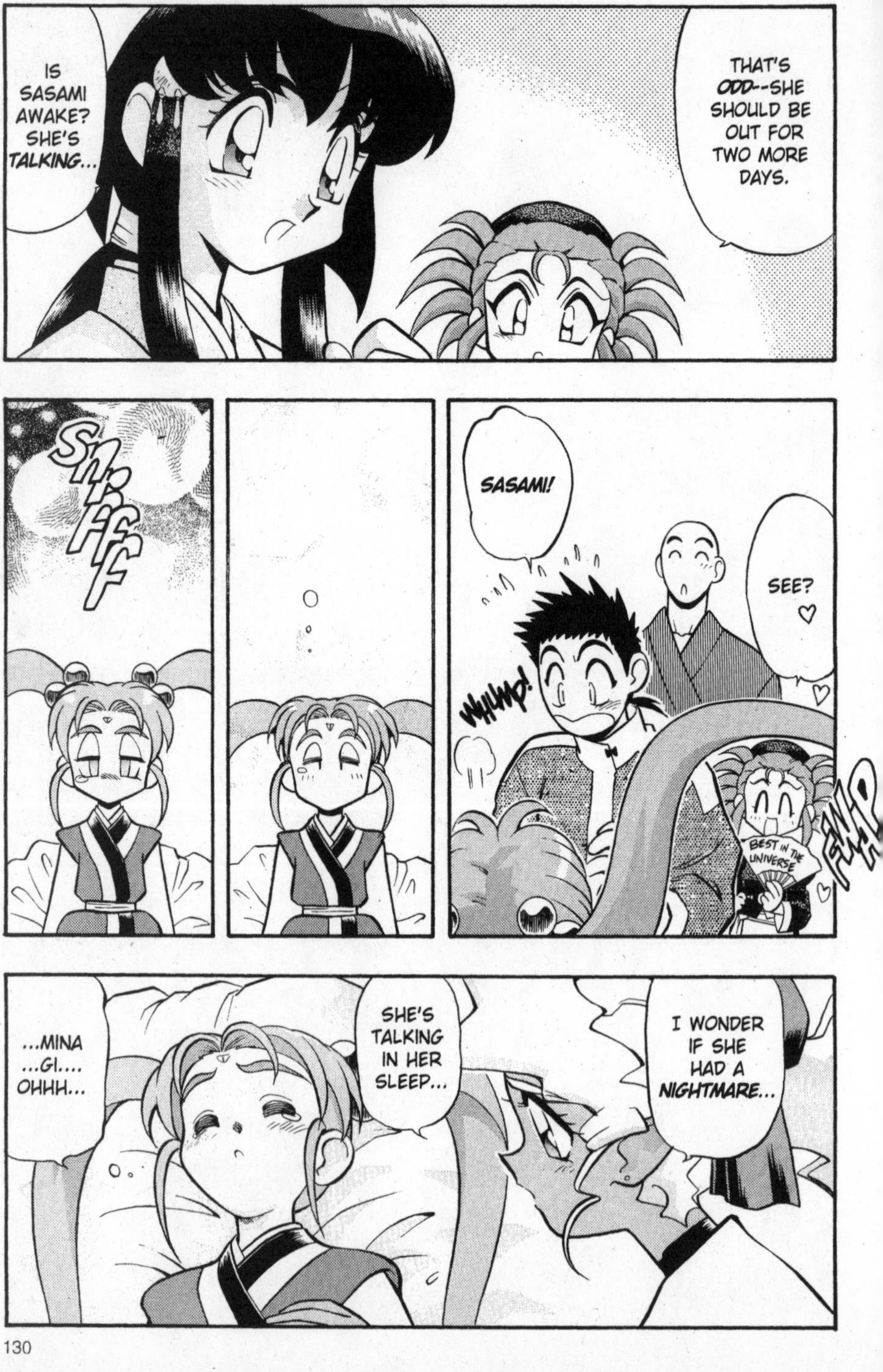
IS SASAMI AWAKE? SHE'S *TALKING*...
THAT'S *ODD*--SHE SHOULD BE OUT FOR TWO MORE DAYS.
Snifff
SASAMI!
WHUMP!
SEE?
BEST IN THE UNIVERSE
FWIP
...MINA ...GI.... OHHH...
SHE'S TALKING IN HER SLEEP...
I WONDER IF SHE HAD A *NIGHTMARE*...

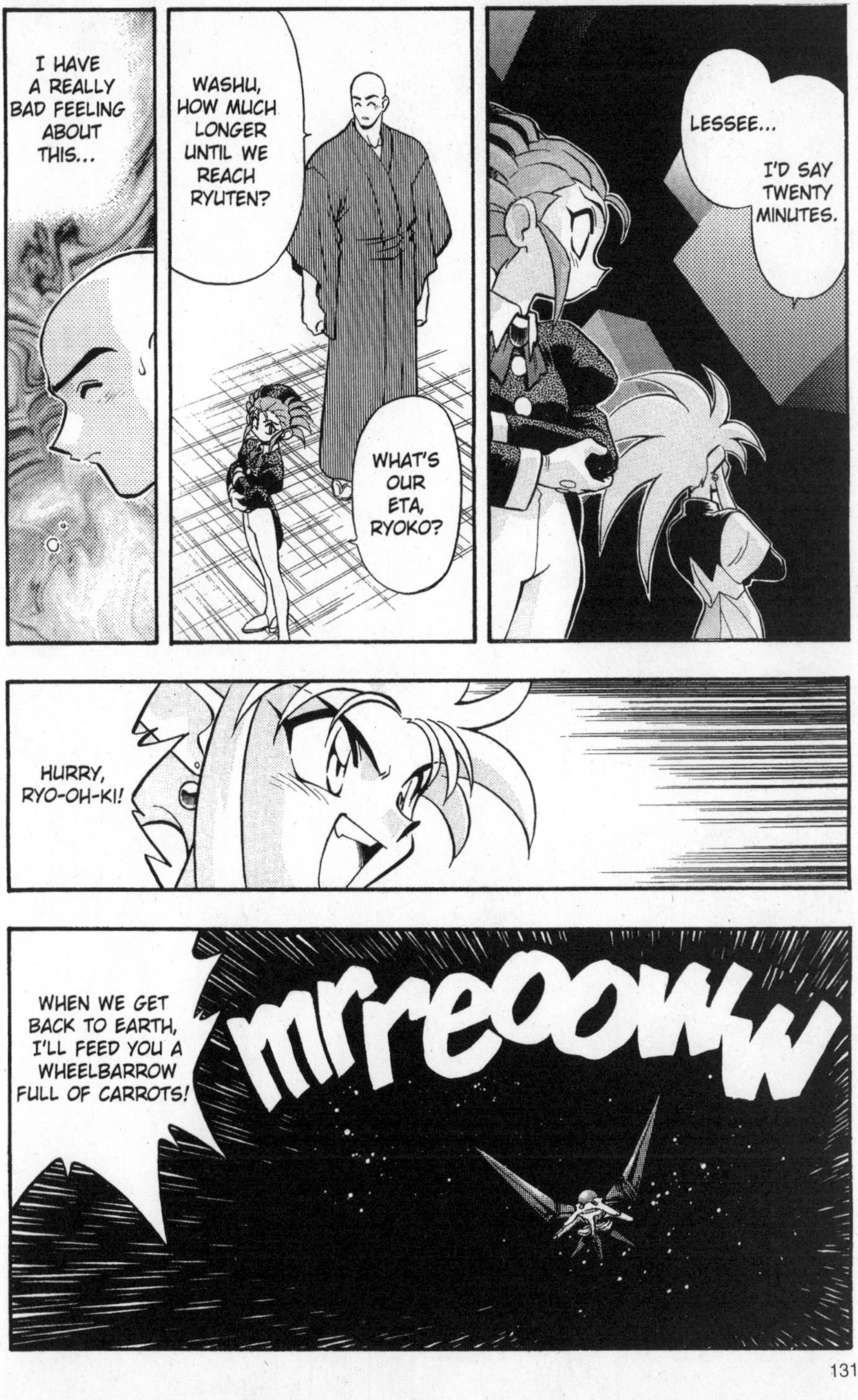
I HAVE A REALLY BAD FEELING ABOUT THIS...
WASHU, HOW MUCH LONGER UNTIL WE REACH RYUTEN?
WHAT'S OUR ETA, RYOKO?
LESSEE...
I'D SAY TWENTY MINUTES.
HURRY, RYO-OH-KI!
WHEN WE GET BACK TO EARTH, I'LL FEED YOU A WHEELBARROW FULL OF CARROTS!
mrreooww

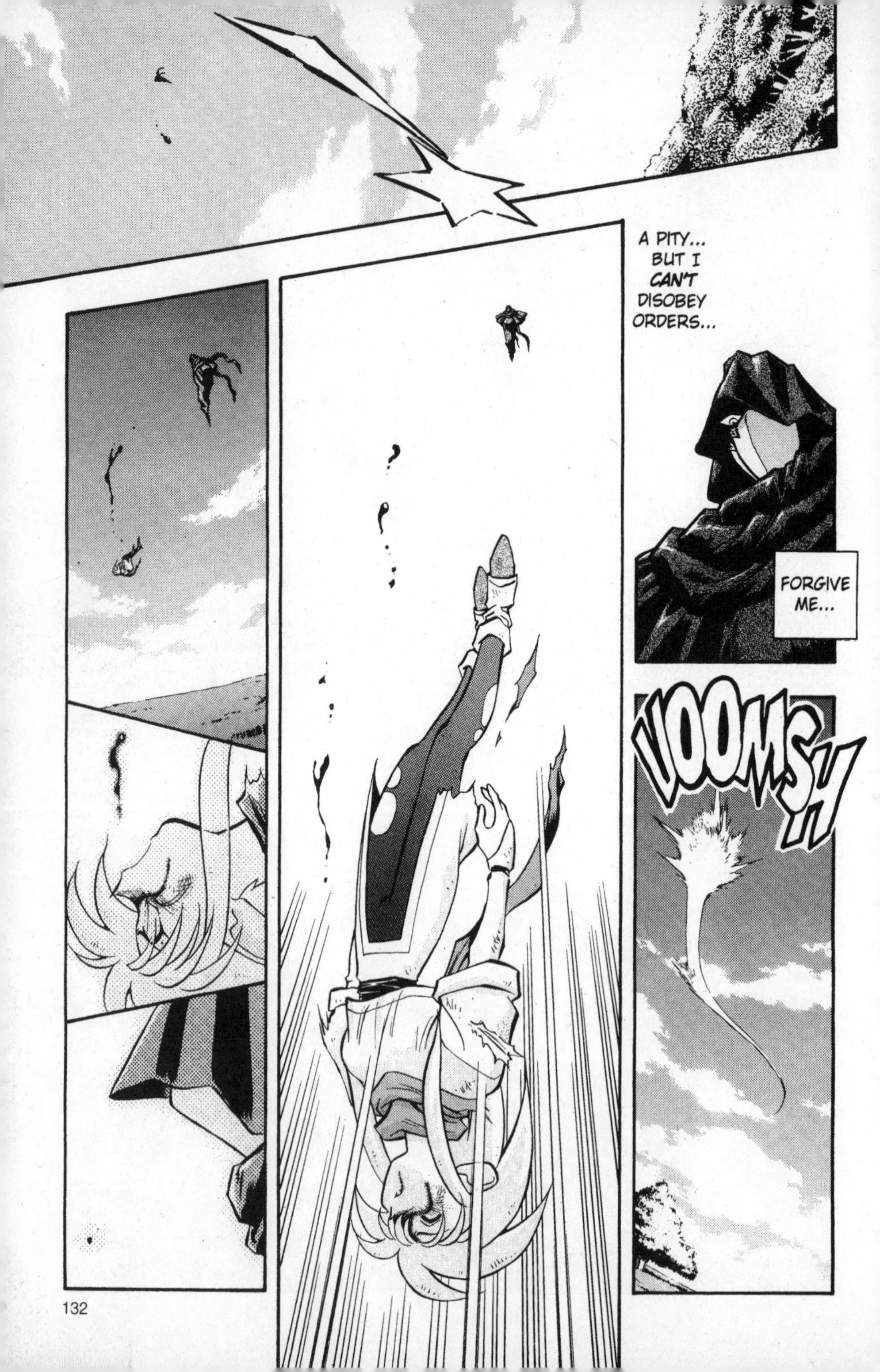
A PITY... BUT I CAN'T DISOBEY ORDERS...
FORGIVE ME...
VOOMSH

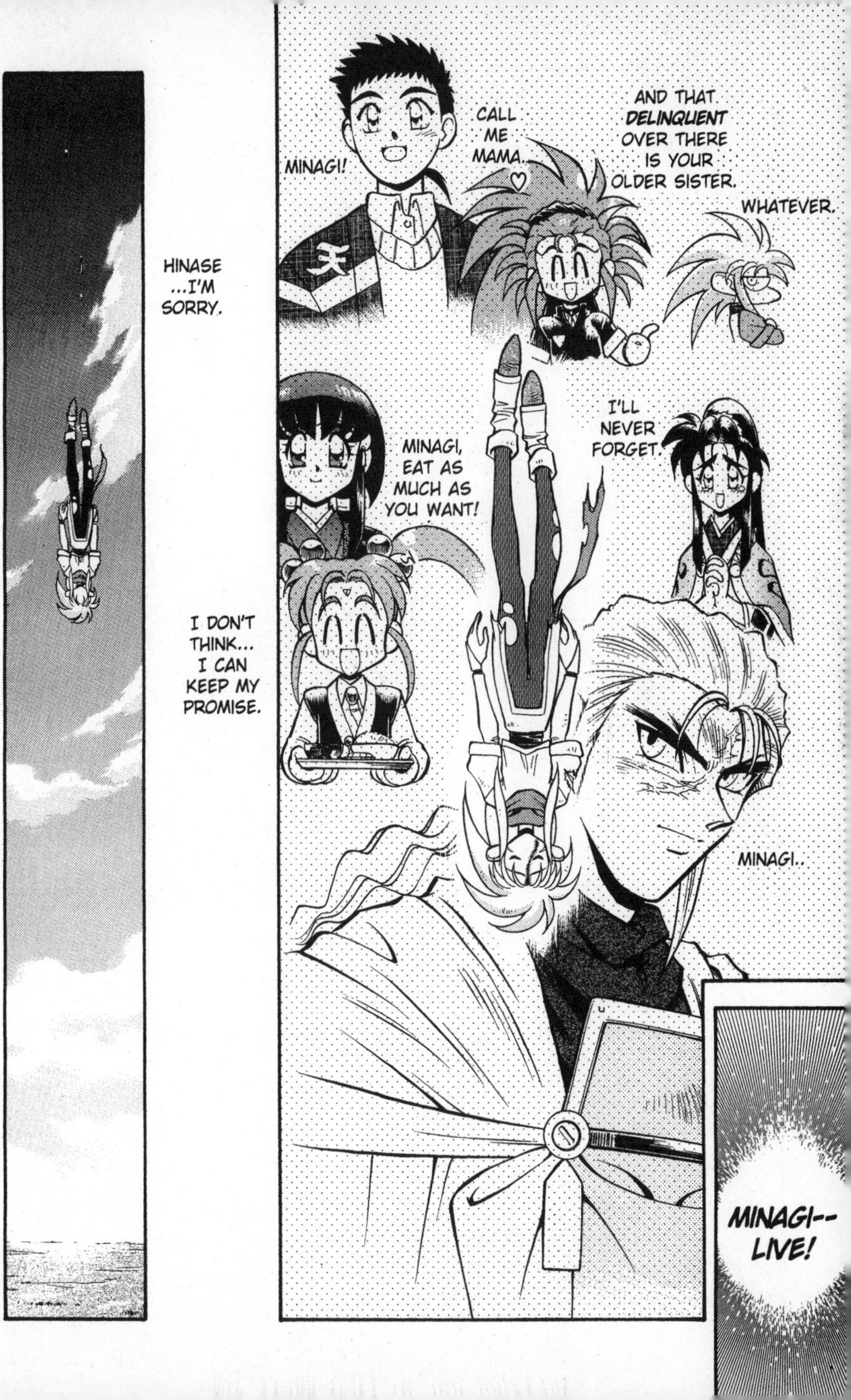
HINASE ...I'M SORRY.
I DON'T THINK... I CAN KEEP MY PROMISE.
MINAGI!
CALL ME MAMA. ♥
AND THAT DELINQUENT OVER THERE IS YOUR OLDER SISTER.
WHATEVER.
MINAGI, EAT AS MUCH AS YOU WANT!
I'LL NEVER FORGET.
MINAGI..
MINAGI-- LIVE!

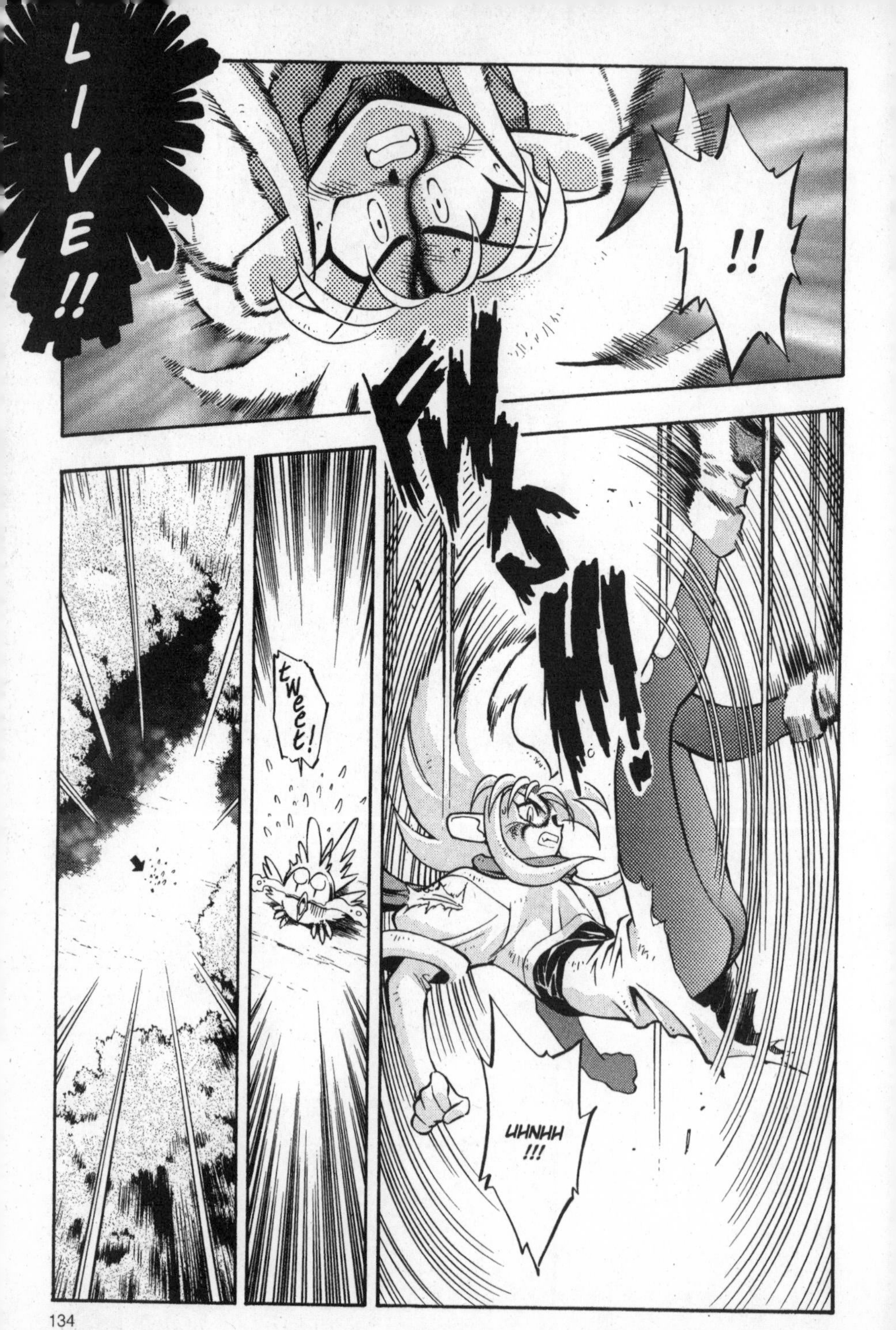
LIVE!!
!!
FWASH!
tweet!
UHNHH!!!

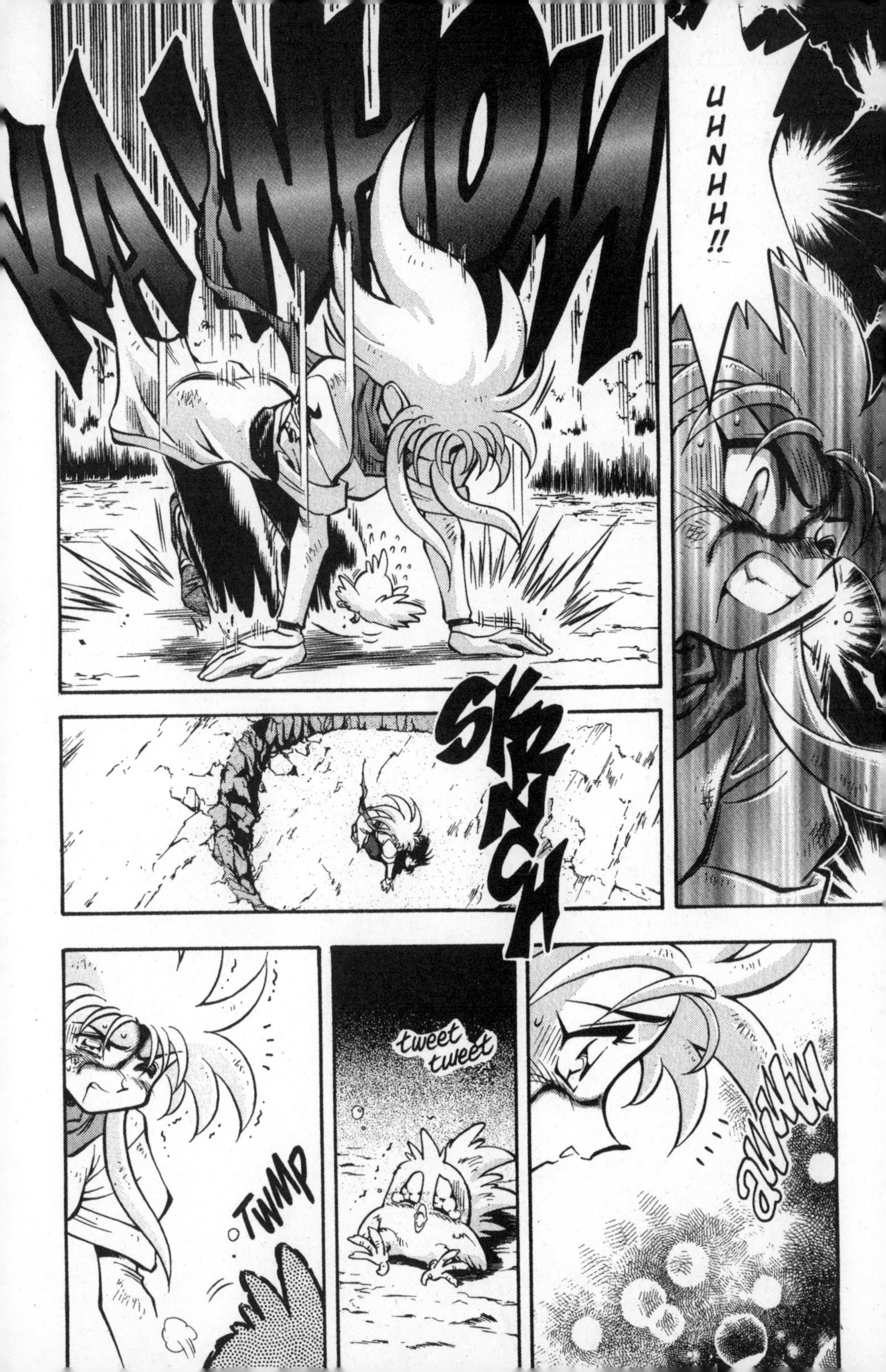
UHNHHH!!
SKRUNCH
TWMP
tweet tweet
awwww

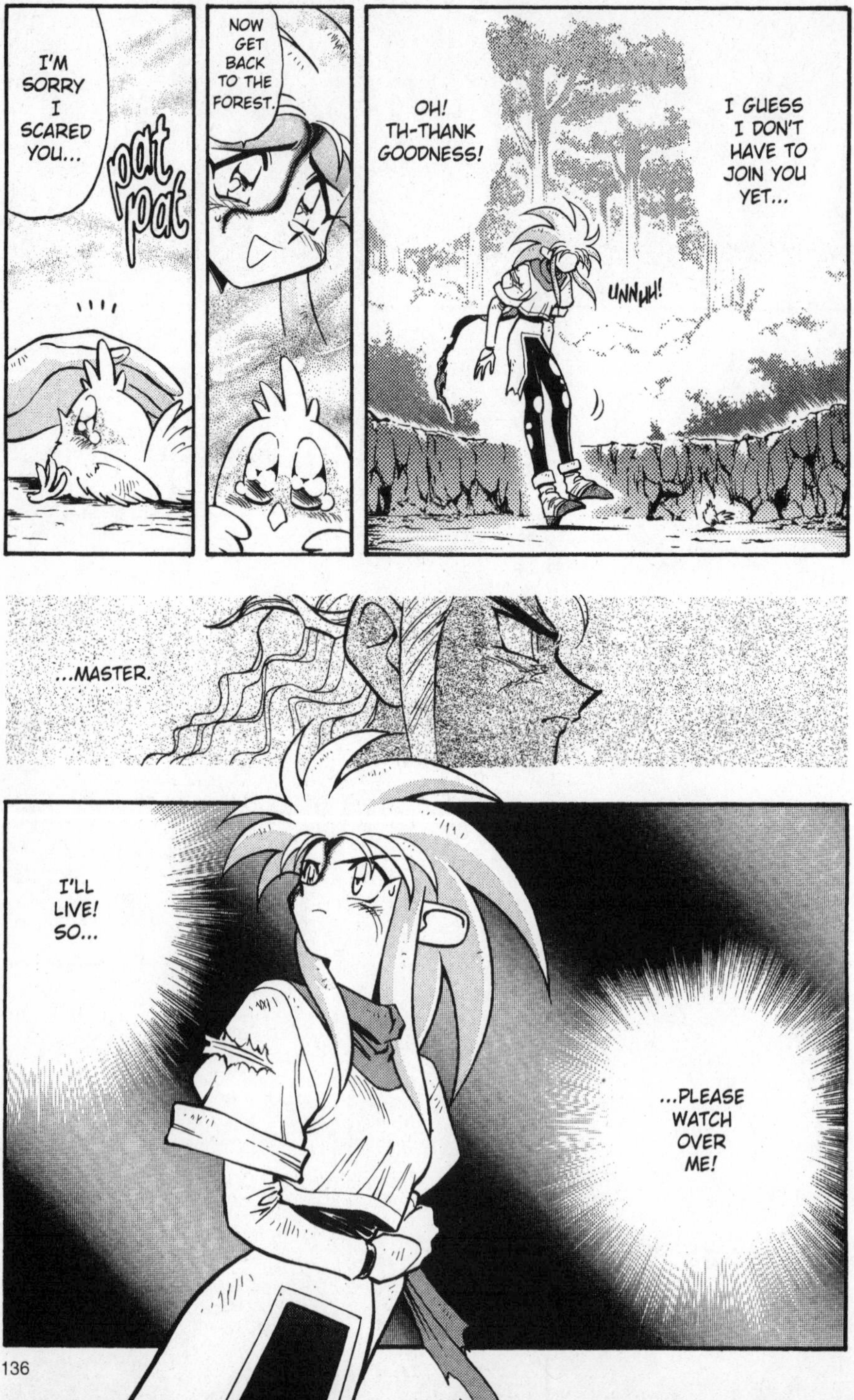
I'M SORRY I SCARED YOU...
pat pat
...!
NOW GET BACK TO THE FOREST.
OH! TH-THANK GOODNESS!
I GUESS I DON'T HAVE TO JOIN YOU YET...
UNNHH!
...MASTER.
I'LL LIVE! SO...
...PLEASE WATCH OVER ME!

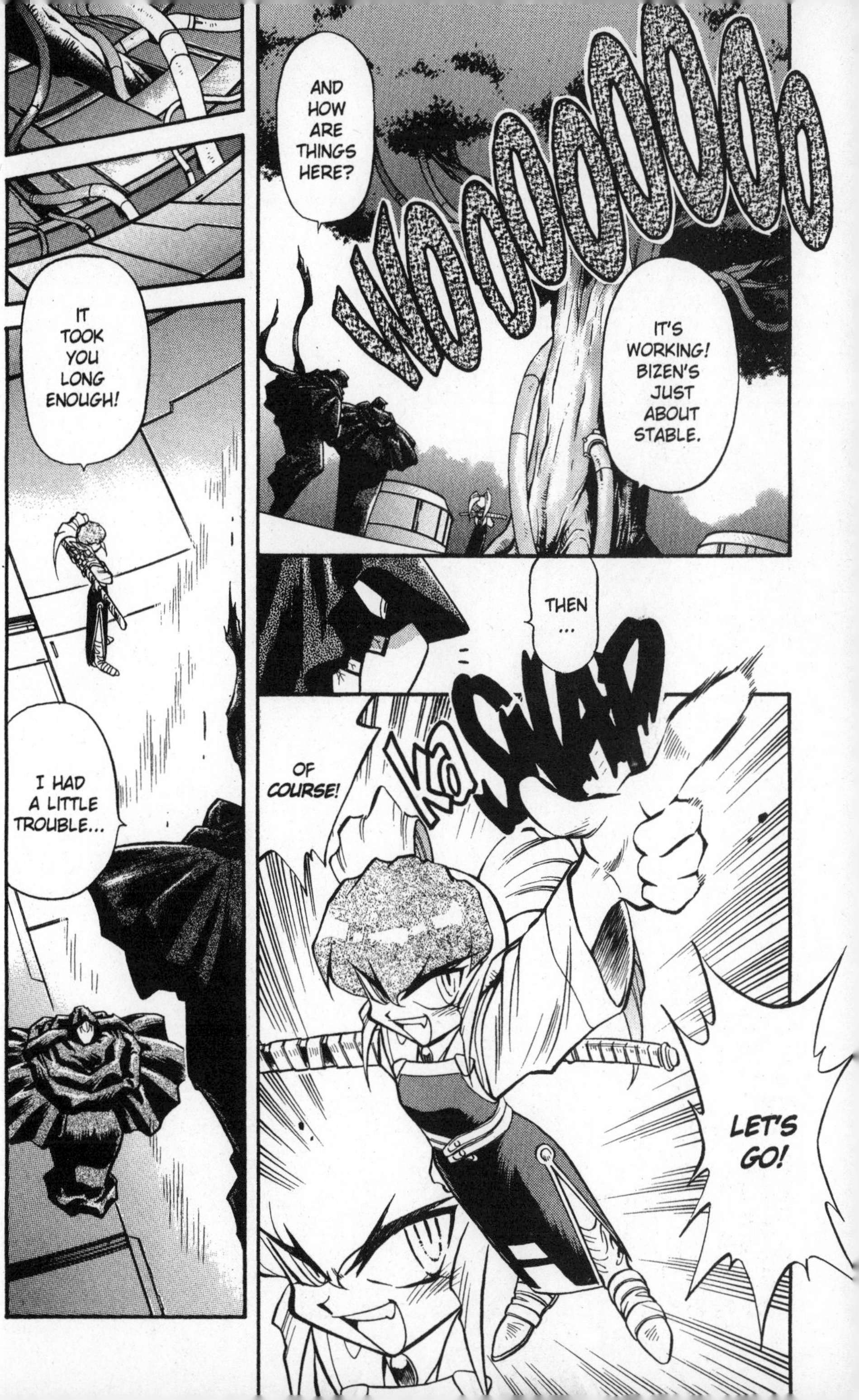
IT TOOK YOU LONG ENOUGH!
I HAD A LITTLE TROUBLE...
AND HOW ARE THINGS HERE?
WOOOOOOOOOO
IT'S WORKING! BIZEN'S JUST ABOUT STABLE.
THEN...
KA SNAP
OF COURSE!
LET'S GO!

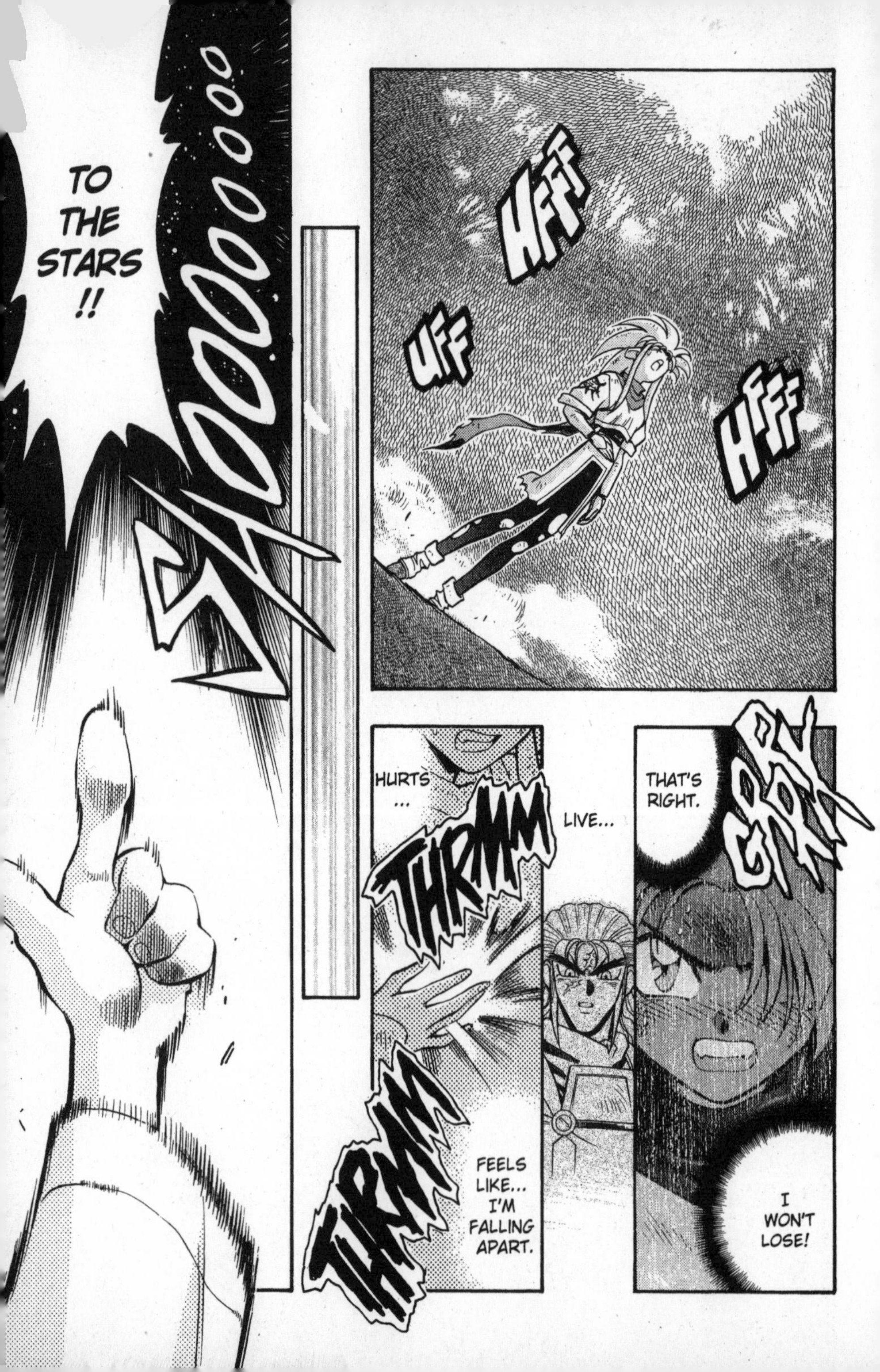
TO THE STARS !!
UFF
HFF
HFF
HURTS ...
THRMM
LIVE...
FEELS LIKE... I'M FALLING APART.
THRMM
THAT'S RIGHT.
I WON'T LOSE!

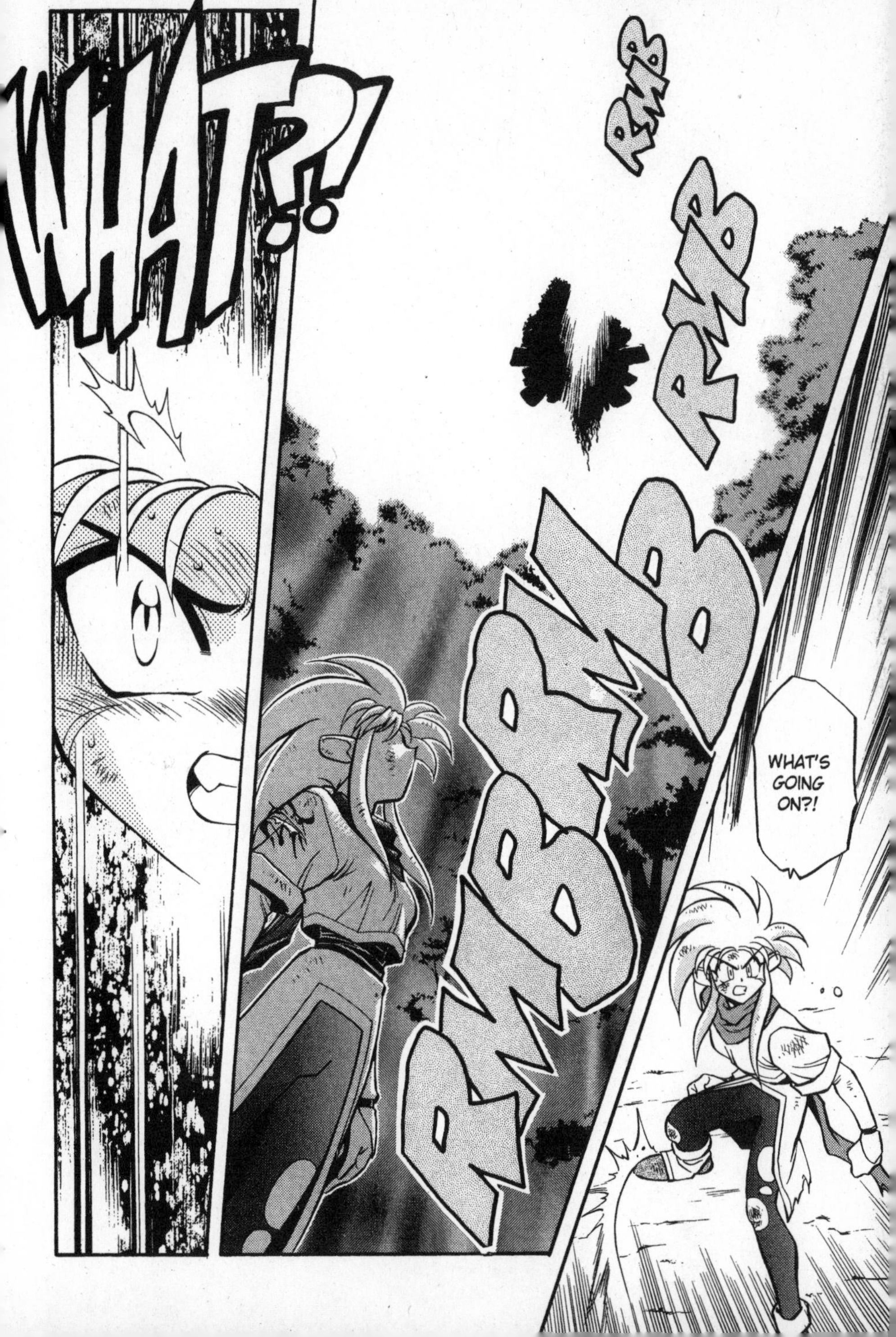
WHAT?!
RMB RMB
RMB
RMBRMB
WHAT'S GOING ON?!

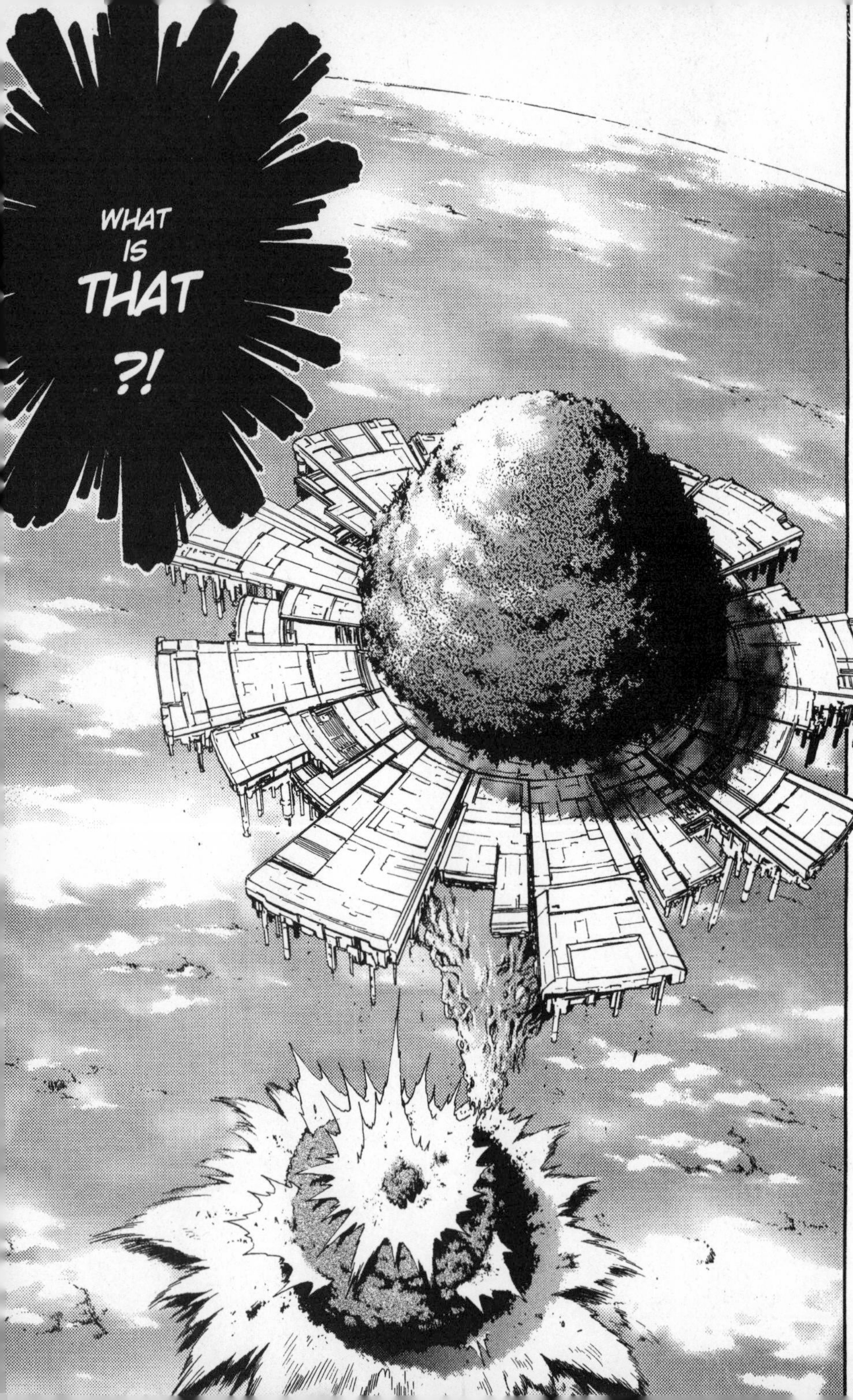
WHAT IS THAT ?!

Tales of Tenchi #7
SHELL GAME

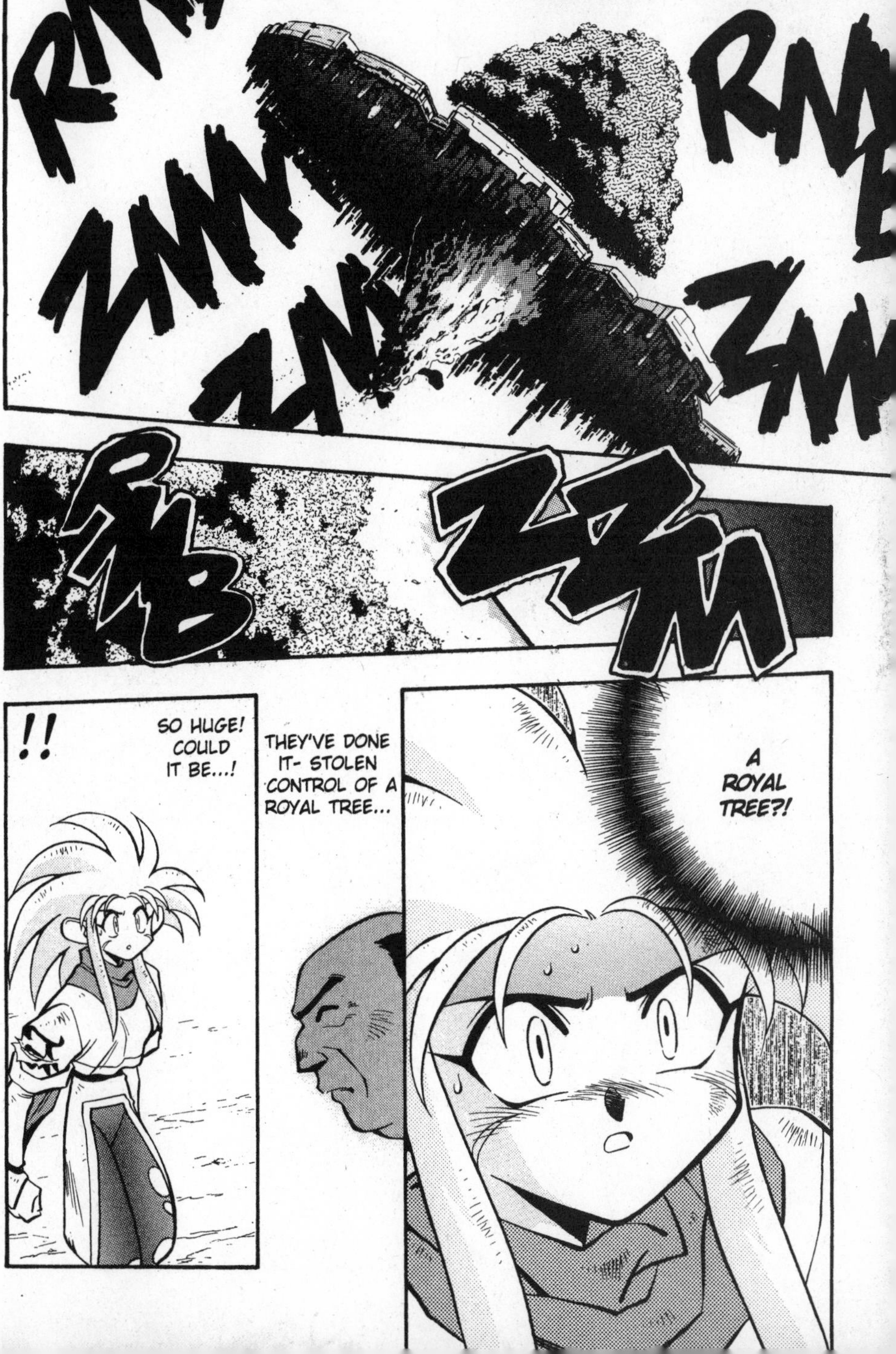
RMB
ZMM
ZM
RMB
ZZM
!!
SO HUGE! COULD IT BE...!
THEY'VE DONE IT- STOLEN CONTROL OF A ROYAL TREE...
A ROYAL TREE?!

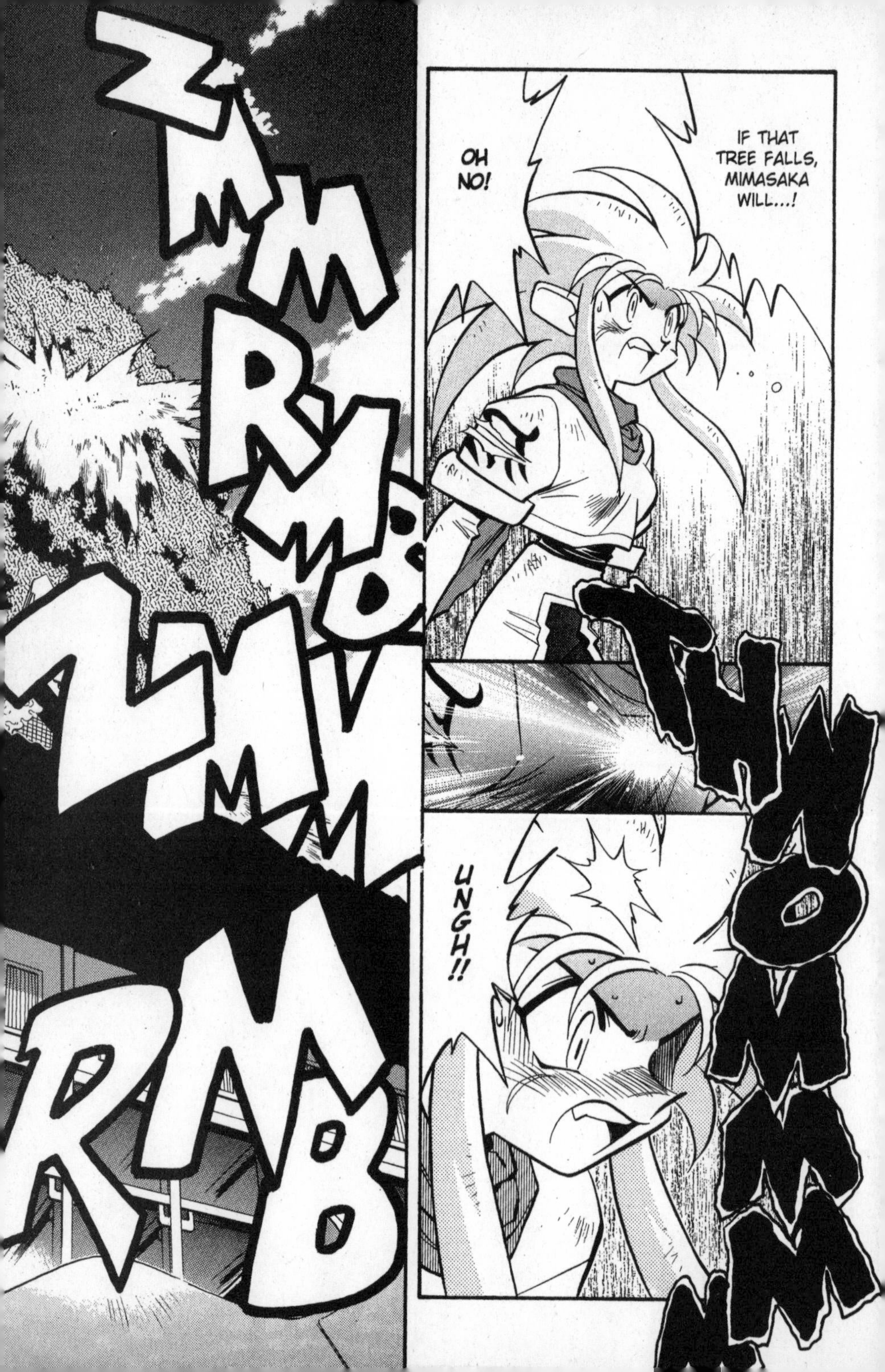
OH NO!
IF THAT TREE FALLS, MIMASAKA WILL...!
THWOMMMM
UNGH!!

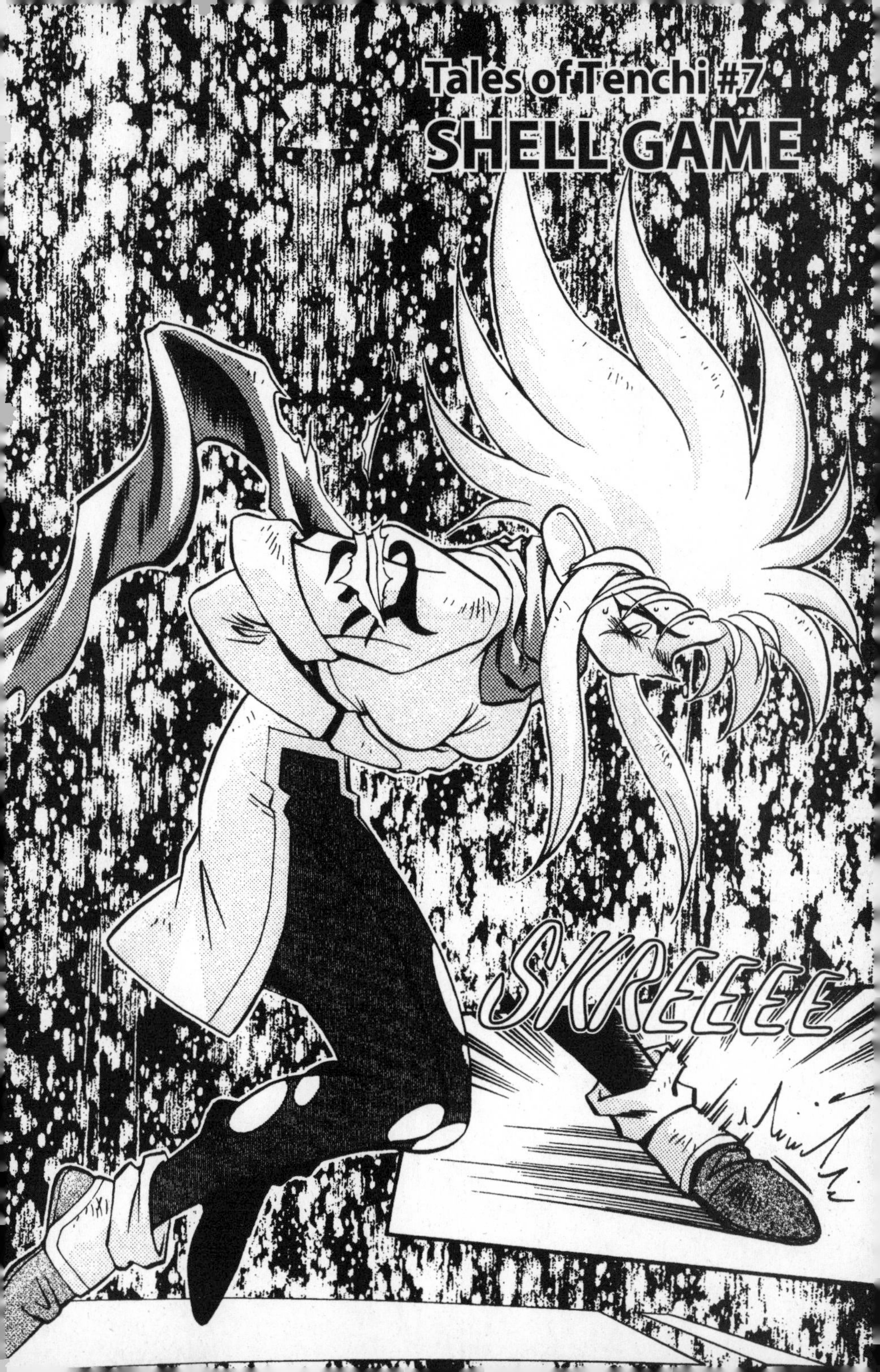
Tales of Tenchi #7
SHELL GAME
SKREEEE

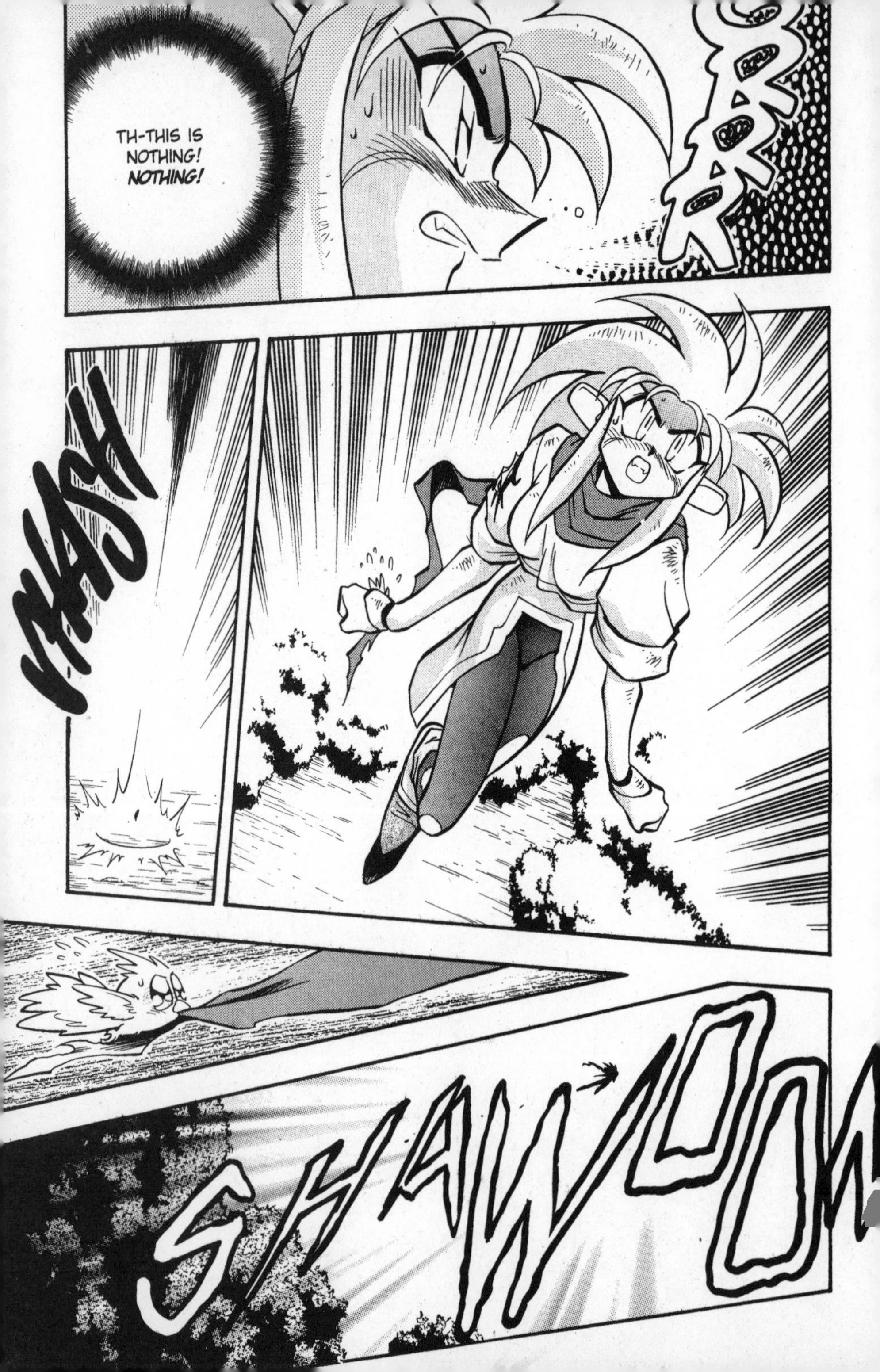
TH-THIS IS NOTHING! NOTHING!

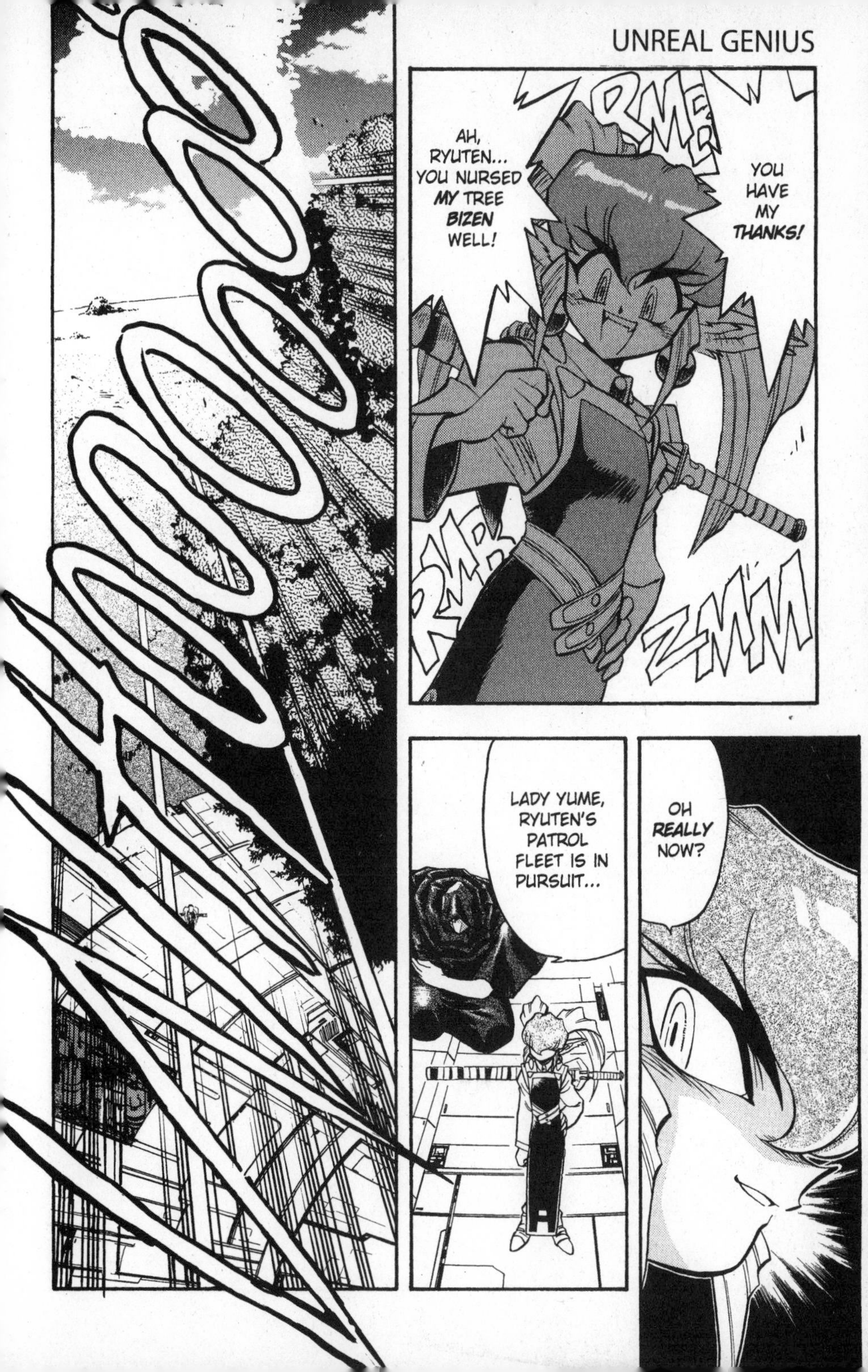
HOOOOOO
AH, RYUTEN... YOU NURSED *MY* TREE *BIZEN* WELL!
YOU HAVE MY *THANKS!*
RMB
ZMM
LADY YUME, RYUTEN'S PATROL FLEET IS IN PURSUIT...
OH *REALLY* NOW?

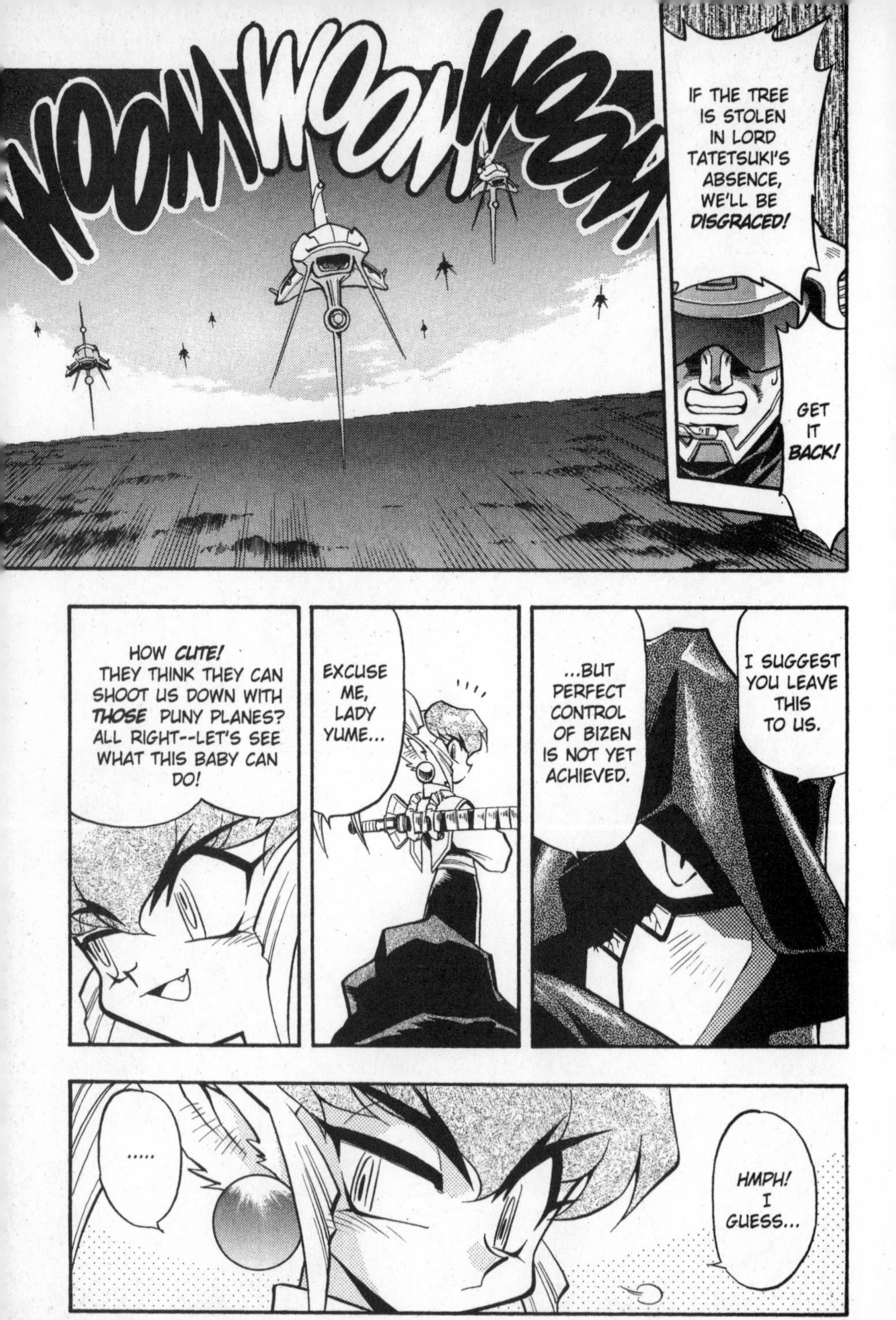
WOOM WOOM WOOM
IF THE TREE IS STOLEN IN LORD TATETSUKI'S ABSENCE, WE'LL BE ***DISGRACED!***
GET IT ***BACK!***
HOW ***CUTE!*** THEY THINK THEY CAN SHOOT US DOWN WITH ***THOSE*** PUNY PLANES? ALL RIGHT--LET'S SEE WHAT THIS BABY CAN DO!
EXCUSE ME, LADY YUME...
...BUT PERFECT CONTROL OF BIZEN IS NOT YET ACHIEVED.
I SUGGEST YOU LEAVE THIS TO US.
.....
HMPH! I GUESS...

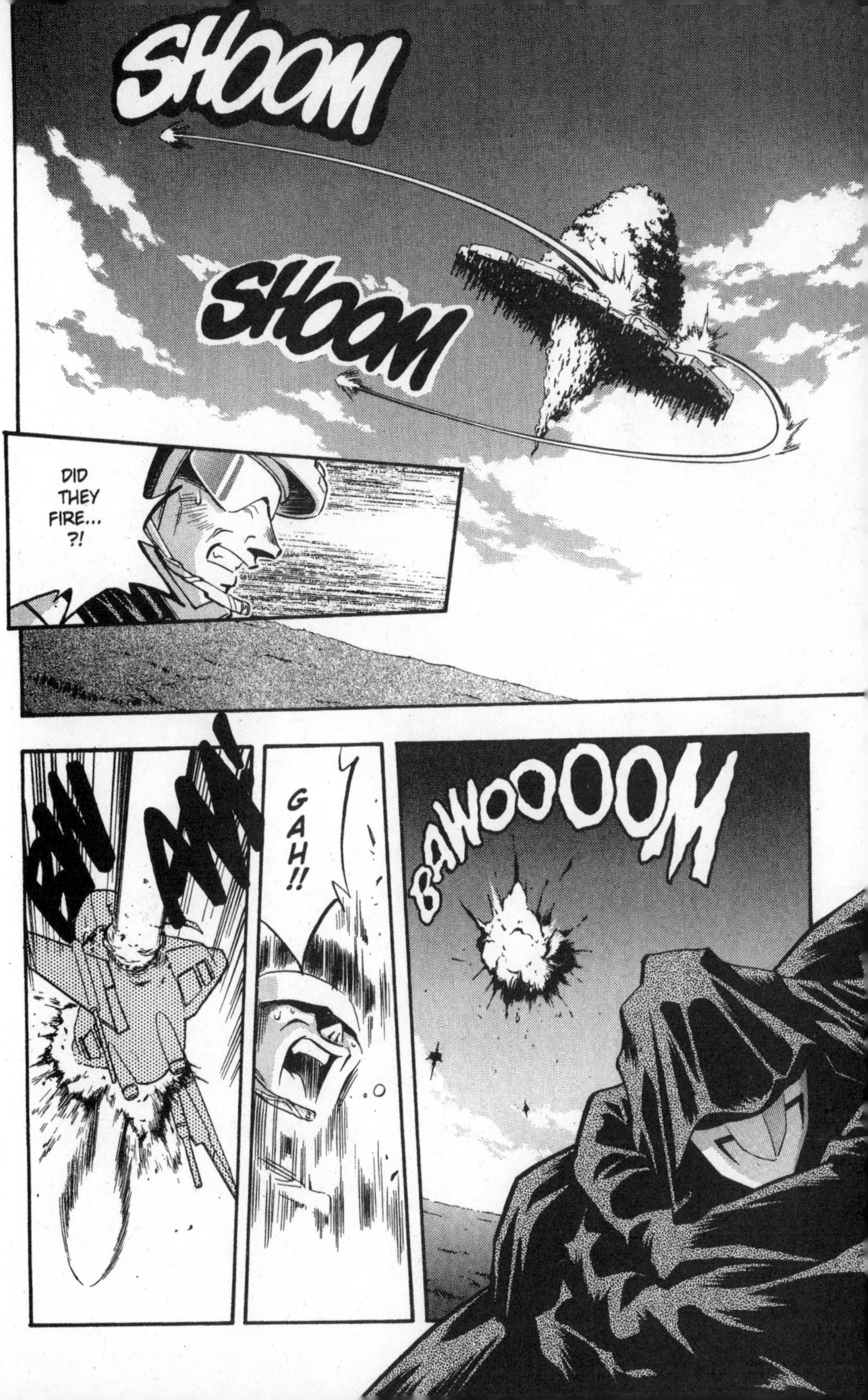
SHOOM
SHOOM
DID THEY FIRE... ?!
BAM!
GAH!!
BAWOOOOM

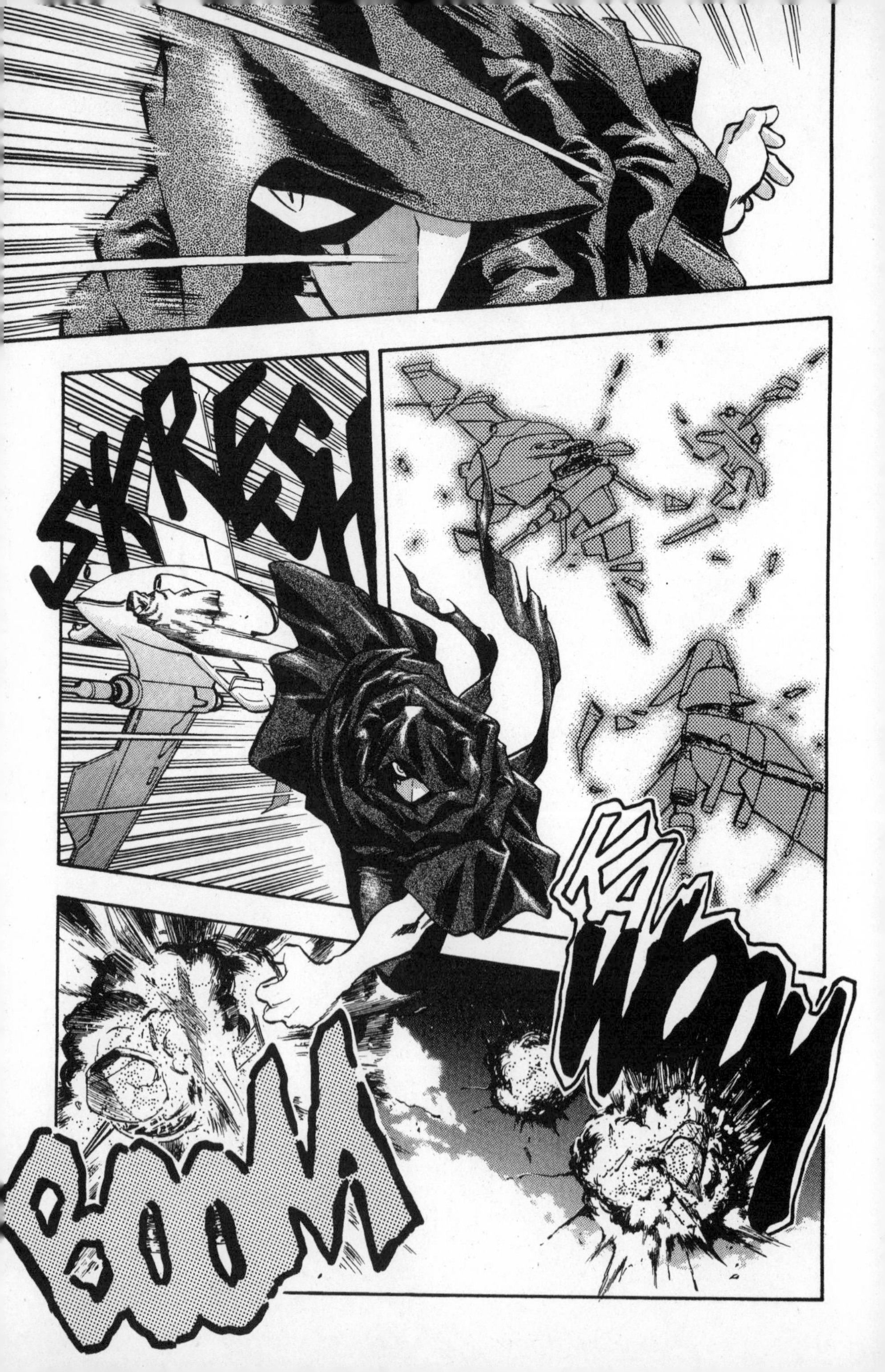
SKRESH
KA WOOM
BOOM!

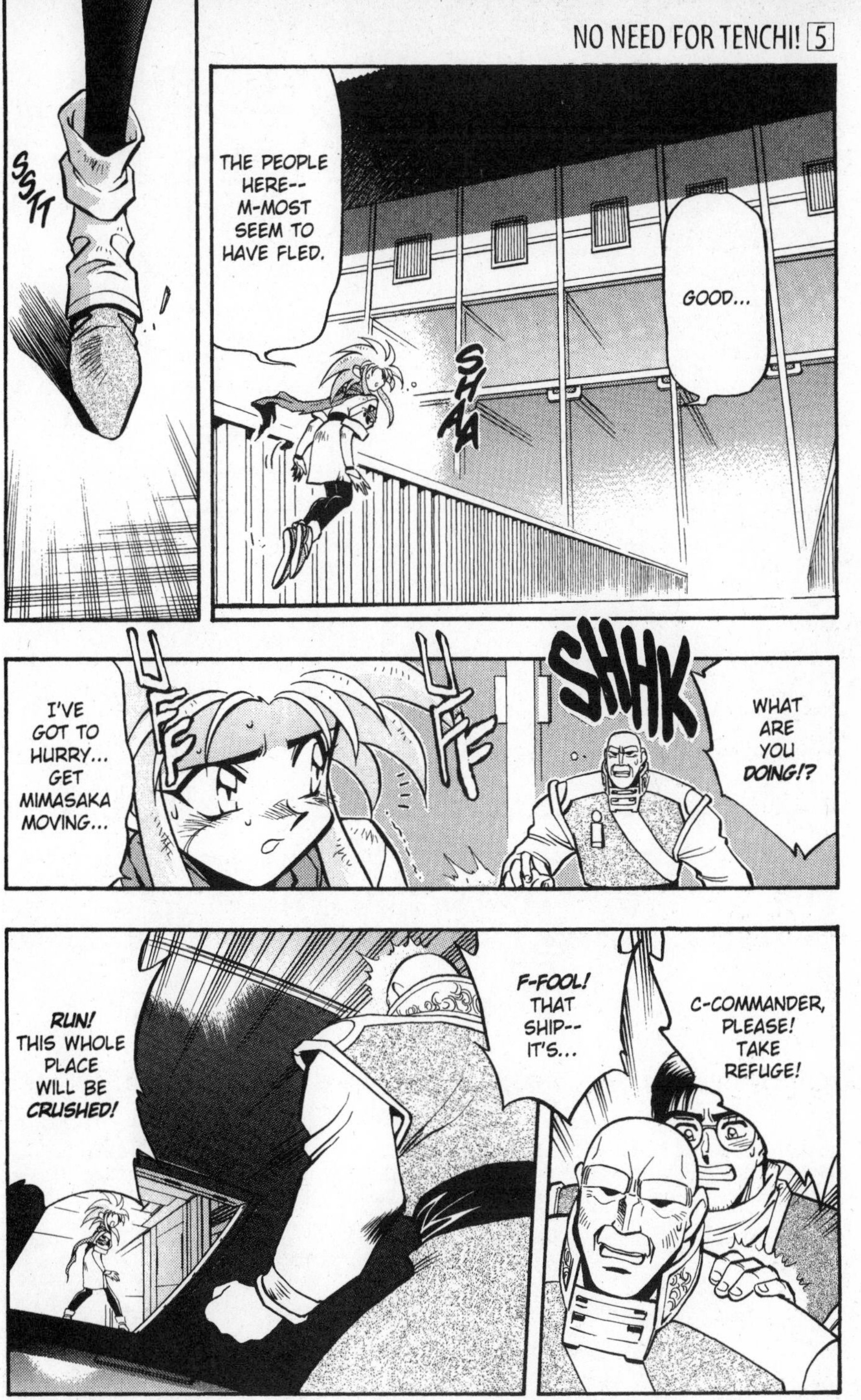
SSTTT
THE PEOPLE HERE-- M-MOST SEEM TO HAVE FLED.
SHAAA
GOOD...
I'VE GOT TO HURRY... GET MIMASAKA MOVING...
UFF
UFF
SHHK
WHAT ARE YOU *DOING!?*
RUN! THIS WHOLE PLACE WILL BE ***CRUSHED!***
F-FOOL! THAT SHIP-- IT'S...
C-COMMANDER, PLEASE! TAKE REFUGE!

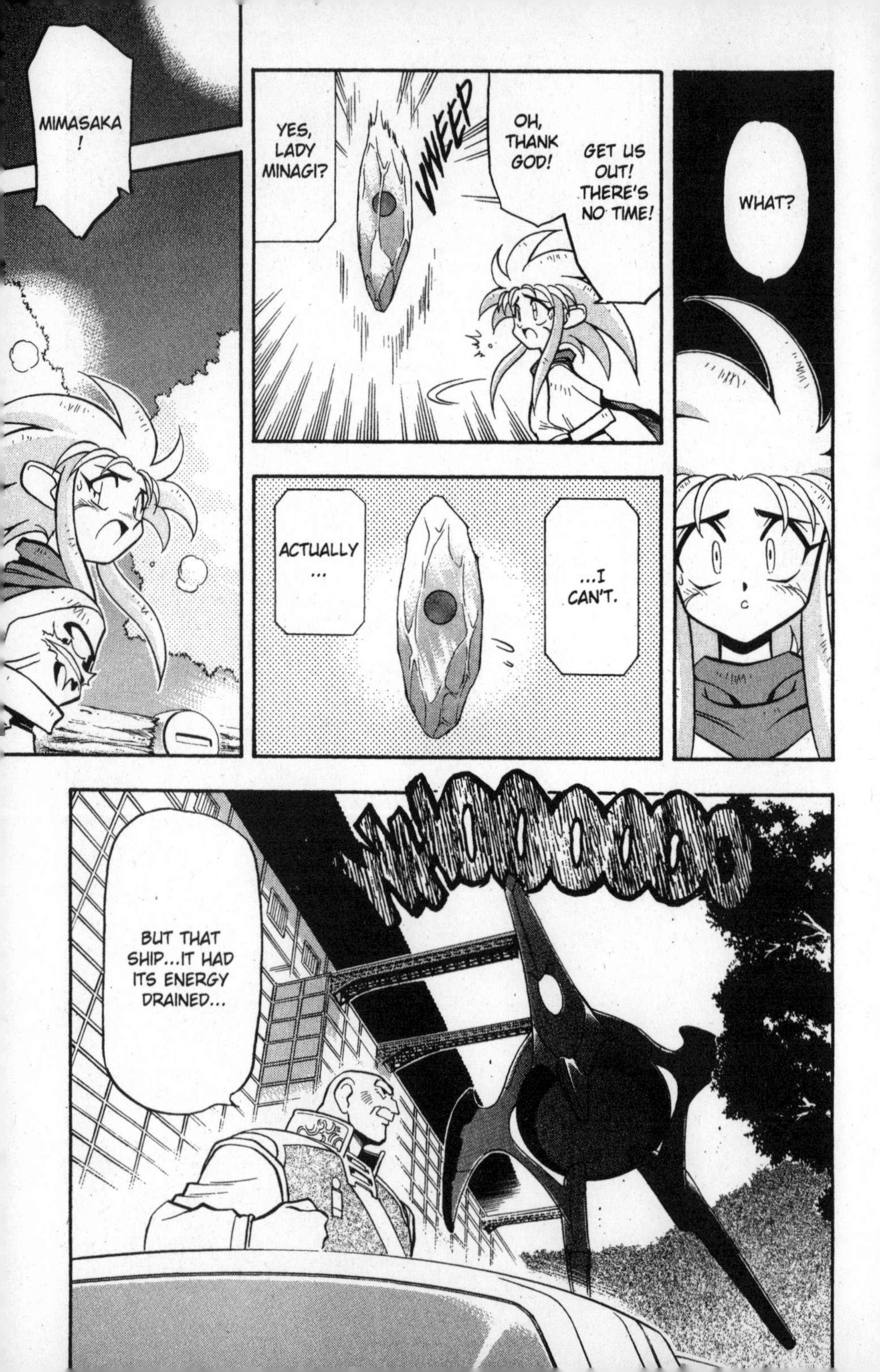
MIMASAKA!
YES, LADY MINAGI?
VWEEP
OH, THANK GOD!
GET US OUT! THERE'S NO TIME!
WHAT?
ACTUALLY...
...I CAN'T.
BUT THAT SHIP...IT HAD ITS ENERGY DRAINED...
WHOOOOOOO

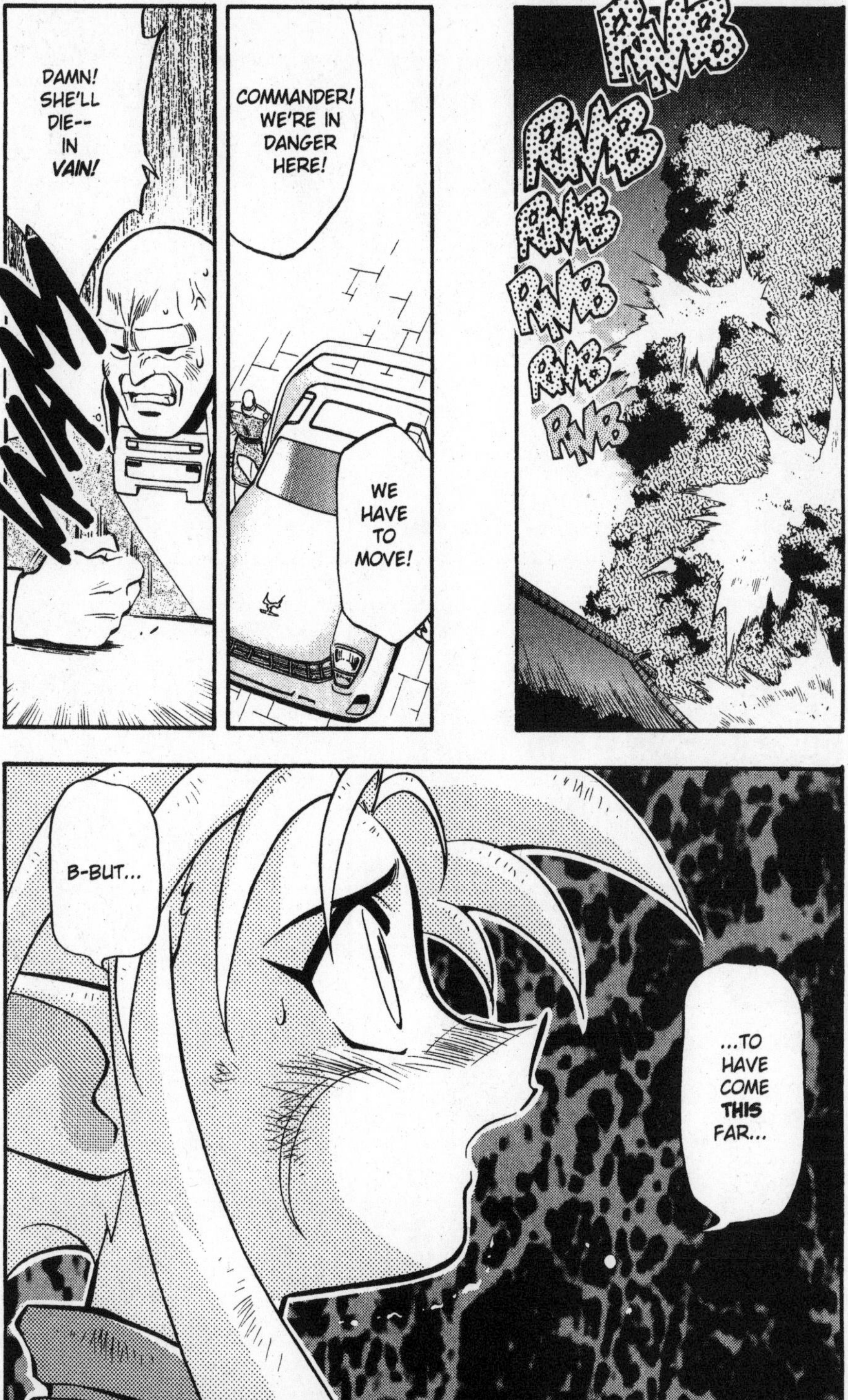
DAMN! SHE'LL DIE-- IN VAIN!
WHAM
COMMANDER! WE'RE IN DANGER HERE!
WE HAVE TO MOVE!
RMB
RMB
RMB
RMB
RMB
RMB
B-BUT...
...TO HAVE COME THIS FAR...

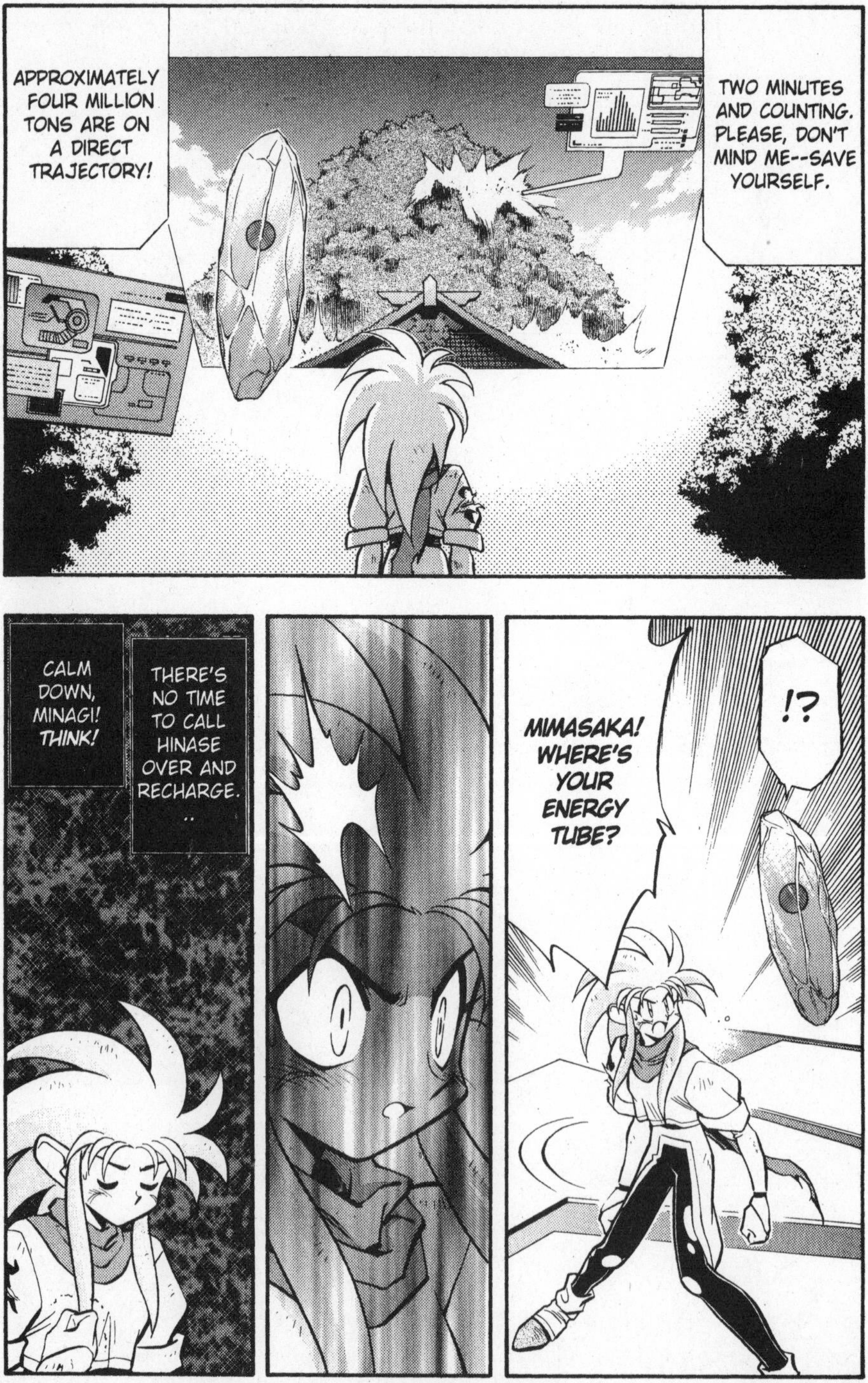
APPROXIMATELY FOUR MILLION TONS ARE ON A DIRECT TRAJECTORY!
TWO MINUTES AND COUNTING. PLEASE, DON'T MIND ME--SAVE YOURSELF.
CALM DOWN, MINAGI! THINK!
THERE'S NO TIME TO CALL HINASE OVER AND RECHARGE. ..
MIMASAKA! WHERE'S YOUR ENERGY TUBE?
!?

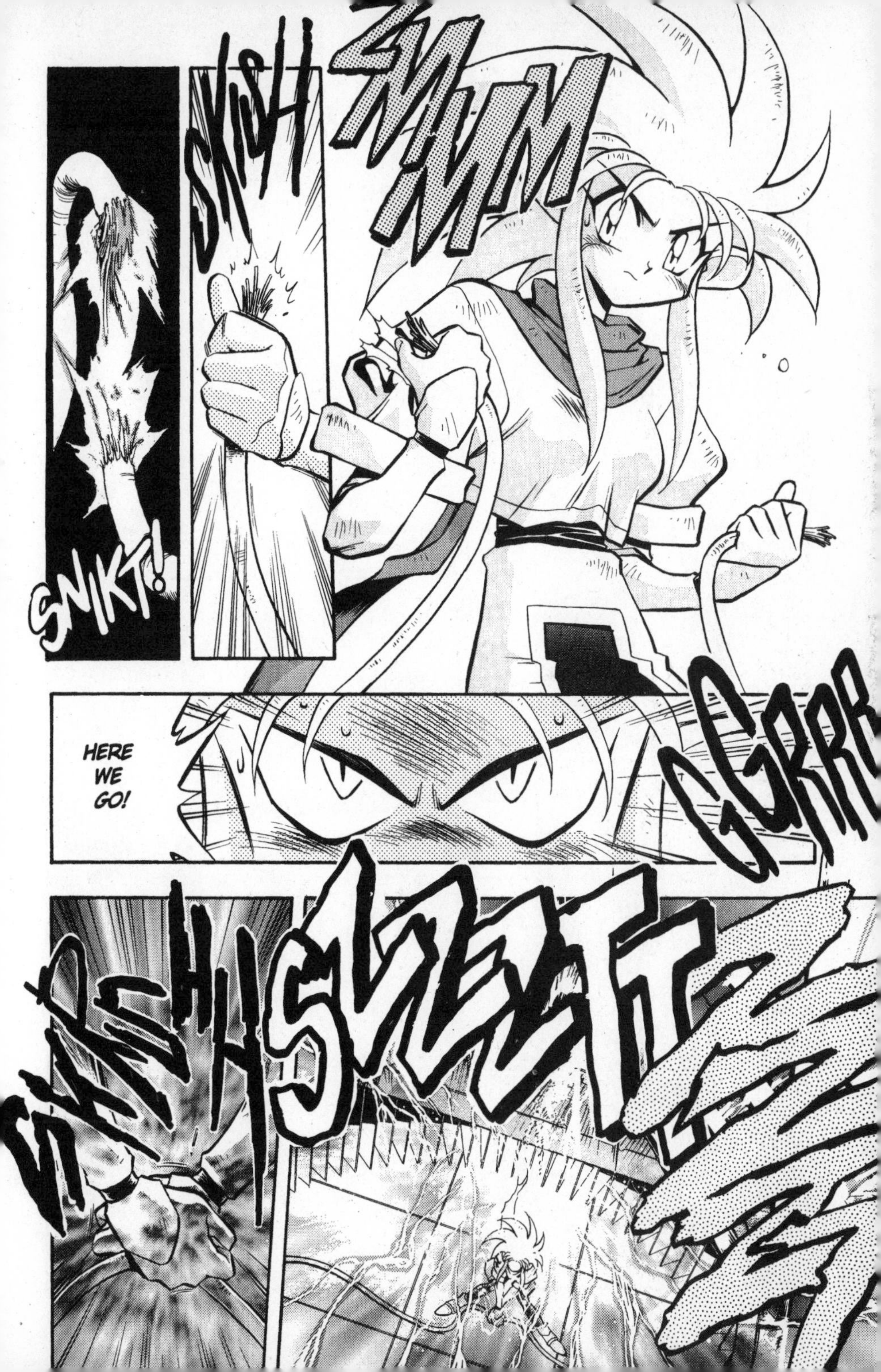
SNIKT!
HERE WE GO!

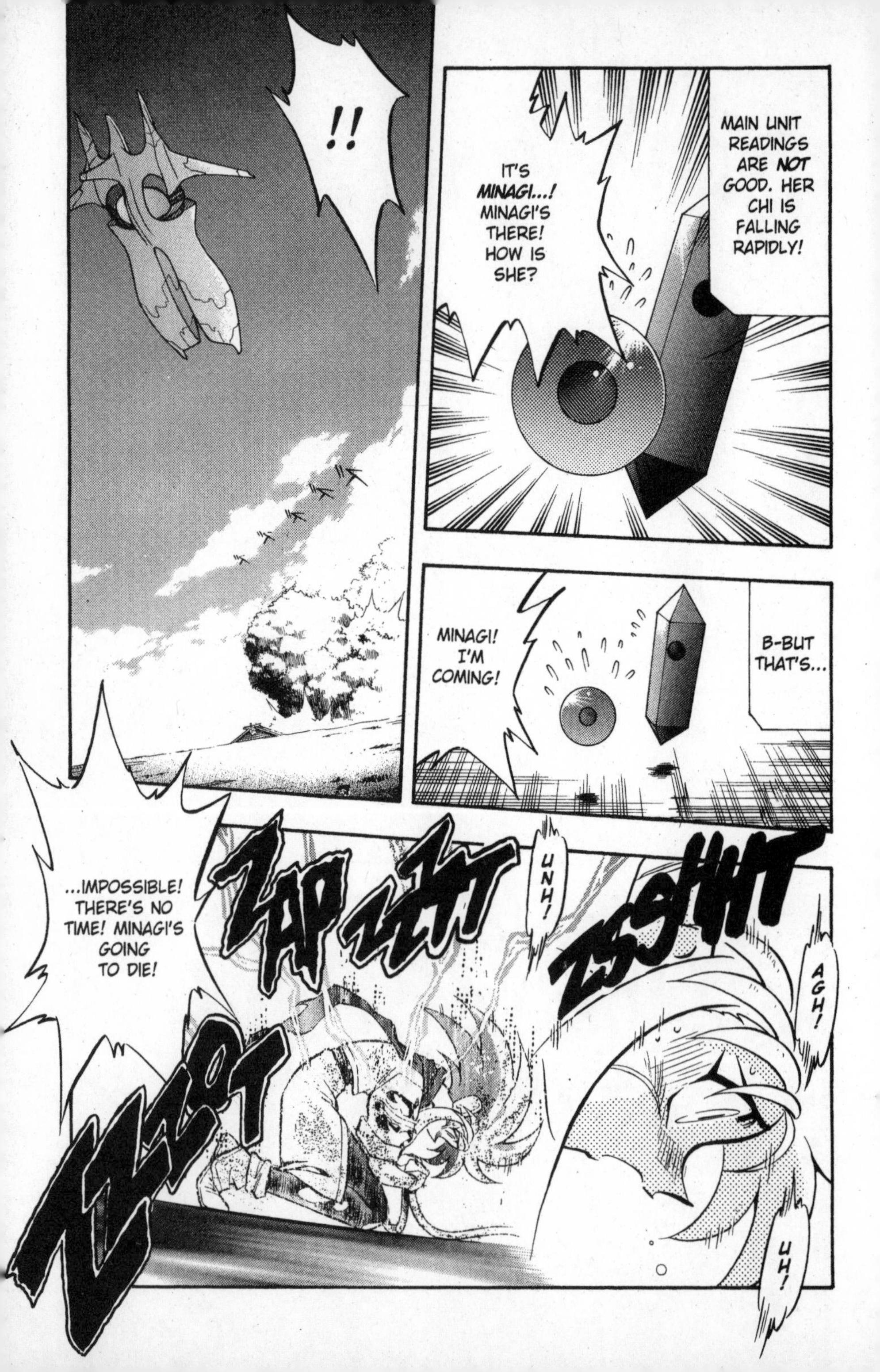
!!
IT'S MINAGI...! MINAGI'S THERE! HOW IS SHE?
MAIN UNIT READINGS ARE NOT GOOD. HER CHI IS FALLING RAPIDLY!
MINAGI! I'M COMING!
B-BUT THAT'S...
...IMPOSSIBLE! THERE'S NO TIME! MINAGI'S GOING TO DIE!
ZAP ZZZT
UNH!
ZSSHHT
AGH!
ZZZAP
UH!

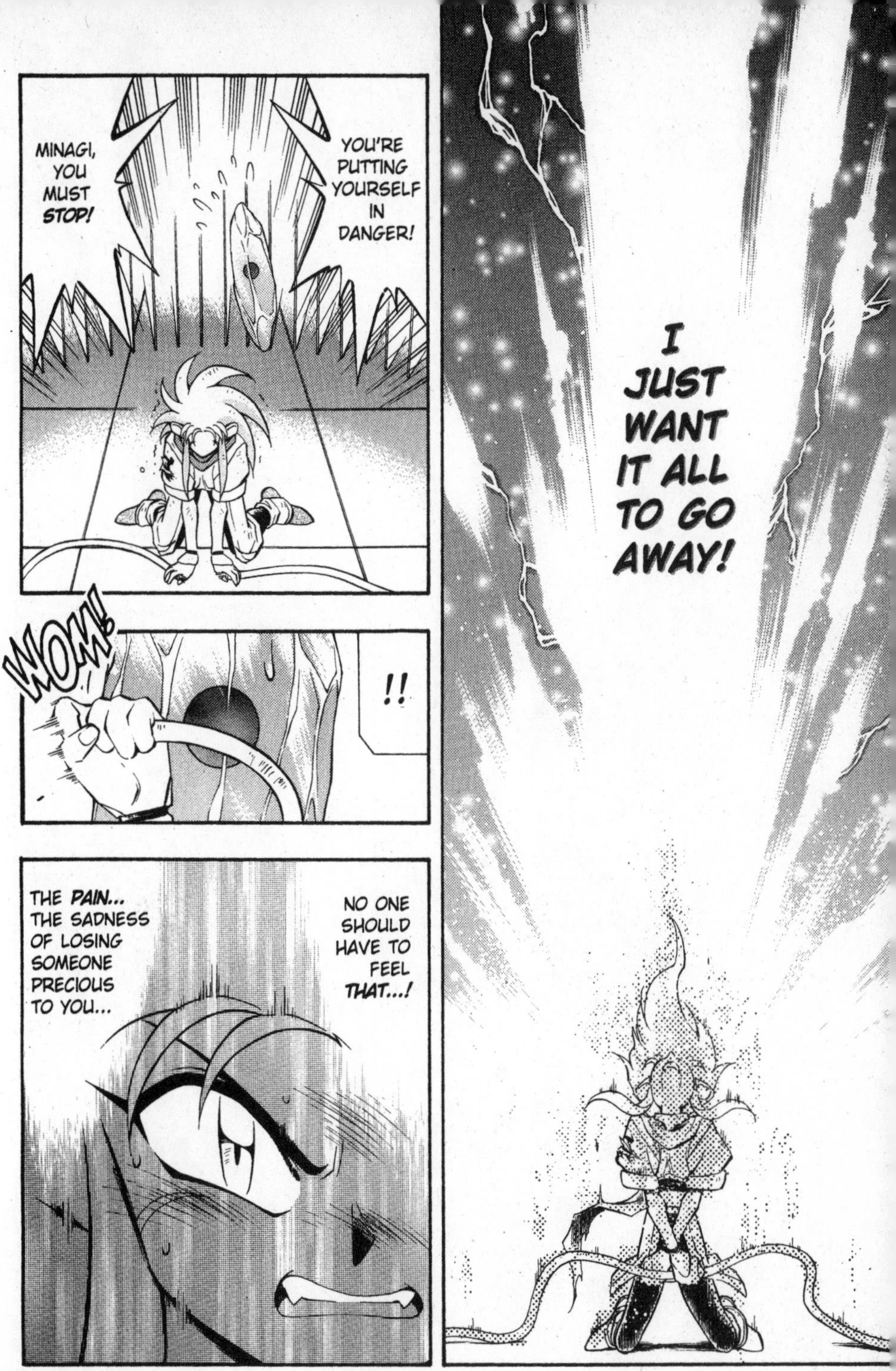
MINAGI, YOU MUST STOP!
YOU'RE PUTTING YOURSELF IN DANGER!
WOM!
!!
THE PAIN... THE SADNESS OF LOSING SOMEONE PRECIOUS TO YOU...
NO ONE SHOULD HAVE TO FEEL THAT...!
I JUST WANT IT ALL TO GO AWAY!

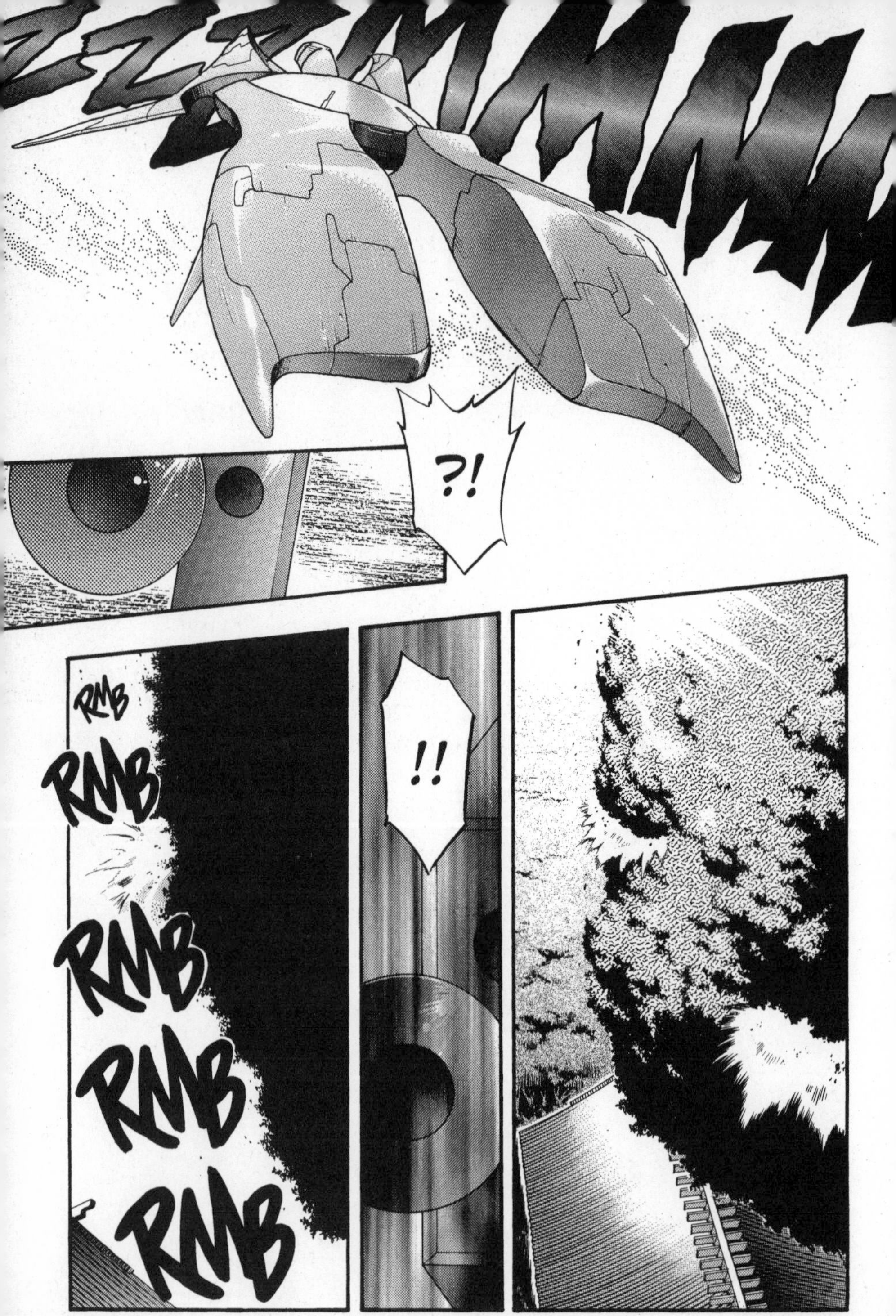

ZZZMMMM
?!
RMB
RMB
RMB
RMB
RMB
!!

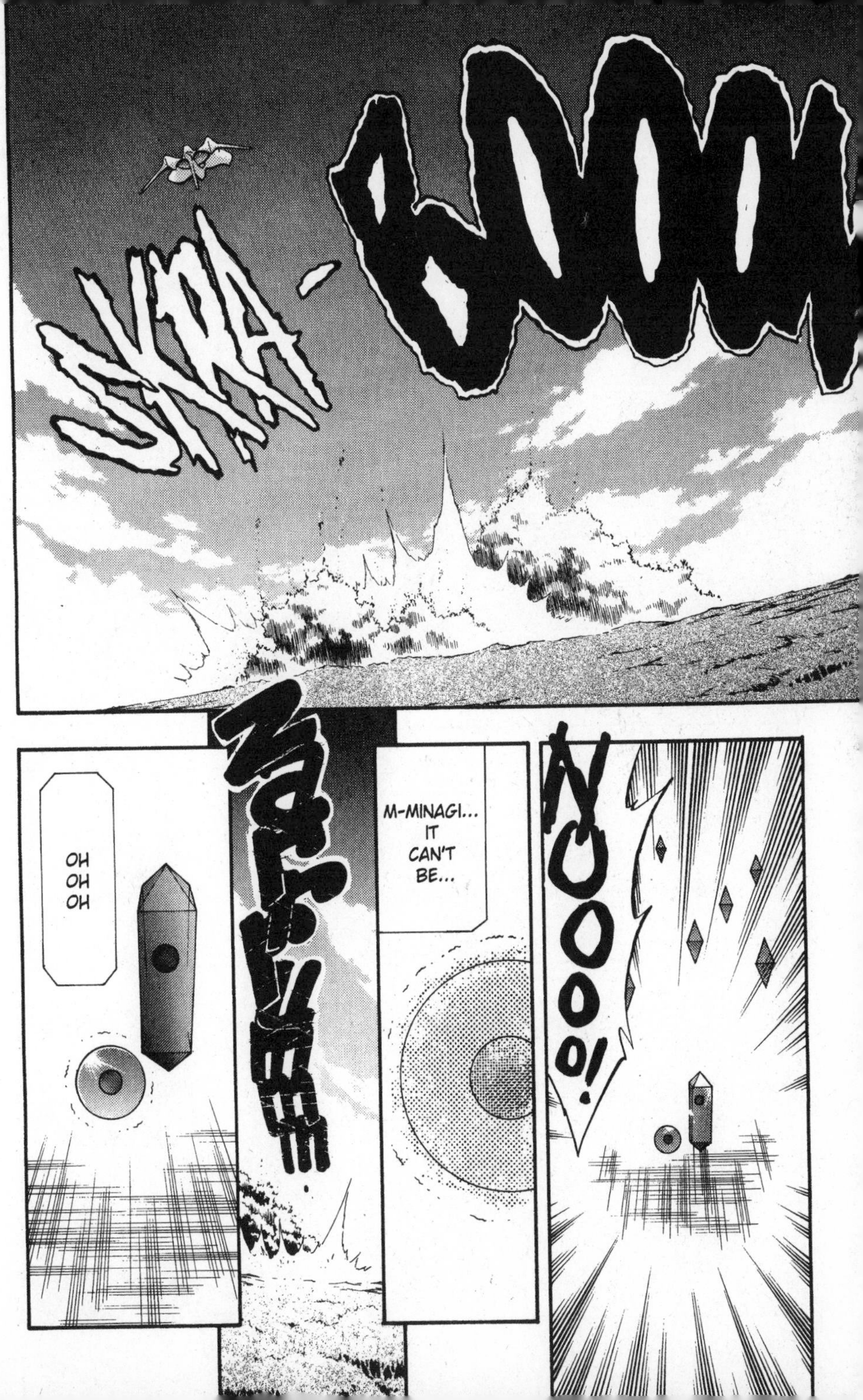
SKRA-BOOM
OH
OH
OH
M-MINAGI...
IT
CAN'T
BE...
NOOOOO!

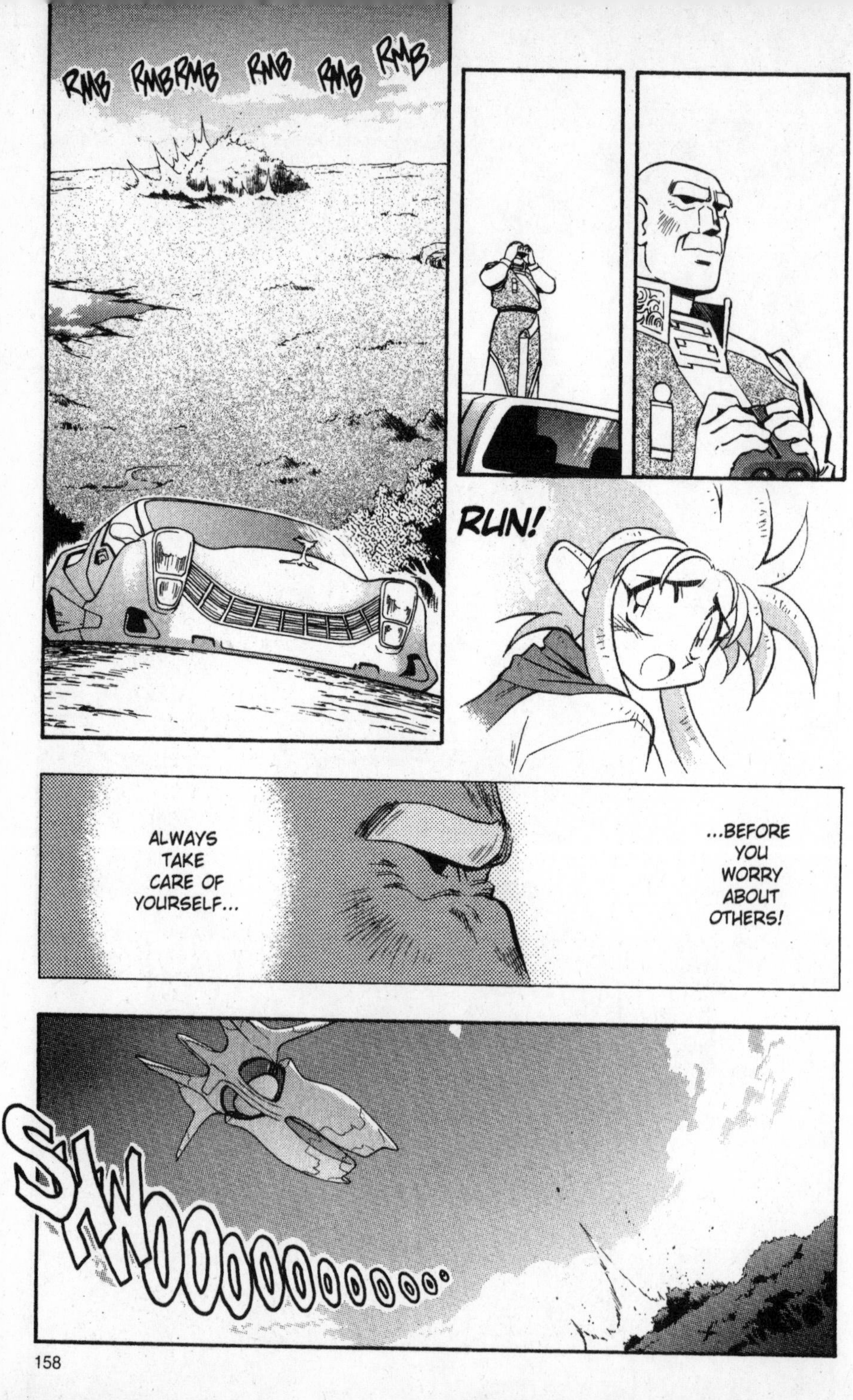
RMB RMBRMB RMB RMB RMB
RUN!
ALWAYS TAKE CARE OF YOURSELF...
...BEFORE YOU WORRY ABOUT OTHERS!
SHWOOOOOOOOOOO

HIC...! >SOB<
!
WAIT, MAIN UNIT! L-LOOK!
TH--
THAT'S... ?!
RMB RMB RMB RMB RMB

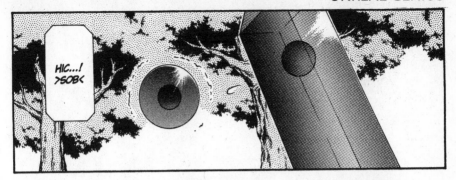

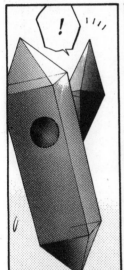

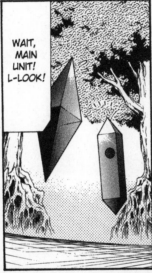

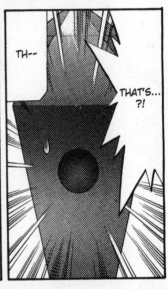

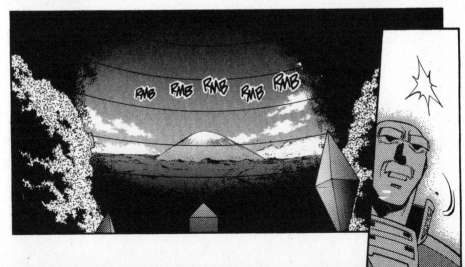

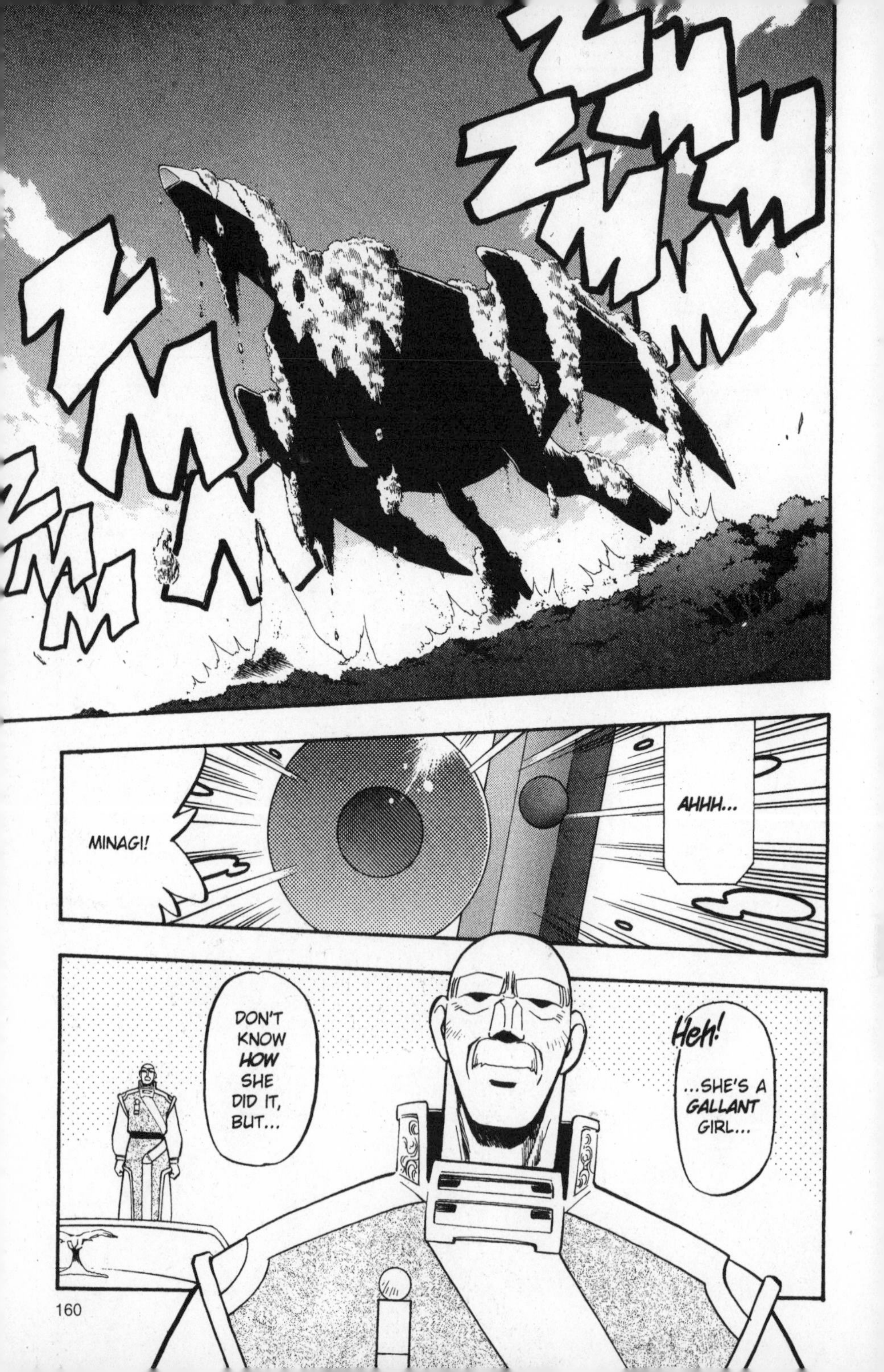
MINAGI!
AHHH...
DON'T KNOW *HOW* SHE DID IT, BUT...
Heh!
...SHE'S A *GALLANT* GIRL...

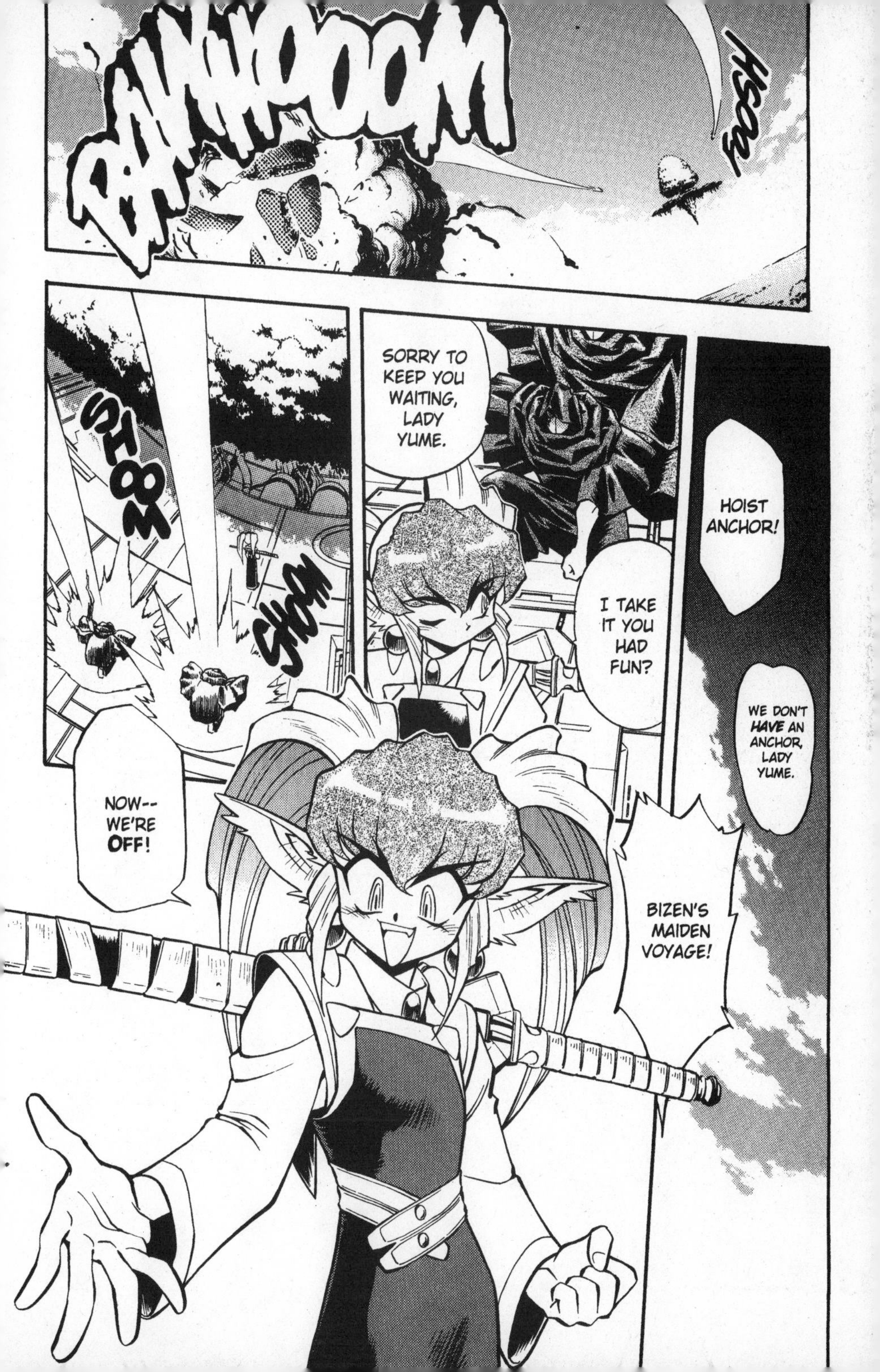
BAHWOOOM
FOOSH
SHOOM
SHOOM
SORRY TO KEEP YOU WAITING, LADY YUME.
I TAKE IT YOU HAD FUN?
HOIST ANCHOR!
WE DON'T **HAVE** AN ANCHOR, LADY YUME.
NOW-- WE'RE **OFF**!
BIZEN'S MAIDEN VOYAGE!

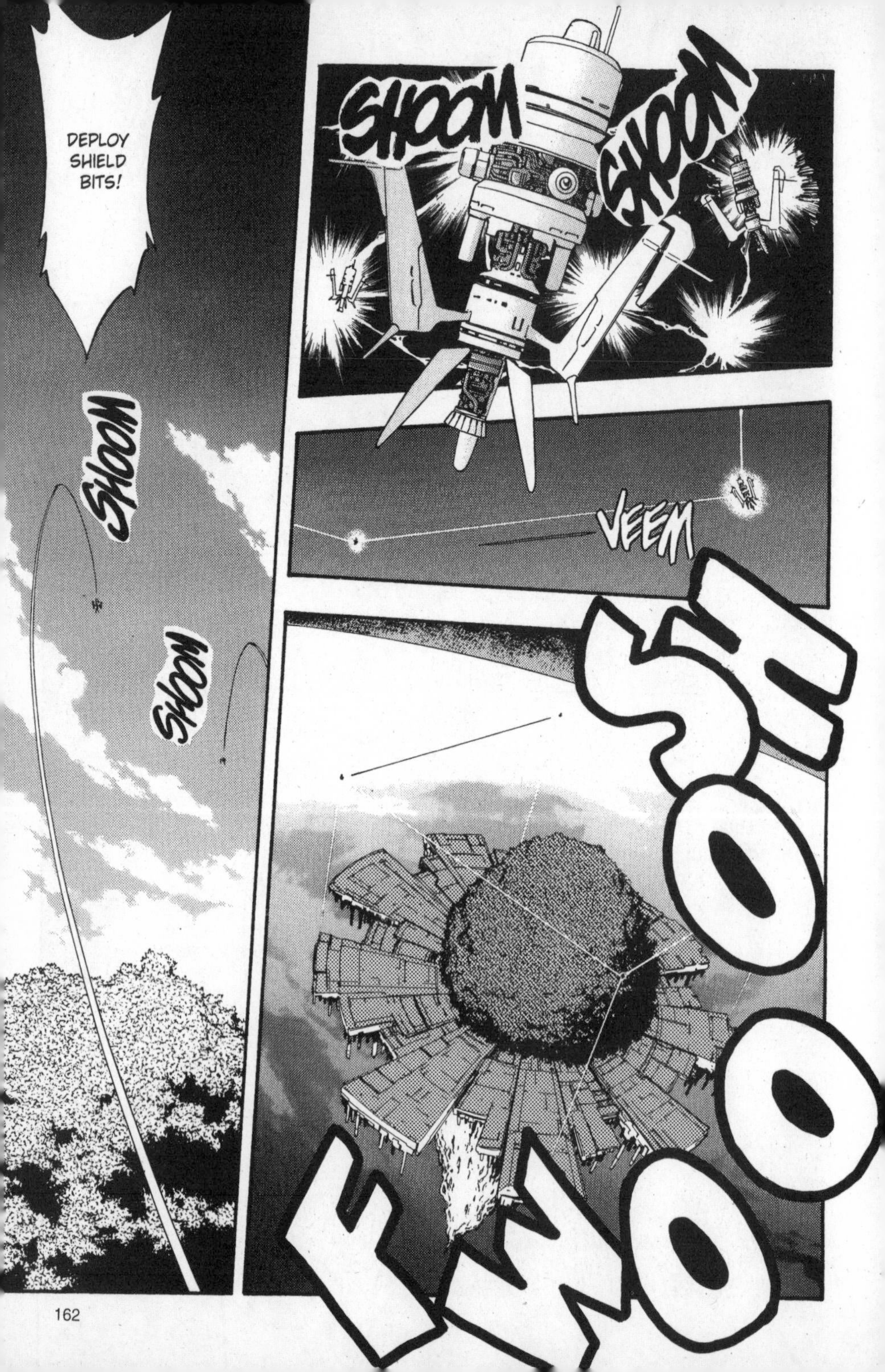
SHOOM
SHOOM
DEPLOY SHIELD BITS!
VEEM
FWOOOSH
SHOOM
SHOOM

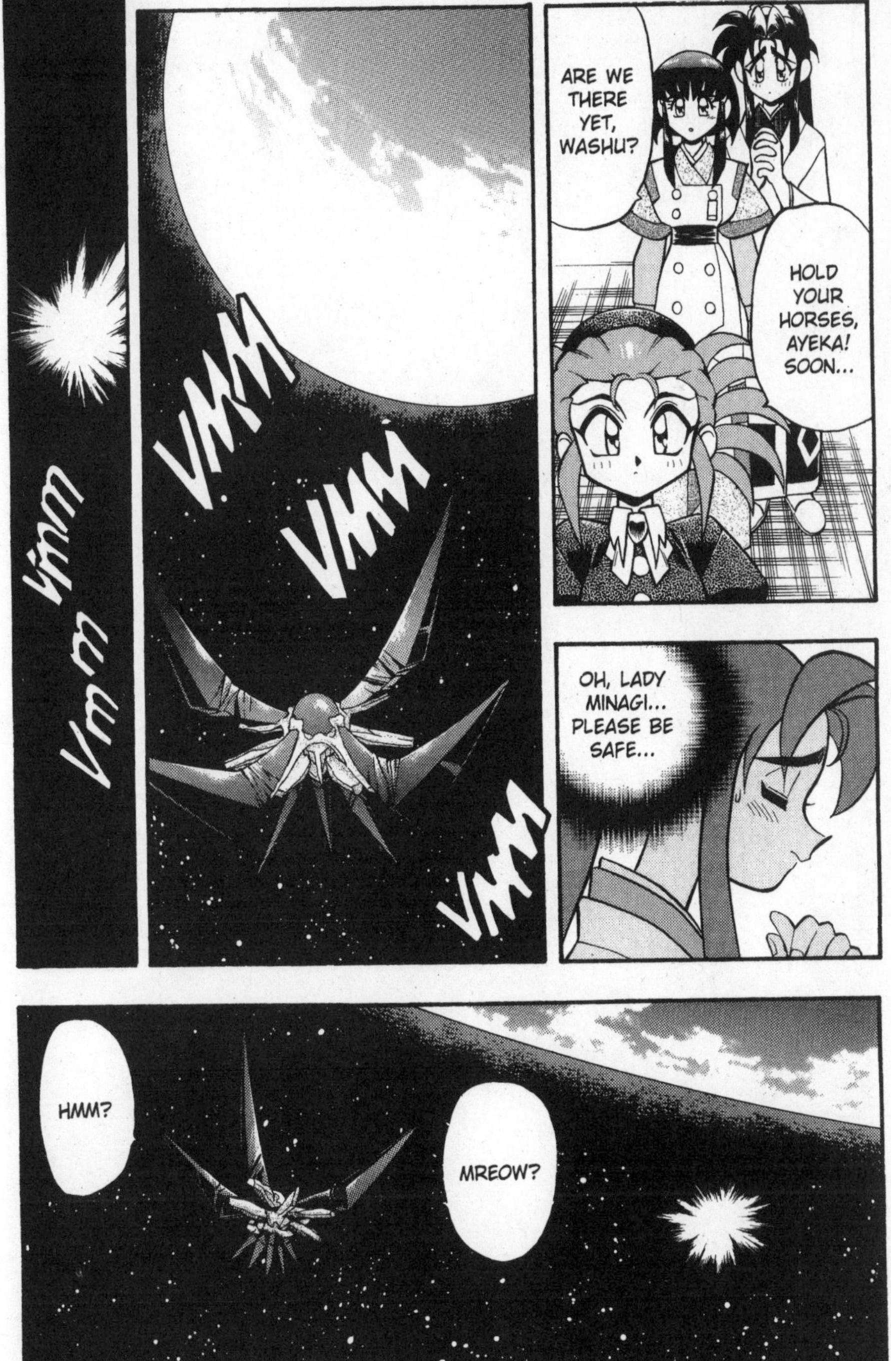
Vmm vmm
VMM
VMM
VMM
ARE WE THERE YET, WASHU?
HOLD YOUR HORSES, AYEKA! SOON...
OH, LADY MINAGI... PLEASE BE SAFE...
HMM?
MREOW?

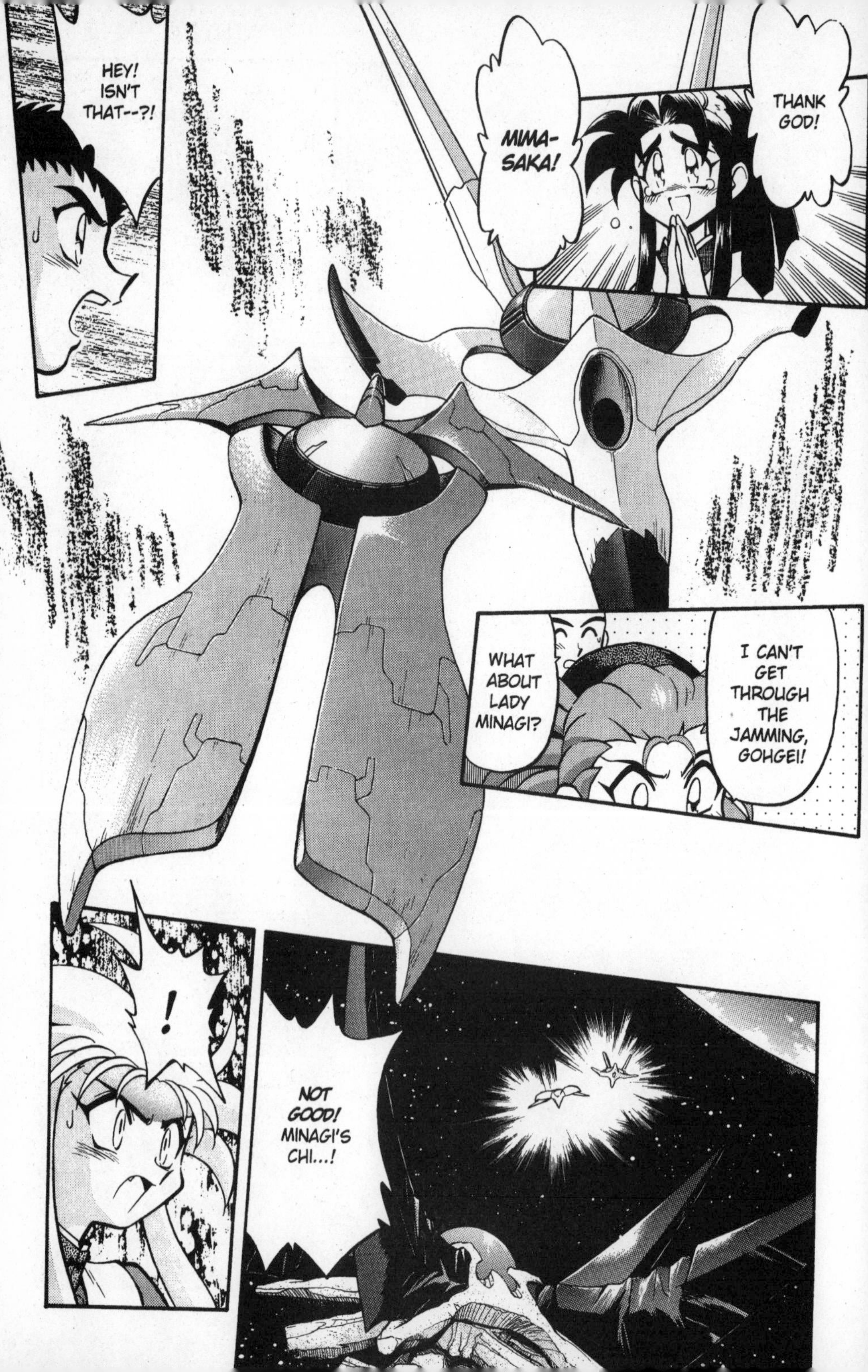
HEY! ISN'T THAT--?!
MIMA-SAKA!
THANK GOD!
WHAT ABOUT LADY MINAGI?
I CAN'T GET THROUGH THE JAMMING, GOHGEI!
!
NOT GOOD! MINAGI'S CHI...!

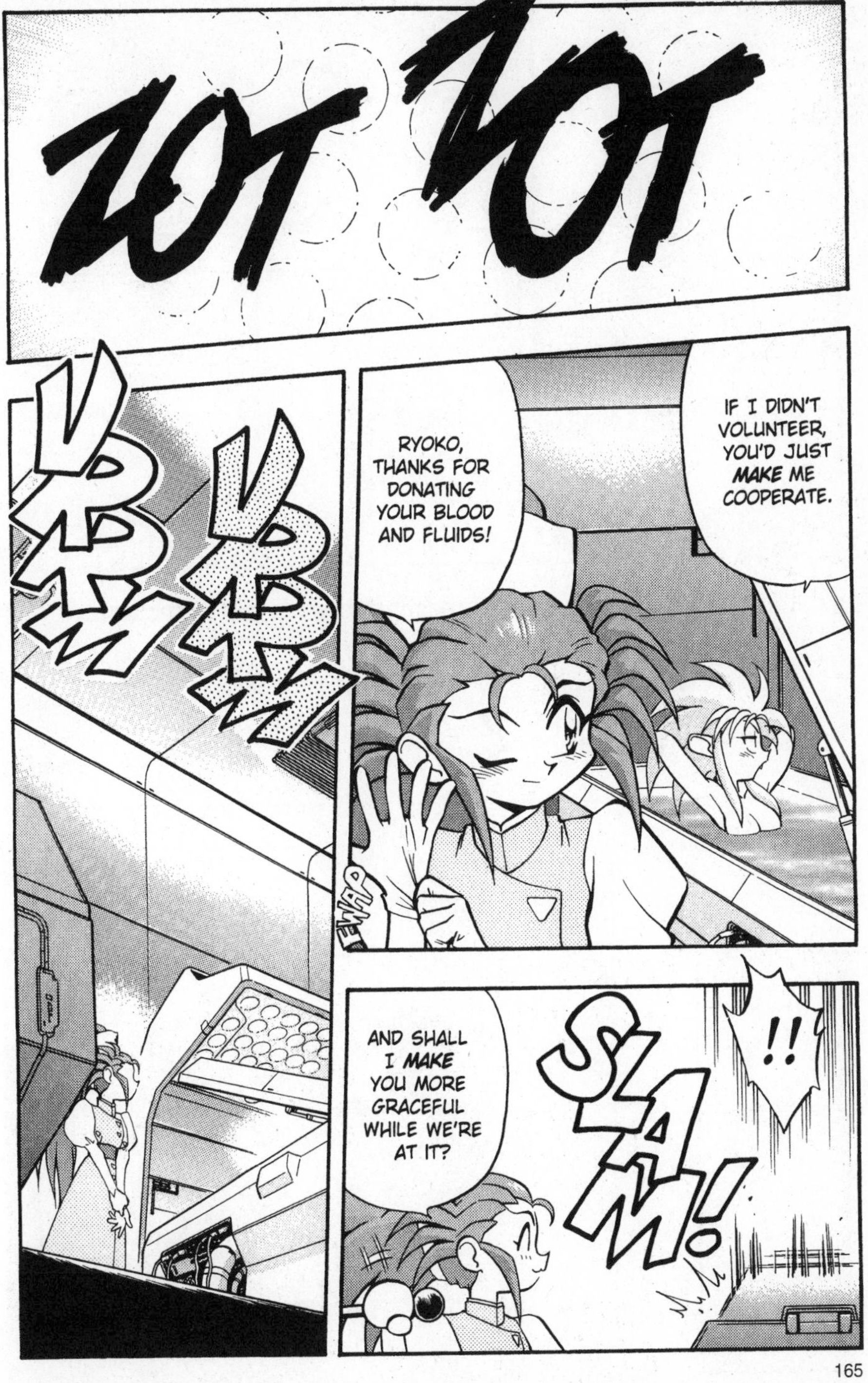
ZOT ZOT
VRRMM
VRRMM
RYOKO, THANKS FOR DONATING YOUR BLOOD AND FLUIDS!
IF I DIDN'T VOLUNTEER, YOU'D JUST MAKE ME COOPERATE.
FWAP
AND SHALL I MAKE YOU MORE GRACEFUL WHILE WE'RE AT IT?
SLAM!
!!

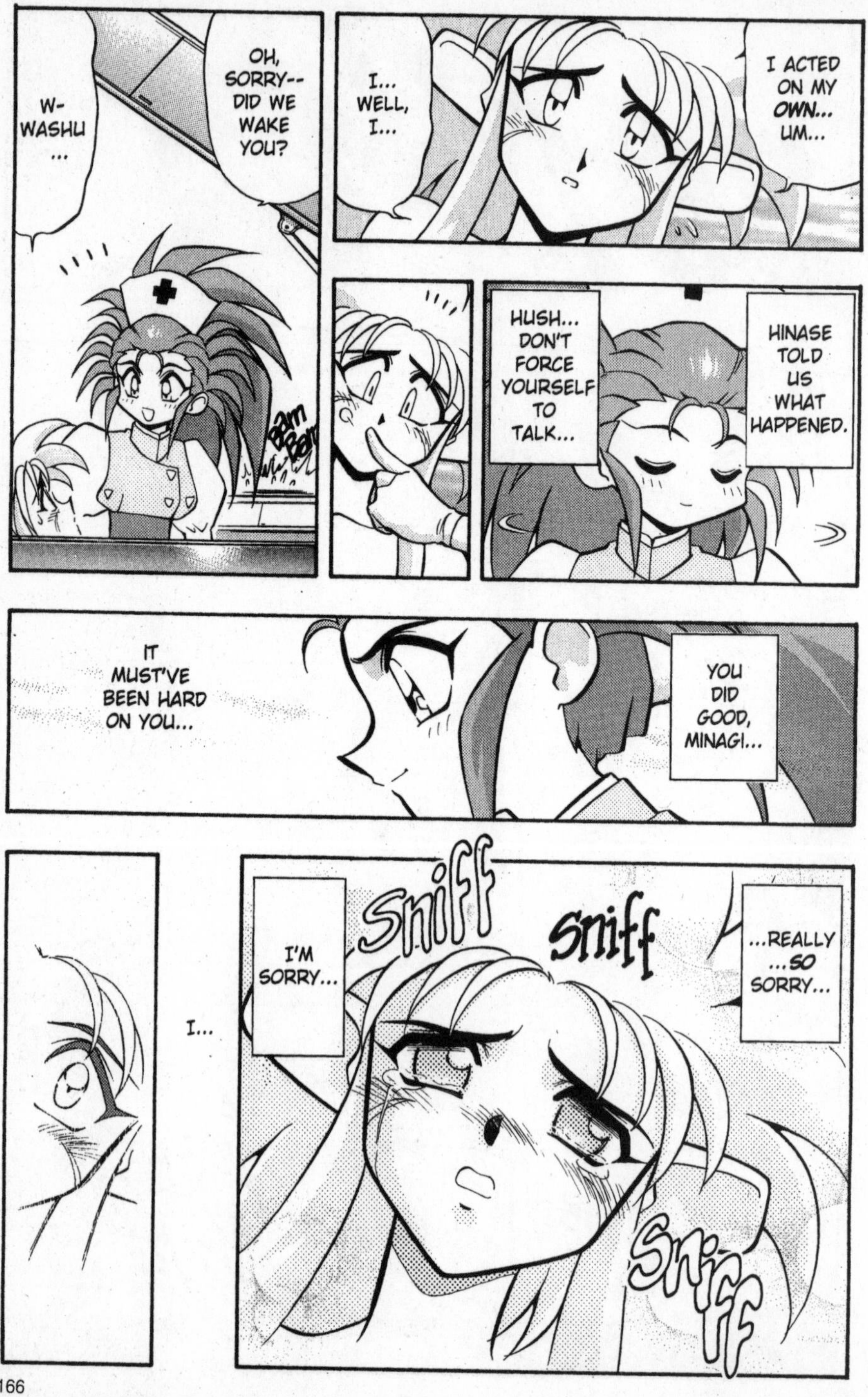
W-WASHU...
OH, SORRY--DID WE WAKE YOU?
Bam Bam
I... WELL, I...
I ACTED ON MY OWN... UM...
HUSH... DON'T FORCE YOURSELF TO TALK...
HINASE TOLD US WHAT HAPPENED.
IT MUST'VE BEEN HARD ON YOU...
YOU DID GOOD, MINAGI...
I...
I'M SORRY...
Sniff
Sniff
...REALLY ...SO SORRY...
Sniff

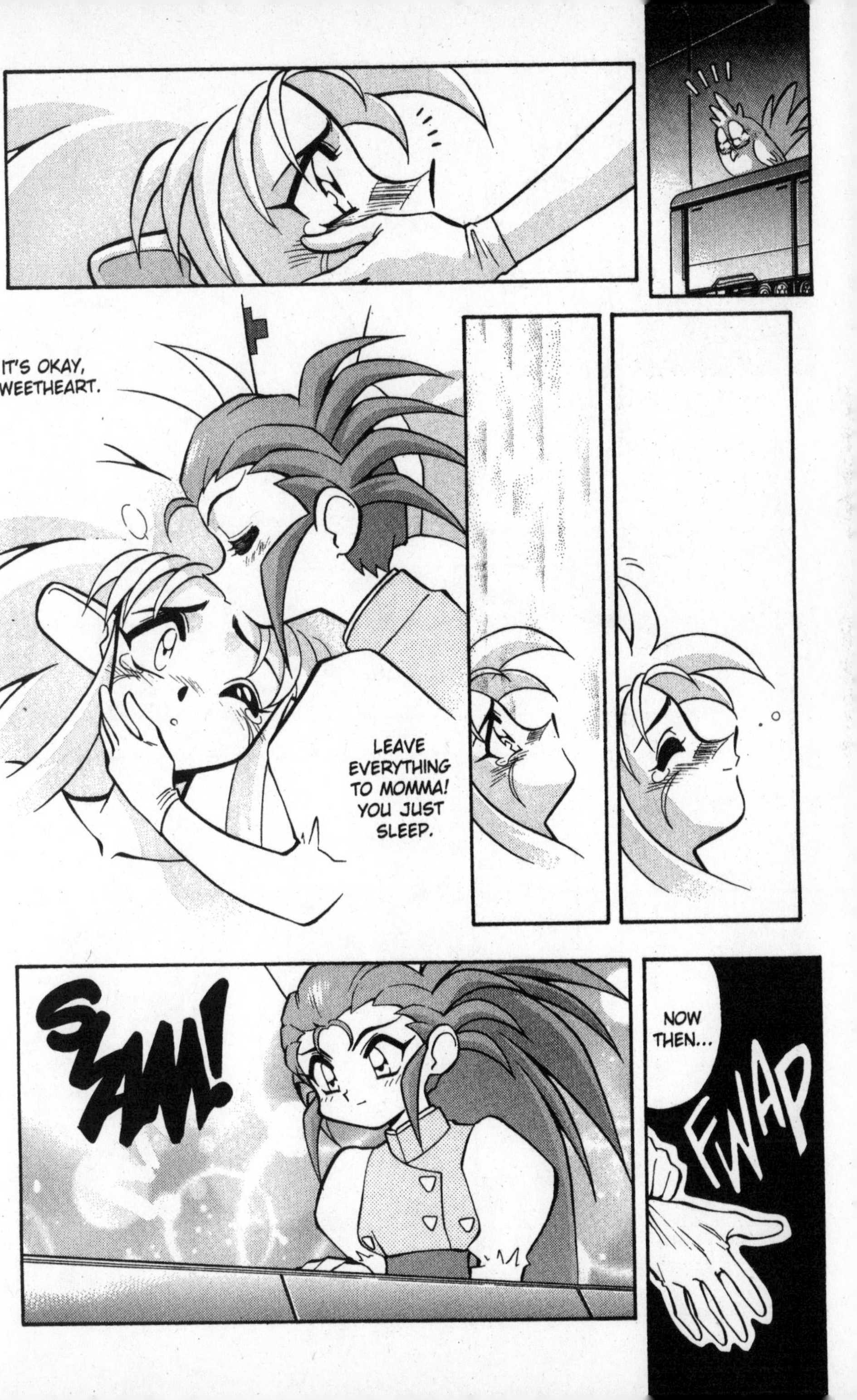
IT'S OKAY, SWEETHEART.
LEAVE EVERYTHING TO MOMMA! YOU JUST SLEEP.
SLAM!
NOW THEN...
FWAP

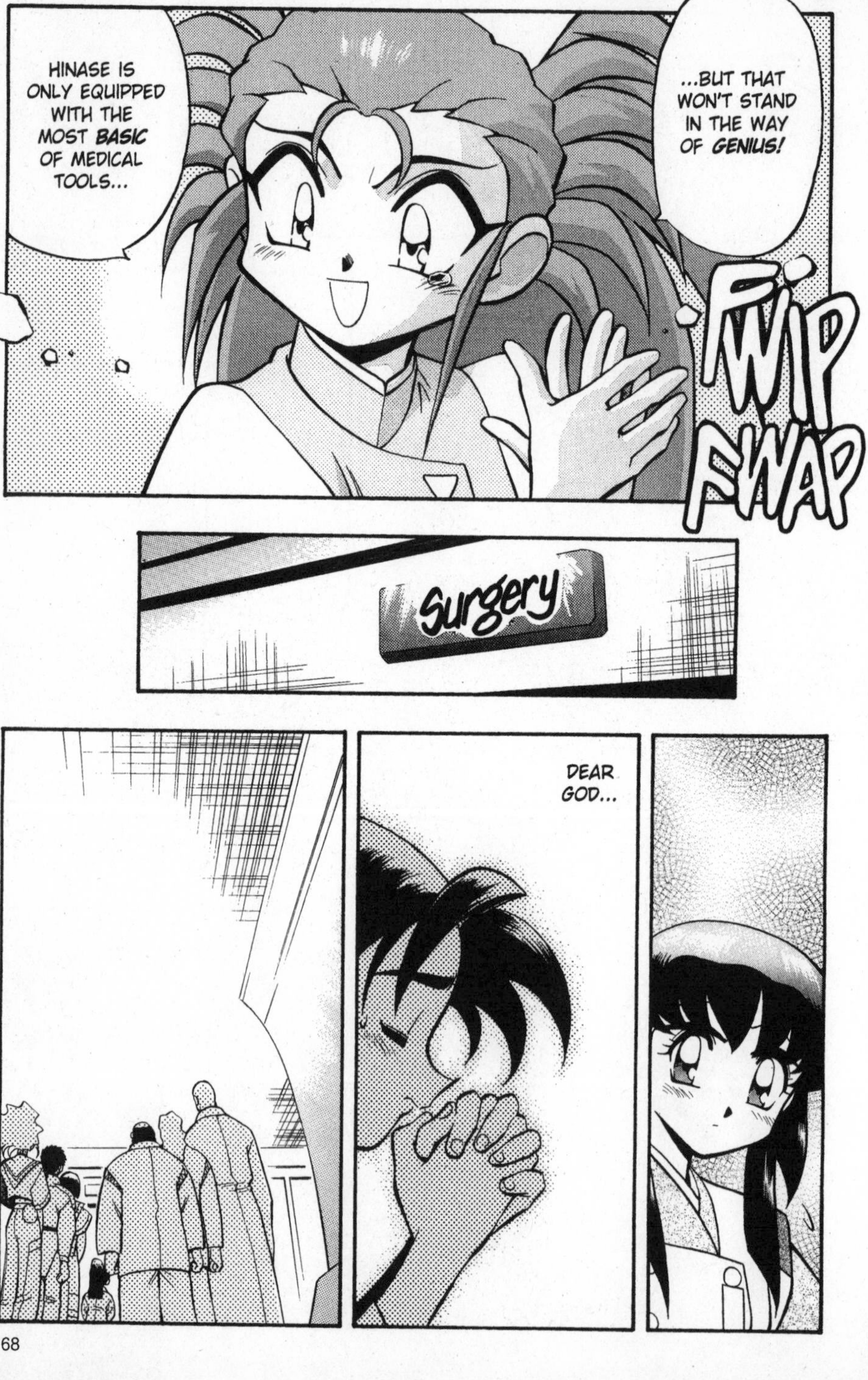
HINASE IS ONLY EQUIPPED WITH THE MOST BASIC OF MEDICAL TOOLS...
...BUT THAT WON'T STAND IN THE WAY OF GENIUS!
FWIP FWAP
Surgery
DEAR GOD...

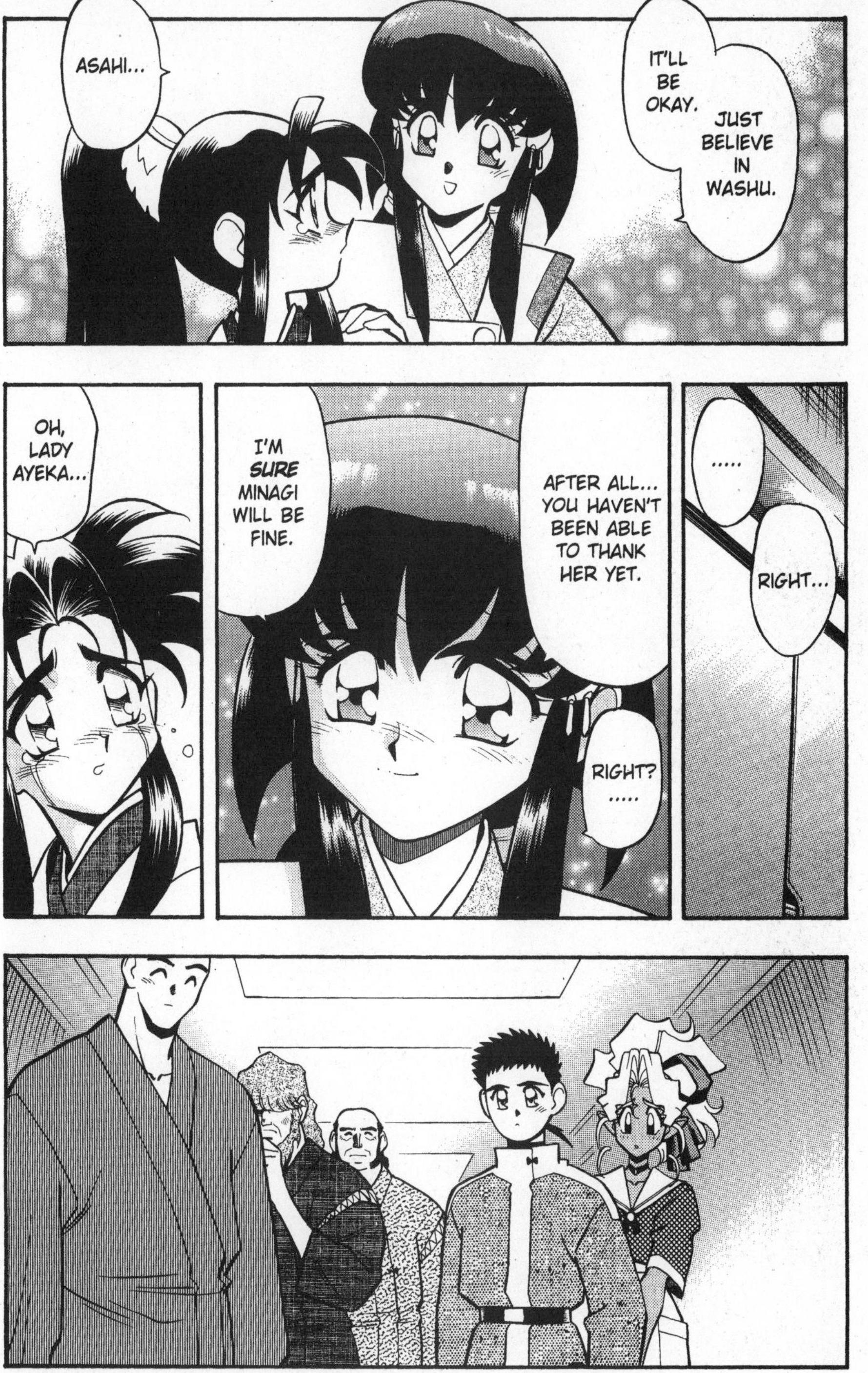
ASAHI...
IT'LL BE OKAY.
JUST BELIEVE IN WASHU.
OH, LADY AYEKA...
I'M **SURE** MINAGI WILL BE FINE.
AFTER ALL... YOU HAVEN'T BEEN ABLE TO THANK HER YET.
RIGHT? .....
.....
RIGHT...

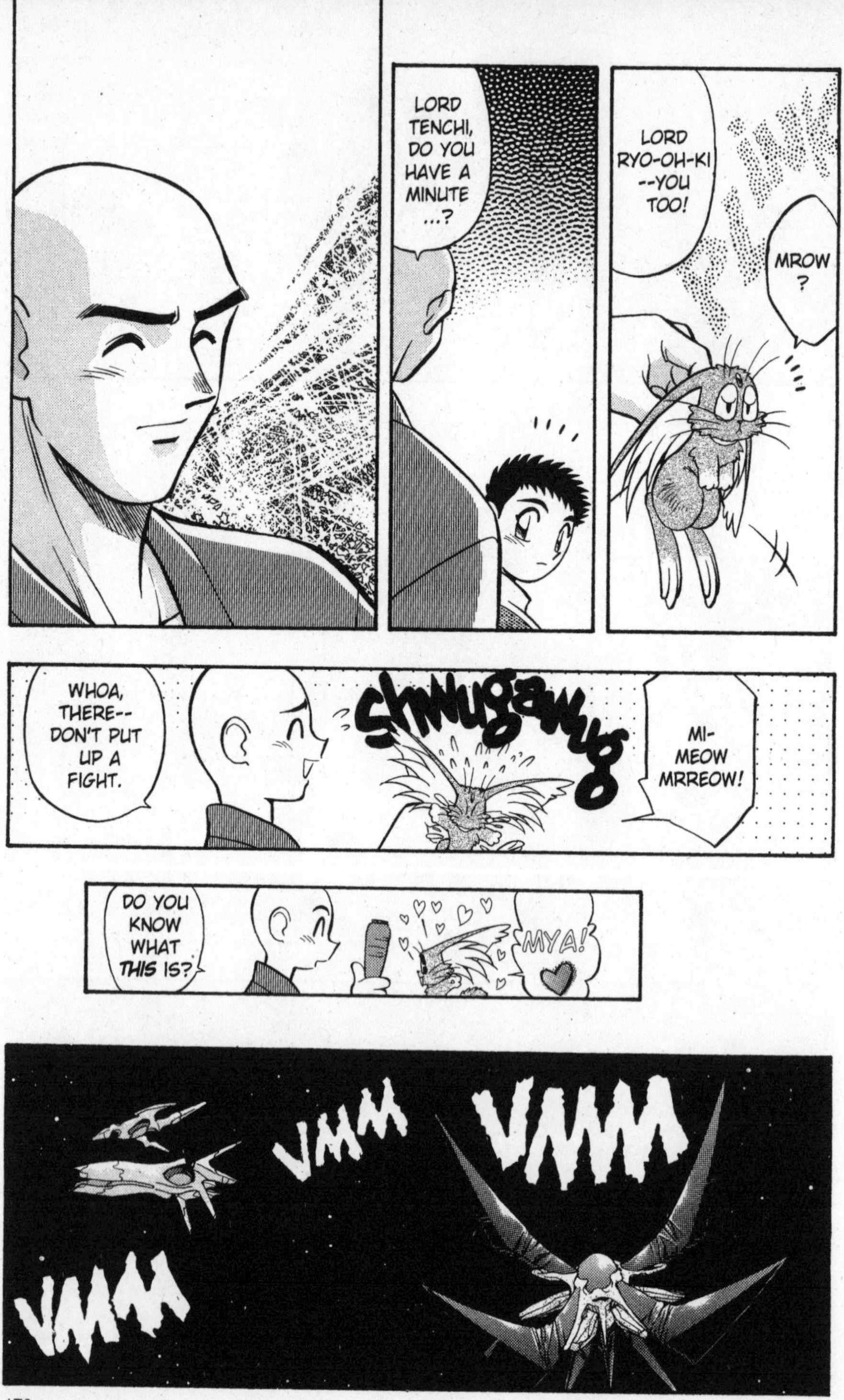
LORD TENCHI, DO YOU HAVE A MINUTE ...?
LORD RYO-OH-KI --YOU TOO!
MROW ?
WHOA, THERE-- DON'T PUT UP A FIGHT.
SHNNUGAWUG
MI-MEOW MRREOW!
DO YOU KNOW WHAT *THIS* IS?
MYA!
VMM
VMM
VMM

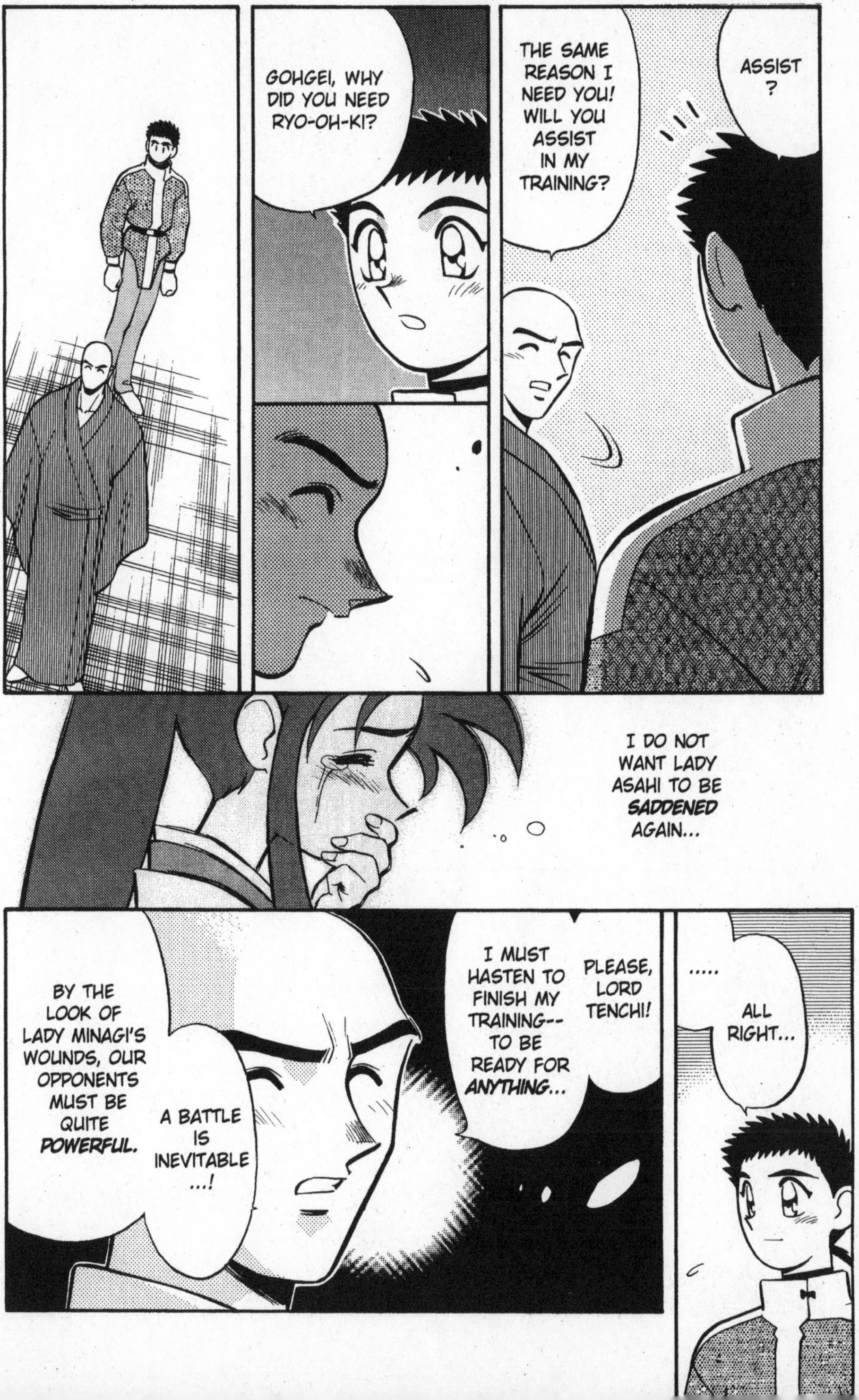
GOHGEI, WHY DID YOU NEED RYO-OH-KI?
THE SAME REASON I NEED YOU! WILL YOU ASSIST IN MY TRAINING?
ASSIST ?
I DO NOT WANT LADY ASAHI TO BE SADDENED AGAIN...
BY THE LOOK OF LADY MINAGI'S WOUNDS, OUR OPPONENTS MUST BE QUITE POWERFUL.
A BATTLE IS INEVITABLE ...!
I MUST HASTEN TO FINISH MY TRAINING-- TO BE READY FOR ANYTHING...
PLEASE, LORD TENCHI!
.....
ALL RIGHT...

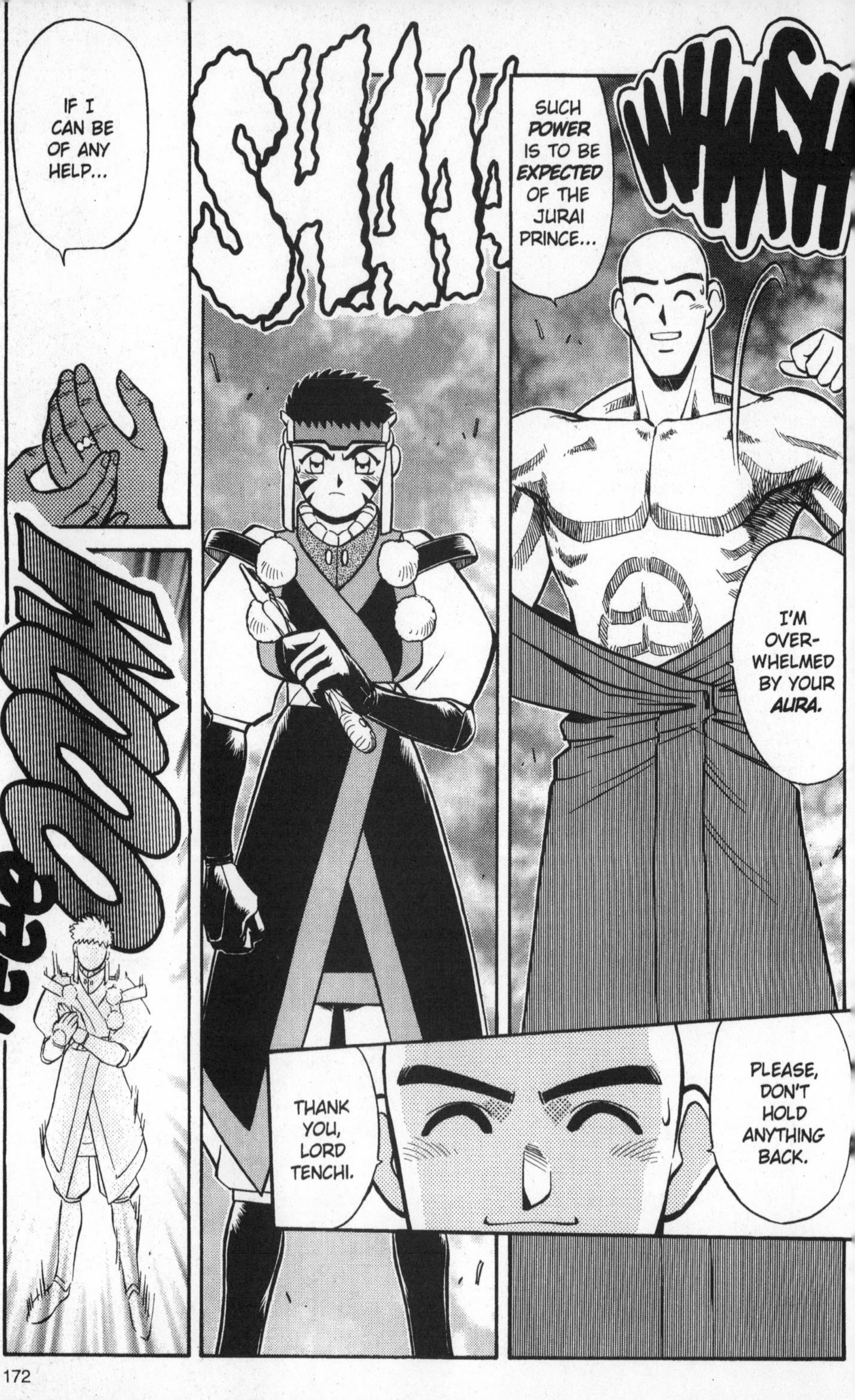
IF I CAN BE OF ANY HELP...
veeOOOM
SHAA
SUCH POWER IS TO BE EXPECTED OF THE JURAI PRINCE...
WHUSH
I'M OVER-WHELMED BY YOUR AURA.
THANK YOU, LORD TENCHI.
PLEASE, DON'T HOLD ANYTHING BACK.

SIGH...

IT'S ALL SO ODD.

THIS INTERFERENCE PATTER-- DEFINITELY *FAR* FROM NORMAL.

I SECRETLY FOLLOWED LADY MIHOSHI HERE BECAUSE I WAS SO WORRIED...

...BUT, OH DEAR, GETTING IN TOUCH WITH HER NOW *WILL* BE DIFFICULT.

BRRRP! BRRRP!

VISUAL CONTACT WITH A SHIP AHEAD-- OFF THE PORT BOW!

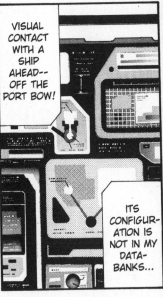

ITS CONFIGUR- ATION IS NOT IN MY DATA- BANKS...

ZMM ZMM ZMM ZMM ZMM

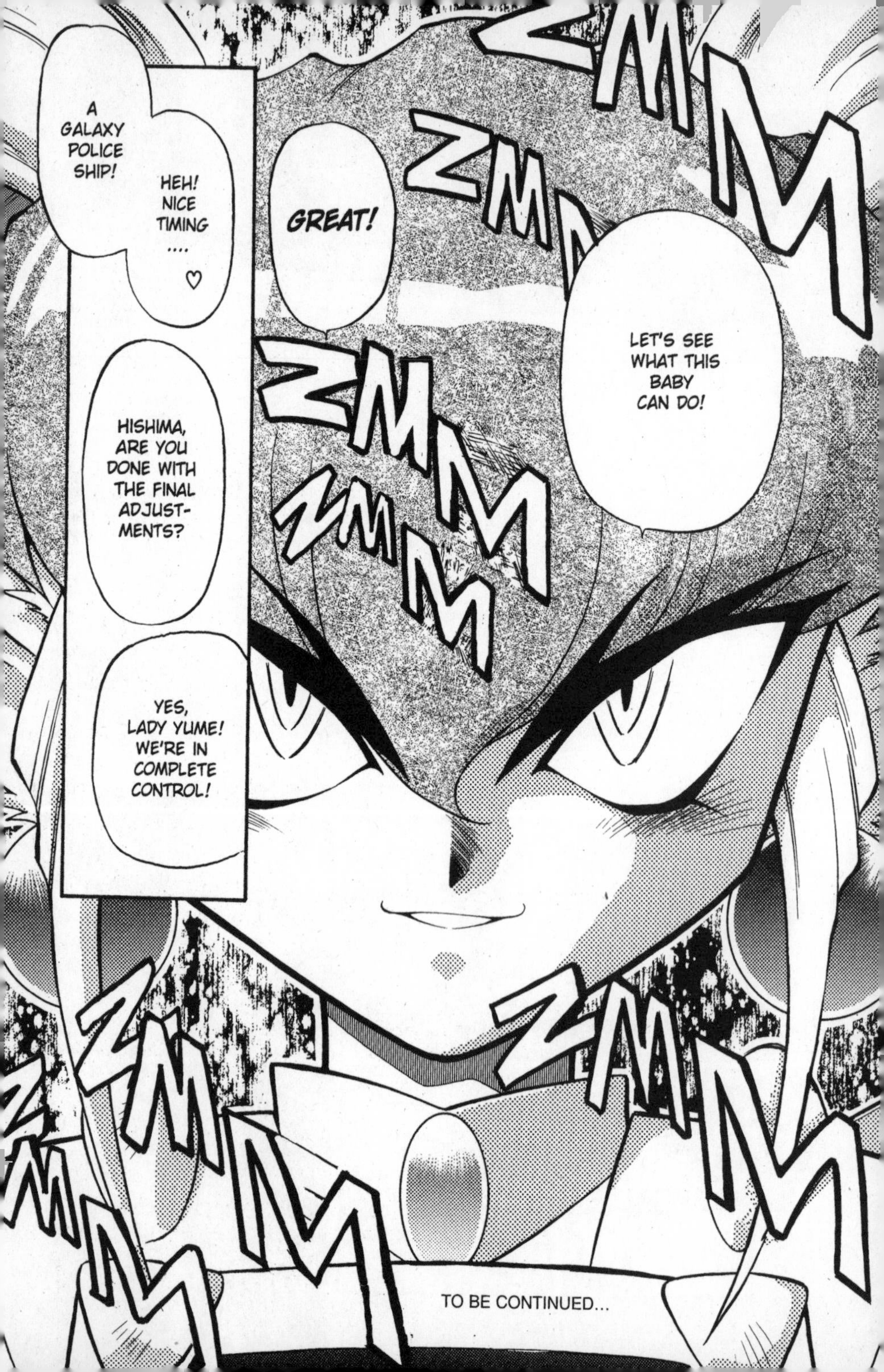
A GALAXY POLICE SHIP!
HEH! NICE TIMING .... ♡
HISHIMA, ARE YOU DONE WITH THE FINAL ADJUSTMENTS?
YES, LADY YUME! WE'RE IN COMPLETE CONTROL!
GREAT!
ZMMM
ZMMM
LET'S SEE WHAT THIS BABY CAN DO!
ZMMM
ZMMM
ZMMM
ZMMM
TO BE CONTINUED...

DISCOVER THE WORLD OF VIZ GRAPHIC NOVELS!

NEON GENESIS EVANGELION

The most controversial anime and manga of the 1990s! In 2015, half the human race is dead, and the survivors face a terrifying last judgment from giant "Angels." Within Tokyo-3 and the headquarters of the secret organization NERV, a handful of teenagers are trained to pilot the colossal "Evangelions" and battle the Angels on their own terms...whatever the cost to their minds and souls.

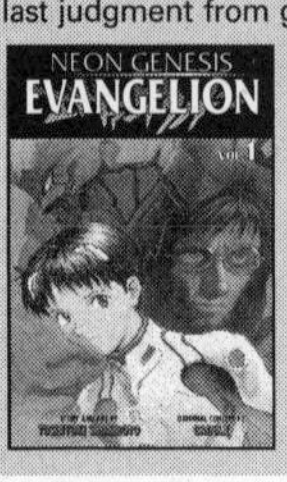
NEON GENESIS
EVANGELION

by Yoshiyuki Sadamoto
168-176 pages each

VOLUME	PRICE
1 (Regular or Special Collectors' Edition)	$15.95
2 (Regular or Special Collectors' Edition)	$15.95

STRIKER

Violent, cinematic action-adventure! The Arcam Foundation ensures that deadly relics of an ancient civilization stay out of the wrong hands. Against zombies, bioweapons, and cyborg troops, one Arcam operative is always on the front lines...Yu Ominae, overworked high school student and super-powered secret agent!

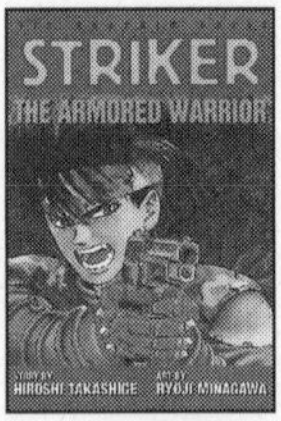
STRIKER
THE ARMORED WARRIOR
HIROSHI TAKASHIGE
RYOJI MINAGAWA

story by Hiroshi Takashige
art by Ryoji Minagawa
160-248 pages each

VOLUME	PRICE
The Armored Warrior	$16.95
The Forest of No Return	$15.95
Striker vs. The Third Reich	$15.95

INU-YASHA

When Japanese schoolgirl Kagome stumbles through a boarded-up well within an ancient shrine, she falls back in time to sixteenth-century Japan. There she becomes the master—and friend—of the feral half-demon Inu-Yasha, and the protector of the magical Shikon Jewel against the demons of the present and past!

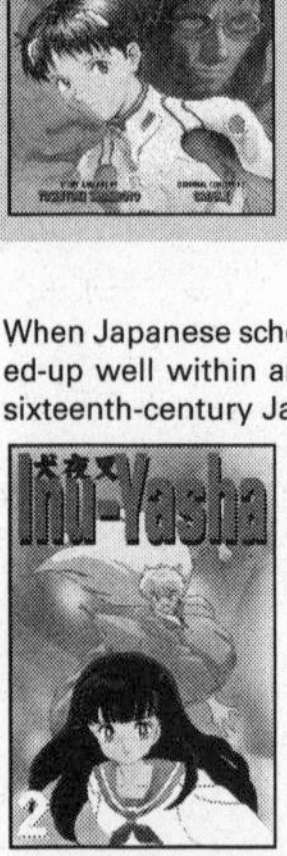
Inu-Yasha

by Rumiko Takahashi
178-192 pages each

VOLUME	PRICE
#1	$15.95
#2	$15.95
#3	$15.95

STEAM DETECTIVES

Cliffhanging retro-future action! It is a past that never was—the Age of Steam—where masked dandies, dastardly supervillains, and sentient machines stalk the Gothic streets of Steam City by night. Are the wits and reflexes of wünderkind detective Narutaki, pretty nurse Ling Ling, and their robot Goriki enough to thwart evil and unravel the mysteries of this strange world?

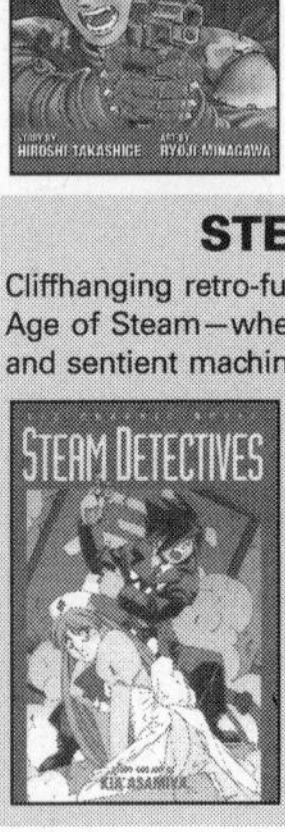
STEAM DETECTIVES
KIA ASAMIYA

by Kia Asamiya
200 pages

VOLUME	PRICE
#1	$15.95

BATTLE ANGEL ALITA

When Doc Ido finds Alita, she's lost all memory of her past—but she still remembers the *Panzer Kunst*, the greatest cyborg martial art ever! Bounty hunter, singer, racer, killer: as Alita's past unfolds, every day is a struggle for survival...

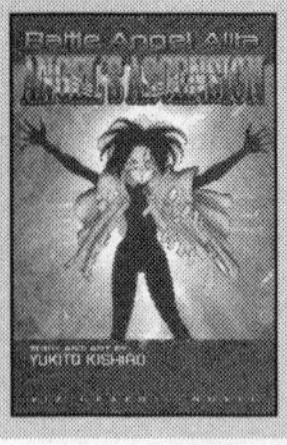
Battle Angel Alita
YUKITO KISHIRO

by Yukito Kishiro **184-244 pages each**

VOLUME	PRICE
Battle Angel Alita	$16.95
Tears of an Angel	$15.95
Killing Angel	$15.95
Angel of Victory	$15.95
Angel of Redemption	$15.95
Angel of Death	$15.95
Angel of Chaos	$15.95
Fallen Angel	$15.95
Angel's Ascension	$16.95

RANMA 1/2

When Ranma and his dad touch cold water, Papa turns into a panda and male Ranma becomes a buxom girl. Hot water reverses the effect—but only until the next time! Chased by suitors of both sexes, challenged by nutty martial artists... What's a half-guy, half-girl to do?

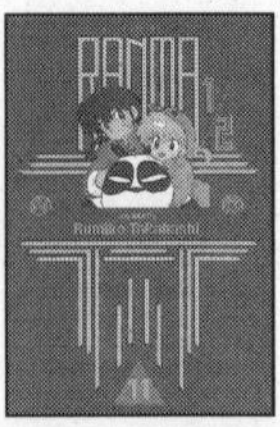

by Rumiko Takahashi **184-302 pages each**

VOL.	PRICE	VOL.	PRICE
#1	$16.95	#7	$15.95
#2	$15.95	#8	$15.95
#3	$15.95	#9	$15.95
#4	$15.95	#10	$15.95
#5	$15.95	#11	$15.95
#6	$15.95	#12	$15.95
		#13	$15.95

NO NEED FOR TENCHI!

New adventures starring the cast of the hit comedy anime ***Tenchi Muyô!*** When schoolboy Tenchi accidentally releases the legendary demon Ryoko from his grandfather's shrine, her friends and enemies soon follow. Now, surrounded by attractive, temperamental alien women, will this poor earth boy stay sane?

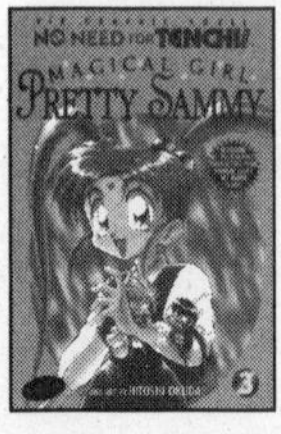
NO NEED FOR TENCHI!
MAGICAL GIRL
PRETTY SAMMY

by Hitoshi Okuda **176-184 pages each**

VOLUME	PRICE
No Need for Tenchi!	$15.95
Sword Play	$15.95
Magical Girl Pretty Sammy	$15.95
Samurai Space Opera	$15.95
Unreal Genius *(available April 1999)*	$15.95

STRAIN

Life in Kuala Lumpur is cheap...and it's about to get cheaper! Assassin Mayo will kill anyone for just $5, and as a Japanese syndicate starts its takeover of Asia, his services are in demand. But even Mayo cannot remain neutral when a teenage prostitute seeks his help in the fight against a megalomanical aristocrat obsessed with purifying his 'strain'...

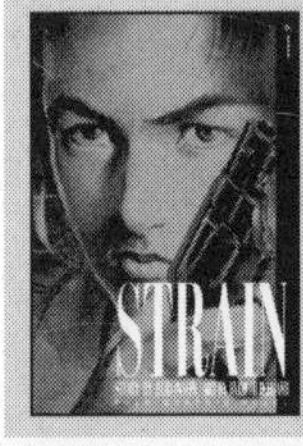
STRAIN

story by Buronson, art by Ryoichi Ikegami
224 pages **MATURE READERS ONLY**

VOLUME	PRICE
#1	$16.95

Check out our whole selection online at www.j-pop.com or order by phone at (800) 394-3042!